'This remarkable, timely, and forward-looking collection is much more than a theoretical analysis of why religious ethics should be opposed to great wealth disparities. It offers an astute, fact-based, and fast-paced diagnosis of the often misunderstood factors that drive inequality in the U.S., including the global financial system, race, class, and gender.'

Lisa Sowle Cahill, *Boston College, USA*

'A book that I thought would be hard to read was one I found hard to put down.'

Kelly Brown Douglas, *Episcopal Divinity School at Union, USA*

'This volume will serve as a critical guide for years to come.'

David Saperstein, *former U.S. Ambassador-at-large for International Religious Freedom, and Director Emeritus at the Religious Action Center for Reform Judaism, USA*

SPIRIT AND CAPITAL IN AN AGE OF INEQUALITY

Spirit and Capital in an Age of Inequality brings together a diverse group of scholars, activists and public intellectuals to consider one of the most pressing issues of our time: increasing inequalities of income and wealth that grate against justice and erode the bonds that hold society together. The contributors think through different religious traditions to understand and address inequality. They make practical proposals in relation to concrete situations such as mass incarceration and sweatshops. They also explore the inner experience of life in a society marked by inequality, tracing the contours of stress, hopelessness and a restless lack of contentment. This book honors the work of Jon P. Gunnemann, who has been a leading scholar at the intersections of religion and economics.

Spirit and Capital in an Age of Inequality will be of interest to undergraduate and postgraduate students and scholars of religion and economics. It will be useful to policy-makers and activists seeking a more thorough understanding of the role of religion and theology in public life.

Robert P. Jones is the founding CEO of the nonpartisan Public Religion Research Institute (PRRI), based in Washington, DC. He previously served as Assistant Professor of Religious Studies at Missouri State University, USA.

Ted A. Smith is Associate Professor of Preaching and Ethics at Emory University's Candler School of Theology, USA.

SPIRIT AND CAPITAL IN AN AGE OF INEQUALITY

Edited by
Robert P. Jones and Ted A. Smith

Routledge
Taylor & Francis Group

LONDON AND NEW YORK

First published 2018
by Routledge
2 Park Square, Milton Park, Abingdon, Oxon OX14 4RN

and by Routledge
711 Third Avenue, New York, NY 10017

Routledge is an imprint of the Taylor & Francis Group, an informa business

British Library Cataloguing-in-Publication Data
A catalogue record for this book is available from the British Library

Library of Congress Cataloging-in-Publication Data
Names: Jones, Robert P. (Robert Patrick), editor.
Title: Spirit and capital in an age of inequality /
edited by Robert P. Jones and Ted A. Smith.
Description: 1 [edition]. | New York : Routledge, 2018. |
Includes bibliographical references and index.
Identifiers: LCCN 2017039759| ISBN 9781138220225 (hardback) |
ISBN 9781138220232 (pbk.) | ISBN 9781315413532 (ebook)
Subjects: LCSH: Economics—Religious aspects—Christianity. |
Economics—Religious aspects.
Classification: LCC BR115.E3 S793 2018 | DDC 261.8/5—dc23
LC record available at https://lccn.loc.gov/2017039759

ISBN: 978-1-138-22022-5 (hbk)
ISBN: 978-1-138-22023-2 (pbk)
ISBN: 978-1-315-41353-2 (ebk)

Typeset in Bembo
by Florence Production Ltd, Stoodleigh, Devon, UK

For Jon, with gratitude.

Jon P. Gunnemann, Professor of Social Ethics, Emeritus
Candler School of Theology, Emory University, USA

CONTENTS

CONTRIBUTORS

Elizabeth M. Bounds is Associate Professor of Christian Ethics at Candler School of Theology and the Graduate Division of Religion at Emory University. She is the author of *Coming Together/Coming Apart: Religion, Modernity, and Community* (1997), and co-editor of *Welfare Policy: Feminist Critiques and Justice in the Making: Feminist Social Ethics* (1999) and *Justice in the Making: Feminist Social Ethics* (2004). Her work focuses on moral questions of incarceration in the United States and on the roles of religion in conflict transformation and peacebuilding.

Keri Day is Associate Professor of Constructive Theology and African American Religion at Princeton Theological Seminary. She has published articles and essays on the how black religion and theology relate to global economics, with a particular emphasis on communities of the African diaspora. She is the author of *Unfinished Business: Black Women, The Black Church, and the Struggle to Thrive in America* (2012) and *Religious Resistance to Neoliberalism: Womanist and Black Feminist Perspectives* (2015).

E. J. Dionne, Jr. is a syndicated columnist for *The Washington Post*, a senior fellow at the Brookings Institution, and university Professor in the Foundations of Democracy and Culture at Georgetown University. He was a visiting Professor at Harvard University in the fall of 2017. He is the author of seven books and has edited or co-edited six other volumes. His most recent books are *One Nation After Trump* (2017), co-authored with Norman Ornstein and Thomas E. Mann, and *Why the Right Went Wrong* (2016). Other works include *Souled Out: Reclaiming Faith and Politics After the Religious Right* (2008); *One Electorate Under God?: A Dialogue on Religion and American Politics* (2004); *Sacred Places, Civic Purposes: Should Government Help Faith-Based Charity?* (2001); and *What's God Got to Do with the American Experiment?* (2000).

William A. Galston holds the Ezra Zilkha Chair in the Brookings Institution's Governance Studies Program, where he serves as a Senior Fellow. Prior to January

2006 he was Saul Stern Professor and Acting Dean at the School of Public Policy, University of Maryland, Director of the Institute for Philosophy and Public Policy and Executive Director of the National Commission on Civic Renewal. Galston is the author of eight books and more than 100 articles in the fields of political theory, public policy and American politics. His most recent books are *Public Matters* (2005), *The Practice of Liberal Pluralism* (2004) and *Liberal Pluralism* (2002). A winner of the American Political Science Association's Hubert H. Humphrey Award, he was elected a Fellow of the American Academy of Arts and Sciences in 2004.

Timothy P. Jackson is Professor of Christian Ethics at Candler School of Theology at Emory University in Atlanta, Georgia. He is also a Senior Fellow at The Center for the Study of Law and Religion at Emory. Professor Jackson has previously held teaching posts at Rhodes College, Yale University, Stanford University and the University of Notre Dame. He has been a Visiting Fellow at The Center of Theological Inquiry, The Whitney Humanities Center at Yale, The Center for the Study of Religion at Princeton and The Program for Evolutionary Dynamics at Harvard. A native of Louisville, Kentucky, Jackson received his B.A. in Philosophy from Princeton and his Ph.D. in Philosophy and Religious Studies from Yale. He is the author of *Love Disconsoled: Meditations on Christian Charity* (1999), *The Priority of Love: Christian Charity and Social Justice* (2003), and *Political Agape: Christian Love and Liberal Democracy* (2015). He is the editor of *The Morality of Adoption: Social-Psychological, Theological, and Legal Perspectives* (2005) and of *The Best Love of the Child: Being Loved and Being Taught to Love as the First Human Right* (2011).

Robert P. Jones is the CEO of Public Religion Research Institute (PRRI) in Washington, DC. Before founding PRRI, he served as Assistant Professor of Religious Studies at Missouri State University. He is the author of three books: *The End of White Christian America* (2016), *Progressive and Religious* (2008) and *Liberalism's Troubled Search for Equality* (2007).

Justin J. Latterell is Assistant Professor in the Practice of Sociology of Religion at Emory University's Candler School of Theology and Alonzo L. McDonald Senior Fellow in Law and Religion at the Center for the Study of Law and Religion. His research focuses on historical interactions among religion, law and politics.

Julie Meadows works as a developmental editor and midwife for scholarly writers at her company, *The Generous Reader*. Her scholarship and writing focus on how we might learn (and learn to teach) skills and practices that enable us to become more humane and more just. Recent articles include '*Mousike* and Bluegrass' (*PES Yearbook*, May 2016) and 'A Quaker Approach to Interreligious Dialogue: Michael Birkel's *Qur'an in Conversation*' (*Quaker Religious Thought*, Spring 2016).

Jonah Dov Pesner serves as the Director of the Religious Action Center of Reform Judaism (RAC), a position he has held since 2015. Rabbi Pesner also serves as Senior Vice President of the Union for Reform Judaism, a position to which he was appointed to in 2011. In 2006, he founded Just Congregations, an organization that engages numerous clergy, professional and volunteer leaders in interfaith efforts for the common good. Named one of the most influential rabbis in America by *Newsweek* magazine, he is an inspirational leader, creative entrepreneur and tireless advocate for social justice.

Christine D. Pohl is Professor of Christian Ethics at Asbury Theological Seminary in Wilmore, Kentucky. She is the author of multiple books, including *Living into Community: Cultivating Practices that Sustain Us* (2012) and *Making Room: Recovering Hospitality as a Christian Tradition* (1999). She is a co-author of several other books. Her research focus is in recovering Christian practices for contemporary life.

Ted A. Smith is Associate Professor of Preaching and Ethics at Emory University's Candler School of Theology. He works in political theology, practical theology and, especially, the spaces where they overlap. He is the author of two books, *The New Measures: A Theological History of Democratic Practice* (2007) and *Weird John Brown: Divine Violence and the Limits of Ethics* (2014), and the editor of two more.

C. Melissa Snarr is Associate Professor of Ethics and Society at Vanderbilt University Divinity School in Nashville, TN. Her research focuses on the intersection of religion, social change and political ethics with particular attention to ethnographic fieldwork and sociological and political theory. She is the author of *All You That Labor: Religion and Ethics in the Living Wage Movement* (2011), *Social Selves and Political Reforms* (2007) and numerous articles in the area of religious ethics and worker justice.

Steven M. Tipton is C.H. Candler Professor of Sociology of Religion, Emeritus at Emory University and its Candler School of Theology. He served as a Senior Fellow at Emory University's Center for the Study of Law and Religion, and he directed Emory's Graduate Division of Religion from 1998 to 2003. Co-author of *Habits of the Heart* (1985) and *The Good Society* (1991), his latest book is *Public Pulpits: Methodists and Mainline Churches in the Moral Argument of Public Life* (2008).

Miguel A. De La Torre is Professor of Social Ethics and Latinx Studies at the Iliff School of Theology. He has served as president of the Society of Christian Ethics, authored over a 100 articles, published over thirty-two books (five of which won national awards) and written the screenplay for the international award-winning documentary *Trails of Hope and Terror*.

John Witte, Jr. is Robert W. Woodruff University Professor of Law, McDonald Distinguished Professor and Director of the Center for the Study of Law and Religion at Emory University. A specialist in legal history, family law, religious liberty and law and religion, he has published over 250 articles, 17 journal symposia and 30 books.

ACKNOWLEDGEMENTS

We are grateful to all the people who helped this *Festschrift* for Jon P. Gunnemann come into being. The authors of the chapters are a remarkable group of thinkers, and we appreciate their taking time to join us in this project. We learned from each essay, and all the more from the conversation they create together. Anne Richardson drew on her encyclopedic knowledge of Western art to suggest just the right cover image. Matthew Erdel and Amelia Thomson-DeVeaux dug into the structure of each argument, edited copy with keen eyes and sustained us with steady good humour. These pages are better because of them. Eve Mayer of Routledge caught our vision for this project and provided crucial early support. Sarah Gore's exceptional organizational skills helped keep the project on track all the way to completion. And Karin Gunnemann deserves the warmest thanks of all. Karin helped conceive the project and offered important guidance as it came together. She has been a generous friend to both of us for many years, and we are thankful for the chance to work with her in preparing this gift for Jon.

———————————————

Parts of Chapter 4 have been adapted from Dionne, E. J. 2015, 'A radical pope', *The American Prospect,* Spring 2015. Parts of Chapter 13 have been adapted from Tipton, S. M. 2007, *Public pulpits: Methodists and mainline churches in the moral argument of public life,* University of Chicago Press, pp. 48–65 and 405–421. In each case, we are grateful to the publishers for permission to reprint material.

INTRODUCTION

Robert P. Jones and Ted A. Smith

This collection of essays is a *Festschrift* to honor Jon P. Gunnemann, Professor of Social Ethics, Emeritus, at Emory University's Candler School of Theology. Across more than three decades of teaching, research and institution building, Gunnemann has developed angles of vision that can discern theological dimensions to basic questions in politics, economics and the social sciences. He has brought that vision to bear on the most pressing questions of the day, from institutional investment and revolution in the 1970s through terrorist attacks in the early years of this millennium. The most fitting tribute, we believe, would not just celebrate but also *extend* this work by addressing one of the most pressing clusters of political and economic questions in our time. And so this book seeks to honor Gunnemann with a series of moral and theological engagements with questions of inequality.

Inequality by the numbers

Numbers only begin to tell the story of economic inequality in the United States. But the story cannot be told without them. In terms of income, the top 1 per cent of earners in the United States now collectively take in almost twice the total amount ✓ of income as the bottom 50 per cent (Piketty *et al.* 2016). Chief Executive Officers of companies now earn, on average, 295 times as much as workers in the companies – a ratio almost ten times as lopsided as it was in 1978 (Davis and Mishel 2014). Years of such disparities in income have generated massive disparities in wealth. In 2010, the wealthiest 1 per cent of households held more wealth than the bottom 90 per cent (Mishel *et al.* 2012). Even among the rich, wealth is concentrated at the top. The wealthiest 0.01 per cent of households now hold 11.2 per cent of all American wealth, all by themselves (Saez and Zucman 2014). Disparities like these give the United States levels of inequality that are a little lower than those in China and Jamaica, but much higher than those in countries like

Germany, Sweden and Finland – higher, even, than the levels of inequality in countries like Russia, Senegal, Turkey, Uganda, El Salvador, Pakistan and Laos (Central Intelligence Agency 2017).

Some inequality has always been a part of American life. But the current level is extraordinarily high. Economists Emmanuel Saez and Gabriel Zucman worked through a century's worth of data to conclude that 'Wealth concentration has followed a U-shaped evolution over the last 100 years: It was high in the beginning of the twentieth century, fell from 1929 to 1978, and has continuously increased since then' (Saez and Zucman 2014). Inequality is now approaching the high level it reached in 1929, just before the stock market crashed. Productivity has improved and the economy has expanded, but the benefits of these gains have not been distributed equally. Almost all of the income growth in the last 25 years has been captured by people at the very top of the income ladder (Leonhardt 2017). The result is a profoundly unequal system that is getting more unequal with every passing year.

Seeing the political causes of inequality

It can be tempting to attribute these trends to technology-driven changes in the nature of economic production. When technology drives increases in productivity, the argument goes, then those who master the technology reap the rewards of productivity gains. Such 'skill-biased technological change' (SBTC) would make manual laborers replaceable – and so less valuable – while designers, engineers and people who worked with ideas became more valuable. This account of inequality became a signature of 'third way' policymakers in the 1990s. It suggested a remedy of programs for retraining that would help workers gain more skills so that they could adapt to an increasingly global, high-tech economy. But these programs did little to slow accelerating inequality. And, over time, the SBTC diagnosis came to be less persuasive. The slowing growth of productivity and the relative lack of investment in new forms of production did not fit the thesis. And the thesis could not explain the fact that laborers at *every* level of skill were losing ground. Most of all, it could not explain the steep slope of the curve that showed more and more income going to the top 1 per cent, 0.1 per cent and 0.01 per cent. After all, there were many highly skilled, highly educated 'symbolic analysts' just a little lower in the income distribution. But they, too, were being left behind by those at the very top (see Krugman 2015).

The real gap was opening up not between unskilled laborers and highly-educated knowledge workers, but between employees of every kind, on the one hand, and the owners and managers of capital, on the other. Economist Paul Krugman argued that such inequality was driven by growing market power – the power to shape the market to one's advantage, to exert undue influence on prices paid and prices received. That market power emerged not through changes in the nature of production, but through *political* changes that did things like weaken unions and lower taxes on the rich. Whether the changes brought more regulation (like those that created near monopolies for cable and internet providers), less regulation (like the weakening of protections for collective bargaining), or oddly specific regulation (like the carried interest loophole that allows managers of capital to be taxed at a lower rate than others), they always seemed to benefit owners over workers (Krugman 2015; see also Reich 2015). As Joseph Stiglitz argued, the steep curve of inequality described by economists like Saez and Piketty 'rests on the ability of wealth-holders to keep their after-tax rate of return high relative to economic growth. How do they do this? By designing the rules of the game to ensure the outcome; that is, through politics' (Stiglitz 2014). Because wealth can influence politics, those with market power can use their wealth to gain political power that they can then use to expand their market power, which generates more wealth, which they can then use to expand political power . . . on and on, in a spiral that would account for just the kind of acceleration that we have seen in inequalities of wealth. Today's economic inequalities have political roots.[1]

Seeing the political causes of inequality matters both morally and politically. We think differently about what Jon P. Gunnemann might call the 'moral meaning' of inequality when we understand it as the product of one group's concerted effort to extract wealth rather than as the unintended by-product of a massively complex system (Gunnemann 1979). But, as Gunnemann sees, the roots of inequality's threat to democracy run deeper even than the behind-the-scenes action of interest-group politics.

Gunnemann has long read Adam Smith not only as an economist, but also as a philosopher of virtue, even a moral theologian. Smith's teacher, Frances Hutcheson, accounted for human capacity to know right and wrong by positing a special 'moral sense' akin to other senses. In Hutcheson's view, this moral sense allowed humans to perceive moral qualities directly. Smith inherited the question of how to account for our moral knowledge, but he proposed what he saw as a more empirical answer. At the centre of his answer was a richly social understanding of the human person. People might not directly perceive moral qualities, Smith thought, but we could project ourselves into the lives of others. We could 'change places in fancy', imagining the world from others' point of view (Smith 1984 §I.i.3). We might not feel directly what other people were feeling, but the faculty of sympathy could represent the feelings of others to us in meaningful ways. These cords of sympathy were strong enough to generate morality, Smith thought. And they were strong enough to knit a group of people together into a society. With increasingly large cities in the early modern period bringing more and more people into community with other people they might not know in person and with whom they might not share ties of kin and clan, bonds of sympathy could still hold people together.

If all people had the capacity for sympathy, in Smith's view, sympathy did not flow towards all people in equal measure. Smith was struck by the ambitions of the people of his time, the desire to get more and to rise in rank. We are ambitious not because material things give us so much more pleasure, Smith wrote, but because we desire the sympathy of other people. And people 'are disposed to sympathize more entirely with our joy than with our sorrow' (Smith 1984 §I.iii.1). Because people are more oriented to sympathizing with joy than sorrow, Smith wrote, we are more likely to sympathize with a rich person than a poor one. This sympathy is what we really desire. 'To be observed, to be attended to, to be taken notice of with sympathy, complacency, and approbation, are all advantages which we can propose to derive' from greater wealth (ibid.). The real glory of wealth is just this attention. A poor person, on the other hand, is scarcely noticed. Being overlooked and being disapproved of 'are things entirely different', Smith wrote. But as 'obscurity covers us from the daylight of honor and approbation, to feel that we are taken no notice of necessarily damps the most agreeable hope and disappoints the most ardent desire of human nature' (ibid.). If other people notice a poor person at all, their aversion to feeling the suffering of poverty – even in fancy – undermines the bonds of sympathy. One need not accept all of Smith's anthropology to agree that wide disparities of wealth make sympathy difficult, and that poor people are especially likely to suffer from this lack of fellow-feeling.

Smith's social account of the meaning of wealth and poverty adds new dimensions to our understanding of the ways that inequality threatens democratic society. It is not just that an interest group translates their economic power into political power to bend policies in their own favour – though this is bad enough, it is that extremes of wealth and poverty fray the cords that hold Americans together as a nation.[2] These strains are exacerbated by increasing segregation by class in every part of our social worlds. Both affluent and poor people are increasingly concentrated in neighborhoods in which the vast majority of people have similar levels of wealth. The number of people living in middle-class neighborhoods, or neighborhoods with a range of incomes, has declined dramatically (Reardon and Bischoff 2016). This geographic segregation reflects and drives further segmentation of schools, networks of socialization, and local political concerns. As Smith knew, it is hard to feel sympathy with people one does not even see. The social effects of inequality thus open wider and wider gaps that the bonds of sympathy have to cross in order to hold society together.

These gaps are especially problematic because of the ways economic inequality arises from and compounds racial inequalities. The systematic, racialized violence of slavery lies at the root of much wealth in America, even more than 150 years after the Emancipation Proclamation. Wealth generated by the violence of slavery – and the many echoes of this violence in the decades since abolition – appears not only in individual family and institutional fortunes, but also in the collective wealth of the nation. That wealth is not distributed equitably, with a massive difference in black and white wealth enduring across many generations. A study by Demos and the Institute for Assets and Social Policy at Brandeis found median wealth of $111,146 in 2011 for white households – an amount that was more than 15 times higher than the $7,113 median for African American households (Sullivan *et al.* 2015, p. 1).

Gaps in household wealth might be expected because they reflect massive injustice across generations. But those who tell narratives of progress in racial justice might expect to see a gradual closing of the gap in present-day income. This has not occurred. African Americans today earn about two-thirds of what white people earn. This is not just a function of concentration in lower-paying sectors of the economy. Something close to this gap plays out in every quintile of the income distribution. And the gap has remained steady for over 50 years. The dismantling of Jim Crow has not made for income equality, let alone equality of wealth ✓ (Campos 2017). And racial self-segregation that accompanies these economic divides remains stark: a 2013 study by the Public Religion Research Institute found that, on average, white Americans' close friendship circles were an astonishing 91 per cent white, and 75 per cent of whites reported not having a single person of color as a close friend (Jones 2014). Racial inequalities stack on top of economic inequalities in ways that compound the effects of each – and further strain the bonds of sympathy on which the sense of being a community that shares a common good depends. Without that sense, it is difficult for a democracy to flourish.[3]

Pope Francis has made the case in even stronger terms. 'Inequality', he wrote in *Evangelii Gaudium,* 'is the root of social ills' (Francis 2013, §202). Pervasive inequality denies not just economic opportunity but also membership in a polity and the recognition – the sympathy – that comes with it. It introduces a kind of violence that permeates the entire society. That violence might be most visible in the actions of those people inequality renders as less than full members of a society. It might be most noticeable in crime or riots. But, Francis wrote, the violence precedes these reactions and runs much deeper. Violence is present 'because the socioeconomic system is unjust at its root' (§59). Unless the root violence of inequality is addressed, 'no political programs or resources spent on law enforcement or surveillance systems can indefinitely guarantee tranquility' (ibid.). The violence at the root of a profoundly unequal society cannot be contained by 'recourse to arms' (§60). If not addressed, it will eventually erupt. Recent empirical studies offer support for the basic contours of the pope's insight. A society that is profoundly unequal is also profoundly unstable (Dutt and Mitra 2008). Even those who care little about justice have reason to work to alleviate inequality.

Thinking religion and economics together

Pope Francis represents one of many people from many different traditions who are reinvigorating religious language to address crises of inequality. As the pope's apostolic exhortation demonstrates, religious criticism of inequality need not undergo a secularizing alchemy that turns it into ethical claims free of all particularity – and theology – in order to be intelligible in pluralistic public spheres around the world. One can speak theologically about economics because the language of theology is already shot through with economics, even as economic discourse is already theological. The relationship is more immediate even than one established through genealogy. It is not just that religious practices and ideas gave rise to economic structures, as Weber argued, it is that – now, in the present tense – the justifications for economic orders engage in theology, even as the first-order speech of religious institutions, is already involved in economic reasoning.

Jon Gunnemann started making this point decades ago. His first book, *The Ethical Investor* (1972), co-authored with Charles Powers and John Simon, was an early challenge to universities to think of decisions about their endowments as more than mere calculus designed to maximize return. The book argued that investments entailed ethical decisions and, more importantly, that the university should recover a sense of itself as a corporate actor with moral responsibilities. This work, gleaned from the insights from a seminar simply titled 'Yale's Investments', which Gunnemann helped lead while still a graduate student, inspired Yale University to be the first major university to bring ethical criteria into investment decisions. It ultimately led the university to divest their interests from companies that were tied to the apartheid system in South Africa.[4] Following Yale's example, hundreds of universities began to rethink their investment responsibilities using *The Ethical Investor* as a blueprint. At Emory, President James T. Laney tapped Gunnemann to counsel the university's leadership in reflecting on the moral dimensions of the university's investments.

In *The Moral Meaning of Revolution* (1979), Gunnemann read Karl Marx and the gospels together and challenged American Christians to see the resonances between the aspirations of the social revolutions in the 1960s and 1970s and the biblical depictions of communal ideals and the Kingdom of God. Gunnemann argued that each radically challenged the status quo with a moral vision of a just social order. These were brave – and, for many, troubling – connections to be making at the height of the Cold War and the beginning of America's heady embrace of capitalism in the 1980s.

In the latter part of his career, Gunnemann's careful conceptual work of thinking theology and economy together was based on his conviction that these discourses were describing the same world. The concept of capital, for instance, so central in modern economics, was a derivative of the Christian conception of spirit; both were ways of talking about stored energy that had the potential to be released for human flourishing. As always, Gunnemann's moral concerns were clear:

> Capital accumulation and formation as a conscious pursuit arrived just a second or so before midnight of the sixth day of creation if those six days are laid on top of the evolutionary timetable. Its arrival has accomplished wonders, but it has also been destructive, chiefly because it has tried to govern alone, living profligately off its natural and social inheritance, not bothering to inquire about its own sources . . . If capital is not to be destructive, it must consciously tend and nurture the sources of its own value.
>
> (Gunnemann 1998)

Gunnemann fleshed out these concepts in the fall of 1998 during a sabbatical at the Center for the Study of Values at Harvard Divinity School. His final lecture at Harvard was immediately recognized as breaking important new ground. It caught the eye of Peter Steinfels, who covered it in *The New York Times* (Steinfels 1999). It also resulted in an invitation to be one of the only Protestant contributors to

The True Wealth of Nations: Catholic Social Thought and Economic Life, an important volume published by Oxford University Press (Gunnemann 2010).

Gunnemann's work challenged economists to make conscious their assumptions about the rationality of markets, their conceptions of the person and the moral responsibilities of corporations; it also challenged theologians to see the ways that religious institutions were structured by economic realities and that theological concepts were shot through with economic ideas. It invited Christians to have a more holistic vision that connected their religious beliefs and practices, on the one hand, and their economic beliefs and practices, on the other.

Gunnemann saw that the reflections of religious institutions were already steeped in politics and economics because religious traditions do not hover above ✔ the ground in some realm of pure ideas. They take the form of institutions. And religious institutions, as institutions, already occupy political and economic space. They do so in particular ways, and they have developed language that both reflects their realities and guides their choices. Therefore, Gunnemann wrote,

> religious traditions do not need to abandon God talk for political talk, or even to translate God talk into political talk, nor to discern the political and worldly implications of the Gospel. All of these assume the division between the Gospel and the political [and the economic]. The point is rather to find a form of discourse in which it is recognized that the society of Christ, like any society, has power relations and thus needs to ask what patterns of authority are just and what unjust.
>
> (Gunnemann 1979, p. 257)[5]

Christian theology already speaks a shared language with economics when it speaks of grace, debt, trespass and redemption. Such theological terms do not need to be translated into economics. They are always already saturated with economics.

Just as theology is already engaged in economics, the language of economics is already involved in theology. In an interview about his 1998 lecture at Harvard, Gunnemann traced the ways that the metaphor of 'capital' has migrated to encompass more and more aspects of life. We speak of 'human capital', 'social capital', 'cultural capital' and more. 'Once we see that the language of capital has migrated to other dimensions of life', Gunnemann said, 'we can turn around and talk about the limitations of the use of traditional economic capital' (Byrd 2000). Ironically, it is just the colonizing sprawl of the economic sphere, its attempt to assume all of life into itself, that opens it to theological criticism.[6]

Shared metaphors become fulcrums for critical leverage. The already theological language of economics invites theological critique. And the economic and political space occupied by religious traditions demands that they reflect on economic and political spheres in which they are already involved. As Gunnemann said,

> The church has to become more conscious of way the economy shapes its practices so that it can shape economic practices. The critical purpose of this

thinking is to re-situate economic activity in relationship to other social institutions, to place it in its broader natural and social – including religious – ecologies.

(Byrd 2000)

The chapters in this book come not just from the church, but from a variety of locations and traditions. But they share a strategy of seizing upon the overlaps Gunnemann named to think religion and economy together for the sake of clearer and better understandings of inequality.

Generative space

Gunnemann's vision of the deep continuities among theology, ethics, economics and politics also informed his work in leading institutions. His leadership helped Yale, Emory and other universities connect their economic lives with their moral purposes. And this was only the beginning. Gunnemann served as president of the Society of Christian Ethics in 1995. His presidential address challenged a guild of scholars mostly ensconced in seminaries to engage in serious thinking about the global economy and its implications for the field of Christian ethics and the church (Gunnemann 1995). In more than two decades at Emory, Gunnemann played a leading role in building the doctoral program in Ethics and Society and the wider Graduate Division of Religion (GDR) into national leaders in graduate study. Reflecting his commitments to thinking across fields, the blueprint for both Ethics and Society and the GDR was, from the beginning, interdisciplinary. Gunnemann's vision for the Ethics and Society area wove together Christian theology, sociology, political theory, moral philosophy and economics. And he helped sustain forms and culture in the GDR that resisted the fragmentation that pitted theological studies against religious studies. Instead, the GDR became a place where empirical work and more normative work – even theological work – could thrive together.

That same interdisciplinary vision and personal generosity shaped Gunnemann's teaching. He did not try to create disciples. He rather used his influence to open spaces in which students could work out of their own deepest convictions in communities of discourse. Gunnemann displayed these open-ended hopes in the classroom, often leaning in to the seminar table and responding with a delighted 'Aha!' when a student made an insightful connection. Because of this intellectual openness, students with a wide range of interests sought Gunnemann out as a dissertation advisor, often as much for the creative process they knew he would foster as for his particular areas of expertise.

We hope the present volume continues the kind of work Gunnemann has done in creating generative communities of discourse. The chapters in this volume work in both descriptive and normative registers, drawing on economics, sociology, historical studies, moral philosophy and theology. Reflecting Gunnemann's combination of intellectual and practical commitments, contributors find their 'first homes' not only in academia, but also in policymaking, advocacy and media. Like

Gunnemann's own work, the book aims to migrate between these different spheres. The contributors also come together to create conversations that go far beyond a single school or centre. Gunnemann understood the need for institutions to aspire to transcend themselves. And so the list of contributors includes not only friends, students and colleagues of Gunnemann, as a traditional *Festschrift* might, but also a wider circle of thinkers whose work shares sources, commitments, or modes of thinking with Gunnemann's own. In word and deed, Gunnemann taught his students that strong communities of discourse can never be narrowly parochial. If the community of contributors to this book still does not include all the voices that should be part of this conversation, it at least suggests the hope that marked the kinds of communities that Gunnemann prized and helped create.

This book of thirteen chapters is divided into four major sections. The first section, 'Thinking with traditions', contains essays that work through histories of specific religious traditions to illumine contemporary thinking about economic inequality. The second section, 'Moral sentiments', consists of essays that reflect on some of the dispositions that inequality generates – and some that might be required for resistance. The third section of the book, 'For the love of the world', contains essays that analyse the role that theology and religious groups can play in specific social movements aimed at reducing economic inequality. Finally, the fourth section, 'Public theology and the common good', articulates a vision of religious engagement calibrated for the complexities of our contemporary pluralistic society.

The first section opens with 'The little Commonwealth: the family as matrix of markets and morality in early Protestantism'. In this chapter, John Witte, Jr. and Justin J. Latterell pick up on Jon Gunnemann's insight about 'the organic ties forged by Protestants between *oikos* and *oikonomiká,* between the household and the market, between the private ethics of the family and the public habits of the economic sphere'. They examine sixteenth century 'household manuals' that provided instructions for ordering domestic life according to Protestant principles. Witte and Latterall point to the power of these manuals in transforming ideals of citizenship, discipleship and economic worldviews, and argue that history suggests that the family may be one of the most overlooked sites for addressing concerns about economic inequality today.

In 'When ancient teachings meet modern problems: Jewish approaches to poverty, inequality, and the market', William A. Galston develops a rich set of resources from Jewish traditions, noting how 'Jewish authorities developed a social theory that rejected hyper-individualism and posited a dense network of mutual responsibilities' that was deeply concerned about economic inequality. Galston's broad, deep history both calls contemporary communities to action and guides them in taking it.

In 'Election, selection and distinction: paradoxes of grace, clan and class', Timothy P. Jackson takes up the problem of distinctions that justify inequality. He argues that such distinctions are entrenched both in Christian theological conceptions of 'the elect' and in ideas of genetic or racial superiority. Jackson argues that this concept strongly undermines economic justice because it attaches divine order, biological destiny, or even merit as justifications for inequality. As a counter-proposal, Jackson develops what he calls political *agape,* a vision of our obligations to others rooted in the egalitarian conviction that all are created in the image of God.

Drawing on Catholic social teaching and its expression during the tenure of Pope Francis, E.J. Dionne, Jr. argues in 'Pope Francis, Catholic social thought and the rejection of fear', that the hallmarks of Francis's leadership are an embrace of mercy and a rejection of fear, which places 'a distinctly Catholic critique of economic inequality at the centre of his papacy'. Francis has become one of the most important leaders in the world today on questions of economic inequality, and Dionne's chapter serves as an essential guide to the contours of his thought.

The second major section opens with Christine D. Pohl's 'More than enough: contentment and the dominance of the economic sphere'. In this chapter, Pohl explores the rich understandings of contentment rooted in the Christian tradition. She argues that contentment, properly understood and linked to other Christian practices such as Sabbath keeping, does not lead to complacency, but rather can serve to generate focus and energy in the service of economic justice.

Julie Meadows, in 'Stress', examines the ways in which the grounds of stress, fear and insecurity, are radically different depending on social location. Examining the experiences of stress in the lives of two women – one richer, one poorer – Meadows traces the difference economic inequality makes for the lived experience of stress. Because these experiences can be so different, simplistic calls to self-improvement and stress management can completely miss the mark for poor people. As Meadows argues, the 'commodified contemplative practices' available to the middle class 'may really help us cope with difficult social circumstances – at least, those of us with the time and the money to access them. But, in the process of translation, they lose their ties to justice'.

Finally, in 'Riots and rip-offs in Baltimore: toward a theology of hopelessness', Miguel De La Torre examines the mischief that theologies of hope can do in the face of pervasive injustice and argues for what he calls 'a theology of hopelessness'. Properly understood, such a theology need not be disabling; rather, De La Torre argues, the moral sentiment of hopelessness 'is fertile ground in which a liberative praxis can grow, as the disenfranchised continue their struggle for justice regardless of the odds against them'.

The third section opens with Elizabeth M. Bounds's chapter, 'Wasting human lives: hyper-incarceration in the United States'. Bounds delivers a sharp critique of the sprawling American prison system, which she argues 'breeds disrespect and wastes human lives, functioning as a powerful engine of ongoing political, social, and economic inequality that excludes whole classes of persons from membership in our democratic social order'.

In 'Challenging a new frontier of market morality: the case of sweatshop economics', Keri Day criticizes an unusual convergence of conservative and liberal economists who are defending the morality of sweatshops with a 'contextual hermeneutic' that lowers the moral bar for developing nations. While Day concedes that sweatshops may offer incremental improvements in already abysmal economic conditions, she argues this moral lens is too narrow to do justice to complex, inter-locking systems of injustice. She draws on Christian theological resources to illu-minate 'a much broader sacred worldview about the meaning of life and our place in the universe as moral agents'.

C. Melissa Snarr, in 'Wage against the machine: wage activism, worker justice and disruptive Jesus in the age of advanced capitalism', draws on fieldwork among religiously-informed living wage activists in Baltimore. Snarr examines how religious connections made a difference in the success of these groups and demonstrates how they reclaimed an egalitarian interpretation of Jesus and discipleship 'where non-elites become co-creators of a more equitable community'.

Finally, in 'Speak up, judge righteously, stand with the poor: the Jewish impera-tive for economic justice', Jonah Pesner narrates an extraordinarily rich account of Jewish traditions that have undergirded past and present activism on issues like workers' rights and universal access to health care. 'Whether we are honouring the legacy of those who died trapped in the stairwells of a New York City factory, marching in the streets of Selma, or advocating in the halls of Congress', he writes, 'American Jews are called by the voices of our tradition to fulfil the visions of the Prophets'.

The final section of the book opens with a chapter by Darryl M. Trimiew entitled 'America, land of the free and home of the poor: inequality as a way of life'. Trimiew argues that despite overt commitments to equality, Americans actually operate with a 'sub-rosa morality', a kind of ethical self-deception, that functions to justify radically unequal outcomes. In the place of an individualistic morality that focuses on equality of opportunity and merit, Trimiew denounces the current, and growing, levels of inequality in the United States. He calls for a return to a shared moral sensibility rooted in a covenantal ideal of the common good.

This volume closes with 'The integrity of the church in a divided society', by Steven M. Tipton. Tipton worked closely with Gunnemann over many years in the Ethics and Society area of the doctoral program at Emory. The steady dialogue between his sociological training and Gunnemann's formation in theology and ethics did much to create the space in which the program continues to flourish. It is fitting that he should have the last word in this volume. In the chapter Tipton argues for the importance of sustaining a shared moral argument about a holistic vision of the common good that can help ground specific policy debates. And, Tipton writes, even if membership numbers are declining, 'communities of faith compose virtually the only modern American institution that cares to accept such responsibility, or indeed that can even recognize its form and grasp its meaning'.

Communities of faith have a critical role in reminding government and corporate leaders that human beings are more than employees and consumers, more even than clients to be satisfied or voters to be persuaded. Jon Gunnemann has made this case across a lifetime of work that challenges actually existing institutions to live out their highest callings in the political and economic spaces that they occupy. Acting on this insight will require doing the kind of work Gunnemann has done and has taught others to do. That work will involve both descriptive and normative dimensions. It will bring together diverse groups of people in conversations about what matters most. It will think theology and economics together. And it will seek more holistic ways of seeing reality, ways that might just let us shape a society that understands radical economic inequality neither as a mysterious accident nor an inevitable, eternal given, but rather as an acute problem that demands a moral response.

Notes

1   Of course factors beyond politics contribute to inequality. For instance, changing visions of marriage are making people more likely to marry people with similar education, income, and class background. The result of such 'assortative mating' is a compounding of class differences and a rise in inequality (see, for instance, Miller and Bui 2016; Watson 2015, p. 75). So, too, an upper and upper-middle class culture of investing heavily in children's development seems, on the aggregate, to pass on social advantages and so transmit inequality across generations (see, for instance, Tavernise 2012). While cultural practices like these contribute to inequality, they do not account for the particular shape of the inequality in the United States today. In particular, they do not account for the widening gap between the very top of the income distribution and those just below. They also cannot account for the magnitude and speed of the expansion in inequality.

2   This section has been informed by Dennis Rasmussen's excellent essay on 'The problem with inequality, according to Adam Smith' in the June 9, 2016 issue of *The Atlantic*.

3   Ganesh Sitaraman makes a distinct but complementary argument in *The crisis of the middle-class constitution* (New York: Knopf, 2017).

4   For the history of Yale University's Advisory Committee on Ethical Responsibility, and the foundational role of *The Ethical Investor*, see the committee's website: http://acir.yale.edu/ [accessed August 13, 2017].

5   This quote from Gunnemann was highlighted for us in Louis A. Ruprecht's excellent article on Gunnemann's work that was published in *Emory Magazine* upon Gunnemann's retirement. The article remains the best overview we know of Gunnemann's career. See Ruprecht 2010.

6   For two other visions of the ways that economic language is already theological, see Walter Benjamin, '*Capitalism as religion*' [(1921, 1972) 1996] and Harvey Cox, *The market as God* (2016).

References

Benjamin, W. ([1921, 1972] 1996) 'Kapitalismus als Religion' in R. Tiedemann (ed.) *Gesammelte Schriften*, 7 vols, Frankfurt a. M.: Suhrkamp, 1972, volume 6:100. English translation: Walter Benjamin, 'Capitalism as Religion', in M. Bullock and M. W. Jennings (eds) *Selected writings, Volume 1: 1913–1926*. Cambridge, MA: The Belknap Press, 1996, 288.

Byrd, C. (2000) 'Jon Gunnemann deals with religious currency', *Emory Report, 52*(20) (7 February). Retrieved from www.emory.edu/EMORY_REPORT/erarchive/2000/February/erfebruary.7/2_7_00gunnemann.html [accessed 10 August 2017].

Campos, P. F. (2017) 'White economic privilege is alive and well', *The New York Times*, 29 July.

Central Intelligence Agency of the United States, 'Country comparison: Distribution of family income: GINI index', Retrieved from www.cia.gov/library/publications/the-world-factbook/rankorder/2172rank.html [accessed 10 August 2017].

Cox, H. (2015) *The market as God*, Cambridge, MA: Harvard University Press, 2016.

Davis, A. and Mishel, L. (2014) 'CEO pay continues to rise as typical workers are paid less', Issue Brief. Washington, DC: Economic Policy Institute, 12 June.

Dutt, P. and Mitra D. (2008) 'Inequality and the instability of polity and policy', *The Economic Journal*, 118 (531) (August 2008): 1285–1314.

Francis (2013) *Evangelii gaudium*. Retrieved from http://w2.vatican.va/content/francesco/en/apost_exhortations/documents/papa-francesco_esortazione-ap_20131124_evangelii-gaudium.html [accessed 3 October 2017].

Gunnemann, J. P., Powers, C. W. and Simon, J. G. (1972) *The ethical investor: Universities and corporate responsibility*, New Haven, CT: Yale University Press.

Gunnemann, J. P. (1979) *The moral meaning of revolution*, New Haven, CT: Yale University Press.

Gunnemann, J. P. (1995) 'Alchemic temptations', *The Annual of the Society of Christian Ethics*, 15: 3–18.

Gunnemann, J. P. (1998) 'Capital ideas: theology engages the economic', working paper presented at Harvard Divinity School, 2 December.

Gunnemann, J. P. (2010) 'Capital, spirit, and commonwealth', in D. Finn (ed.), *The true wealth of nations: Catholic social thought and economic life*, New York: Oxford University Press. pp. 289–318.

Jones, R. P. (2014) 'Self-segregation: Why it's so hard for whites to understand Ferguson', *The Atlantic* (August 21). Retrieved from www.theatlantic.com/national/archive/2014/08/self-segregation-why-its-hard-for-whites-to-understand-ferguson/378928/ [accessed 10 August 2017].

Krugman, P. (2015) 'Challenging the oligarchy', *The New York Review of Books*, 17 December.

Leonhardt, D. (2017) 'Our broken economy, in one simple chart', *New York Times*, 7 August.

Miller, C. C. and Bui, Q. (2016) 'Equality in marriages grows, and so does class divide', *The New York Times*, 27 February.

Mishel, L., Biven, J., Gould, E. and Shierholz, H. (2012) *The state of working America*, 12th edn, Ithaca, NY: Cornell University Press, for the Economic Policy Institute.

Piketty, T., Saez, E. and Zucman, G. (2016) 'Distributional national accounts: methods and estimates for the United States', Working paper series, Washington, DC: Washington Center for Equitable Growth.

Rasmussen, D. C. (2016) 'The problem with inequality, according to Adam Smith', *The Atlantic*, 9 June.

Reardon S. F. and Bischoff K. (2016) 'The continuing increase in income segregation, 2007–2012'. Stanford Center for Education Policy Analysis. Retrieved from: http://cepa.stanford.edu/content/continuing-increase-income-segregation-2007–2012 [accessed 3 October 2017].

Reich, R. B. (2015) *Saving capitalism: For the many, not the few*, New York: Knopf.

Ruprecht, L. A. (2010) 'Moral meaning and social change', *Emory Magazine*, Spring. Retrieved from www.emory.edu/EMORY_MAGAZINE/2010/spring/gunnemann.html [accessed 15 May 2017].

Saez, E. and Zucman, G. (2014) 'Wealth inequality in the United States since 1913: Evidence from capitalized income tax data', National Bureau of Economic Research working paper series, Cambridge, MA: National Bureau of Economic Research.

Sitaraman, G. (2017) *The crisis of the middle-class constitution: Why economic inequality threatens our republic*, New York: Knopf.

Smith, A. ([1759] 1984) *The theory of moral sentiments*, D. D. Raphael and A. L. Macfie (eds), Indianapolis: Liberty Fund.

Steinfels, P. (1999) 'Beliefs: A social ethicist carries the language of economics into the world of religion, and, though history's tide opposes him, finds benefits for both', *The New York Times*, 30 January.

Stiglitz, J. E. (2014) 'Inequality is not inevitable', *The New York Times*, 27 June.

Sullivan, L., Meschede, T., Dietrich, L. and Shapiro, T. (2015) 'The racial gap: Why policy matters'. Retrieved from https://iasp.brandeis.edu/pdfs/2015/RWA.pdf [accessed 10 August 2017].

Watson, W. (2015) *The inequality trap: Fighting capitalism instead of poverty*, Toronto: University of Toronto Press.

PART 1
Thinking with traditions

1

THE LITTLE COMMONWEALTH

The family as matrix of markets and morality in early Protestantism

John Witte, Jr. and Justin J. Latterell

One of the hallmarks of early modern Protestantism was its view of the family as a 'little commonwealth' – the most primal school of justice and mercy, morality and virtue and education and welfare in a Godly republic. Martin Luther called the marital household the 'mother of all earthly laws'; John Calvin called it 'the first covenant of a covenant community'; Anglican divines called it 'the seminary of the republic'.[1] All these metaphors were designed to underscore the early modern Protestant belief that a stable and well-functioning marital household (the '*oikos*') was an essential foundation of a well-ordered church, state, society and economy.

In his early work, Jon Gunnemann highlighted the foundational role of the family in the early modern Protestant world, including for the development of economic life. In *The Moral Meaning of Revolution*, for example he wrote:

> What made the Puritan revolutionaries of the seventeenth century successful was the power of Calvinist theology with its special emphasis on discipline and organization. This discipline found its focus in the Puritan families and local churches . . . Calvinism organized life around the family and voluntary religious organizations from which educational and political institutions evolved, as well as economics.
>
> (Gunnemann 1979, p. 168)

In a later lecture, he said, memorably:

> To understand the rise of modern capitalist economics, we need to understand the organic ties forged by Protestants between *oikos* and *oikonomiká*, between the household and the market, between the private ethics of the family and the public habits of the economic sphere.[2]

In this brief chapter, dedicated to Professor Gunnemann in admiration, appreciation and affection, we illustrate how the early modern Protestant family was structured and schooled to cultivate the critical habits of 'discipline and organization' in the economic and moral lives of its members. We turn for evidence to early modern Protestant household manuals that set out in detail the moral and religious rules, rights and responsibilities of husbands and wives, parents and children, and masters and servants to each other and to their neighbors in different stages of life. It is here, in the elementary ethics and experiences of the Protestant household, that so many of the basic norms and habits of modern economic life were slowly instilled and cultivated in each new generation.

Professor Gunnemann, among many others, has made clear that any analysis of the interactions of Protestantism and economic life must deal with Max Weber's seminal work on the topic. We thus begin with a brief excursus on Weber's theory on the Protestant spirit of capitalism, and then turn to the Protestant household manuals as an underexplored form and forum of economic 'rationalization'. It was not just the mystical spirit of capitalism in Protestantism, as Weber posits, or the ironic convergence of new Protestant teachings on vocation, predestination and asceticism that helped to ground and guide early modern economics, it was also the role that the Protestant household played as an important site of economic activity and an incubator of market morality.

Max Weber and the Protestant spirit of capitalism

In a series of writings at the turn of the twentieth century, German social scientist Max Weber observed that the most highly-developed (or 'rationalized') economies in his day correlated with regions and cultures in which Protestant reform movements had developed most fully and forcefully; and that, within those contexts, the 'business leaders and owners of capital, and even more the higher technically and commercially trained personnel of modern enterprises' were 'overwhelmingly Protestant' (2003, p. 35). This seemed paradoxical since the 'spirit' of modern capitalism – often characterized by unrepentant utilitarianism and relentless acquisitiveness – seemed to contradict traditional Christian values and virtues that Protestants so strongly emphasized. Yet, to Weber, the correlation between Protestantism and capitalism was no coincidence. It was precisely the ideas, anxieties and institutional forms of Protestantism that had helped drive and direct the emergence of the modern capitalist order and the displacement of the traditional feudal economies and church-dominated monopolies that dominated medieval Catholic life.

Three Protestant teachings were particularly important, said Weber. First, Martin Luther's conception of the Christian vocation (*Beruf*) leveled the professional and spiritual hierarchies of his day and catalyzed greater participation by all in disciplined work, professionalized labor, and a market economy. Medieval Catholics regarded the clergy as superior to the laity in virtue and spiritual attainment; the lowliest parson was thought to be closer to God than the highest emperor. Luther, by contrast, insisted that priests and monks were no more virtuous or near to God than soldiers or maidservants. All were equally slaves to sin and equally dependent upon divine grace for their salvation. And all were equally entitled and equipped to pursue the Christian vocation that best suited their talents and stations in life. Christians were not called to leave their secular callings of the world for a cloistered life of self-sanctifying religious asceticism. They were faithfully and dutifully to serve God and neighbor in the ordinary vocations, firm in the knowledge that the work of the butcher, housewife, or soldier was just as spiritual and conducive to salvation as that of the bishop, abbot, or priest. The same devotion and discipline that a cleric directed to spiritual and ecclesiastical ends could be devoted to secular and material ends, with equal assurance of salvation by grace through faith. The broad effect of this teaching, Weber concluded, 'as compared to the Catholic attitude' of the Middle Ages, was that 'the moral emphasis on and the religious sanction of, organized worldly labor in a calling was mightily increased' (ibid., p. 83).

Second, Weber argued, John Calvin's doctrine of predestination engendered religious anxieties that fueled the development of an intense and systematic work ethic among subsequent generations of believers. Lacking the sacramental means of grace that provided Catholics with a reassuring certitude of salvation, Calvinists were anxious to know whether they were among those whom God had elected for eternal salvation, rather than eternal damnation. Over time, Weber argued, Calvinists came to view diligent and productive labor and success in one's vocation as, on the one hand, a non-negotiable religious duty and, on the other hand, a reliable indicator of one's election. The 'systematic self-control' and discipline that Calvinists consequently applied to their lives and work thus served 'as the technical means, not of purchasing salvation, but of getting rid of the fear of damnation' (ibid., p. 115). 'The God of Calvinism demanded of his believers not single good works, but a life of good works combined into a unified system [and] subjected to a consistent method for conduct as a whole' (ibid., p. 117). Soteriological anxieties, then, fostered a form of economic asceticism and organization that impacted broader economic structures.

Third, it was this progressively systematic rationalization of life and work, Weber contended, that drove Protestant societies away from late-medieval feudalism dominated by church monopolies and clergy-dominated guilds towards the highly rationalized and competitive capitalistic economies of Protestant lands in Western Europe and North America. Protestant individuals and communities, spurred on by a sense of vocation and a burning need to prove their state of grace, adopted a feverish and systematic work ethic that subsequently transformed the economic ethos and institutions around them. Even those who did not share the Protestant faith and zeal were forced to embrace the same ethic in order to compete. The institutional dynamics of Protestant sects in the American colonies further catalyzed this process by enforcing strict moral standards for membership and participation in sacramental rites, which allowed, in turn, for fuller participation in the economic life of the community.[3] Feudal traditions and small-scale guilds gave way to the breakneck pace of modern factories and finance. Even as its religious underpinnings and trappings faded from view, the Protestant ethic and the institutions it created remained in place as the basic socio-economic framework into which all were now born. Ironically, where early Protestant reformers sought to elevate the work of ordinary people, emerging economies made the so-called Protestant work ethic all but compulsory. The burgeoning 'spirit of capitalism' – ultimately a denatured and perverted caricature of earlier forms of Protestant asceticism – was hollow and mundane: 'The Puritan wanted to work in a calling', Weber (2003, pp. 181–182) concluded, whereas now

> we are forced to do so. For when asceticism was carried out of monastic cells into everyday life, and began to dominate worldly morality, it did its part in building the tremendous cosmos of the modern economic order. This order is now bound to the technical and economic conditions of machine production which today determine the lives of all the individuals who are born into this mechanism, not only those directly concerned with economic acquisition, with irresistible force. Perhaps it will so determine them until the last ton of fossilized coal is burnt. In Baxter's view the care for external goods should only lie on the shoulders of the 'saint like a light cloak, which can be thrown aside at any moment.' But fate decreed that the cloak should become an iron cage.
>
> Since asceticism undertook to remodel the world and to work out its ideals in the world, material goods have gained an increasing and finally inexorable power over the lives of men as at no previous period in history . . . Where the fulfilment of the calling cannot directly be related to the highest spiritual and cultural values, or when, on the other hand, it need not be felt simply as economic compulsion, the individual generally abandons any attempt to justify it at all. In the field of its highest development, in the United States, the pursuit of wealth, stripped of its religious and ethical meaning, tends to become associated with purely mundane passions, which often actually give it the character of sport . . .
>
> For of the last stage of this cultural development, it might well be truly said: Specialists without spirit, sensualists without heart; this nullity imagines that it has attained a level of civilization never before achieved.

The 'Baxter' whom Weber mentions in this famous 'iron cage' passage is Richard Baxter (1615–1691), a distinguished English Puritan theologian who penned exhaustive practical guides for faithful living. If Baxter thought that care for external goods should rest but lightly on the shoulders of God's predestined believers, his writings suggest that the Christians' responsibility to order their daily lives, especially their households, constituted a much weightier responsibility. Baxter is a prime example of the rationalizing and systematizing impulses that Weber attributes to Protestantism generally, and especially to seventeenth-century Calvinism. Yet, the title of the 504-page volume in which Baxter discusses most thoroughly the Christian's economic life offers an important clue about the real locus and focus of early Protestants' 'economic' reform efforts. Baxter's volume was entitled *Christian Economics (or, Family Duties)*,[4] showing his straightforward equivalence of Christian economics and Christian family life.

Baxter's treatise is only one of scores of extant Protestant household manuals and family directories from the sixteenth to eighteenth centuries.[5] These under-studied texts show that, insofar as Protestants did help to shape the 'spirit' and institutions of early modern capitalism, they did so first of all by rationalizing the household (the *oikos*) and teaching its members the meanings and measures of vocation, discipline and work. Indeed, the birth of capitalism rested not only on the reorganization of guilds and church monopolies into highly rationalized factories and competitive markets of supply and demand, but also, and more basically, on the radical rationalization of the home – an institution that many Protestants viewed as sociologically, politically and theologically prior to all other social institutions, including the economy. Household manuals taught the Christian faithful how to manage the interlacing rights and responsibilities of husbands and wives, parents and children and masters and servants. They offered guidelines for everything from table manners to clothing, diet, work habits, worship and prayer. They instructed parents how to instil virtues and combat vices in their children and exhorted children to heed the word (or suffer the rod) of their elders and to tend to them in old age. And they exhorted parents and children and masters and servants to develop mutual habits of order and discipline that allowed everyone to produce good work in their unique Christian vocations, knowing that hard work was a reflection and affirmation of divine favor.

These household manuals both confirm and qualify some of Weber's key insights into the relationship of markets and morality in the early Protestant world. Weber's and, later, Weberian accounts of economic rationalization were focused on the 'public' economy – the productive activities of tradesmen and merchants, buyers and sellers, and others (mostly men) who made, exchanged, sold and purchased goods and services in the marketplace. Early modern Protestants who engaged in such activities may well have been guided, to varying degrees, by the religious motives and beliefs that Weber highlighted, including the idea of the Christian vocation and the good works and moral discipline that it fostered. Yet early modern Protestant conceptions of vocation were, emphatically, not limited to a person's public work or career. Fatherhood, motherhood and childhood were regarded as important vocations for early Protestants no less than the vocations of blacksmiths or bakers, bankers or barristers. Moreover, a great deal of economic activity in early modern Europe and North America occurred within the household, which often included servants, apprentices and students along with blood relatives, and which provided a great deal of the nurture, education, social welfare and moral discipline historically furnished by the medieval Catholic Church and later provided by the modern welfare state. The norms and habits that each household member learned in this carefully structured domestic sphere formed an important part of their preparation for public economic life. And the rationalization of the early modern Protestant household was an important step in the gradual rationalization of early modern economies in the later institutionally differentiated societies on both sides of the Atlantic.

Illustrations from the Protestant household manuals

We could, and ideally would, duplicate examples to drive home this thesis. But in the small space available here, let us take three Protestant household manualists as illustrations: Heinrich Bullinger, Robert Cleaver and William Perkins. All three of these writers built their manuals on biblical, classical, patristic and humanist learning. All three wrote in highly accessible terms for all pious persons to understand either by reading or hearing their instruction. All three were highly influential writers throughout Great Britain, the European Continent and colonial North America; their works were reprinted often, and in multiple languages. Finally, all three of these manualists anticipated many of the formulations of Richard Baxter's *Family Directory* that Max Weber would later hold up to illustrate his theory of the Protestant ethic.

Heinrich Bullinger (1504–1575)

A good example of an early Protestant household manual comes from the pen of Zurich Reformer Heinrich Bullinger, whose work on the family bridged Lutheran, Calvinist and Anglican worlds. Bullinger wrote extensively on the theology and law of marriage and family life, but his most popular writing was *The Golde Boke of Christen Matrimonye* (1540), written in German but translated into English by the famous Bible translator Miles Coverdale.[6] Here, Bullinger set out a covenantal model of marriage and family life at the foundation of the covenant community of church, state and workplace. 'Wedlock', he wrote, 'is a covenant, a coupling or yoking together' of one man and one woman 'by the good consent of the both' (Bullinger 1542, folio v). 'Holy wedlock was ordained of God himself in Paradise' (ibid., folios i.b–ii, iii). It is thus an 'honourable and holy' estate, enjoyed by the 'holiest, and most virtuous, the wisest and most noble men' in the Bible, and commended to all persons today – clerical and lay, young and old, single and widowed, rich and poor. For Bullinger, the single adult man or woman living outside a marital household was an aberration (ibid., folios xxi.b, xxiii, xxxvi.b, lxxvii.b–lxxviii).

God created marriage so that a man and a woman 'may live together honestly and friendly the one with the other, that they may avoid uncleanness, that they may bring up children in the fear of God, that the one may help and comfort the other' (ibid., folios bv–v.b.). Bullinger followed conventional Protestant arguments regarding the marital purposes of protection from lust and procreation of children, arguing that marriage is God's 'remedy and medicine unto our feeble and weak flesh' and that children are 'the greatest treasure' of a marriage (ibid., folios xix, xxi.b). But he placed special emphasis on marital love and friendship, returning to this theme several times (ibid.).[7] At creation, he insisted, God planted in Adam and Eve 'the love, the heart, the inclination and natural affection that it beseems the one to have toward the other'. The 'mouth of God thereby declares the duty knot and covenant of married folks, namely that the highest love, bond and unite among them should be this, that no man separate them asunder, but only death . . . The love therefore in marriage ought to be (next unto God) above all loves', with couples rendering to each other 'the most excellent and unpainful service, diligence and earnest labor, . . . one doing for another, one longing, depending, helping and forbearing another, suffering, also like joy and like pain one with another' (ibid., folios iii.b–iiii; xxii–xxiiii; xxxvi.b–xxxviii).[8] Thus, for Bullinger, the marital household was the principal social welfare institution for adults, the nerve centre for intimacy and kinship networks that were of vital importance to human flourishing.

Such an ideal state of matrimony, Bullinger insisted, could be achieved only if the covenant of marriage was 'framed right according to the word and will of God' (ibid., folios vi, vii). Bullinger recognized the conventional steps of betrothal, wedding and consummation, and glossed each step with ample pastoral advice and biblical texts. The first few months of cohabitation are a 'most dangerous' time, he believed, and he thus devoted a third of his tract to describing the interlocking 'duties of domesticity' required by the marital covenant between husband, wife and God (ibid., folio l.b). Bullinger went on for several pages advising couples about sex, food, dress and other details of domestic economy, warning against excess in any of these. He then set out the couple's respective duties of 'ordinate obedience and conjugal love mutual', following New Testament leads, and holding up the relationship of Yahweh and ancient Israel, and Christ and his Church as a 'mirror to the state of wedlock and conjugal covenantal love' (ibid., folios liii, lv.b).

The wife owes her husband the duties of obedience, service, respect, devotion, modesty, courtesy, support, faithfulness and honesty (ibid., folios liii–lv, lxii–lxiii.b). The husband is the head of the wife, 'her defender, teacher, and comforter' called to exhibit the selfless sacrificial love of Christ himself and the virtues of clemency, wisdom, integrity and faithfulness (ibid., folios lv–lvi). The wife must give proper care to the home, exhibiting cleanliness, industry, thrift and judiciousness in her treatment of servants and neighbors. The husband must 'labor for the common weal' of his family, exhibiting industry, honesty, integrity and charity (ibid., folios lxvr–lxvii).

Marital couples blessed with children could find ample instruction in Bullinger's *Golde Boke* (1542) on the parental duties of breast-feeding, nurture, protection, discipline, education and dress of children, and, later, their courtship and contracting of marriage with a suitable partner. Bullinger's comments on discipline and training were typical of the sixteenth-century household manuals. He encouraged parents from the start to engage their children with 'godly, honest, grave and fruitful' instruction and example. Parents should teach their children by word and example all the cardinal virtues, lead them in memorizing and reciting the Ten Commandments, Apostle's Creed and other apt texts from the Gospels and Epistles. They should teach their children to 'spend all the time in virtuous uses and never be idle', nor steal, fight, gossip, or harm others or themselves. When children did stray, parents should

> correct them duly and discretely for their faults, so that they stand in great fear and awe of them, and if words will not reclaim them, then take the rod

or whip of correction discretely used. For the rod of correction ministers
wisdom.

(ibid., folio lxxii.b)

Bullinger also encouraged parents to instill industriousness in their children by
helping each child 'learn that science or handicraft . . . whereunto the child is
naturally inclined and unto that occupation let him be put to'. It was not good
enough just to teach children literacy and numbers, said Bullinger, or to set them
up in their own home and marriage in due course, important as all those steps
were. A child also needed the preparation, encouragement, and means to thrive
in his or her own vocation. Parents who failed to provide and emphasize proper
education and vocational training were, in fact, 'ungodly destroyers of themselves,
their children, and of all commonwealths and congregations' who need well-trained
leaders and members to function, conversant not only with 'God's Law, Prophets,
and Gospel', but also the methods and means to succeed in their occupations. 'What
is the cause of all this dissension, cruel persecution, tyranny, evil laws making unjust
acts, false religion, wicked ordinances and ungodly decrees and institutions, but
only the blind ignorance of unlearned rulers' and undereducated citizens unable
to fend properly for themselves or stand up for each other when buffeted by tyrants
or ill-served by incompetent officials (ibid., folio lxxii.b).

Bullinger connected this new understanding of vocation to broader economic
reforms, calling for a system of universal education and vocational training to
replace the medieval system of church-based education for service in the church's
bureaucracy. 'In times past, when men saw so many spiritual promotions unto rich
bishoprics, benefices, deaneries, abbeys, priories, chancellorships, etc., then they did
set fast their children to schools to make them popish priests, idly to live by other
men's sweat'. But with advent of the Reformation, this clerical exploitation of the
laity was over, Bullinger argued. Now 'the common labor, godliness, and the public
profit of all commonwealths and congregations depend upon' all citizens and subjects
being trained in proper schools in all manner of vocations, including but going well
beyond work within the church. 'Now, therefore, O ye Christian parents: seeing
that your youth is now by the favor of God endowed with so good wits and inclined
unto good letters, let not the graces and gifts of God be offered you in vain, but
exercise them' in such a way that your children can 'come to be profitable unto
the commonwealth, whereunto they be born'. Indeed, train them at home and let
them be further trained by teachers and masters in 'all just and true occupations
justly exercised and used' knowing that 'God's blessing maketh them to prosper' if
they remain 'true doers and laborers in their calling' (ibid., folios lxxiii-lxxiii.b).

Thomas Becon, Thomas Cranmer's chaplain, published an edition of Bullinger's
tract in 1542, and it was regularly reprinted and used thereafter.[9] Becon added his
own long foreword to the 1542 edition in which he extolled marriage not only
for the spiritual good of the couple and their children, but also for the civil good
of the commonwealth and church. With a properly functioning marital household,
Becon wrote with ample bombast,

many noble treasures chance unto us, virtue is maintained, vice is eschewed, houses are replenished, cities are inhabited, the ground is tilled, sciences are practiced, kingdoms flourish, amity is preserved, the public weal is defended, natural succession remaineth, good arts are taught, honest order is kept, Christendom is enlarged, God's word promoted, and the glory of God highly advanced and set further.

(Bullinger 1542, folio Aiiii.b)

Indeed, on the strength and stability of 'this household's common weal' hangs the security and success of the whole commonwealth of England (ibid.).[10]

Robert Cleaver (b. ca. 1561)

This emphasis on the public utility of the private marital household was a central theme in Robert Cleaver's hefty tome on *A Godly Form of Householde Gouernment* (1598). Cleaver was a Puritan preacher in Drayton, Oxfordshire who wrote popular tracts on the Ten Commandments, Sabbath Day observance and other aspects of Christian piety. In *A Godly Form of Householde Gouernment,* Cleaver worked hard to systematize and rationalize domestic life, expanding on the themes illustrated by Bullinger. 'All government of a family must be directed to two principal ends', Cleaver wrote: 'First Christian holiness, and secondly the things of this life'. 'Religion must be stirring in Christian families, and that good government looketh to bring godly behavior into families, as well as thrift and good husbandry' (Cleaver 1598, pp. 6–7).[11]

The paterfamilias must play the leading role in the 'good government' of the family, Cleaver believed. As a husband, he must 'live with his wife discreetly'. He must 'cherish and nourish' her as Christ loves and supports his Church. He must work with her 'in all due benevolence, honestly, soberly, and chastely'. And he must 'govern her in all duties, that properly concern the state of marriage, in knowledge, in wisdom, judgment, and justice'. A husband must not be 'bitter, fierce, and cruel' to his wife and must 'never beat her' even if he, as her head, must reproach and admonish her. Instead, 'as a man of knowledge', he must 'edify her, both by a good example, and also, by good instructions' (ibid., p. 92, p. 114, pp. 159ff., pp. 202ff.).[12] As a father, the married man must lead his household in private devotions, daily prayer, catechization and Bible reading. He must ensure that children and servants are faithful in public worship and Sabbath observance. He must be vigilant in offering his children instruction and admonition with wisdom, and punishment and rebuke with patience (ibid., pp. 9–42).

If husbands were to govern the household, the duty of the married woman was to be 'faithful and loving' to her husband and 'wise and prudent' to her family. She must 'reverence her husband' and 'submit herself unto him', as the Bible enjoins. She must dress and deport herself and her children in accordance with the family's means and station in life. She must avoid sloth and not keep idle, lazy, or untoward company. She must be thrifty, just, charitable and prudent in her choice of friends. She must keep order and help maintain 'the exercise of religion within the household'. She must tend especially to the care of her daughters and maidens, teaching them and exemplifying for them the norms and habits of Christian womanhood (ibid., pp. 52–91, pp. 203–222).[13]

Husband and wife also have mutual duties to each other and to their children. They 'must love one another with a pure heart fervently'. They must be 'faithful' to each other, constantly 'bending their wits, and all their endeavors, to the help each of other, and to the common good of the family'. They must pray together, 'admonish one another', and serve as 'mutual helps to each other in matters concerning their own salvation, and the service of God'. Together, they must 'instruct and bring up their children even from their cradle, in the fear and nurture of the Lord, . . . in shame fastness, hatred of vice, and love of all virtue'. Such virtues were to be carried out of the home and into the extended economic sphere. As children mature, parents must 'bring them up in some profitable and lawful calling, by which they may live honestly and Christianly, and not be fruitless burdens of the earth . . . or commonwealth'. They must also 'provide for the disposing of them in marriage', counselling them in their courtship and consenting to their marriage when they come of age and have chosen wisely among available spouses (ibid., pp. 188–191, pp. 243ff.).[14] In response to this, 'the duties of the natural child' are very simple: 'reverence, obedience, and thankfulness' – exemplified notably in seeking their parents' consent to their own marriage, and in caring for their parents when they become elderly or disabled (ibid., p. 186).

In many households, the man and woman are also the 'masters and mistresses' of servants and apprentices, who work and sometimes live within in the home or are a daily part of the family business (Cleaver 1600, pp. 363–383).[15] Cleaver saw the master-servant relationship as a natural and necessary extension of the parent-child relationship. Masters and mistresses must teach their servants diligence and discipline, and keep them from idleness and sloth. They must bring up their servants 'in honesty, and in comely manners, and in all virtues'. They must 'instruct their servants and apprentices in the knowledge of their occupations and trades, even as parents would teach their own children, without all guile, fraud, delaying, or concealing'. And they must discipline them with 'such discretion, pity, and desire of their amendment, as loving parents use to deal with their own dear children'. They must maintain order, courtesy, respect and diligence, and peace among children and servants, and work 'to banish sin and corrupt religion out of their dwellings' (ibid., pp. 364–372).

The household was to be not only an incubator of Christian morality, but also a model of a good Christian business, said Cleaver. In taking on servants and apprentices, for example, the master must be as sure of 'their honest, godly conversation and how they have profited in the knowledge of God' as he is of their skills and strengths and how they have excelled in their craft or profited in their work. For the two are 'closely tied': 'such servants that take in hand the Lord will much better prosper and give success unto him than otherwise'. Once he hired his servants, the master thus was obliged to tend to his servants' souls as much as their bodies. Indeed, he was called to discharge the three-fold office of Christ at home and in business: 'rule like a King, teach like a Prophet, and pray like a Priest to show how a godly man should behave himself' at home and at work. Alongside this spiritual leadership, the master must set rules and create conditions of labor that provided servants with adequate food and shelter, rewarded hard work, paid fair wages, maintained reasonable hours and granted weekly Sabbath rest to all. He must strike a balance between lawful acquisition and proper accumulation of wealth, on the one hand, and 'profligacy' and 'niggardliness' on the other hand. He must promote collaboration among the workers, and throw himself into the work 'so that their necessary affairs and business are dispatched well' (ibid., pp. 372–373). Servants, laborers and apprentices, in turn, must 'cheerfully and willingly from their hearts perform the labors and works' they are assigned. Calling to mind Weber's observation that prosperous work eased spiritual anxieties, Cleaver urged workers to 'be faithful in all things committed to them' knowing that ultimately 'they are serving the Lord, not men; and not only have respect of the earthly reward, but because they know, and are assured, that of the Lord they shall receive the reward of inheritance, in as much as they serve the Lord Christ' (ibid., 378–383).

Faithful maintenance of all these household duties and offices was the best guarantee of productive order within the broader commonwealths of church and state, Cleaver insisted. Indeed, properly functioning households were indispensable to civic flourishing. '[I]f masters of families do not practice at home catechizing, and discipline in their houses and join their helping hands to magistrates and ministers', social order and stability will soon give way to chaos and anarchy (Cleaver 1598, preface, A4). '[I]t is impossible for a man to understand to govern the commonwealth, that doth not know to rule his own house, or order his own person, so that he that knoweth not to govern, deserveth not to reign' (ibid., pp. 4–5).

This was common lore among Cleaver's fellow English divines. 'There was never any disorder and outrage, in any family, church, or commonwealth' when domestic offices were respected and domestic duties discharged, Robert Pricke insisted. For domestic duty and discipline allow persons 'to rise up to the knowledge of the sovereign Lord, and to give unto him the reverence and honor due to his divine majesty'. It also teaches them the personal virtues and civic habits that 'upholdeth, and continueth all these estates, degrees, and orders' of the broader commonwealth (Pricke 1609, p. B2). Daniel Rogers wrote further that a stable household served as 'the right hand of providence, supporter of laws, states, orders, offices, gifts, and services, the glory of peace, . . . the foundation of countries, cities, universities . . . crowns, and kingdoms' (Rogers 1642, p. 17). 'A conscionable performance of household duties . . . may be accounted a public work,' Puritan divine, William Gouge (1622, p. 17), wrote in his massive 800-page, eight-book treatise *Of Domesticall Duties*. For 'good members of a family are likely to make good members of church and commonwealth' (ibid., p. 27).

Gouge zeroed in on the master-servant relationship, devoting more than 100 pages to describing their respective duties. Like Cleaver, Gouge called masters to serve as 'prophets, priests, and kings' within their households, and to cater to the soul, mind and body of their servants and apprentices:

> Masters themselves reap great benefit by a faithful discharge of this duty . . . by bringing their servants to do more faithful service to them. For there is no such means to stir up servants to do all good duty, as the fear of God planted in their hearts. That servant that shall find true grace either first wrought, or further increased in him by his master's means, will think himself so beholding to such a master, as he has never been able to make any sufficient recompense, and therefore will endeavor to do what good service he can in way of thankfulness: he will not only be faithful and diligent in his business, but he will call upon God to prosper his services for his master's good . . . Servants well instructed in piety are likeliest to prove most profitable not only to the family, but also to the Church and the Commonwealth where they live.
>
> (Gouge 2006, p. 484)[16]

Servants so trained will also be able to find their own 'true calling' or 'vocation', Gouge continued.

> God by his providence so ordereth men's affairs, that masters who from time to time train up and send forth many [ap]prentices well exercised and skillful in their trade, do hold on and yea increase their own dealing and gain which they get thereby; and yet withal their apprentices also come well forward . . . This is an especial means to make everyone the more diligent and faithful. For when everyone hath his peculiar work, they know, that they in particular have to give an account thereof to themselves, to their fellow servants, to their master and family, and ultimately to God himself who has called them to this vocation.
>
> (ibid., pp. 495–496)[17]

William Perkins (1558–1602)

This concern for the 'Christian vocation' was a special focus of another Anglo-Puritan, William Perkins, Fellow of Christ College, Cambridge, and rector of St. Andrew's Church in Cambridge. Perkins wrote a famous *Treatise of the Vocations*, published posthumously in 1605, as well as books on other themes that Weber would later highlight: *Damnation or Salvation; How to Live Well; A Christian and Plain Treatise of the Manner and Order of Predestination;* and *Economy, or Household-Government: A Short Survey of the Right Manner of Erecting and Ordering a Family, According to the Scriptures.*

Perkins' description of the well-ordered household was very much like Cleaver's and Bullinger's. '[M]arriage was made and appointed by God himself to be the foundation and seminary of all sorts and kinds of life in the commonwealth and the church', Perkins declared. '[T]hose families wherein the service of God is performed are, as it were, little churches; yea, even a kind of paradise on earth' (Perkins 1631, pp. 418–419). In a well ordered Christian household, worship of God must come first and undergird all family relationships, duties and activities:

> Common reason and equity showeth it to be a necessary duty: for the happy and prosperous estate of the family, which consisteth in the mutual love and agreement of the man and wife, in the dutiful obedience of children to their parents, and in the faithful service of servants to their Masters, wholly dependeth upon the grace and blessings of God: and this blessing is annexed to his worship.
>
> (ibid., p. 669)

Like Cleaver, Perkins emphasized that the parent's and master's responsibilities to children and servants were not only to love, nurture, feed, clothe, and protect them. They were also to 'observe both the inclination and the natural gifts of body and mind, that are in the child, and accordingly to bestow it in some honest calling and course of life' (ibid., p. 695).

In his 1605 *Treatise of the Vocations*, Perkins homed in on the need for an 'honest calling' for all members of the community. 'Every person of every degree, state, sex, or condition, without exception, must have some personal and particular calling to walk in', Perkins wrote. And he or she must discharge that calling with diligence and zeal, and to the glory and honor of God and neighbor, church and state, family and self.

> Sloth and negligence in the duties of our callings, are a *disorder* against that good order which God set in the societies of mankind, in both church and commonwealth. And indeed, idleness and sloth are the causes of many damnable sins. The idle body, or the idle brain, is the workshop of the devil.
>
> (Perkins 2015 [1626], p. 9, p. 13, pp. 17–18)

Each person must 'shake off that spiritual drowsiness' and be constantly ready to answer the question '*What have I done?* or *How does it stand between God and me?*' (ibid., p. 50)

Piling up biblical and classical verses that reflected this vocational ideal, Perkins took sharp aim at those who, in his view, betrayed it. The first were idle beggars and drunks, itinerant vagabonds and mendicants, and others who wrongly exploited the charity of others. These are the 'undeserving poor', Perkins wrote. They should be put to hard work to restore the charitable and diaconal coffers they emptied so these alms may properly serve the 'deserving poor' – that is widows, orphans and the injured and disabled. The second were the 'idle rich', who had inherited or earned 'great livings and revenues, [and now] spend their days in eating and drinking, in sports and pastimes, not employing themselves in service for church or commonwealth'. From those who have been given much, much is expected,

Perkins argued, citing Scripture. And those with wealth or time to spare are obliged to 'set it in motion' to provide opportunities for others and to enhance the common good. The third and most egregious betrayers of vocational ideals, are 'monks and friars' and other 'popish votaries' who 'live apart from the societies of men in fasting and prayer'. 'This monkish kind of living is damnable', Perkins wrote, for it is sloth and idleness masquerading as a spiritual vocation. In fact, 'all monks a[re] thieves and robbers' living on the tithes of others, rather than as 'good and profitable member[s] of some society and body' (ibid., p. 13, pp. 16–17).

'Every man must judge that the particular calling in which God has placed him, is the best of all callings for him. I do not say simply *best*, but best *for him*.' At minimum, this requires each Christian to 'join the practice of his personal calling, with the practice of the general calling of Christianity . . . [I]n his personal calling, he must show himself to be a Christian' (ibid., pp. 14–15). Furthermore, a person has to pick a vocation that best suits his inclinations and gifts. Here, Christian parents and masters must play a key role, said Perkins. They must be attentive to their child's inclinations: 'some are affected with music more than others; some with merchandise; some with a more liberal kind of learning'. Their training must follow these inclinations. The parents must also discern the 'natural gifts' of their children.

> Those children who excel in the gifts of the body are to be brought up in callings performed by the labor of the body, as in mechanical arts. And those who excel in the gifts of the mind, are to be applied to those sciences that are performed by wit and learning.
>
> (ibid., pp. 17–19)

A parent's failure to encourage and prepare the child for his or her proper vocation 'is a great and common sin', Perkins argued:

> For the care of most is that their children may *live* – not regarding at all whether they live *well*, and do service to God in a fit calling or not. And the truth is, parents cannot do greater wrong to their children, and to the society of men, than to apply them to unfit callings – as when a child is fit for learning, to apply him to a trade, or other bodily service; or contrariwise, to apply him to learning when he is fit for a trade. For this is like a man applying his toes to feeling, and not his fingers; and to go about on his hands and not his feet; and to set the members of the body out of their proper places.
>
> (ibid., pp. 18–19)

Perkins used this metaphor of the body and its members to argue further that when a person has properly prepared and pursued a vocation most suitable to his talents, that person must 'keep himself within the compass, limits, or precincts of it', following the rules of his vocation. Much like a body needs each member to do its own function, or an army needs each soldier to follow his orders, so a properly running society and economy need workers in their places. If a man stays within his calling, he will be blessed, and all society with him. If he strays 'outside the compass of his calling, he is out of the way, and by this means he bereaves himself of the protection of the Almighty; and he lies open and naked to all the punishments and plagues of God' (ibid., p. 8).

Summary and conclusions

Jon Gunnemann was quite right to stress 'the organic ties forged by Protestants between *oikos* and *oikonomiká*, between the household and the market, between the private ethics of the family and the public habits of the economic sphere'. The Protestant household manuals that we have sampled mandated a form of rationalization and routinization of the home that would prove critical for the early modern economy. The Protestant home was to be a little church and state that provided much of the nurture, education, social welfare and moral discipline that was historically furnished by the medieval Catholic Church and later provided by the modern welfare state. The Protestant home was also to be a little business, with the family farm, shop, estate, or service giving servants and laborers the space and time to learn their craft and earn their keep, ideally under the benign Christian rule of the master. And the Protestant home was to be a little school, where children and apprentices were first taught and disciplined to pursue that vocation that best suited their inclinations and gifts, and learned to excel in that vocation as a form of loving service to God, neighbor, and self.

Like Max Weber's famous thesis in *The Protestant Ethic and the Spirit of Capitalism*, the real impact of these household manuals is difficult to quantify with precision. Numerous scholars have challenged Weber's claim that Protestant ideals and anxieties played a significant role in the emergence of modern economies.[18] If theology affected this transformation at all, they say, its effects were secondary to other innovations in technology, law and politics. Similarly, sociologists after Weber have shown that the early modern household was one of many new institutions that cultivated the norms and habits of market morality, not least the new public schools that emerged out of the Renaissance and Reformation. And it is doubtful that every Protestant household lived up to the ideals put forth in these manuals. The sheer prevalence of the manuals may, for example, indicate how often Protestants fell short of these norms and thus required constant instruction from authors like Bullinger, Cleaver, Perkins and Baxter. More research is needed to determine how widely and fully the teachings of these manuals were adopted in practice.

Despite these caveats, household manuals like the ones sampled above clearly illustrate the type of rationalizing impulse that Weber attributed to early modern Protestantism, and they represent one of the means by which this impulse took institutional form. Protestants' elevation of ordinary jobs to divine 'callings' transformed the social and religious status of important economic roles and relationships; importantly, this transformation required a thoroughgoing reinterpretation of how ordinary people could fulfil these roles and relationships in practice. Household manuals served this interpretive function. Written for a lay audience, they defined the metes and bounds of household economies. They provided a detailed, scalable model of organizational hierarchy. They furnished a work ethic and a corresponding moral argument for the wellbeing of the individual, the family and the broader community: industry, discipline, frugality and mutual care were sacred duties, while idleness and profligacy were unholy vices. Household manuals thus sought to structure domestic life and its constituent economies to the finest detail. To the extent that people implemented these instructions, households contributed more or less to the tide of economic transformation that washed over Protestant lands in the early modern period. Protestant households alone do not explain the emergence of modern capitalism. But they are an important part of that story.

Are there lessons in this story for contemporary scholars and readers? How should we understand the roles in and of families in our own contexts, where we find vast disparities of wealth and income, new methods of mass production, growing levels of gloabl connectivity, dizzyingly dynamic financial systems, unprecedented divorce rates, rising numbers of out-of-wedlock births, same-sex marriage and much more?

We may start simply by noticing the new depths of irony in Weber's observations about the 'iron cage' of modern economic systems. Weber pointed out the paradox in Protestants' remaking of the economic order: new forms of economic insecurity replaced Protestants' spiritual insecurities, making a once-voluntary Protestant work ethic all but compulsory to survive in the new economic order. Once-meaningful work now took on the character of bald necessity or mere sport. An important corollary is the havoc that economic systems have waged on the institution that early Protestants viewed as prior to all others – the family household. We do not lament that the patriarchal authority prescribed in these manuals has been replaced with relatively benign and egalitarian gender norms, or dismiss the moral importance of other recent changes to the laws of marriage, divorce and child-rearing. A simplistic return to the norms espoused in these manuals will not solve many challenges facing modern families, which now include a broader array of relationships and legal arrangements than our forebears could have imagined.

We do lament, however, that modern economies and cultural norms often impair the formation of strong and well-ordered households, as such. For all but the most affluent of families, the conscious formation of the household as a place of nurturance and care, of religious and secular education, of training in the virtues, practical wisdom and trades and more, has become an unaffordable luxury. The household, for many, has become a mere way station between long shifts; a place where children receive more commercially mediated 'screen time' than quality time with their parents and elders; where streams of short-term lovers stand decrepitly in the place of steady love from a lifelong spouse; where intergenerational ties are weak or non-existent; and where the relationships that matter most in life are afforded the least veneration, and the fewest public and private resources. Even in affluent homes, where resources are not scarce, parenting and household management are relegated to an army of professional staff while the nominal heads-of-house work long hours away from home.

Weber's *Protestant Ethic* was, in part, a refutation of Marx's claim that material institutions and interests, alone, are decisive factors in economic history. It was also a subtle and profound critique of the modern economic order and its ethos. If today we live amidst a complex of interlocking 'iron cages' that demand vocational mania and foster familial atrophy, Weber reminds his readers that there was a time, at least, when ideas and ideal interests – theological ones, no less! – also mattered. 'No one knows who will live in this cage in the future', he pondered, 'or whether at the end of this tremendous development entirely new prophets will arise, or there will be a great rebirth of old ideas and ideals, or, if neither, mechanized petrification, embellished with a sort of convulsive self-importance' (Weber 2003, p. 182). Is it conceivable that our households can be reincarnated as incubators of a new social transformation? Might modern households one day be reimagined as a basic and humane institution that reflects and instills our best values? Will communities, large and small, begin to invest more resources and implement better laws to support strong and stable families – especially on the bottom rungs of the socioeconomic ladder? We hope so. And if this hope is naïve, the story of Protestant household manuals should at least remind us that we are not the first to try. It should also encourage researchers to investigate more fully the ties between religious world views and economic orders today. For the family is one significant place to look for the ways in which religion and economy come together and shape one another. *Oikos* and *oikonomiká* still matter for one another, and religion runs through them both.

Notes

1 See detailed references in Witte (2012).
2 This statement came in a seminar on 'Calvinism and Politics', taught by Professor Gunnemann in 1989 or 1990, during a session when John Witte participated.
3 See Weber (1946).
4 This was one volume in Baxter's (1678) much-read set of publications. The first two parts were on *Christian Ethics (or Private Duties)*; the third on *Christian Economics (or Family Duties)*; the fourth on *Christian Ecclesiastics (or, Church Duties)* and the fifth on *Christian Politics (or, Duties to Our Rulers and Neighbors)*. Each volume was 500–700 pages long.
5 On household manuals, which also had earlier Catholic and later liberal forms, see Witte and Good (2008, pp. 266–294).
6 Bullinger (1540), translated as Bullinger (1541) and then as Bullinger (1542) under Thomas Becon's pseudonym, Theodore Basille. Throughout this chapter, we have retained the archaic spelling of the book titles, but modernized the spelling and punctuation in all quotations.
7 See, for example Bullinger (1849, pp. 397–398).
8 Contemporaneous Tudor divines sometimes offered similar sentiments on the purposes of marriage, with an emphasis on marital affection, love and companionship. See, for example Tilney (1571, folios Biiibv–Biiic, Biiia).

9 The work is summarized in Bullinger (1849, pp. 393–435). In the 1586 Convocation, Archbishop Whit gift directed the lower clergy to study Bullinger's *Decades* as part of their theological training (Vidler 1963, p. 34).

10 See also Thomas Becon (1560, folio DCxlix):

> For being that a city standeth of houses, and the common weal of private things, and of ruling of a household and family, the discipline to govern a common wealth is ordained: how shall he rule a citye that hath not learned to rule a house: how shall he govern a common weal that never knew his private and familiar business . . . For truly matrimony giveth a great exercise to moral philosophy. For it has a certain households commonwealth annexed, in ruling that which a man may soon learn and have experience of wisdom, temperance, love to god and his kin, and all other virtues.

See also Becon (1560, folios CCCClxcvii–CCCClxcvix):

> The order of wedlock . . . maketh kingdoms populace great . . . [It] bringeth forth children, sons and daughters, to the commonwealth . . . which at all times are not only ready to do good to the commonwealth but also to do for the conservation of the same . . . [T]hey refuse no labor, no pain, to show their obedience toward their superiors, . . . to do good to all men, . . . to do God's good will & pleasure, in laboring, in calling upon God, in thanking God for his benefits, in mortifying the filthy lusts of the flesh, in wearing such apparel, as becometh godliness, in relieving the poor and the needy, in visiting the sick, in dying unto sin and living unto righteousness.

11 See further Dod and Cleaver (1604, p. 181).

12 See further Dod and Cleaver (1604, p. 24, pp. 226–228).

13 See further Dod and Cleaver (1604, pp. 221–222).

14 See further Dod and Cleaver (1604, pp. 174–222).

15 For this section on masters and servants, see the expanded edition, Cleaver (1600).

16 Cf. Gouge (1622, bk. 8, p. 21).

17 Cf. Gouge (1622, bk. 8, p. 37).

18 See, for example Stanislov (1984); Barbalet (2008); Delacroix and Nielsen (2001); Becker and Woessmann (2009).

References

Barbalet, J. M. (2008) *Weber, passion and profits: 'The protestant ethic and the spirit of capitalism' in context*, New York: Cambridge University Press.

Baxter, R. (1678) *A Christian directory: Or, a summ of practical theologie, and cases of conscience: Directing Christians, how to use their knowledge and faith; how to improve all helps and means, and to perform all duties; how to overcome temptations, and to escape or mortifie every sin*, 2nd edn, 5 vols, London: Robert White for Nevil Simons.

Becker, S. O. and Woessmann, L. (2009) 'Was Weber wrong? A human capital theory of protestant economic history', *The Quarterly Journal of Economics*, *124*(2): 531–596.

Becon, T. (1560) *The booke of matrimonie both profitable and comfortable for all them that entende quietly and godly to lyue in the holy state of honorable wedlocke, in The first part of the bokes, which Thomas Becon made*, 1560–1564, vol. 1, item 12, London: John Day.

Bullinger, H. (1540) *Der christlich eestand*, Zurich: Christoffel Froschouer.

Bullinger, H. (1541) *The Christen state of matrimonye*, n.p., London. STC 4045.

Bullinger, H. (1542) *The golde boke of Christen matrimonye*, Ioh[a]n Mayler for Ioh[a]n Gough, London. STC 1723.

Bullinger, H. (1849) 'Second decade, tenth sermon', in T. Harding (ed.), *The decades of Henry Bullinger: The first and second decades*, Cambridge, UK: Cambridge University Press, pp. 393–435.

Cleaver, R. (1598) *A godly form of householde gouernment*, London: Thomas Creede.

Cleaver, R. (1600) *A godlie forme of hovseholde government: For the ordering of private families according to the direction of God's word*, London: Felix Kingston.

Delacroix, J. and Nielsen, F. (2001) 'The beloved myth: Protestantism and the rise of industrial capitalism in nineteenth-century Europe', *Social Forces, 80*(2): 509–553.

Dod, J. and Cleaver, R. (1604) *A plaine and familiar exposition of the ten commandments, with a methodicall short catechisme, containing briefly all the principall grounds of Christian religion*, London: Thomas Man. STC 6968.

Gouge, W. (1622) *Of domesticall duties: Eight treatises*, London: John Haviland. STC 12119.

Gouge, W. (2006) *Of domestical duties*, G. Fox, (ed.), Pensacola, FL: Chapel Library.

Gunnemann, J. P. (1979) *The moral meaning of revolution*, New Haven, CT: Yale University Press.

Perkins, W. (1631) 'Economy, or household-government: A short survey of the right manner of erecting and ordering a family, according to the scriptures', in M. W. Perkins (ed.), *The workes of that famous and worthy minister of Christ in the Universitie of Cambridge*, vol. 3, London: J Haviland.

Perkins, W. (2015 [1626]) *A treatise of the vocations, in the works of that famous and worthy minister of Christ in the University of Cambridge, Mr. William Perkins*, vol. 1, pp. 750–759. John Legatt, London: Modernized by WH Gross, Digital Puritan Press, pp. 1–52. Available from: www.digitalpuritan.net/Digital%20Puritan%20Resources/Perkins%20William/Treatise%20of%20the%20Vocations%20(OTW%20Version).pdf.

Pricke, R. (1609) *The doctrine of superioritie, and of subjection, contained in the fifth commandment of the holy law of almightie God*, London: Ephraim Dawson & T. Downe.

Rogers, D. (1642) *Matrimoniall honour or, the mutuall crowne and comfort of godly, loyall, and chaste marriage*, London: Th. Harper for Philip Nevelm.

Stanislov, A. (1984) *Max Weber's insights and errors*, London: Routledge and Kegan Paul.

Tilney, E. (1571) *A brief and pleasant discourse of duties in marriage, called the flower of friendshippe*, London: Henrie Denham.

Vidler, A. R. (1963) *Christ's strange work: An exposition of the three uses of God's law*, rev. edn, London: SCM Press.

Weber, M. (1946) 'The protestant sects and the spirit of capitalism', in H. H. Geerth and C. W. Mills (eds), *From Max Weber: Essays in sociology*, New York: Oxford University Press, pp. 302–332.

Weber, M. (2003 [1958]) *The protestant ethic and the spirit of capitalism*, T. Parsons (trans.), repr edn, Mineola, NY: Dover Publications.

Witte, J. Jr. (2012) *From sacrament to contract: Marriage, religion, and law in the western tradition*, 2nd edn, Louisville, KY: Westminster John Knox Press.

Witte, J. Jr. and Good, H. M. (2008) 'The duties of love: The vocation of the child in the household manual tradition', in P. M. Brennan (ed.), *The vocation of the child*, Grand Rapids, MI: Wm. B. Eerdmans, pp. 266–294.

2

WHEN ANCIENT TEACHINGS MEET MODERN PROBLEMS

Jewish approaches to poverty, inequality and the market

William A. Galston

Introduction: the Constitution and the Torah

The Constitution is a spare, terse document. The framework it established must be applied to issues and circumstances that the Framers could have anticipated only in the most general terms, if at all. So the process of interpretation is crucial. Indeed, it is not misleading to suggest that the Constitution is the text plus its tradition of interpretation, principally though not exclusively by the courts. This tradition contains not only judgements but also the reasons for them; not only the victorious majority views but also those of the minority.

Constitutional judgements require more than constitutional premises. As every judge knows, these judgements arise in the context of specific cases and controversies, and the facts of the case shape (sometimes drive) the conclusions. This encounter between general guidelines and concrete particulars is at the heart of the process of judging. So is debate about analogies: is X similar enough to Y, which the court has already decided, to be governed by the same arguments, or is it dissimilar enough to require fresh consideration?

I am hardly the first to discern the similarity between the US process of constitutional interpretation and the kinds of arguments that form the heart of the Jewish tradition. The Constitution finds its equivalent in the Torah – the five books of Moses. Cases decided under the Constitution, memorialized in thick volumes of decisions stretching back more than two centuries, stand in roughly the same relationship to the Framers' document as does the Talmud to the Torah – with the not insignificant difference that the Talmud reflects, and to some extent codifies, nearly a millennium of interpretive argumentation.

The Talmud is relentlessly particular. It examines each issue on its own terms, with sometimes maddening thoroughness, from every possible angle. Rabbis may concur in judgements while disagreeing about the reasons for them. Typically, it is difficult to discern the more general principles at work; the bottom-line judgements – the kinds of propositions that modern lawyers call 'black-letter law' – possess a clarity that the principles often lack.

This is especially the case when the principles at work are moral. Some prominent Jewish thinkers – Yeshayahu Leibowitz, for example – have gone so far as to argue that their tradition contains no general premises of morality other than what can be gleaned from the particulars of the law.[1] Others disagree, citing not only the prophets but also passages from the Torah itself.

Although no direct inferences can be drawn from the laws governing ancient Jewish communities to the resolution of modern policy disputes, the Jewish tradition does provide a framework for understanding contemporary issues of wealth, poverty and the free market. I shall argue that Judaism combines an affirmative stance towards the understanding of work, property and competition embraced by today's conservatives with an endorsement of the stance towards regulating markets and limiting extremes of wealth and poverty more characteristic of liberals and social democrats. This unique blend is embedded in a theological anthropology that interprets this-worldly economic behaviour as *imitatio dei*, with human work and innovation understood as analogies to the work of God the Creator.

Law and morality

As is well known, the stance of traditional Judaism on economic life and most other matters is expressed through law (in Hebrew, *halacha*). This creates a problem at the threshold – legalism, a charge prominent in texts of the Christian New Testament and levelled against Judaism for two millennia. A focus on the minutiae of law and observance, the allegation runs, comes at the expense of the spirit of the law, its higher moral and spiritual significance.

Every philosophical and religious tradition has a characteristic excess, and Judaism is no exception. Concern about this tendency towards legalism was not invented by the New Testament writers, however. It has been evident to Jewish leaders through the ages, and they have done their best to lean against it.

The Roman destruction of Jerusalem and the Second Temple in 70 CE was one of the great catastrophes of Jewish history and required theological explanation. How could God permit such a disaster? For what sins were the Jews being punished? The leader of the surviving Jewish community in Palestine after the destruction of the Temple, Rabbi Yochanan ben Zakkai, said that Jerusalem had been destroyed because Jews 'based their judgements solely on the law of the Torah and did not act beyond the requirements of the law' (b. B Mets 30b). The law, he suggested, provided at most a minimum standard of required conduct; often adhering to it would not be enough.

In taking this position, Rabbi Yochanan was drawing on a rich tradition. It suffices to mention the prophet Isaiah's famous castigation of his community for adhering to the letter of the Yom Kippur fast while ignoring its moral significance:

> This is the fast I desire: to unlock the fetters of wickedness, and untie the cords of the yoke to let the oppressed go free . . . It is to share your bread with the hungry and to take the wretched poor into your home.
>
> (Isaiah 58:5–6)

And there is the Torah itself. Deuteronomy 6:18 reads, in part: 'Do what is right and good in the Lord's sight, so that it may go well with you'. Reflecting on this passage, Nachmanides, the great medieval interpreter, commented that

> It is impossible to mention in the Torah all of a person's actions toward his neighbours and acquaintances, all of his commercial activity, and all social and political institutions. So after God had mentioned many of them . . . God later said that one should do the right and the good in all matters through compromise and conduct *beyond the letter of the law.*
>
> (cited in Hartman 2012, p. 44, italics mine)

It is possible to be a scoundrel within the bounds of the Torah. The rabbis often endorsed, and sometimes enforced, conduct guided by moral principles that goes beyond the requirements of the law. The Talmud records a famous application of this broader stance to relations between employers and employees:

> Some porters working for Raba bar bar Chanan broke a jug of wine. He seized their clothes. They came before Rav, and Rav said to Raba bar bar Chanan, 'Give them their clothing'. Raba bar bar Chanan said to him, 'Is this the law?' Rav said, 'Yes, because of the principle, "You should walk in the ways of the good"' (Proverbs 2:20). He gave them back their clothes. They said to him, 'We are poor, and we troubled ourselves to work all day, and we are needy – do we receive nothing?' Immediately Rav said to Raba bar bar Chanan, 'Go, give them their wages'. He said to Rav, 'Is this the law?' Rav said, 'Yes, [because of the principle], "You should keep the ways of the righteous"' (Proverbs 2:20).
>
> (b. B. Met. 83a)

The point of the employer's question was that as a matter of law, he was entitled to compensation for the loss of the wine. The point of Rav's response is that there is a distinction between what you have a right to do and what the right thing to do actually is. Sometimes moral considerations require you not to press your legal claims to the hilt; all the more so when the person affected by your actions is of lower wealth and status.

To be sure, a core principle of Jewish adjudication, grounded in the Torah, is that the judge should incline neither towards the rich nor towards the poor. When the issue is the rightful owner of a disputed piece of property, this stance of impartiality must govern the result. Although the poor man may need the property more than the rich man, the judge has no choice but to find for the latter if the facts so require. On charitable grounds, the rich man could have chosen not to press his claim. But he was not morally culpable for doing so. And once he did, the judge had no choice.

As one of the great leaders of Babylonian Jewry, Rav possessed enormous moral authority, which he used to bring about the morally correct result. By presenting themselves before him, both parties agreed to be bound by his judgement. Against a moral backdrop, Rav transformed the dispute into a matter of equity rather than settled law. And once he pronounced judgement, the employer had no choice but to comply.

Applying the Torah to contemporary society

Since the Enlightenment, many prominent Jews have been political radicals, often combining that radicalism in politics with socialism in the economic domain. This reflects, in part, the continuing influence of the prophetic tradition, and even more, the historic identification of the Jewish people with outcasts and underdogs. Over and over again in the Torah, Jews are commanded to remember that they were strangers and slaves in Egypt. Often this injunction is linked to norms of behaviour towards others of oppressed or subordinate status within the community. This history imparts a distinctive cast to the characteristic Jewish social outlook, down to the present day. It is no accident that American Jews played a prominent role in the civil rights movement of the 1950s and early 1960s.

Nonetheless, many leading authorities caution against a literalist link between the Jewish tradition and modern politics. According to Rabbi Lord Jonathan Sacks (1985), the former Chief Rabbi of the United Kingdom, 'There never has been, and could not be conceived, an identification of Judaism with any particular political stance'. The same is true of economics, he argues: 'It would be quite wrong to identify a great religious tradition with any particular set of economic institutions' (Sacks 2000). Yes, the Talmud contemplates, and seeks to guide, transactional, market-based communal economic life. On the other hand, Sacks notes, the biblical story of Joseph in Egypt depicts a successful advocate and practitioner of central planning, and the collectivism of kibbutz life in Mandatory Palestine was squarely within the Jewish pale. For this reason, he concludes, 'Judaism has no specific answers to the economic and social problems of our time' (Sacks 1985). In the same vein, Joseph Isaac Lifshitz (2010), the author of a careful study of Jewish law and the free market, argues that 'Jewish thinkers should be cautious about the economic inferences they draw from Jewish [legal] sources. Instead, we should focus on and learn from the moral principles that generated those laws' (p. 88).

This sensible proposal will not necessarily end disputes, however, because scholars writing from conservative and progressive perspectives can offer different accounts of Judaism's underlying morality. Defending a free market interpretation, Corinne and Robert Sauer (2006) discern five principles at the heart of the tradition.

- Through work, human beings are called upon to participate in the creative process. As an ancient rabbinic interpretation of Genesis states, 'All that was created during the six days that God created the world still requires work' (*Genesis Rabbah* 11:6).
- Orderly and viable human societies require the vigilant protection of private property – the subject of two of the ten commandments.
- Accumulating wealth is a virtue, not a vice.
- Caring for the needy is a moral, not legal principle, and it is not guided by the aim of reducing inequality.
- Although government is necessary, it must be strictly limited, because concentrated power threatens oppression, including the taking of personal property to satisfy the aims (or even whims) of the sovereign.

From a progressive perspective, Rabbi Jill Jacobs (2009), author of *There Shall Be No Needy: Pursuing Social Justice through Jewish Law and Tradition*, offers a very different list (p. 22):

- The world, and everything in it, belongs to God; human beings do not necessarily 'deserve' the wealth in their possession.
- The fates of the wealthy and the poor are linked.
- Law must prevent the gap between the rich and the poor from becoming too wide.
- Even the poorest member of society possesses inherent dignity, which every other member is bound to respect and preserve.
- Poverty relief is an obligation, not a choice, an essential part of bringing about a perfected world. Not doing so would fail the obligation to uphold the dignity of the poor and to love them as oneself.

Notably, each of these lists is squarely grounded in traditional texts, even where (as in the case of relieving poverty) they contradict one another. This opens up space for a similarly grounded synthesis, along the lines Rabbi Sacks offers. On the one hand, he argues, there is an 'elective affinity' between Judaism and the market economy, rooted in respect for labor and property rights, openness to creativity and innovation, and unswerving insistence of rule of law (Sacks 1985). On the other hand, he points out, economic laws in the Torah – especially the idea of the year of Jubilee when debts are forgiven and land restored to original owners as spelled out in Leviticus 25 – aim to 'correct the tendency toward radical and ever-increasing inequality that result from the unfettered play of free market economics' (Sacks 2012). This legislation, Sacks (2012) says, tells us that an economic system

> must exist within a moral framework. It need not aim at economic equality but it must respect human dignity. No one should become permanently imprisoned in the chains of debt. No one should be deprived of a stake in

the commonwealth . . . None of this means dismantling the market economy, but it may involve periodic redistribution.

Some thinkers try to blunt the force of tradition-based syntheses such as Sacks' by sharpening the distinction between principles and practises. In the course of a systematic effort to construct a modern Jewish conservatism, Eric Cohen (2015) states that 'Many Biblical precepts, whatever their merits within the agricultural order of the time, are not compatible with modern capitalist life'. The reason, he argues, is the progress of human understanding:

> [E]ven the rabbis, who knew how to adapt to the times, could not have grasped what Adam Smith and F. A. Hayek eventually discovered and explained to the world: the complex mechanisms by which markets channel self-interest to create economic progress, spur entrepreneurial creativity, leverage investment capital, and promote the efficient division of labour.

As we shall see, it is not so clear that the rabbis failed to understand the positive impact of self-interest and competition on the economy. But the deeper difficulty with Cohen's argument lies elsewhere. If biblical precepts challenge contemporary capitalist practises, is it so obvious that we should discard the precepts? Perhaps we should question the practises instead. For example Cohen questions the concept of periodic debt relief. But setting aside the specifics of the every-fifty-years Jubilee, the Jewish tradition might lead us to wonder whether excluding student loans from the bankruptcy code, rendering them lifelong burdens, is the most humane and productive course. It might even lead us to doubt the unyielding moral proposition – debts must be repaid – at the heart of Europe's response to the Greek crisis.

As Rabbi Sacks (1985) puts it, 'The Jewish encounter with the policy issues of an age . . . occurs when an expert in the facts seeks the guidance of an expert in the values'. This often means that the experts in the values must immerse themselves in the facts, as today's judges wrestling with complex problems of intellectual property or telecommunications regulation have discovered. Even on social issues such as homosexuality and same-sex marriage, the Jewish tradition does not simply invoke stark biblical precepts but examines the practical consequences of competing legal regimes.

Even though traditional Judaism endorses a version of *stare decisis* – the presumption in favour of past decisions – it is not rigidly inflexible when confronting unexpected difficulties, especially when adhering to the strict letter of the law does not work in practice and could even undermine the entire legal system. Two examples suffice to make the point.

In the times when indentured servitude was a common practice, the labour of such servants could be jointly owned by two masters. What should happen when one master but not the other released a servant from his indenture? The followers of Rabbi Hillel said that he should work one day for the remaining master and one day for himself. The followers of Shammai countered that servitude is more than a relationship of subordination; it is a legal status with broad implications. For example, a man who is half slave and half free could marry neither an enslaved woman nor a free one, rendering legitimate reproduction impossible. So the right course is a legal innovation: the remaining master should be required to release the servant from his bonds, and in return the liberated man should be obligated to repay the master over time for the forfeited value of the indenture. The tradition records that when confronted with these practical exigencies, the Hillelites changed their mind and agreed to the innovation (m. Git. 4:5).

A more famous example involves Hillel himself. The Torah mandates that, every seventh year, the land should lie fallow and debts should be forgiven. But this injunction creates incentive problems: as the seventh year approaches, why would anyone lend? Although the Torah explicitly forbids people with resources to take this into account, Hillel noticed that the fear of Divine punishment was not enough to counter the promptings of self-interest. So he invented a procedure by which the creditor transferred ownership of the debt to a court, which was not bound to forgive debts. After the end of the seventh year, the court could collect the debt and repay the creditor (b. Git. 36a-b).

Hillel's innovation contradicted the spirit, and arguably the letter of the Torah. It was nonetheless accepted as legitimate, not only because it solved a practical problem but because it helped preserve the viability of – and respect for – the legal system as a whole. In a similar vein, when Abraham Lincoln's suspension of *habeas corpus* at the beginning of the Civil War came under attack, Lincoln countered with a rhetorical question: 'Are all the laws, but one, to go unexecuted, and the government itself go to pieces, lest the one be violated.'? (Lincoln, A. 1953, p. 430). Exigent circumstances can sometimes bring out latent tensions within legal codes. And when that happens, those with responsibility for administering those codes must do their best – even when their acts break with the past, and even (as in Hillel's case) when the code is of Divine origin.

So, Cohen is not wrong in principle to suggest that innovations in economic organization may necessitate changes in Jewish law. The issue is whether he is right in practice. That depends on how comfortable one is with the consequences of contemporary capitalism. Although the tradition provides some guidelines for making that judgement, it may not resolve the dispute.

This is nothing new: the Talmud records many instances when good arguments are offered on both sides but the question remains unsettled. When the rabbis disagreed, they sometimes voted, and the majority prevailed – a decision procedure they derived from the Torah itself. Even though human reason is imperfect, in practice some questions must be resolved. The rabbis could find no better way of doing this than voting, and neither have the legislators and judges of our day.

Theological anthropology

Although the Jewish tradition does not speak clearly on every current economic dispute (or on every past dispute, for that matter), there are some fixed points that constitute the perimeter of debate. Of these, the most fundamental is that human beings are made in the image of God. Not only does this proposition undergird the moral equality of all people, but also – and more important for our purposes – it shapes our understanding of what human beings are.

In the beginning of Genesis, God is depicted as creatively active, a principle that has done more than any other to shape Jewish anthropology. As God works, so does man. Far from being a curse, work is the opportunity God has given man to imitate Divine activity. That is why a leading rabbi in the Talmud calls on the Jews to 'love work', and why we read in an important commentary on the Talmud, the Avot d'Rabbi Natan, that 'Just as the Torah was given through the covenant, so too, work was given through the covenant'.

As God is creative, so are human beings. Indeed, the Jewish tradition depicts humans as co-creators of the world, a role that God's beneficence has made possible. As Rabbi Sacks (2000) states, summarizing Rabbi Akiva, 'God has handed the world over to human stewardship . . . and deliberately left the world unfinished so that it could be completed by the work of man'.

Humanity's creative work begins with procreation. A rabbinic commentary on Genesis says that 'The Holy One creates worlds and so, too, your father creates worlds' (Gen. Rab. 99). Human creativity also extends to the economic realm. One of the Talmud's most famous sentences states that work makes human beings 'partner with the Holy One . . . in the work of creation' (b. Sabb. 10). This applies also to wealth creation, which occupies a respected place in Jewish morality. As the thirteenth century commentator Rabbenu Bachya puts it, 'The active participation of man in the creation of his own wealth is a sign of his spiritual greatness' (Rabbenu Bachya, cited in Sacks 1995, p. 197).

Not all work leads to wealth, of course. But even the humblest profession is honourable, both because it allows us to imitate God but also because it helps us avoid unnecessary dependence on our fellows. This theme recurs throughout the Talmud, as three representative quotations show. In one, Rav says, 'Skin carcasses in the market-place and collect your wages, and do not say, I am a priest and a great man, and this is below my dignity' (b. Pesah. 113a). In another passage, we read that 'R. Yehuda used to go into the house of study carrying a pitcher on his shoulders. He would say, "Great is work, as it gives honour to the one who does it"' (b. Ned. 49b). And R. Chiyya ben Ammi declares: 'Greater is the one who benefits from the work of his hands than one who fears heaven' (b. Ber. 8a). This tradition is reflected in the New Testament practises of the apostle Paul, a Jew who worked as a tentmaker to support himself even as he was working to establish early communities who were following the teachings of Jesus (Acts 18:1–3).

One interpretation of these arresting statements is that work shapes our life and character in ways that help us surmount the temptation to do wrong. Talmudic discussions of one of the fruits of work – namely, property – add support to this interpretation: property enables us to avoid dependence and wrongdoing. Rabbi Akiva taught his son that 'It is better to profane your Sabbath than to become dependent on others' (b. Pesah. 112b). And Rabbi Elazar said that 'For the righteous, their property is dearer to them than their own body. Why so? Because they do not stretch out their hand to steal' (b. Hul. 91a).

From the beginning, Judaism has acknowledged the inevitability of dependence and has created a system of norms and practises designed to address it in ways that respect the dignity of dependent persons. This is, so to speak, the liberal side of the tradition. At the same time, the tradition insists on the obligation to work if one is able and to do one's best to avoid becoming dependent on others. Dependence is sometimes inevitable, but it should not be a voluntary status.

There is one intensely controversial exception to this principle – scholars who devote their full attention to the study of the Torah and the Talmud. On one point there is no dispute: the study of God's Word, and of human efforts to understand it, is the highest form of human activity, the nearest we can get to God. But as far back as Talmudic times, some authorities said that to pursue this activity full-time, scholars are permitted to accept charity, while others said the opposite. Rabban Gamliel, a leader of the Jewish community, declared that 'Beautiful is the study of Torah combined with a worldly occupation, for the toil of them both causes sin to be forgotten'. At the same time, he issued a warning: 'Ultimately, all Torah study that is not accompanied with work is destined ... to cause sin' (b. Abot 2:2). This issue – the financial dependence of scholars – continues to be actively debated today, and it figures centrally in Israeli politics.

An orientation towards this world is a second key feature of Jewish theology. Looking on His Creation, God affirms its goodness. Who are we to argue? Jews are commanded to believe that this world reflects God's beneficence and act accordingly, not only by expressing our gratitude but also by enjoying our world's distinctive satisfactions. For this reason, Judaism has no problem with legitimate pleasures – eating and drinking, sexuality within marriage, the joys of parents and grandparents, and the satisfactions of friendship. And it is mostly opposed to asceticism, which it understands as a rejection of what God has given us. For this reason, says the Jerusalem Talmud, 'Man will have to account for all that he sees with his eyes and does not partake of' (y. Qidd. 4:12).

Judaism regulates desire, of course, and it prescribes carefully measured doses of self-denial – fast days, for example – as opportunities for reflection and spiritual renewal. But the Torah treats the Nazarite – the only category of longer-term asceticism it recognizes as legitimate – with decided ambivalence.

The belief in the goodness of God's creation also explains why Judaism regards theodicy as a difficult problem. It would be one thing if this world were just a vale of tears, a torment to be endured in anticipation of the world to come. But if the world is presumed to be good, then the misfortunes of virtuous individuals cry out for justification, as does the prosperity of the evildoers. Rabbi Yannai threw up his hands: 'We cannot understand the tranquillity of the wicked', he sighed, 'or the suffering of the righteous' (b. Abot 4:15). Nor, he might have added, has God given us an explanation – even though He owes us one. God's denial that He does owe human beings an explanation (see the conclusion of the book of Job) does not make its absence any easier for Jews to bear.

A third key element of Judaism's theological anthropology is the implicit rejection of the doctrine of original sin. The Jewish tradition regards human beings as endowed with a mixed nature, combining positive elements such as generosity and justice with negative elements such as self-interest, envy and lust. In Ecclesiastes 4:4, we read that 'All labour and all achievement spring from man's envy of his neighbour', rendering it pointless – 'chasing after the wind'. The rabbinic tradition had a more benign interpretation: God has so arranged the world that even man's ✔ negative side has positive consequences. As a rabbinic interpretation of Genesis puts it, 'Were it not for the evil inclination, no one would build a house, marry a wife, have children, or engage in business' (Gen. Rab. 9:9). Far from recoiling in dismay, traditional Judaism anticipates and accepts Adam Smith's famous dictum that 'It is not from the benevolence of the butcher, the brewer, or the baker that we expect our dinner, but from their regard to their own interest'. Self-interest is natural and ineradicable. If religion demands saintliness, it condemns believers to unending guilt. At best, it can restrain self-interest and arrange the world so that it works to benefit others as well.

The same stance leads to a realistic interpretation of human altruism. Yes, we are commanded to love others as we do ourselves. That does not mean that we are forbidden to love ourselves and to act on that self-regard. It does mean that we are not free to ignore the claims of others, which reflect their self-regard, as we pursue our own. But faced with those claims, we are not required to abnegate ourselves; the claims of other-regardingness on us end where serious harm to oneself begins. It may sometimes be virtuous to go farther and set aside one's own interests in favour of others'. But it does not take formal psychological training to understand that those who do not love themselves will have a hard time loving others. Like so much else in the Jewish tradition, altruism begins at home.

Poverty

Within Judaism, concern for others manifests itself above all in individual and collective responses to poverty, which is first and foremost seen as a communal concern. In Deuteronomy 15:4–5, God promises the Jewish people that once they enter the land of Israel, 'There will be no needy among you'. But the promise is conditional: '*if* you diligently heed the voice of the Lord to observe all that I command you to do this day'. Two verses later, we encounter another conditional statement: 'If there is a needy man among you', followed by a mandatory response: 'you shall not harden your heart nor withhold your hand from your needy brother'. And in Deuteronomy 15:11 we are told that 'the poor shall never cease out of the land'. The inference is unavoidable: the Jewish people will never reach the level of obedience to God's law that is the prerequisite for ending poverty. There is no suggestion, at least in this key passage, that poverty is a punishment for individual wrongdoing; the error is collective.

Isaac Caro, a medieval commentator, suggests that the problem is structural: wealth and poverty go together. 'The reason that the poor person is poor', he says, is because 'the rich person is rich; when your star ascends, his star descends . . . You [the rich person] are the reason that he is poor' (Isaac Caro, cited in Jacobs 2009, p. 17). If so, this would be another basis for the obligation of the rich towards the poor.

This is not to say that individuals bear no responsibility for their own misfortune; often they do. Weakness of will and bad choices can leave potentially self-supporting individuals dependent on others. But as Rabbi Jacobs points out, whatever may be the case in theory, traditional Judaism refuses in practice to distinguish between the deserving and the undeserving poor. A rabbinic commentary on Leviticus contains the following parable:

> If [a] rich man says to [a] poor man, 'Why do you not go and work and get food? Look at those hips! Look at those legs! Look at that fat body! Look at those lumps of flesh!' I, the Blessed Holy One say to him, 'Is it not enough that you have not given him anything of yours, but you must set the evil eye upon what I have given him!'
>
> (Vay. Rab. 34:4)

In the tradition, we occasionally find theological justifications for poverty. One commentator says that if the Jews 'have no food to eat, or clothing to wear, or oil for anointing, they will plead for mercy and will find it, and because of poverty they will come to fear God' (Jacobs 2009, pp. 54–55). Poverty is good for the poor, because prosperity leads to forgetfulness of their dependence on God. A rabbinic commentary on Leviticus suggests that poverty is even more beneficial for the character of the rich because it induces them to help and care for others: 'More than the wealthy person does for the poor, the poor person does for the wealthy' (Vay. Rab. 34:8).

In the main, however, the Jewish tradition refuses to regard poverty as ennobling. 'Poverty is worse than fifty plagues', says the Talmud (b. B. Bat. 116a). A rabbinic commentary on Exodus says that 'Poverty is worse than all of the other sufferings in the world' (Sh. Rab. 31:12). Indeed, it continues, 'If all the other troubles were placed on one side and poverty on the other, poverty would outweigh them all' (Sh. Rab. 31:14).

Conversely, there is nothing intrinsically wrong with wealth. The key question is how the wealthy use it. There is nothing in the Jewish tradition that corresponds to Jesus' claim that 'It is easier for a camel to go through the eye of a needle than for a rich man to enter the kingdom of God' (Matthew 19:24).

We have a good intuitive idea of what it means to be wealthy (as opposed, say, to merely well-off). But what exactly is poverty in the Jewish tradition? On the conceptual level, there are three different approaches. The first, most familiar to us today, equates poverty with dire need – lack of access to the basic requisites of human life such as food, shelter, medicine, primary education – and, the rabbis add, what individuals need to fulfil the ritual obligations incumbent on every Jew.

By contrast, the second approach to poverty is distinctly unfamiliar, at least at first. The tradition often discussed cases of men who had lost a great deal – but not all – of their former wealth. The rabbis focused on the human consequences of this loss – a fall in social status, but even more, a sense of shame and humiliation. Although there was no obligation to restore what had been lost, some rabbis – most famously, Hillel – tried to do so. Although there is nothing in contemporary anti-poverty programmes that corresponds to this idea, there is a controversial vestige of it in the sense, deeply felt by some and fervently deplored by others that the perpetrators of financial crimes who lose their jobs and assets should not be sent to jail. To be stripped of status and resources, some insist, is punishment enough.

A third rabbinic approach is moral and psychological. 'Who is rich?' Ben Zoma asked rhetorically: 'One who is satisfied with his lot' (b. Abot 4:1). We are poor, he implies, when we are dissatisfied. Daily experience suggests that he was on to something. Even if we live comfortably, we often feel deprived when we encounter those who are better off. Comparison leads to envy, and envy to dissatisfaction. Since the eighteenth century, economists have sought to harness this psychology of comparison to the work that produces more wealth for everyone. But much social commentary regards this envy-driven striving as a source of permanent unhappiness – the notorious 'rat race'. This probably accounts for the perennial appeal of 'Eastern' religions such as Buddhism in modern capitalist societies. (The unforgettable closing scene of *Mad Men*, in which the tortured advertising executive Don Draper ends up chanting 'Om . . .' at Esalen, pivots on this.)

But let us return from the spiritual to the material. In a manner familiar to modern policy-makers, the rabbis wrestled with defining the 'poverty line' – a task complicated, as in our time, by the different kinds of poverty relief. The criteria for emergency food aid were relatively straightforward; for longer-term assistance, less so. In the latter case, the rabbis began with a specific level – denominated in currency – of income and wealth but moved on to make distinctions among kinds of assets. In a striking anticipation of today's policies, they ended up excluding certain kinds of holdings, such as a home and cooking utensils, from the calculation of assets on which the determination of eligibility for assistance was based (Jacobs 2009, pp. 68–70).

This brings us to the heart of the matter – the Jewish response to poverty, *tzedaka* in Hebrew. Although this term is etymologically related to *tzedek* (justice), it is usually translated as charity. Yet *tzedaka* doesn't mean charity in the Christian sense, but rather a transfer made in response to an objective obligation.

Modern commentators disagree about the nature of this obligation. We begin with a premise not in dispute – the status of property in the Jewish tradition. Rabbi Sacks argues that Judaism has a high regard for private property as an institution governing the relations among human beings. But when it comes to the relation between man and God, there has been 'an equal insistence that what we have we do not unconditionally own. Ultimately everything belongs to God. What we have, we hold in trust' (Sacks 2000). According to Rabbi Yechiel Epstein

> One should not say, 'How can I take away from my own money to give to the poor?' For this person should know that the money is not his own, but

> rather is a deposit left for safekeeping in his hand in order that he may do the will of the one who left it. And [God's] will is that the person should give *tzedaka*.
>
> (Jacobs 2009, p. 86)

For Rabbi Sacks (2012), the implication is clear: 'Those who are blessed by God with more than they need should share some of that surfeit with those who have less than they need. This, in Judaism, is not a matter of charity but of justice . . .' According to Sacks

> *Tzedakah* belongs to the notion of justice rather than benevolence . . . and reflects the idea that since all property ultimately belongs to God, it is a sense of equity rather than generosity that commands giving it to others. The giving of charity could therefore be coerced by communal sanction and was formally organised on a community basis.
>
> (Sacks 1985)

In the same vein, another leading scholar, Meir Tamari (1987), says that

> The divine origin of wealth is the central principle of Jewish economic philosophy. All wealth belongs to God, who has given it temporarily to man, for his physical well-being . . . The 'haves' in Judaism have an obligation to share their property with the 'have-nots', since it was given to them by God partly for that purpose. Charity is not simply an act of kindness but rather the fulfilment of a legal obligation.
>
> (p. 26, p. 52)

Although Joseph Lifshitz (2010) insists that strong rights of private property govern relations among human beings, he does not deny that all we have, including property, is ultimately God's. Nonetheless, he takes the analysis of *tzedaka* – charity – in a different direction. Charity, he says, is 'something that flows not from a sense of justice but from the goodness of one's character or the generosity of one's heart . . . For this reason, the Sages defined charity foremost as a moral principle, not a juridical one' (p. 17). Nonetheless, he acknowledges, it is neither optional nor supererogatory, but rather obligatory and enforceable. This reflects the rabbinic understanding of the legitimate role of coercion in moral matters, which differs from the contemporary liberal understanding.

Still, Lifshitz (2010) insists

> Curtailing man's mastery over his possessions is derived solely from man's religious obligations [to God] and not from his status *vis-à-vis* another human being . . . Hence, any interpretation that claims the existence of distributive justice in Jewish Law as separate from the individual's religious identity . . . must be merely a reduction of Jewish Law's theological principles to an anachronistic political position.
>
> (pp. 34–35)

The collectively enforceable obligations to assist the poor that do exist stem from the religious significance of Jewish peoplehood – in particular, the importance of its survival and unity.

This is a genuine debate: the 'sense of equity' that Sacks places at the core of *tzedaka* is different from the 'generosity' to which Lifshitz gives pride of place. Nonetheless, the practical consequences of this disagreement may be modest. If Sacks means that the difference between justice and charity is between what is enforceable and what isn't, then the dispute is largely verbal; Lifshitz acknowledges that charity as he understands it is enforceable. And if Lifshitz means that the right relationship between man and man rests on the right relationship between man and God, then we are arguing about the basis of social obligation, not about its content. This is a distinction with a difference, however: the Jewish account of social justice, which reflects the vertical relationship between man and God, is incompatible with any argument – such as John Rawls's (1971) theory of justice – that it can be adequately grounded in the horizontal relationship among fellow citizens.

When it comes to the principles governing the practice of *tzedaka*, there is less dispute. In the Jewish tradition, concentric circles of responsibility shape charitable giving: family in the innermost circle, then members of one's immediate community, then others. But the dire needs of strangers can trump the lesser needs of those closer to you (Jacobs 2009, p. 90). There is a tension, moreover, between individual obligation, which typically reflects relationships, and collective obligation, which must be based on membership rather than personal ties.

There are minimum standards for charitable giving, but also limits. No one should impoverish himself to relieve the poverty of others. Individuals are not allowed to divest themselves of wealth to the extent to which they risk becoming dependent on others (call it the King Lear principle). Collectors of charity should not make such requests, and individuals who for whatever reasons want to go too far should be restrained from doing so. Nothing in the mainstream Jewish tradition corresponds to Jesus' admonition to 'Go, sell what you possess and give it to the poor, and you will have treasure in heaven' (Matthew 19:21). Part of the reason is practical: if the wealthy divest themselves of their property, they will become dependent in turn, and the poor would have ended up worse off. Would it have been better for the sick and hungry in Africa if Bill Gates had distributed all his wealth to the poor after he made his first million dollars?

Finally, forms of charity differ qualitatively; the best kind helps the poor dispense with it altogether. Moses Maimonides, the great medieval codifier of Jewish law, states that

> The highest degree of charity, exceeded by none, is that of a person who assists a poor Jew by providing him with a gift or a loan or by accepting him into a business partnership or by helping him to find employment – in a word, by putting him [in a position] where he can dispense with other people's aid.

> (Sacks 2000)

This view has become canonical among Jews, and it finds its correlates in contemporary American culture. Give a man a fish, goes the saying, and you feed him for a day; teach him to fish, and he can feed himself for life – or at least until the fish run out.

Economic management

Although I have focused thus far on *tzedaka*, it is not the only way in which the Jewish tradition seeks to alleviate poverty and economic oppression. As Tamari (1987) points out, the community's responsibility for the welfare of its members gives it the corresponding right, when circumstances require, to finance those needs through taxation 'over and above the individual's duty to contribute to charity' (p. 240). In addition, the Talmud addresses issues such as wages, working conditions, prices and unfair manipulation.

I begin with some general considerations about the market. The Jewish tradition is not inhospitable to the idea of an invisible hand that transmutes self-interested action into broadly beneficial results. In that spirit, Judaism recognizes the contribution that competition can make to progress. For example an established teacher could not object to a newcomer hanging out his own shingle: 'Jealousy among scholars', it was said, 'increases wisdom' (b. B. Bat. 21a).

Nor is the tradition hostile, at least in principle, to the more tangible fruits of competition. On the contrary, says Sacks (2000)

> From a Jewish perspective, economic growth has religious significance because it allows us to alleviate poverty . . . [The rabbis] sought to create a society in which the poor had access to help when they needed it, through charity to be sure, but also and especially through job creation.

At the same time, there are limits to market relationships. The domain of the 'holy' has a measure of value wholly independent of price. Holiness includes not only sanctified rituals but also intimate human ties and our understanding of ourselves. If we are made in the image of God, then *homo economicus* cannot be an adequate conception of human beings. The market undermines not only the holy but also itself when it expands beyond its due bounds and becomes an imperialist cast of thought.

In practice, the Jewish tradition employs numerous strategies to mitigate the adverse consequences of markets for workers and the poor. Although Lifshitz (2010) offers a generally pro-market interpretation of the tradition, he notes that 'Laissez faire is hardly a Jewish motto!' (p. 84).

Indeed not. For example price controls are sometimes appropriate, especially to prevent gouging. Merchants are not allowed to exploit a superior bargaining position at the expense of the economically vulnerable. 'Whatever the market will bear' is not a principle of Jewish economics.

A remarkable story from the Talmud illustrates this point. Because Jews cannot consume anything leavened on the 8 days of Passover, during this period they cannot use cookware that has absorbed traces of leaven from pre-Passover use. Rav, a great rabbinic authority, ruled that such cookware must be broken and replaced each year. This produced a sudden spike in demand, permitting merchants to jack up their prices. In response, Rav's friend and colleague Shmuel assembled the merchants and read them the riot act: if they did not bring their prices down, he would suspend Rav's ruling and allow families to store their regular cookware rather than destroying it. Faced with the prospect of a total collapse in demand, the merchants complied (b. Pesah. 30a).

This is hardly an isolated story. Throughout the Talmud and its commentaries we find discussions of profiteering in its various modes – hoarding, price manipulations, exploitation of crises and others – along with legitimate communal responses to them. Local monopolies may establish minimum prices, but only in some circumstances. After taking the cost of materials and labour into account, merchants are limited to a 20 per cent profit on their sales.[2] For contemporary purposes, the point is not to mimic the specific limit on profits but rather to note the underlying principle that such limits are legitimate restraints on market outcomes.

In a similar vein, we find numerous Talmudic discussions of wages and working conditions. Employers must always respect the dignity of their workers, and local communities are sometimes permitted to set minimum pay levels. Anticipating recent research on the effects of the US minimum wage, there are even subtle discussions of the relation between wages and workers' productivity. And contemporary rabbinic authorities see the workers' guilds of Talmudic times as precedent for today's trade unions. (Whether and under what circumstances Jewish law permits strikes and work stoppages is a matter of dispute, however.)[3]

In Talmudic times, Jews enjoyed substantial autonomy within larger imperial structures. Individual local communities would often adopt measures to protect local merchants against competition from imports and new market participants, and Jewish law endorsed these practises, within limits. There is even a dispute – redolent of the current strife between Uber and the taxi drivers – about the extent to which harm to the livelihood of current participants in an economic sector warrants the prohibition of new entrants into that sector. The underlying Talmudic principle seems to have been that local protectionism is warranted when outside competitors are playing by rules that give them an unfair structural advantage.

Conclusion

It is a mistake to read today's conceptions of social justice into the Torah and Talmud, or to straightforwardly apply ancient Jewish law to contemporary economic circumstances. As we have seen, the tradition's understanding of economic relations has theological underpinnings alien to today's secular philosophy. Jewish authorities did not determine the presence of injustice by examining income distribution tables. Although they deplored poverty and sought to alleviate it, they cared much more about how the rich used their wealth than about how much they had. They were concerned with individual character, human ties and man's relationship to God, and they examined economic practises from this perspective.

The Jewish tradition provides a framework for thinking about these issues. We find a theological anthropology – man made in God's image – that calls upon human beings to participate actively in the process of Creation. Whatever its kind, work is an expression of dignity as well as a source of income and wealth, which the law defines and society protects.

We are required to respect the property of others, the tradition teaches, but we are constantly reminded that the world and everything in it ultimately belongs to God. We are stewards of Creation, and what we have made of it, in God's service, which involves service to our fellow human beings. Accumulating wealth is no vice, provided that those who do so use it appropriately.

Jewish authorities developed a social theory in light of these principles. Rejecting hyper-individualism, they saw a dense network of mutual responsibilities, not all of which were limited to fellow Jews. Every person has a duty to become self-supporting to the greatest extent possible but also to help others who are not, regardless of how they ended up in a position of dependence. Levels of expected contribution are established, usually by social norms, but only through collective decisions. Communities may regulate the operations of the market, not only to prevent outright fraud, but also to police against the exploitation that occurs when the economically powerful can take advantage of their stronger bargaining position. Wages, working conditions, prices and monopolistic practises are all subject, within limits, to communal control.

Although the Jewish tradition is far from egalitarian in economic matters, it is concerned about extremes of wealth and poverty, especially those that are self-perpetuating across generations, even if they have come about through a sequence of legitimate transactions. The cancellation of debts every 7 years, and the broader reversions to earlier conditions every 50 years are intended as counterweights to these tendencies, which the tradition saw as threats to the survival of the community. Today, as the impact of the circumstances of one's birth increasingly shape our lives and as advantages and disadvantages are handed down more and more from parents to children, we would do well to reflect on these questions and to develop responses appropriate to our circumstances. The alternative is the arrogance of the strong and the suffering of the weak against which the prophets warned.

Notes

1 For a lucid summary of Leibowitz's forbidding position, see 'Yeshayahu Leibowitz', *Stanford Encyclopedia of Philosophy*, available from: https://plato.stanford.edu/entries/leibowitz-yeshayahu/.
2 These and other issues are authoritatively treated by Itamar Warhaftig (1987).
3 For a thorough discussion of these issues, see Chapter 5 in Jacobs (2009).

References

Cohen, E. (2015) 'The spirit of Jewish conservatism', *Mosaic*, 6 April. Available from: http://mosaicmagazine.com/essay/2015/04/the-spirit-of-jewish-conservatism/ [accessed 21 April 2015].

Hartman, D. (2012) *From defender to critic: The search for a new Jewish self*, Woodstock, VT: Jewish Lights Publishing.

Jacobs, J. (2009) *There shall be no needy: Pursuing social justice through Jewish law & tradition*, Woodstock, VT: Jewish Lights Publishing.

Lifshitz, J. I. (2010) *Judaism, law & the free market: An analysis*, Grand Rapids, MI: Acton Institute.

Lincoln, A (1953[1861]), 'Message to Congress in special session', in *Collected works of Abraham Lincoln, vol. 4*, New Brunswick, NJ: Rutgers University Press.

Rawls, J. (1971) *A theory of justice*, Cambridge, MA: Harvard University Press.

Sacks, J. (1985) *Wealth and poverty: A Jewish analysis*, London: Social Affairs Unit. Available from: http://socialaffairsunit.org.uk/digipub/index2.php?option=content&do_pdf=1&id =16 [accessed 7 May 2015].

Sacks, J. (1995) *Faith in the future: The ecology of hope and the restoration of faith, community, and family*, Macon, GA: Mercer University Press.

Sacks, J. (2000) 'Markets and morals', *First Things*, vol. 105. Available from: www.firstthings.com/article/2000/08/markets-and-morals [accessed 23 June 2015].

Sacks, J. (2012) 'The limits of the free market', *Covenant & Conversation*, 14 May. Available from: http://rabbisacks.org/covenant-conversation-5772-behar-bechukotai-the-limits-of-the-free-market/ [accessed 7 May 2015].

Sauer, C. and Sauer, R. (2006) *Judaism, markets, and capitalism: Separating myth from reality*, Grand Rapids, MI: Acton Institute.

Tamari, M. (1987) *With all your possessions: Jewish ethics and economic life*, Northvale, NJ: Jason Aronson.

Warhaftig, I. (1987) 'Consumer protection: Price and wage levels', in Rosenfeld, E. (ed.), *Crossroads: Halacha and the modern world*, vol. 1 Alon Shvut-Gush Etzion, Israel: Zomet Institute, pp. 49–69.

3

ELECTION, SELECTION AND DISTINCTION

Paradoxes of grace, clan and class

Timothy P. Jackson

> And if the Lord had not cut short those days, no one would be saved; but for the sake of the elect, whom he chose, he has cut short those days.
>
> (Mark 13:20)

> So too at the present time there is a remnant, chosen by grace. But if it is by grace, it is no longer on the basis of works, otherwise grace would no longer be grace. What then? Israel failed to obtain what it was seeking. The elect obtained it, but the rest were hardened.
>
> (Romans 11:5–7)

> As they went away, Jesus began to speak to the crowds about John: 'What did you go out into the wilderness to look at? A reed shaken by the wind? What then did you go out to see? Someone dressed in soft robes? Look, those who wear soft robes are in royal palaces'.
>
> (Matthew 11:7–8)

> Then Jesus said to his disciples, 'Truly I tell you, it will be hard for a rich person to enter the kingdom of heaven. Again I tell you, it is easier for a camel to go through the eye of a needle than for someone who is rich to enter the kingdom of God'.
>
> (Matthew 19:23–24)

Introduction

My purpose in these pages is to criticize two classical foundations of elitism: the theological notion of election and the social idea of distinction. In addition, I take aim at a modern source of bias based in genetics: racial superiority. Racism-astribalism is ancient, but reference to genetic selection as the rationale for hubris is only approximately 150 years old. All three phenomena – functions of grace, class and clan – are inspired, I argue, by ubiquitous human anxiety over finitude. We dread our various vulnerabilities and ultimately our mortality and, in an effort to deny or evade these, we project them onto others. We are made anxious by the prospect of our own suffering and death, so we hurt and kill our neighbors. Here is the original sin: trying to elevate ourselves, we denigrate others; trying to liberate ourselves, we enslave others. This makes possible a kind of perpetual *Schadenfreude*: we take joy at others' permanent (or deeply entrenched[1]) inferiority. *In extremis*, we insist that our salvation justifies, even *requires*, the damnation of others.

The divide between 'the elect' (a.k.a. 'the saved') and 'the reprobate' (a.k.a. 'the damned') is referred or alluded to at least fifteen times in the New Testament[2] and runs through the subsequent writings of most Christian theologians, including Saint Augustine, Thomas Aquinas, Martin Luther, John Calvin and Karl Barth. Details vary, especially as to how fixed and resistible membership in these groups may be. But, to this day, Christians tend to relate to the divide between the elect and the reprobate in much the same way that some relate to the distinction between royal and commoner – with unquestioning acceptance or even overt celebration. The idea of royalty, 'people of distinction', is also present in both the Hebrew Bible and Christian Scripture, with the early church concerned about establishing Jesus' hereditary connection to the House of David.

These facts ought to be more surprising and distressing to us than they usually are. On the face of it, both contrasts are profoundly inegalitarian and contrary to the universalist spirit of Christ and the democratic spirit of many countries that retain a royal/commoner distinction, like Britain. In Matthew 11, Christ even explicitly contrasts royalty with prophecy. Yet, the invidious dichotomies are assumed as given by many and even hailed as sites of virtue and tradition. Indeed, Christianity initially founded its church on a profound gulf between 'the children of light' (a.k.a. 'us') (Luke 16:8) and 'the children of the evil one' (a.k.a. 'them') (Matthew 13:38), even as Great Britain built its empire on what Rudyard Kipling would eventually call 'the White Man's burden' and a sense of the intrinsic inferiority of plebeian races.

Many Christians, especially Protestants, will protest that reference to immutable 'election' is an admirable expression of humility, a denial of works righteousness and an affirmation of God's sovereignty. The rub, however, is that this inevitably entails both elitism and fatalism. For this reason, Arminians insist that Christ's Atonement was not limited and that God's grace is not irresistible. Even if all people might in principle and freely be saved, however, the fact that some should contingently be bound in an agonizing hell forever remains a challenge to the goodness of God and the justice of the human condition. (How can a temporal sin warrant an eternal punishment?) And the paradoxes multiply. The country that most conspicuously sought to 'abolish' both divine election and social class – Russia via the Communist Revolution – ended up being one of the most economically stratified and undemocratic nations on earth. Add to the sins of theological election the fact that natural selection and Social Darwinism are often its secular successors and you begin to sense the worm at the heart of human nature: the inclination to glorify self by demeaning others.

Many Anglo Americans, especially entrepreneurs, will protest that reference to personal 'distinction' is an admirable expression of ambition, a goad to achievement and a recognition of merit. The rub, however, is that when distinction is understood biologically – as in master races and royal families – it again entails both elitism and fatalism. One cannot appreciably change one's genes, and blood prejudices are among the most insulting and violent. When distinction is construed politically or economically, as a matter of power or possessions, it frequently becomes spiteful as well. One can celebrate the efforts and contributions of a successful politician or businessperson, of course, even as one may applaud heroism in combat or medical prowess. Not all honoring of merit is false or offensive. But when individual worth is seen as a direct function of high office or income, then something has gone badly wrong. The rich and famous look down their noses at the poor and marginal, and shared human sanctity and dignity is ignored or violated. Why should all this be? And what, specifically, ought to be our normative reaction to it?

Let me begin by narrating a brief theological history of election, taking Saint Augustine, Thomas Aquinas, Julian of Norwich, Martin Luther, Jacob Arminius and Søren Kierkegaard as signposts. This will be a didactic tale of progress from two static cities determined by God to one dynamic self responding to God. I will then elaborate further Luther's views on righteousness and note analogies with biological distinctions between the noble and the lowly, the selected and the unfit. Next, I will examine capitalism and political and economic distinctions between the powerful and the weak, the rich and the poor. These latter analyses will amount to a didactic tale of decline. Far too often, natural selection or market distinction supplants supernatural election as the occasion for contumely. I conclude with the hope that most clan-based and class-based divisions, like the elect versus reprobate dichotomy, can be overcome in time. Such hope is dictated by the revolutionary conception of God embodied in and taught by Jesus Christ. This conception affirms, paradoxically, that God 'elects' everyone, power is made perfect in weakness and poverty is wealth. Because God loves me, I need not repress my insignificance at your expense. Indeed, I can will your good.

Against irresistible election as the source of inequality

For Saint Augustine (354–430), humanity was divided into two discrete and unequal camps. His City of God is composed of those who love God even to the contempt of self, while the city of this world is made up of those who love self even to the contempt of God (Augustine 1972 [426], XIV.28, pp. 593–594). The membership of each group is fixed and non-overlapping, with the elect being irresistibly chosen by God for the heavenly City and the reprobate being ineluctably forsaken by God to the earthly city. The drama of history is generated, in large measure, by the interaction of these two diverse communities. The former is oriented towards God and the rational governance of the soul (*caritas*), and it is destined for eternal Beatitude. The latter is oriented towards humanity and the wanton indulgence of bodily desire (*cupiditas*), and it is destined for perpetual damnation (Augustine 1971 [426/427], p. 481).[3] Both populations are 'born of Adam', and, having been bequeathed original sin biologically, both are justly in 'the mass of perdition' and due everlasting punishment (Augustine 1971 [418], II.36, p. 250). But, *mirabile dictu*, some are saved by God as 'vessels of mercy', while others are condemned by God as 'vessels of wrath' (Augustine 1972 [426], XV.2, p. 598). Why God-in-Christ does not redeem all souls is a mystery, but we cannot complain because all deserve to die. We can only be impressed by the sovereign power of God's providence: all those elected cannot but be saved, and all those reprobated cannot but be damned.

Early in his authorship, such as his *Commentary on the Sentences of Peter the Lombard* and parts of *De Veritate*, Thomas Aquinas (1225–1274) limited God's causal agency to creation and sustaining grace. Bernard Lonergan (1971) points out that by the time of *Summa Contra Gentiles* and *Summa Theologiae*, however, Thomas judged that God's will had to be brought into line with His intellect. Just as God knows all things, so God causes all things. This is what Lonergan (1971) calls the 'universal instrumentality' thesis. God is the sufficient reason for everything that happens. Moreover, 'God moves man to act, not only by proposing the appetible to the senses, or by effecting a change in his body, but also by moving the will itself' (Aquinas 1981, Ia-IIae, Q. 6, art. 1, reply obj. 3, p. 617). Even so, God respects 'inferior' causes and gives creatures 'the dignity of causality', bringing about necessary things necessarily and contingent things contingently (ibid., Ia, Q. 22, art. 3, p. 124). The mature Thomas agrees with Augustine that God can move the will irresistibly and yet preserve the voluntariness of human agency (ibid., Ia-IIae, Q. 6, arts. 4–5, pp. 618–620). To hold that God can necessitate a free and responsible action in this way is commonly called 'compatibilism'. In addition to compatibilism, Thomas also agrees with Augustine that there are two fundamentally discontinuous human groups: the elect and the damned.

Julian of Norwich (1342–1416) is both compelling and vexing in bending Augustinian and Thomistic orthodoxies without quite breaking them. She avers that 'God is the focal point of everything, and he does it all', which sounds like universal instrumentality, but she suggests as well that all might be redeemed in the end (Norwich 1966 [1395], p. 80). Her claim that 'everything is included in the "mankind who are to be saved"' sounds rather like universal atonement (ibid., p. 75). And her contention that 'all shall be brought to joy' smacks of universal salvation (ibid., p. 95). To raise even the possibility of universal salvation is to challenge two fundamental assumptions endorsed by much of Western Christianity from the beginning: (1) that God is elitist and aims only to save a few and (2) that human beings are inherently unequal, with some fated to heaven and others fated to hell. It does not seem accidental that a fourteenth-century religious woman might see existence from the margin so as to butt up against invidious contrasts between 'us' and 'them'. To be sure, Julian announces her fidelity to the official teachings of Mother Church, but her 'showings' have a life of their own. They tend to displace an accent on divine power and condemnation and replace it with an accent on divine goodness and mercy. Compare in this connection her remarks on both God and Jesus as 'Mother' (ibid., p. 151, p. 164). Julian describes a nurturing and merciful God.

Martin Luther (1483–1546) begins Part One, Section III of 'Secular Authority' along Augustinian lines: 'We must divide all the children of Adam into two classes; the first belong to the kingdom of God, the second to the kingdom of the world' (Luther 1961 [1523], p. 368). The Godly kingdom is composed of all true Christians and ruled by Christ-like love and non-violence; the worldly kingdom is comprised of everybody else and ruled by coercive law and the sword. As 'Secular Authority' and later works unfold, however, many have perceived a shift in Luther's position. When he claims that a Christian is *simul justus et peccator* (simultaneously justified and a sinner) and that a Christian may violently defend others (including other Christians) just not himself or herself, he effectively embraces what some commentators call 'the two hats theory' (ibid., p. 381). On this account, a Christian is in both kingdoms at once. In 'outer' political relations, a Christian seeks to restrain evil and governs behavior according to strict rules of justice; in 'inner' spiritual matters, a Christian 'turns the other cheek' and relies on mercy and forgiveness. Luther thus transmutes various medieval hierarchical unities – gospel over law, eternity over time, mind over body, etc. – into more dualistic tensions – gospel versus law, eternity versus time, mind versus body, etc. He also gives up on the compatibilism of Augustine and Aquinas regarding irresistible divine grace and meaningful human freedom. Luther sometimes expresses misgivings about the word 'necessity' and admits 'free will' with respect to things 'below' man, but he typically affirms necessity and denies freedom: 'We do everything of necessity, and nothing by "free will"; for the power of "free will" is nil, and it does no good, nor can do, without grace' (Luther 1961 [1525], p. 182, p. 189, p. 188). His considered opinion is that, after the Fall, there is no meaningful human freedom. God's grace moves our actions ineluctably: 'All we do, however it may appear to us to be done mutably and contingently, is in reality done necessarily and immutably in respect of God's will. For the will of God is effective and cannot be impeded, since power belongs to God's nature' (ibid., p. 181).

Jacob (a.k.a. James) Arminius (1560–1609) is the first of our authors emphatically to deny unconditional election, limited atonement and irresistible grace. He was asked, while serving as a pastor in Amsterdam, to write a refutation of Dirck Volckertszoon Coornheert's critique of Calvinism. Coornheert had rejected the strict Calvinist doctrines of predestination and irresistible grace, and Arminius seemed like a good candidate to write a refutation. After reading Coornheert's argument, though, Arminius came generally to side with Coornheert. He discerned in traditional Calvinism what I call '*the fundamental paradox of election*': it makes God arbitrary and responsible for evil. Hence, Arminius began to preach that God's offer of salvation was universal and human beings were free to accept or reject that offer. He rejected what he saw as the stronger forms of free will at work in Pelagianism and semi-Pelagianism, inasmuch as he denied that we can even turn to God on our own in the fallen state. He granted that God must turn us, but he insisted that we could say 'yes' or 'no' to the turning, that we could accept or reject the indispensable (but not ineluctable) offer of grace (Arminius 1996, pp. 150–264). After Arminius died in 1609, his followers composed a summary of their position entitled 'the Remonstrance' and called for a synod to adjudicate the central theological disputes. In spite of being condemned by the Synod of Dort in 1618–1619, the theology of Arminius and 'the Remonstrants' was judged biblical (cf. John 3:16) by its adherents and was influential especially on Anglicanism and Methodism.

By the time Søren Kierkegaard (1812–1855) writes *The Sickness unto Death* under the pseudonym Anti-Climacus, the story has come full circle and the original Augustinian contrasts are explicitly internalized and delivered from fatalism. For Kierkegaard, 'a human being is a synthesis of the infinite and the finite, of the temporal and the eternal, of freedom and necessity, (Kierkegaard 1980, p. 13). The Kierkegaardian 'self' or 'spirit' does not belong to one Augustinian city or the other; nor does it juggle two sets of Lutheran roles or forms of membership; rather, it is *constituted* by two opposing poles. The poles of the self may be united dialectically, so they do not constitute a hard contradiction, but they are nevertheless divergent. They must be continuously integrated by passionate choices, and these free choices generate the drama of history. This final turn of the screw, so to speak, delivers us from prideful distinctions between 'us-the-elect-of-God' and 'them-the-poor-damned-wretches'. 'Every human being is a psychical–physical synthesis intended to be spirit' (ibid., p. 43). Becoming spirit, in turn, is a matter of an egalitarian and recognizably Arminian subjectivity. In 'The Expectancy of Eternal Salvation', Kierkegaard (1990, p. 271) writes:

> We are all unprofitable servants, and even our good deeds are nothing but human fabrications, fragile and very ambiguous, but every person has heaven's salvation only by the grace and mercy of God, and this is equally close to every human being in the sense that it is a matter between God and him.

In his *Journals and Papers*, Kierkegaard (1975, p. 352) observes:

> In order to constrain subjectivity, we are quite properly taught that no one is saved by works, but by grace – and corresponding to that – by faith. Fine.
>
> But am I therefore unable to do something myself with regard to becoming a believer? Either we must answer this with an unconditional 'no', and then we have fatalistic election by grace, or we must make a little concession. The point is this – subjectivity is always under suspicion, and when it is established that we are saved by faith, there is immediately the suspicion that too much has been conceded here. So an addition is made: But no one can give himself faith; it is a gift of God I must pray for.
>
> Fine, but then I myself can pray, or must we go farther and say: No, praying (consequently praying for faith) is a gift of God which no man can

give to himself; it must be given to him. And what then? Then to pray aright must again be given to me so that I may rightly pray for faith, etc.

There are many, many envelopes – but there must still be one point or another where there is a halt at subjectivity. Making the scale so large, so difficult, can be commendable as a majestic expression for God's infinity, but subjectivity cannot be excluded, unless we want to have fatalism.

The Arminian vision, completed in Kierkegaard, emerged over centuries and was not proposed primarily for the sake of political ends, but one might still suspect that something like this vision provides a necessary but not a sufficient condition for liberal democracy, especially civic equality. This is a debatable point – the Puritans, after all, both believed in election and overthrew a monarchy – but the practical implications of Arminianism have certainly been profound for Western culture. For his part, Kierkegaard helps us see more clearly who God is and how God's grace operates. For him, divine power is made perfect in weakness (2 Cor. 12:9) and primarily bestows worth rather than appraising it. 'Love is a giving of oneself', and everyone is capable of faith in God, 'the highest' (Kierkegaard 1995, p. 264, p. 27, p. 79). True holiness as seen in Christ on the cross is inclusive and kenotic, rather than exclusive and cavalier. Christianity upholds 'the kinship of all human beings', and allows that 'every person is God's bond servant' (ibid., p. 69, p. 107). Relatedly, 'Christian love teaches us to love all people, unconditionally all' (ibid., p. 49). 'Every human being is the neighbour', and 'in being the neighbour we are all unconditionally like each other' (ibid., p. 89). Again, history is not a divinely foreordained conflict between two cities ('us' vs. 'them') – that way lies crusade and *jihad* – but rather a divinely assisted overcoming of egotism in favor of altruism within each human spirit. Thus are human equality and freedom fully affirmed, thereby realizing the modern theological vision adumbrated by Jacob Arminius and the Remonstrants. As Kierkegaard's *Attack on Christendom* insists, the kingdom values of faith, hope and love must freely govern all dimensions of every human life and every human institution, including church and state.

Against irresistible selection as the source of inequality

Martin Luther was particularly concerned with shielding the salvation of the elect from what we would call market mechanisms: monetization and choice. Johann Tetzel's notorious sale of plenary indulgences, with no apparent need for repentance, was deeply offensive to Luther. The idea that one could buy one's own or a dead loved one's way out of temporal punishment for sin helped prompt the 1517 posting of his ninety-five theses. Relatedly, the notion that one could select actions or habituate virtues that would please God and earn heaven profoundly misunderstood the nature of divine judgment. For Luther, money and merit have nothing to do with justification before God. Righteousness in the primary sense is imputed to believers as something 'alien', based on Christ's atoning sacrifice and at the Father's merciful discretion. It is 'instilled in us without our works by grace alone' (Luther 1961 [1519], p. 88). Moreover, the second kind of righteousness, 'proper righteousness', is not the Christian's sole possession. It 'work[s] with that first and alien righteousness' and is 'that manner of life spent profitably in good works' (ibid.). Luther's views here made impossible any theological class stratification among the faithful. No Christian – pope, priest or layman – was closer to God by virtue of income, social status or ethics. All were one in depending entirely on God's gift of faith, and any discriminations based on morals and behavior were secondary and unrelated to salvation.

The irony is that this radically egalitarian vision of those within the fold entails an equally inegalitarian perception of those outside the fold. The elect is on a par theologically, but the reprobates are hopelessly lost and 'other'. Their terrible fate is through no individual fault of the damned but rather the combination of original sin and the absence of saving grace. Because the elect are lifted out of perdition by God alone, there is no *ethical* reason to boast or feel superior, but there is inescapably an *ontological* reason. Non-Christians are fundamentally different and destined to spend eternity in hell rather than heaven, agonizingly estranged from God instead of in Beatitude. That proposition cannot help but generate a despite of unbelievers by believers, even if who is never fully clear. (How many of those who talk of 'election' think they are excluded from the category?) As I say, this fact ought to be more surprising and distressing than it usually is. How a loving God can condemn some to perpetual torment, independent of any personal responsibility on their part, is not a mystery; it is a scandal. Hence the Arminian alternative, which is dialectically related to capitalism's accent on free choice and upward mobility but which is only partly realized within Christianity. Yet, again, even if the Arminian endorsement of a universal offer of salvation and of uncoerced human responses is accepted, one still has the problem of an endless punishment for a temporal crime (unbelief). More on this later.

Consider the troubling parallels with verdicts of biological inequality.[4] From Plato to Hitler, traditional or classic clan-based contrasts between the noble and the lowly appeal to family or race. The upper crust or master folk comes from a superior stock, it is said, and breeding warrants the hierarchy in social standing and political power. Royals are inherently different from commoners and deserve to rule and revel in opulence. The lowborn may not be culpable for their condition, but they are unlovely and expendable, like a base metal compared to gold.[5] Jorge Garcia (2001, p. 259) plausibly defines racism 'as fundamentally a vicious kind of racially based disregard for the welfare of certain people. In its central and most vicious form, it is a hatred, ill will, directed against a person or persons on account of their assigned race'. In spite of Christ and, I suspect, partially because of the Christian dualism of elect versus reprobate described above, it took Western civilization several centuries to overcome ontological prejudice even to a degree. Indeed, royalty worship, caste discrimination and racism abide to this day. *Yet the fundamental paradox of clan-based superiority is that, though believed in for centuries, it is manifestly false and unjust.* Jesse Owens and World War II helped give the lie, at least anecdotally, to the myth of the Aryan Superman, and some argue that race does not even exist as a biological category.[6] But Bernard Boxill (2001, p. 42) makes a crucial general point:

> The possible existence of race raises no fundamental difficulties for any moral-ity that rejects bigotry, favouritism, injustice, and disrespect. If, conceivably, there are biological races, and there are important intellectual differences between them on average, it still remains that what the races have in com-mon, their capacity for rationality and morality, remains a solid basis for maintaining that every human being has equal moral rights to life, liberty, and respect.

My only misgiving with this statement is that it risks being overly intellectualist. The shared human need and ability to give and receive agapic love is even more fundamental than rationality and morality. For Christians, it is arguably constitutive of the image of God.[7]

Whether or not races exist, families do, but after Prince Charles's treatment of Princess Diana, how anyone can consider Queen Elizabeth's line intrinsically noble or otherwise elect is beyond me. Ontological prejudice is not limited to the European past, of course – *vide* America's sad history from the Charleston slave mart to Wounded Knee to Ferguson, Missouri – and some argue that a tendency to be biased against 'outgroups' is hardwired into human nature.[8] So let us look more closely at biology and 'nature'.

Ontological chauvinism often stands behind theories of biological (a.k.a. genetic) and cultural (a.k.a. mimetic) evolution. The similarities and differences between these types of evolution have been commented on anecdotally for millennia but studied scientifically for only a little over a century and a half. In the nineteenth century, theorists of the Lamarckian school stressed cultural development, involving the transmission of acquired or learned traits, while Darwinists stressed biological development, involving random mutation and natural selection. One of the deepest questions in both domains remains: What is the basic unit of importance? Who counts and is the subject of divine *election* for salvation, eternal life, etc.? What counts and is the subject of natural *selection* for reproduction, historical survival, etc.? At times, these two questions seem one, or, rather, natural selection seems to have succeeded supernatural election as the prime mover in history and the putative explanation for why some people are 'chosen' and others are 'unfit'.

Charles Darwin published *The Origin of Species* in 1859, 7 years prior to Gregor Mendel's presentation of his work on dominant and recessive traits in peas in 1866; thus, Darwin knew nothing about modern genetics. (In fact, Mendel's findings were not appreciated until rediscovered some 30 years later.) Referring to 'the good of each being', Darwin generally assumed that individuals were the main entities whose fitness was selected for in the competition for reproductive success, though he did speculate on the possibility of 'family' or 'community' selection (1964 [1859], p. 84, pp. 201–203, pp. 237–238). In *The Descent of Man*, published in 1871, Darwin explicitly wondered how the social virtues of 'sympathy, fidelity, and courage' could be cast up by a natural selection that seems to favor individual selfishness (2004 [1871], p. 155). One tribe might out-compete another by having more loyal and self-sacrificial members that defend it to the death, but how can 'survival of the fittest (being)' pass on such virtuous dispositions to future generations? As Darwin (ibid.) realized,

> It is extremely doubtful whether the offspring of the more sympathetic and benevolent parents, or of those who were the most faithful to their comrades, would be reared in greater numbers than the children of selfish and treacherous parents belonging to the same tribe. He who was ready to sacrifice his life, as many a savage has been, rather than betray his comrades, would often leave no offspring to inherit his noble nature.

Darwin's somewhat tentative answer was to suggest two things: (1) that altruistic traits might actually benefit their bearer because others will tend to reciprocate and assist or reward the person (what later came to be called, in a misnomer, 'reciprocal altruism'); (2) that beyond individual benefit, group selection might be operating. It is worth emphasizing that (1) is not true self-sacrifice, since it does not involve uncompensated loss by one in order to aid another. With the neo-Darwinian synthesis of modern genetics and evolutionary theory in the twentieth century, in any case, the focus shifted away from both individuals and groups to chromosomal DNA and RNA. For many decades thereafter, (fit) genes or alleles were considered the basic units of selection and this made it even more difficult to account for altruism defined as expensive service to the neighbor.

So entrenched and reductionistic did this gene-centric paradigm become that, as late as 1976, Richard Dawkins could maintain that 'universal love and the welfare of the species as a whole are concepts that simply do not make evolutionary sense' (1976, p. 2). For Dawkins, 'the fundamental unit of selection, and therefore of self-interest, is not the species, nor the group, nor even, strictly, the individual. It is the gene, the unit of heredity' (ibid., p. 11). The individual is really epiphenomenal to his or her genes, with the person being a 'survival machine', nothing but the genes' way of making duplicates of themselves (ibid., p. 19). Metaphysical and moral notions like God, personal agency and inter-personal altruism are finally illusory or deluded (Dawkins 2006); it is the 'replicators' (a.k.a. 'genes') that drive evolution, with freedom and morality belied by the imperative of genetic continuity (ibid., p. 15). For Dawkins, in effect, genes replace the Lutheran God as the supreme arbiter of time, agency and meaning. 'A body is really a machine blindly programmed by its selfish genes' (ibid., p. 146). 'The fundamental unit, the prime mover of all life, is the replicator' (ibid., p. 264). '[Genes] created us, body and mind; and their preservation is the ultimate rationale for our existence' (ibid., p. 20). Dawkins (ibid., p. 2) protests that he is 'not advocating a morality based on evolution', and he ends *The Selfish Gene* with a call for people voluntarily to resist genetic egotism, but everything he has said previously about biology and selection implies that such resistance is impossible. Biological determinism can no more be reconciled with human moral responsibility than can theological determinism. Dawkins' compatibilism is no more plausible than that of Augustine or Aquinas.

Jesus, of course, thought otherwise about God, life and love. Like Socrates, Jesus published nothing during his earthly life. Being the pre-existent Word, he himself was a First Edition, according to the Gospel of John (1:1–4), but, again like Socrates, Jesus awaited others to transmit his temporal sayings via posthumous texts. How true to the original was Plato? How true to the original were Matthew, Mark, Luke and John? We will never know for sure, but the verbal traditions that grew up around Jesus' life and death suggest that he taught a rigorous but inclusive form of Torah piety. He was a Jew and evidently upheld the basic Law of Moses (Mark 10:17–19), but he radicalized its demands and extended them to include both Jews and Gentiles. All persons were called to love God and the neighbor, even unto self-sacrifice, and all were potentially members of a 'kingdom' very different from Rome – the kingdom of God – that is proclaimed to all nations and is both here and not yet (Matthew 22:36–40, Matthew 16:24, Matthew 8:11, Matthew 24:14).[9] Some 30 years after Jesus' crucifixion, however, the first Gospel, Mark, vilified the Jews as Christ-killers and effectively limited election to Jewish converts and righteous Gentiles. The subsequent Gospels differ in important ways, but Matthew, Luke and especially John also denigrated 'the Jews' and made the Gentiles the recipient of a new and largely Law-free covenant. For centuries thereafter, Christians broadly denied human freedom in favor of overriding grace for those favored by God and unavoidable damnation for the reprobate (see section II above). The most reprobate group of all, of course, was the perverse and unbelieving Jews.

So entrenched and reductionistic did this paradigm become that, as late as 1925, Adolf Hitler could contend that the Jews were a false or epiphenomenal people, a *Scheinvolk*, to be unmade by predatory Nazis in obedience to *Natur*. Fate and healthy Aryan instinct rule the world, not biblical faith, hope and love. As Hitler (1971, p. 65) averred,

> Eternal Nature inexorably avenges the infringement of her commands. Hence today I believe that I am acting in accordance with the will of the Almighty Creator: *by defending myself against the Jew, I am fighting for the work of the Lord.*

Any worldview that gainsays 'the basic aristocratic pri2nciple of Nature' is guilty of 'decadence' (ibid., p. 81).

Both Jesus and Darwin would have trouble recognizing long stretches of the revolutions they supposedly initiated. The perfidy of talk of hard 'election' is that it always invites invidious and fixed contrasts between 'us-the-beloved-of-God' and 'them-poor-bastards-denied-by-God'. Similarly, the danger of talk of hard 'selection' – what Stephen Jay Gould (2002, p. 41) calls 'selectionist absolutism' or 'panadaptationism', what I and others call 'panselectionism' – is that every physical or behavior trait is seen as solely a function of reproductive advantage for the 'fit'. Both forms of election and selection would make altruism (a.k.a. '*hesed* and *agape*') impossible,[10] thus both are incompatible with the life and teaching of Christ. Christ made a point of supping with women, publicans and sinners, and of loving the 'unfit'. Sometimes his love took the form of healing physical infirmity or satisfying bodily hunger, but often he blessed the needy and despised by accepting and affirming them as they are (see the Beatitudes of Luke 6:20–22). Even leprosy and Ebola are easier to bear when you are not shunned or abandoned.

Against irresistible distinction as the source of inequality

So far, I have tried to deflate objectionable theological and biological bases of inequality. We come now to a third basis: economics. Since my focus is on the West, I consider in this section, in very broad terms, mixed-market democratic capitalism. I have defended such a system in the past, and I continue to deem it a preferable economic arrangement to any feasible alternative. Capitalism, broadly speaking, is our best economic safeguard of personal freedom and buffer against political tyranny,[11] but it requires a theological framework and underpinning. The equality of opportunity claimed by the system is manifestly in tension with the inequality of starting points and end results within the system. The genius of the free market, at least among producers and consumers, is its sensitive pricing and incentives for profit; monetary exchange rather than payment in kind is indispensable to economic growth; the efficient production of commodities – including food, shelter, medicine, clothing – is a service to embodied human beings of all faiths and the protection and cultivation of individual choice is a necessary condition for key virtues, including faith, hope and love. What is unacceptable, however, is valorizing the market, money, commodities and autonomy as the highest or self-sufficient goods. Without love of God and neighbor, capitalism produces forms of class distinction that are cruel and corrupting.

Capitalist righteousness is not enough. Left to itself, a laissez faire economy produces disparities of income, power and status that are insidious – a kind of material royalty that can be as threatening to self-respect and other-regard as any predestined hell or inherited crown. 'The rich are different from you and me', Scott Fitzgerald is said to have opined, eliciting Ernest Hemingway's deflating rejoinder: 'Yes, they have more money'.[12] Any more substantive interpretation of class-based superiority is as untrue as the clan-based variety, but *the fundamental paradox of economic class is that trying to eliminate it typically exacerbates it.* As I note below, taxation, antitrust laws and the Federal Reserve have their proper place, but more thoroughgoing legislative efforts to level income, control prices and redistribute wealth tend to require concentrations of power (political and economic) that are themselves threatening to equality and freedom. A command economy not only centralizes undue authority in the state, which authority is used in turn to enrich bureaucrats, but also stifles initiative and dampens material production in ways that impoverish the majority both economically and morally. In the extreme, a centralized economy can lead to the extermination of the 'peasants', as in the Soviet starvation campaign in the Ukraine (1932–1933) and the broader-based Great Terror (1937–1938).[13] To repeat, however, the market is not God, and capitalist righteousness is not enough. To substantiate this claim, let me tell a second didactic tale, but this time of decline. To do so, I draw heavily on Daniel Bell (1976).

In *The Cultural Contradictions of Capitalism*, Bell (1976, p. 10) argues that contemporary (Western) society is characterized by the absence of a holistic vision of the true, the good and the beautiful, plus the presence of three 'disjunctive realms': the techno-economy, the polity and the culture. Each realm has its own axiological principles and values and its own axiological structures and mechanisms, and, though it overlaps with the other two realms, it operates with considerable independence. The main value of the economy is utility or productivity, with the chief structure being hierarchical bureaucracy operating within a free market. The central good of the polity is legitimacy, with the main mechanism being equal citizens holding free and open elections. The norms and instruments of the cultural arena are harder to specify, but Bell suggests that 'self-realization' and 'self-fulfillment' are the key ideals and freedom of speech and expression their means (ibid., pp. 10–14).[14] Again, there is overlap, which I would elaborate as follows:

1   The polity impacts and constrains the economy to some degree via taxation, antitrust laws, food and drug safety regulations, the Federal Reserve's control of interest rates, and the like.
2   The polity also impacts and constrains the cultural sphere via laws against slavery, prostitution, child pornography, murder, etc.
3   The economy impacts and constrains the political order in that citizens can donate money to political candidates of their choice; the average consumer is not dependent upon the government for his employment and daily bread and so can speak and vote his conscience without fear of official reprisal; etc.
4   The economy also impacts and constrains the cultural ethos in so far as authors, actors, artists, singers, *et al.* typically must sell their creations or performances and will go under without adequate finances; etc.
5   The culture impacts and constrains political life, given that religious and ethical commitments often dictate voting patterns; a particularly heinous transgression of either law or morality can get one impeached; etc.
6   The culture impacts and constrains the economy when buyers boycott irresponsible or inept businesses, when sellers give discounts to charitable organizations, etc.

With these important exceptions, however, one can, in theory, buy and sell whatever commodities one wants and can afford, vote for whatever official one wants and can get nominated, and pursue whatever life plans one wants and can realize. The central government does not dictate all aspects of life and neither does the market or the church/synagogue/mosque. This, at any rate, is the ideally pluralistic scheme of checks and balances.

In reality, of course, there are tensions – what Bell calls 'contradictions' – within this arrangement that can precipitate abuse, even collapse. The hierarchy of the economy is at odds with the egalitarianism of the polity, for instance. Thus, one of five scenarios might unfold. Either (a) the realms float completely free of each other, such that political activities are thought entirely amoral, economic exchanges are judged beyond positive or natural law, and/or moral-cultural goals become purely inward or sectarian. Here we get Machiavellian statesmen and stateswomen, the 'business is business' mentality, and/or religious and ethical teachers who think that they must escape the profane world and withdraw from society into an imagined purity. Or (b) the prime principle or mechanism in the polity colonizes or co-opts the other realms: a fairly elected president tries to pack the Supreme Court; a duly appointed Chancellor declares martial law and assumes dictatorial power; etc. Or (c) the economy turns omnivorous, as some fear is happening in America: the rich buy elections; the poor must sell their bodies; etc.[15] Or (d) the culture becomes overweening: a religious sect tries to make a creedal affirmation essential to political membership; a secularist insists on banishing religious language from the public domain; etc. Or (e) the culture implodes: values drift towards nihilism or solipsism, which leads to instability in the other realms.

Many of Bell's readers conclude that he blames capitalism for the major disharmonies in modern liberalism. He faults capitalist society's making accumulation an end in itself, but he actually points an even more accusing finger at modernism in culture (Bell 1976, p. xii). 'Modernism has . . . been the seducer. Its power derived from the idolatry of the self' (ibid., p. 19). The emerging exhaustion and nihilism of the modernist ethos has created an axiological vacuum that pushes or pulls the other realms into instability, imploding into chaos or exploding into various forms of totalitarianism. I, too, hold that we should not fault the free market for achieving what it is designed to achieve: efficient production of material goods and monetary profits. Still more positively, economic growth, properly moderated, promotes geopolitical and cultural (including moral) progress. Benjamin M. Friedman (2005, p. 4) is worth quoting at some length in this connection:

> Moral thinking, in practically every known culture, enjoins us not to place undue emphasis on our material concerns. We are also increasingly aware that economic development – industrialization in particular, and more recently globalization – often brings undesirable side effects, like damage to the environment or the homogenization of what used to be distinctive cultures, and we have come to regard these matters too in moral terms. On both counts, we therefore think of economic growth in terms of material considerations *versus* moral ones . . . I believe this thinking is seriously, in some circumstances dangerously, incomplete. The value of a rising standard of living lies not just in the economic improvements it brings to how individuals live but in how it shapes the social, political, and ultimately the moral character of a people. Economic growth – meaning a rising standard

of living for the clear majority of citizens – more often than not fosters greater opportunity, tolerance of diversity, social mobility, commitment to fairness, and dedication to democracy.

I would add, in the spirit of Bell, that it is modernist philosophy (or anti-philosophy) that strips souls of the capacity to delay gratification and to relativize commodities and cash in favor of more spiritual and communal goods. Religious faith used to provide this capacity, but it has been eclipsed by other axial allegiances.

Martin Heidegger (1968, p. 24) writes: 'Our age is not a technological age because it is the age of the machine; it is an age of the machine because it is the technological age'.[16] The market is one more machine, I believe, as are free elections. Both are essentially amoral mechanisms without a conscience, which therefore cannot guarantee virtuous outcomes. (As we know, Hitler came to power via free elections and parliamentary processes.) So I would paraphrase Heidegger thus: 'Our age in not a consumerist age because it is the age of the market; it is an age of the market because it is a consumerist age'. It is our hearts and minds, our Nietzschean wills, that have strayed, not our artefacts as such. One should no more indict capitalism and free markets for materialism than one should indict science and free inquiry for technology. Admittedly, the atomic bomb is a technical machine and, once built, it is intrinsically dangerous, but bombs do not manufacture or drop themselves any more than economies advertise or purchase themselves. Arrogance and the abuse of others are an ethical affair. Markets, free choice in the agora, and elections, free choice in the polis, may help avoid some vicious results, but they need to be brought under moral governance by thoughtful human beings.

There are different kinds of markets, of course. Jon Gunnemann (2015, personal correspondence, 5 Oct.) identifies four – the consumer market, the labor market, the market among producers, and the financial market – commenting: 'Each of these markets functions differently and the classic ideas of supply and demand, which supposedly produce efficiency, operate very differently in each, and with different effects as regards not only efficiency but other possible measures'. I recognize that each market may be rendered unfree by a host of factors: force, fraud, manipulation, secrecy, monopoly or even the gradual usurpation of resources. Thus, I emphasize that I want to rein in both big government and big business, including, for example, the largely unregulated creation of money by commercial banks.[17] The weak and vulnerable should be protected, from womb to tomb, but they should also be empowered for individual self-reliance. To this end, I affirm 'mixed-market democratic capitalism', wherein the state regulates the economy to some degree, and the economy escapes the state to some degree, but my main point in what follows is that both domains are dependent on a moral-cultural – a.k.a., religious – vision that must not be subservient to either. *All* forms of concentrated power – *political, economic and cultural* – need to check each other and be checked by something higher. The challenge is to keep governments, markets and, yes, churches and universities democratically accountable without creating a monster that makes the problem of tyrannical power worse. Whether we call this 'democratic socialism', 'mixed-market democratic capitalism', or some third option, is irrelevant.[18]

The agora is no more divine or incorrigible than the polis or the ecclesia, but just as Dawkins focuses on the unit of *selection*, Bell (1976, p. 16) zeroes in on the unit of *distinction*:

> The fundamental assumption of modernity, the thread that has run through Western civilization since the sixteenth century, is that the social unit of society is not the group, the guild, the tribe, or the city, but the person. The Western ideal was the autonomous man who, in becoming self-determining, would achieve freedom.

At the extreme, 'the untrammelled self' becomes Deity, and a constant craving for pleasure and novelty means that old institutions, roots and relationships are jettisoned in favor of remaking oneself, flaunting society and dominating nature (ibid.). The consequence is that nothing and no one is truly distinguished, much less graceful. Yet, to update Bell's references, everybody thinks themselves 'simply irresistible' (Robert Palmer). Donald Trump or even Bernie Madoff becomes the quintessential entrepreneur, Madonna or even Marilyn Manson the most celebrated artist, and any of the above can become the next President of the 'Dis-United' States.

The dilemma of modernity is a function of thinking that the three realms of society – the polity, the techno-economy and the culture – can be sustained without a universal set of values in which they are embedded and by which they are regulated. The center cannot hold without such values. The straightforward lesson I draw from Bell and others is that the isolation of the economy from ethico-religious considerations, together with the cultural segregation of the individual from the common good, has led to notions of distinction that are deluded and degrading. Material wealth or business clout or aesthetic pleasure is simply not a reliable measure of virtuous character or social contribution. It is tragic when one judges others or oneself based on material possessions or will to power; it is equally pathetic when one judges others or oneself in terms of election or selection.

The main problem with traditional doctrines of election, selection and distinction is that the 'us vs. them' contrasts they generate are false. They take what is passing or contingent as eternal and essential; they deny our common humanity. More specifically, election by irresistible grace makes God arbitrary and finally responsible for evil, since the reprobate could not be otherwise; election by irresistible genes, in turn, makes persons and their worth epiphenomenal to blind biological mechanisms; distinction by the irresistible self makes an idol of the market and the pursuit of happiness. Finally, all three bases of inequality tend to foment animosity and aggression towards those deemed inferior or outré.

Ted Smith (2017, personal correspondence, 18 February) has forcefully argued that 'it took Calvinist traditions with a strong sense of election to topple monarchies and start democracies. As those democracies matured, some kind of Arminianism arose as their natural complement. But it took election to get them going'. I readily grant the historical point that a doctrine of election in which God chooses a limited yet large group of individuals for salvation, including commoners and laypersons, is more amenable to democracy than the idea of absolute monarchy and the divine right of kings. But Calvinist election, with its corollaries of limited atonement and irresistible grace, was only a half cure for unjust hierarchy. Smith himself notes the importance for political equality of Arminian denials of Calvinist orthodoxy, but he adds that

> an Arminian notion of salvation offered to all, inviting a free decision, fits with a modern meritocracy . . . That notion of meritocracy has had some emancipatory potential. But now it serves to create and legitimate profound inequality. After all, the reasoning goes, all parties are just getting what they deserve (ibid.).

I have significant reservations about Smith's association of Arminianism with meritocracy. I have noted that Arminius rejects both (1) the Pelagian view that we can, on our own, overcome sin and win heaven without special grace and (2) the semi-Pelagian view that we can freely begin the process of justification but then need God's help to complete it. Arminius does not deny total depravity, meaning he affirms that we can do *nothing* on our own even to turn towards God, much less to achieve salvation. God must convert us, but, crucially, we can accept or reject the conversion. Some of my Calvinist friends argue that such consent opens the door to works righteousness and boasting, but I just don't see it. Consent to God's grace does not constitute merit, any more than accepting an indispensable gift makes one the author of the gift.

Equally key in Arminius is his denial of (3) irresistible grace and (4) limited atonement.[19] Both of these moves seem most consistent with the life and teachings of Jesus, the former denial being an affirmation of freedom of conscience and the latter denial being an affirmation of human equality. Arminius's concern was not merely anthropocentric, however. His was a defence of theonomy not autonomy, of God's love rather than human merit. I would concede to Smith that the actual impact of Arminianism may have been to help entrench the sovereign self of unbridled capitalism, but I would also insist that this is an irony of history, as Smith himself realizes (2017, personal correspondence, 19 February). Elsewhere, I have contended that liberal democracy itself is a 'prodigal son' to Christianity, transmuting emphasis on the faithful individual before God, active in the world, into individualism, fideism and materialism.[20] Obviously, neither Jesus nor Arminius intended this. To reiterate, the chief reasons for Arminius's rejection of (3) and (4) were both moral and theological: irresistible grace and limited atonement imply a fatalism that undermines ethics and ultimately makes God cavalier and evil.

Political *agape* as an alternative

The alternative to the rule of election, selection and distinction is a political *agape* that governs all aspects of life by attending to the image of God. If God is agapic love (1 John 4:8), then the *imago Dei* is plausibly seen as the need or ability to give or receive such love.[21] Bestowed by the Creator and shared by all human lives (Gen. 1:26–27), the call to love and be loved undercuts all discriminatory social labels. It constitutes a sanctity that precedes any merit or achievement (a.k.a., dignity) and that transcends all theological, biological and economic differences and hostilities. Tempered judgments of merit and reward are legitimate – who is so jaded or jealous as to deny that Socrates, Saint Francis, Da Vinci, Shakespeare, Gandhi, Einstein, *et al.* were extraordinary talents? – even as prudent judgments of demerit and punishment are appropriate. But the gift of sanctity both empowers and obliges us to love God unconditionally and our neighbor as ourselves (Deuteronomy 6:5, Leviticus 19:18 and Matthew 22:37–40). All the great geniuses only became such because God, their parents and/or their earthly fellows first gave them unmerited favor. A similar debt to charity is owed by us all, and such equality is chronologically prior and axiologically fundamental.

To appeal to the image of God in this way is anything but metaphysically neutral, but there is nothing wrong in that. The time is perhaps past when a detailed axiological picture can be widely shared in a pluralistic context, but this does not mean that individuals can sustain integrity without such a picture. Nor does it mean, *pace* John Rawls, that such a vision must be privatized and excluded from public discourse about basic matters of justice.[22] Civil debate, persuasion, compromise and dissent are the orders of the day in democratic countries. Christians will wear lightly all worldly distinctions – nationality, office, race, class, sex and sexual orientation – even as they care profoundly about and lobby for others' well-being. 'There is no longer Jew or Greek, there is no longer slave or free, there is no longer male and female; for all of you are one in Christ Jesus' (Gal. 3:28).[23] But Christians cannot muzzle their consciences and prescind from theological virtue in any quarter of existence. So, I would redraw Bell's initial schema by drawing on Jewish and Christian traditions in which faith, hope and love are the universal set of values that hold the different domains together and order relations between them. This redrawing retains the relative autonomy of the political, economic and cultural domains, but it subordinates them to a comprehensive religious covenant with God and neighbor.

This is not a prescription for theocracy or for tearing down the wall of separation between church and state. I endeavor, instead, to convey the integrity of a Christian believer committed to liberal democracy without naiveté or idolatry. First God, then the neighbor, family, country, alma mater and self – with only God commanding unconditional obedience. Some liberals (e.g. Rawls and Richard Rorty) seem to think that no general perspective on the universe and other people is needed or appropriate for a viable modern society, but, in my estimation, the music of the spheres is more elusive than that.[24] It cannot be heard in a vacuum.

Bell acknowledges the dialectical overlap of the realms, but his descriptive model leaves large portions of politics and economics outside of moral-cultural governance. This is a dangerous idea. Not every political or economic decision need be self-consciously or laboriously examined, but 'permissibility' remains a crucial ethical and theological category. If an attitude or behavior cannot pass that presumptive minimal muster, it ought not be embraced, no matter how expedient or efficient or popular it may be.

All creatures are sinful, and not all citizens will aspire to biblical norms. But all will bring some metanarrative to bear on the source and end of communal existence – neo-Darwinism being an increasingly influential one – and no metanarrative is beyond contestation. It is precisely because of Hebrew and Christian Scripture – most specifically, the revelation of God in Christ – that I reject oppressive social distinctions in favor of human equality and liberty before God. Genesis, Leviticus, Isaiah, Jesus, Paul, Lincoln and King all declare: 'Down with all fatalistic and hate-inspiring "us vs. them" divides, and up with "charity for all"'. Rumi and the Dalai Lama say much the same thing.

Conclusion

I have tried to adumbrate the falsity, evil and ugliness of three things: election-cum-irresistible-grace, selection-cum-irresistible-genes and distinction-cum-the-irresistible-self. *These three are basically the same hubristic phenomenon expressed in different disciplines and applied to different contexts.* I have also attempted to intimate an alternative: what I call 'political *agape*'. This is a Christian vision, but I have no illusions about the Christian church and its traditions. That church has blood on its hands, from violent anti-Semitism to chattel slavery to gay bashing. But Christ lived and taught the brotherhood and sisterhood of humanity, and he called for uncoerced love of God and neighbor, all of which must condition the whole of a believer's life. Even in a liberal society, I see no way to escape political victimization of the weak by the powerful or economic exploitation of the poor by the rich without fidelity to certain basic truths. One of these truths is *'prima caritas, inde jus'*. We live first by the grace of others, especially the Holy Other, and only secondarily do we benefit from distributive and retributive justice. Another basic truth is that the inequalities cast up by democratic governments and capitalist markets must be mitigated and compensated for by a prior allegiance to something larger than our cupidinous selves. This requires transcendence of the modernist emphasis on 'me' and my control of things. Political *agape* looks first to the holiness of God, second to the sanctity of life and only third at the dignity of choice.[25] It is by thus reminding us of our finite creatureliness that we can counter both *hubris* and despair.

This is not to neglect or deny the import of the individual and his or her freedom. Quite the contrary. I am Arminian and Kierkegaardian enough to affirm both of these goods but to see them as transmuted by faith in the Good. When God is the 'middle term' in our relations to other people, as well as to our own selves, we can have *individuality without individualism and freedom as theonomy rather than autonomy* (Kierkegaard 1995, p. 107). Individuality stems from each human life bearing the image of God, but we all bear it equally and vulnerably before God. True freedom is not arbitrary license or self-assertion but, rather, the consent to be used by God's grace. This everyone can do. The traditional theological doctrine of election versus reprobation has caused no end of human (and divine) grief, but it is in the process of being transcended. One can only speak and act in such a way that the clan-based and class-based distinctions that have so troubled human history, especially the last two centuries, will meet a similar end. Racism remains a major problem in the United States – as the long-running, freshly visible crisis of racially motivated shootings by white police officers attests – and theological, biological and economic biases interact synergistically. But the thing perhaps most needful in the twenty-first century is a zeal to surmount class-based inequality. An egalitarian cultural revolution is called for analogous to the civil rights movement and feminism, and it will not come by centralizing the economy in an omni-competent state. A grace-filled opening of the heart is required, and one of the virtues of liberal democracy, suitably reformed, is that it permits and even encourages this.

Many will judge my recommendations utopian, doubting that love can be made politically and economically salient without paternalism or worse. (I certainly fail to live up to the demands of *agape* personally.) No less a historian and social critic than David Nirenberg (2007, pp. 575–576) contends that

> far from being an antidote to instrumental reason or to relations of possession and exchange, the fantasy that love can free interaction from interest is itself one of the more dangerous offspring of the marriage of Athens and Jerusalem that we sometimes call the Western tradition.

I cannot respond adequately to Nirenberg's argument here, but I hasten to emphasize that I endorse the *regulation* of 'instrumental reason' and 'relations of possession and exchange', not their elimination. I champion the *priority* of agapic love in relation to 'interest' (a.k.a. *eros*), not the latter's exclusion or vilification. We all live in and through the mechanisms of preferential desire, including politics and markets, and we all rely on police and armies to defend our well-being. I merely propose to *relativize and limit* these things, not destroy or demonize them.[26] Jesus himself took embodied human existence and its wants and needs seriously: 'Is there anyone among you who, if your child asks for bread, will give a stone? Or if the child asks for a fish, will give a snake?' (Matthew 7:9–10) Nevertheless, he decentered them:

> Do not keep striving for what you are to eat and what you are to drink, and do not keep worrying. For it is the nations of the world that strive after all these things, and your Father knows that you need them. Instead, strive for his kingdom, and these things will be given to you as well. (Luke 12:29–31)

That is *the Christian counter-paradox*: 'Those who try to make their life secure will lose it, but those who lose their life will keep it' (Luke 17:33). Jesus' teachings frequently contain stunning reversals of hierarchy; consider the blessings and curses of the Sermon on the Plain (Luke 6:20–26):

> Then he looked up at his disciples and said: 'Blessed are you who are poor, for yours is the kingdom of God. Blessed are you who are hungry now, for you will be filled. Blessed are you who weep now, for you will laugh. Blessed are you when people hate you, and when they exclude you, revile you, and defame you on account of the Son of Man. Rejoice in that day and leap for joy, for surely your reward is great in heaven; for that is what their ancestors did to the prophets. But woe to you who are rich, for you have received your consolation. Woe to you who are full now, for you will be hungry. Woe to you who are laughing now, for you will mourn and weep. Woe to you when all speak well of you, for that is what their ancestors did to the false prophets'.

But the cross is our most staggering icon and neglected principle of social ethics. Far from being a symbol of merely private devotion, it highlights the hollowness of election, selection and distinction as commonly conceived. The subversive fact that God's grace is long-suffering and prejudiced in favor of everyone is the key to the moral meaning of the Christian revolution.[27] *Omnipotence freely sacrificed for us all* (John 3:16), *while we are yet sinners* (Romans 5:8), *and we show our gratitude by un-coercively building up the neighbour* (1 Cor. 8:1). The close of Saint Francis's cruciform prayer applies to communities as well as individuals: 'It is in giving that we receive; it is in pardoning that we are pardoned; it is in dying that we are born again to eternal life'. Thus divine paradox overcomes all vanities of grace, clan and class.

Notes

1   Social distinction based on economic class is somewhat mutable, especially in free-market contexts, but even there it can be quite difficult to escape various kinds of poverty. Capitalist upward mobility of income is real, though the degree and causes are debated. (See Chetty *et al.* 2014). But even the *nouveau riche* are often looked down on culturally. 'The rich get rich and the poor get poorer' is not a hard-and-fast rule for individuals, but the rich will seemingly always disdain the poor as a group. That is the enduring sensibility I am trying to isolate and criticize.

2   See Matthew 24:22, Matthew 24:24, Matthew 24:31, Mark 13:20, Mark 13:22, Mark 13:27, Romans 8:33, Romans 9:11, Romans 11:28, 1 Timothy 5:21, 2 Timothy 2:10, Titus 1:1, 2 Peter 1:10, 2 John 1:1, and 2 John 1:13.

3   Augustine (1971 [426/427], p. 481) writes: 'Whosoever . . . in God's most providential ordering are foreknown, predestinated, called, justified, glorified . . . are already children of God, and absolutely cannot perish'. Those not so predestinated 'shall perish' (ibid.). Quoting Philippians 2:13, Augustine (ibid.) assures the elect: 'For it is God that worketh in you, both to will and to do for His good pleasure'.

4   Sexism is, of course, a form of biological devaluation, but I focus in this chapter on family and race rather than gender.

5 Cf. Plato's 'noble lie' in *The Republic* (1968, 414c–415c, pp. 93–94).

6 Naomi Zack (2001, pp. 44–45) writes: 'It is now accepted by scientists that there are no racial essences which inhere in individuals and determine their racial membership'. Citing Anthony Appiah, Garcia (2001, p. 260) makes the relevant point: 'Even if it were true that race is unreal, what we call racism could still be real'.

7 See Jackson (2015), especially Chapter 2.

8 See Marsh, Mendoza-Denton and Smith (2010).

9 In *A Marginal Jew: Rethinking the Historical Jesus*, John P. Meier (1994, p. 450) writes: 'A number of sayings and actions of Jesus argue strongly for the view that Jesus at times spoke of the kingdom as already present in some way or to some degree in his ministry. Some of the sayings refer only in a vague, global way to Jesus' ministry as the sign or vehicle of the kingdom's presence: "The kingdom of God is in your midst" (Luke 17:21) . . . "Happy the eyes that see what you see" (Luke 10:23). Other sayings focus more specifically on particular actions of Jesus as manifestations or instruments of the kingdom's presence. The most important witness . . . is found in Luke 11:20: "If by the finger of God I cast out the demons, the kingdom of God has come upon you." Effectively, Jesus declares his exorcisms to be both manifestations and at least partial realizations of God's coming in power to rule his people in the end time'.

10 See Jackson (2016).

11 In *The Capitalist Revolution: Fifty Propositions about Prosperity, Equality and Liberty*, Peter Berger (1986, p. 79) argues that 'the modern state has the innate tendency to project its power further and further into society, *unless* it meets up with institutionalized limits. Capitalism, by providing a social zone relatively independent of state control, facilitates this limit'. Correlatively, he defends the hypothesis that '*capitalism is a necessary but not sufficient condition of democracy*' (ibid., p. 81).

12 This oft-cited exchange never took place in actual conversation; it is a loose splicing together of quotes from two short stories: Fitzgerald's 'The Rich Boy' and Hemingway's 'The Snows of Kilimanjaro'.

13 See Timothy Snyder (2010). Snyder reminds us that, in the 1930s, it was the Soviets who first organized mass shootings of ethnicities judged to be unprofitable or burdensome. I am less convinced than Snyder that Stalin's eliminationist actions directly triggered Hitler's, and I am well aware of the United States' genocidal assault on Native Americans and protracted enslavement of Africans. But the point is that concentrated power, political or economic or cultural, is hazardous whenever and wherever it occurs and that making the state omnicompetent exacerbates the abuses of the rich. We must not forget that National Socialism, like Soviet communism, involved massive state control of markets and production, even before World War II, and that this control crucially facilitated the Holocaust.

14 Bell gives a slightly different account in his Preface. There the economy is associated with the axial principle of 'efficiency', the polity with 'equality', and the culture with 'self-realization (or self-gratification)' (ibid., pp. xxx–xxi).

15 For Christians, Jesus' vigorously forbidding economic transactions in or near the temple sanctuary (Mark 11:15–19) is the preeminent example of what Michael Walzer calls a 'blocked exchange'. See Walzer (1983, pp. 100–103). For all his historical insights, however, Walzer declines to leave Plato's cave (p. xiv). His normative judgements are based on social consensus, internal criticism, rather than on substantive theses about God's will, human nature, natural law, or objective goods. Like Richard Rorty and the later John Rawls, Walzer describes the logic of certain ideas and practices prevalent in Western societies, leaving one to wonder how he can fault injustice so long as it is triumphant or conventional. Such pragmatism would defend tolerance but ends up, despite protests, entailing a self-defeating relativism. I champion here a fallibilist, yet more realist, version of liberal democracy; see also Jackson (2015), Chapters 3–6.

16 Heidegger's Nazism, including his valorizing of the German language, people and state, has rightly tainted his legacy, but his comments on technology remain perceptive.

17 On this increasingly recognized issue, see Ib Ravn (2015).
18 See, in this connection, Alec Nove (1983).
19 See Arminius (1996).
20 See Jackson (2015, pp. 116–151).
21 See Jackson (2003).
22 See Jackson (2015, pp. 155–185).
23 Admittedly, 'all of you' may originally have referred only to the baptized or, again, 'the elect', but I have underscored the tradition's slow overcoming of such parochialism.
24 See Jackson (2015, pp. 155–185, pp. 214–236).
25 See ibid. (pp. 84–115, pp. 186–213).
26 See Jackson (2003, pp. 28–69) and Jackson (1999).
27 Cf. Gunnemann (1979). Professor Jon Gunnemann was one of my teachers at Yale and a colleague for many years at Emory. I am delighted and honoured to dedicate this chapter to him.

References

Aquinas, T. (1981) [1265–1274] *Summa theologica*, vol. 2, Fathers of the English Dominican Province (trans.), Westminster, MD: Christian Classics.

Arminius, J. (1996) [1608–1609] 'Disputations on some of the principal subjects of the Christian religion', in *The works of James Arminius*, vol. 2, J. Nichols (trans.), Grand Rapids, MI: Baker Book House.

Augustine (1971) [418] 'On original sin', in P. Schaff (ed.), *The Nicene and post-Nicene fathers*, vol. V, Grand Rapids, MI: Eerdmans, pp. 237–255.

Augustine (1971) [426/427] 'On rebuke and grace', in P. Schaff (ed.), *The Nicene and post-Nicene fathers*, vol. V, Grand Rapids, MI: Eerdmans, pp. 471–491.

Augustine (1972) [426] *City of God*, H. Bettenson (trans.), London: Penguin Books.

Bell, D. (1976) *The cultural contradictions of capitalism*, New York: Basic Books.

Berger, P. (1986) *The capitalist revolution: Fifty propositions about prosperity, equality, and liberty*, New York: Basic Books.

Boxill, B. (2001) 'Introduction', in B. Boxill (ed.), *Race and racism*, Oxford: Oxford University Press, pp. 1–42.

Chetty, R., Hendren, N., Kline, P. and Saez, E. (2014) 'Where is the land of opportunity? The geography of intergenerational mobility in the United States', *The Quarterly Journal of Economics*, *129*(4): 1553–1623.

Darwin, C. (1964) [1859] *On the origin of species*, Cambridge, MA: Harvard University Press

Darwin, C. (2004) [1871] *The descent of man*, London: Penguin Books.

Dawkins, R. (1976) *The selfish gene*, Oxford: Oxford University Press.

Dawkins, R. (2006) *The God delusion*, New York: Houghton Mifflin.

Friedman, B. M. (2005) *The moral consequences of economic growth*, New York: Knopf.

Garcia, J. L. A. (2001) 'The heart of racism', in B. Boxill (ed.), *Race and racism*, Oxford: Oxford University Press, pp. 257–296.

Gould, S. J. (2002) *The structure of evolutionary theory*, Cambridge, MA: Harvard University Press/Belknap.

Gunnemann, J. P. (1979) *The moral meaning of revolution*, New Haven, CT: Yale University Press.

Heidegger, M. (1968) *What is called thinking?* J. G. Gray (trans.), New York: Harper & Row.

Hitler, A. (1971) *Mein Kampf*, R. Manheim (trans.), New York: Houghton Mifflin Company.

Jackson, T. (1999) *Love disconsoled: Meditations on Christian charity*, Cambridge, UK: Cambridge University Press.

Jackson, T. (2003) *The priority of love: Christian charity and social justice*, Princeton, NJ: Princeton University Press.

Jackson, T. (2015) *Political agape: Christian love and liberal democracy*, Grand Rapids, MI: Eerdmans.

Jackson, T. (2016) 'Evolution, agape, and the image of God: a reply to various naturalists', in F. Simmons and B. Sorrells (eds), *Love and Christian ethics: Tradition, theory, and society*, Washington, DC: Georgetown University Press, pp. 226–251.

Julian of Norwich (1966) [1395] *Revelations of divine love*, C. Wolters (trans.), London: Penguin Books.

Kierkegaard, S. (1975) *Journals and papers*, vol. 4, H. V. Hong and E. H. Hong (eds) (trans.), assisted by G. Malantschuk, Bloomington, IN: Indiana University Press.

Kierkegaard, S. (1980) *The sickness unto death*, H. V. Hong and E. H. Hong (eds) (trans.), Princeton, NJ: Princeton University Press.

Kierkegaard, S. (1990) 'The expectancy of eternal salvation,' in H. V. Hong and E. H. Hong (eds) (trans.), *Eighteen upbuilding discourses*, Princeton, NJ: Princeton University Press, pp. 253–274.

Kierkegaard, S. (1995) *Works of love*, H.V. Hong and E.H. Hong (eds) (trans.), Princeton, NJ: Princeton University Press.

Lonergan, B. (1971) *Grace and freedom: Operative grace in the thought of St. Thomas Aquinas*, J. P. Burns (ed.), London: Darton, Longman & Todd.

Luther, M. (1961) [1519] 'Two kinds of righteousness', in J. Dillenberger (ed.), *Martin Luther: selections from his writings*, Garden City, NY: Doubleday, pp. 86–98.

Luther, M. (1961) [1523] 'Secular authority: to what extent it should be obeyed', in J. Dillenberger (ed.), *Martin Luther: Selections from his writings*, Garden City, NY: Doubleday, pp. 363–402.

Luther, M. (1961) [1525] 'The bondage of the will', in J. Dillenberger (ed.), *Martin Luther: Selections from his writings*, Garden City, NY: Doubleday, pp. 166–206.

Marsh, J., Mendoza-Denton, R. and Smith, J. A. (eds) (2010) *Are we born racist?: New insights from neuroscience and positive psychology*, Boston, MA: Beacon Press.

Meier, J. P. (1994) *A marginal Jew: Rethinking the historical Jesus*, vol. 2, New York: Doubleday.

Nirenberg, D. (2007) 'The politics of love and its enemies', *Critical Inquiry*, *33*(3): 573–605.

Nove, A. (1983) *The economics of feasible socialism*, London: George Allen & Unwin.

Plato (1968) *The republic*, A. Bloom (trans.), New York: Basic Books.

Ravn, I. (2015) 'Explaining money creation by commercial banks', *Real-World Economics Review*, (71), pp. 92–111.

Snyder, T. (2010) *Bloodlands: Europe between Hitler and Stalin*, New York: Basic Books.

Walzer, M. (1983) *Spheres of justice: A defense of pluralism and equality*, New York: Basic Books.

Zack, N. (2001) 'Race and philosophical meaning', in B. Boxill (ed.), *Race and racism*, Oxford: Oxford University Press, pp. 43–57.

4

POPE FRANCIS, CATHOLIC SOCIAL THOUGHT AND THE REJECTION OF FEAR

E. J. Dionne, Jr.

The philosopher Michael Walzer argues that a passionate approach to politics is always risky, but its hazards 'cannot be avoided altogether, unless one gives up the hope for great achievements'. This quest for greatness ends, he adds, 'when conviction and passion, reason and enthusiasm, are radically split and when this dichotomy is locked onto the dichotomy of the holding centre and the chaos of dissolution' (Walzer 2005).[1]

Whether or not Pope Francis has read Walzer, this passage offers a key to the success of his papacy and to the astonishing popularity he enjoys around the globe. The pope is not conflicted: His convictions are harnessed to a powerful passion for a merciful God, and he reasons his way to an infectious enthusiasm for life, love and justice.

But even more important is his rejection of fear – fear that modernity has called forth an onslaught of secularism that threatens to undermine Christianity's cultural and social role, and fear that Catholicism itself is endangered by these larger forces which some fear worked their way into the Church in the name of reform. This rejection of fear means that he rejects framing the Church's mission around the culture wars that have been so central to religious arguments over the last three decades. His differences with his immediate predecessors involve less a fundamental change in Church doctrine than a radical shift in emphasis. Francis is putting a distinctly Catholic critique of economic inequality at the centre of his papacy. And while he does not court chaos, he certainly believes in the saving power of surprise.

'If the Church is alive, it must always surprise', he said on Pentecost Sunday in 2014. 'A Church that doesn't have the capacity to surprise is a weak, sickened, and dying Church. It should be taken to the recovery room at once' (Francis 2014). Michael Gerson, the conservative columnist who writes frequently about social justice, has called Francis a 'troublemaker' (Gerson 2013). He meant it as a compliment.

'Be not afraid' was one of Saint Pope John Paul II's signature exhortations, and it certainly captured his buoyant personal spirit and his fearless opposition to communist dictatorship in Poland. Yet his papacy and also Pope Benedict XVI's were rooted in a strategy of consolidation and restoration that reflected deep alarm over what had happened to the Church – and what was happening outside its doors.

Theirs was a plausible approach if one assumed that the Church's central task was to preserve its 'deposit of faith' at a time of growing doubt. If those assumptions were true, Catholicism's obligation was to be 'countercultural' in offering an antidote to the acids of modernity and in establishing a community of uncompromising believers who would hold fast to the institution and to the truths it taught. In the West especially, this might lead to a smaller church in the medium term. But by being tough-minded and coherent, the Church would put itself in a better position to evangelize and prosper again in more congenial times. Not for nothing did Cardinal Joseph Ratzinger take the name Benedict – after an earlier pope but also after the saint who founded the religious order that bears his name. Pope Benedict XVI explained that Saint Benedict's 'life evokes the Christian roots of Europe' (Benedict, cited in *New York Times* 2005). Europe, he believed, was straying far from its Christian underpinnings.

Pope Francis's Catholicism is also 'countercultural', but in an entirely different way. What he preaches is decidedly out of tune with the advertisements bombarding contemporary men and women, particularly in the wealthy nations; with the direction of economic globalization and with a culture of instant gratification and instant profit. In his statements and writings on capitalism and economic inequality, Francis declares plainly that unfettered capitalism and the 'deified market' will inevitably exclude and deplete the powerless (Francis 2015). This critique is moral and theological: 'We cannot understand the new Kingdom offered by Jesus if we do not free ourselves of idols, of which money is one of the most powerful', he told a gathering of entrepreneurs in 2017 (Francis 2017). Like his predecessors, he sees the Catholic Church, whose roots long predate the Enlightenment, as necessarily in a dialectical relationship with modernity. The Church criticizes modernity and learns from it, but never capitulates to it.

The contrast with his predecessors comes partly in Francis's less gloomy outlook on the Church's relationship to our time. Even his darkest denunciations of economic inequality are suffused with confidence that his listeners can – and will – rise to the challenge of engaging in 'generous solidarity' with the poor. He has spoken out against 'querulous and disillusioned pessimists', and is certainly the only pope ever to take people to task for being 'sourpusses' (Francis 2013). As the columnist Mark Shields has observed, in a Church and a world often divided between those who hunt heretics and those who look for converts, Francis is resolutely a convert-seeker. He seems to be speaking especially to those who identify with Kanye West's plea: 'I want to talk to God, but I'm afraid 'cause we ain't spoke in so long' (West 2004).

When it comes to his own institution, Francis most emphatically rejects the idea that 'the holding centre' should be his priority. On the contrary, Francis sees 'the centre', including the Vatican itself and the traditional ways of the Church's leaders and priests, as in great need of reform. He speaks of 'a conversion of the papacy' itself and has argued that 'excessive centralization, rather than proving helpful, complicates the Church's life' (Francis 2013).

A commitment to reforming the Church from within

If you didn't know he was the pope, you'd assume Francis was anticlerical. He has argued that 'the spirit of careerism' in the Church 'is a form of cancer' (Francis 2013). He excoriates the 'theatrical severity and sterile pessimism' and the 'funereal face' of those who exercise power in the Church (Francis 2014). He has warned against the pursuit of 'an exaggerated doctrinal "security"', and has criticized 'those who stubbornly try to recover a past that no longer exists'. He sees the Church not as a throne from which to judge sinners but as a refuge for them, 'a field hospital after battle' (Spadaro 2013).

Who ever imagined a pope would use the words 'Who am I to judge' (Donadio 2013)? Many of us thought that is what popes do for a living. The quickly famous line won him the broad affection of gays and lesbians even though he has yet to alter a comma in the Church's formal teaching on homosexuality.

He called for a Church that is 'bruised, hurting and dirty because it has been out on the streets' (Francis 2013). If Francis is declared a saint someday, he might become the patron of community organizers.

The pope has backed up his words with actions that point down a new path. He tossed away the trappings of piety and might, disdaining the ornate regalia that appeal to so many prelates. The joke in Rome was that as priests got on board with the new pope's programme, many lacy surplices went on sale at steep discounts on eBay. He gave up the papal apartments and is known to treat the Vatican staff more as co-workers than employees.

On his first Holy Thursday, Francis washed the feet not of the usual group of priests gathered at St. Peter's or another basilica, but of a dozen young people being held at a juvenile detention centre, including two women and two Muslims (Peralta 2013). In the foreword to Elisabetta Piqué's biography of Francis, Cardinal Seán O'Malley, the Archbishop of Boston and a close Francis adviser, noted that this act scandalized many traditionalists, much as Jesus's original washing of the Apostles' feet stunned them. The pope, O'Malley said, 'replicated the surprise and shock of the apostles even as he dismayed those who preferred the stylized liturgy in a Basilica' (O'Malley, in Piqué 2014).

And, yes, Francis also declared that Jesus Christ has redeemed everyone, 'including atheists' (Poggioli 2013), even if the atheists might insist they are not interested and many theological conservatives might be horrified at the suggestion of salvation without conversion.

Francis has captured the world's imagination. Global polling finds his popularity to be nearly universal. He is certainly loved in the United States. In January 2017, a Pew survey found that 70 per cent of Americans had a favorable opinion on

Francis, including 87 per cent of Catholics (Gecewicz 2017). Intriguingly but not surprisingly, Francis is more popular among American liberals than conservatives. A 2015 PRRI survey (Jones and Cox 2015) found that 76 per cent of liberals have a favorable view of Francis, compared to 62 per cent of conservatives. Francis is also slightly more popular among Democrats than Republicans: More than three-quarters (76 per cent) of Democrats view him favorably, while 69 per cent of Republicans say the same.

The perception shared across the dividing lines of politics, philosophy and theology is that the first Latin American and first Jesuit pope is moving the Catholic Church in a progressive direction. This statement is true by many measures, but it is also incomplete.

Understanding Francis's radicalism

A strong case can be made that Francis is not a liberal but a radical. His radicalism is obvious in his pronouncements on the injustices of capitalism, which please so many on the left. But Austen Ivereigh, whose recent biography is subtitled 'Francis and the Making of a Radical Pope', takes the R-word in a direction that is not, shall we say, universally associated with liberalism or the left. 'Francis's radicalism', Ivereigh writes, 'is born of his extraordinary identification with Jesus after a lifetime of total immersion in the Gospel and mystical prayer' (Ivereigh 2014).

Any attempt to come to terms with who Francis is and what he is doing must bear Ivereigh's observation in mind. It is a reminder that the pope is motivated primarily by his relationship with Jesus Christ and his faith in a God of mercy. 'If you understand that preaching a God of mercy is central to his ministry', said the Catholic writer Michael Sean Winters, 'everything else falls into place' (Dionne 2014). Much of the discussion of Francis understandably relates to his political views, to his recasting of the Church's leadership around the globe, and to what is in many ways a break with the last 35 years of Church history. Yet his profound spirituality, of an old-fashioned sort rooted more in popular devotion than in high theology, is central to everything about him. When he takes on 'the individualism of our postmodern and globalized era', he is speaking about more than just economics (Francis 2013). And when he describes 'a vacuum left by secularist rationalism', he is reminding us of the Catholic dialectic with modernity (Francis 2013).

But neither should his spiritual radicalism be used to downplay how much change he is bringing about, and how he is moving a profound critique of economic injustice to the Church's centre stage. These are other aspects of his radicalism.

He has explicitly denounced 'trickle-down' economics by name. It is, he says, a system that 'expresses a crude and naïve trust in the goodness of those wielding economic power', a view that 'has never been confirmed by the facts' and has created a 'globalization of indifference' (Francis 2013). That conservatives like Rush Limbaugh have declared the pope's approach 'pure Marxism' (Burke 2013) should not be surprising; yet Francis sent a powerful message when he responded not with defensiveness but with a surprising declaration about the capaciousness of his friendships. 'The Marxist ideology is wrong', he told the Italian daily, *La Stampa*. 'But I have met many Marxists in my life who are good people, so I don't feel offended' (Davis 2013).

Lest anyone misunderstand him, he used the interview to give an additional spin to the trickle-down metaphor by way of describing the mystery of economic growth detached from rising wages. 'The promise was that when the glass was full, it would overflow, benefitting the poor', he observed. 'But what happens instead is that when the glass is full, it magically gets bigger, nothing ever comes out for the poor' (Davis 2013).

Francis worries about not only the market's injustices, but also its role as the primary source of values and meaning in advanced societies. 'We are thrilled if the market offers us something new to purchase', he said. 'In the meantime all those lives stunted for lack of opportunity seem a mere spectacle; they fail to move us' (Francis 2013).

He is also skilled at linking disparate issues under the umbrella of economic injustice. For example, Francis has explicitly characterized climate change as a 'sin' that disproportionately affects the poor. 'Developing countries, where the most important reserves of the biosphere are found, continue to fuel the development of richer countries at the cost of their own present and future', he wrote in *Laudato si*, his 2015 encyclical on the environment (Francis 2015).

And try to imagine an American liberal politician – even Bernie Sanders, who was invited to speak at the Vatican during the 2016 campaign – who would dare say something like this: 'In this system, which tends to devour everything which stands in the way of increased profits, whatever is fragile, like the environment, is defenceless before the interests of a deified market, which become the only rule' (Francis 2013).

'How can it be', Francis has asked, 'that it is not a news item when an elderly homeless person dies of exposure, but it is news when the stock market loses two points?'

I have offered only a small selection of Francis's observations on economic justice, but it's obvious that this cause is central to his papacy. Yet while he speaks with exceptional passion and urgency, what Francis says is consistent with a long tradition of Catholic social teaching. Both John Paul II and Benedict could be fiercely critical of the injustices of unregulated capitalism. John Paul regularly decried 'imperialistic monopoly' and 'luxurious egoism' (Dionne 1984), and he memorialized his friendship with unions and workers in his powerful 1981 encyclical, 'On Human Work' (John Paul II 1981). Benedict's 2009 economic encyclical, 'Charity in Truth' (Benedict XVI 2009), put him well to the left of Barack Obama. Market systems, Benedict said, needed to be tempered by 'distributive justice and social justice'. He condemned 'corruption and illegality' in 'the conduct of the economic and political class in rich countries', spoke approvingly of 'the redistribution of wealth', and warned that nations should not seek to become more competitive by 'lowering the level of protection accorded to the rights of workers'.

Francis is like his predecessors in another important way: he continues to preach the Church's opposition to abortion. 'Unborn children', he says, are 'the most defenceless and innocent among us' (Francis 2013). He insists that the Church's position is not 'ideological, obscurantist, and conservative', but rather is 'linked to the defence of each and every other human right' (Francis 2013). Even after extending priests' ability to grant absolution for abortion – another example of his dedication to emphasizing mercy over condemnation, especially for Catholics who might be alienated from the church – he reaffirmed his total opposition to abortion as 'a grave sin, since it puts an end to an innocent life' (D'Emilio 2016).

So why is Francis's papacy so different? The key is not only the concreteness and fervour of his language about justice, but also the priority he gives to economic and social questions. He signalled this early on in an interview with Father Antonio Spadaro, published in Jesuit publications around the world. Here are the words, in English, from the magazine *America* in the fall of 2013, which shook the church, cheered liberals and alarmed conservatives:

> We cannot insist only on issues related to abortion, gay marriage, and the use of contraceptive methods. This is not possible. I have not spoken much about these things, and I was reprimanded for that. But when we speak about these issues, we have to talk about them in a context. The teaching of the church, for that matter, is clear and I am a son of the church, but it is not necessary to talk about these issues all the time.

He added: 'The dogmatic and moral teachings of the church are not all equivalent. The church's pastoral ministry cannot be obsessed with the transmission of a disjointed multitude of doctrines to be imposed insistently' (Spadaro 2013).

With these words, Francis moved Catholicism decisively away from the culture wars. His comment about being 'reprimanded' was important, too, since conservative Catholics, including key bishops, were unhappy with the papacy's new focus. They were even more troubled after the interview.

In the American Church in particular, conservative bishops appointed in the John Paul and Benedict years had moved the focal point of public Catholicism away from its long-standing emphasis on economic justice and towards what many of them called the 'non-negotiable' issues: abortion, euthanasia, embryonic stem cell research, cloning and gay marriage. They did not abandon the commitments of Catholic social thought. But they made them far less central to the Church's public mission.

This was a sharp break from where the Church had stood as recently as the 1980s, when Chicago's Archbishop Joseph Bernardin argued for what he called the 'seamless garment' that linked the Church's opposition to abortion and euthanasia with questions he and his allies argued should also be part of a 'consistent ethic of life' (Hyer 1983). These included opposition to capital punishment, an embrace of economic justice with a 'preferential option for the poor', and a sceptical view of war (Bernardin 1983). The US Conference of Catholic Bishops caused a major stir in the mid-1980s with two pastoral letters, one on nuclear war widely seen as implicitly critical of the Reagan administration (National Conference of Catholic Bishops 1983), and another letter on economic justice that was broadly progressive and even social democratic in outlook (National Conference of Catholic Bishops 1986).

Catholic conservatives pushed back then, and they gained considerable ground within the hierarchy in subsequent years as Bernardin-era bishops were replaced by more conservative appointees. The views of the conservatives were reflected well by George Weigel, a leading Catholic intellectual who was personally close to John Paul II. His *Evangelical Catholicism*, published in 2013, not long before Francis's election (Weigel 2013), was a book for the John Paul–Benedict Era.

Weigel argued that the Church's public witness should focus on 'first principles' and 'areas of the Church's special competence'. He did not place war and peace issues within these parameters. Weigel had taken sharp issue with the Church's opposition to the Iraq War in 2003 and scolded bishops in the process. The Bush White House, he argued, enjoyed the 'charism of political discernment', a gift 'not shared by bishops'. Elected officials, he had insisted, were 'more fully informed about the relevant facts' (Weigel 2003).

Weigel did not mention Iraq or who was 'more fully informed' in his book 10 years later, but he did emphasize 'the limits of the social doctrine' and criticized a 'lack of discipline in identifying and relentlessly pursuing those issues on which the Church has competence to speak' (Weigel 2013, p. 225). Going broader – meaning, in effect, emphasizing the areas related to social justice on which the Church had been historically progressive – 'dissipates energies that could be better applied in a more focused way', Weigel wrote (Weigel 2013, p. 228).

Francis's *America* interview could only be read as a rejection of the idea of limiting the church's witness to the 'non-negotiables' and as a rebirth of Bernardin's 'seamless garment' idea. Clearly, Francis does not see his emphasis on economic justice and poverty as a dissipation of his or the Church's energies.

The influence of liberation theology

And here, the Pope's status as a son of Argentina and Latin America is key. His radical language about poverty is the language of the progressive wing of the Church in his region. This represents another break with John Paul and Benedict.

In 1968, Father Gustavo Gutiérrez, a Peruvian, wrote a paper entitled 'Toward a Theology of Liberation', urging Christians to take on the economic injustices of Latin America and to battle the privileged. It grew into a book published in 1971 (Gutiérrez 1971). Liberation theology was unapologetically radical and its advocates often found themselves in alliance with Marxists in opposition to right-wing Latin American dictatorships. The repression of the progressive church was brutal. In El Salvador, Archbishop Óscar Romero was gunned down in 1980, and four churchwomen from North America, including two Maryknoll sisters, were also killed (Connor 1980).

The link between liberation theology and Marxism was certainly troubling to John Paul, a veteran of resistance to the communist dictatorship in Poland, and also to Benedict, a West German who started life as a relative liberal and acknowledged that he – like many subsequently neoconservative intellectuals – became more conservative in response to what he saw as irrational and even nihilistic aspects of the student uprisings in the late 1960s ('The pope: from liberal to conservative' 2013). John Paul had named Benedict, then Cardinal Joseph Ratzinger, as prefect of the Congregation for the Doctrine of the Faith, the Vatican office that arbitrates orthodoxy. In 1984, Ratzinger sharply admonished Gutiérrez and criticized liberation theology for its links to Marxism and materialism (Novak 1984).

As the leader of the Jesuits in Argentina, Francis, then Jorge Mario Bergolio, was ambivalent about liberation theology – he neither supported nor attacked its advocates – and more radical Jesuits criticized him for failing to come to the defence of two priests sought by the Argentinean junta (Otis 2013). (Francis's defenders insist that he sought to protect rebel priests and the ensuing reporting suggests that he did so.) But as pope, Francis did something quite astonishing in light of the recent past: one of his first acts was to invite Gutiérrez to Rome (McElwee 2013). They celebrated Mass and had breakfast together. The gesture did not represent a formal revocation of what Benedict had written, but it sent an important signal. So did the pope's move to speed the beatification and sanctification process for Romero. It had been blocked. He unblocked it (Dada 2015). The importance of this move cannot be overstated.

Leonardo Boff, another liberation theologian condemned by the Vatican in the John Paul years and forced into 'penitential silence', has re-emerged as a staunch defender of Francis. Boff praised Francis as 'a pope who comes from the Great South' and who has a 'new view of things, from below'. With this perspective, Francis will 'be able to reform the Curia, decentralise the administration and give the Church a new and credible face' (Boff 2013).

Francis and the divisions in the Church

Boff's comments speak to the extravagant hopes Francis has inspired. Can he live up to them? He has moved deliberately to reshape the Vatican, to reform a Vatican Bank that had been riddled with corruption (Kahn 2013), and to appoint new officials sympathetic to his reforms. He has broadened representation from outside Europe and North America in the College of Cardinals, in order to more closely reflect the truly global nature of the church's flock (Goodstein 2016). He has used his power to appoint bishops to send strong signals to local hierarchies.

The appointment of Blase Cupich as archbishop of Chicago – and his subsequent elevation to the rank of cardinal – was an especially powerful signal to an American hierarchy that includes many conservatives who have been openly sceptical of the direction Francis has taken (Krashesky 2016). Inside the Bishops' Conference, Cupich has been a courageous voice against the culture-war approach championed by so many of his colleagues, and he was as outspoken and candid as any prelate in condemning the crimes committed in the sex-abuse crisis. Breaking with many of his colleagues, he emphasized dialogue rather than confrontation with the Obama administration over the contraception mandate in the Affordable Care Act (Dizikes 2014). In the aftermath of the Supreme Court's ruling legalizing gay marriage, Cupich refrained from condemning the decision, emphasizing instead that gay people 'must be accepted with respect, compassion, and sensitivity' ('Archbishop speaks about Supreme Court rulings' 2015).

In March 2015, Francis followed up the Cupich appointment with another that sent a message, naming Robert McElroy as bishop of San Diego. McElroy has urged the Church to 'elevate the issue of poverty to the very top of its political agenda' and has specifically argued that issues such as abortion and same-sex marriage should not eclipse its commitments to economic justice (McElroy 2013). In a speech in February 2017, he took on President Donald Trump's agenda openly, declaring that Catholics needed to 'disrupt' the policies implemented by 'those who would take even food stamps and nutrition assistance from the mouths of children' ('Transcript of speech by Robert McElroy' 2017).

And Cardinal Joe Tobin, who took over the troubled archdiocese of Newark late in 2016, signalled a similar turn away from the issues of the culture wars. Tobin, who is known for helping with dishes after lunch and driving himself to and from meetings rather than using a driver, ministered to dying patients in Chicago during the height of the AIDS epidemic, saying that despite the church's stance on homosexuality, it was 'important to be there for people'. He, too, was open about his distress over Donald Trump's campaign rhetoric, especially on refugees and immigrants, telling the *New York Times* that Trump was 'appealing to the dark side of the divisive forces, to the unredeemed part of us' (Otterman 2016).

Perhaps the clearest sign that Francis's progressive moves are real and substantive is the pushback he is encountering from conservative prelates. Massimo Faggioli, one of the most important scholars of the changes wrought in the Church by the Second Vatican Council, wrote extensively in *Commonwealth* about the resistance to the new pope's initiatives inside the Vatican and the Italian Catholic Church (Faggioli 2014). As he noted, Francis's critics began speaking out very early in his papacy. And their criticism has continued.

Archbishop Charles Chaput of Philadelphia is one of the most outspoken conservative voices in the Church. In 2013, he said that what he called 'the right wing of the church' was uneasy with Francis. 'They generally have not been really happy about his election, from what I have been able to read and to understand', Chaput told the *National Catholic Reporter* (Allen 2013). Bishop Thomas Tobin of Providence was blunter, declaring himself 'a little bit disappointed in Pope Francis', adding that 'he hasn't, at least that I'm aware of, said much about unborn children, about abortion' (Winters 2013).

Even before the release of *Laudato si*, which warned against the 'grave implications' of climate change and condemned richer countries for exporting toxic substances to poorer nations (Francis 2015), some conservatives were already engaging in defiance-in-advance. It is highly unusual for Catholics to pre-spin against a papal document, but American conservatives who had been down-the-line loyalists to John Paul and Benedict felt no compunction about challenging Francis on issues where he seemed likely to part company with the political and economic right.

In January 2015, Robert P. George, a professor at Princeton University and one of the leading intellectual lights of Catholic conservatism, engaged in what might be called papal pre-emption in a piece for the right-of-centre journal *First Things*. 'There is no area of morality in which the papal writ does not run', George wrote (George 2015), suggesting he endorsed the same sort of loyalty to Francis that Catholic conservatives had demanded towards Benedict and John Paul. But loyalty in this case came with an asterisk. 'The Pope has no special knowledge, insight, or teaching authority pertaining to matters of empirical fact of the sort investigated by, for example, physicists and biologists, nor do popes claim such knowledge, insight, or wisdom', George wrote.

> Pope Francis does not know whether, or to what extent, the climate changes (in various directions) of the past several decades are anthropogenic – and God is not going to tell him. Nor does he know what their long-term effects will be.

Which presumably means that conservatives could dissent to their heart's content. Liberal Catholics have begun to joke that they are now the true 'ultramontanes' preaching loyalty to Rome against conservative dissidents.

And dissent there is. Stephen Moore, a Catholic and a leading advocate of supply-side thinking who served as an economic adviser to Trump during his campaign, called Francis 'a complete disaster' on public policy. The Pope, he said, 'has allied himself with the far left and has embraced an ideology that would make people poorer and less free' (Moore 2015). John Gehring, the author of *The Francis Effect: A Radical Pope's Challenge to the American Catholic Church* (Gehring 2015), cited Moore in arguing that Francis could matter a great deal to American politics – even if the papacy is primarily about something other than politics. 'The right is rattled', Gehring wrote, 'because a popular pope is shifting the power dynamics in the church and emphasizing priorities that could lead to a different kind of values debate in American politics'.

Francis particularly alarmed his conservative critics by signalling a more conciliatory attitude ('pastoral' is the operative Catholic word) towards divorced and remarried Catholics. Following a 2015 synod on family life, he released a document called *Amoris laetitia* that opened the door for priests to lift the ban on Communion for these Catholics – at least, on a case-by-case basis (Francis 2016). Some bishops welcomed the opportunity to bring divorced and remarried parishioners back into the fold (Morris-Young and Morris-Young 2016), but others spoke out forcefully against the 'great disorientation and grave confusion' spur red by the document. In November 2016, four cardinals – including the conservative Raymond Burke, one of Francis's sharpest American critics – issued a set of questions, known formally as a *dubia*, challenging the pope to clarify whether the Church's stance on divorce and remarriage had, in fact, changed (Pentin 2016).

The ongoing feud between Francis's supporters – some of whom went so far as to accuse Burke and his allies of heresy for questioning the pope – sharpened the rhetorical skirmishes around Francis. Ivereigh, Francis's biographer, wrote that in the wake of the *dubia*, the 'tone of disrespect and contempt' from Burke's supporters had 'plumbed shockingly new lows' (Ivereigh 2017). Ross Douthat, the *New York Times* columnist, had predicted before *Amoris laetitia* was released that changes in practice towards divorced and remarried Catholics 'would put the church on the brink of a precipice' (Douthat 2014). As bishops like Robert McElroy began to interpret the document to allow – or even encourage – priests to discuss the possibility of Communion with divorced and remarried congregants, Douthat declared that such churches were no longer supporting the institution of Catholic marriage (Douthat 2016).

The shift towards elevating more progressive voices in Church leadership will likely continue throughout Francis's papacy as he continues to appoint both bishops and members of the College of Cardinals who are more in line with his focus on pastoral care and social justice. Early on, he removed Cardinal Burke from the Vatican Congregation for Bishops, the committee that supervises the selection of new bishops, a move widely seen as signalling Francis's desire to limit the influence of the culture warriors (Yardley and Horowitz 2013). And in July 2016, the pope appointed Cardinal Cupich to that body, ensuring that a close ally of his would wield significant power in shaping the future of the Church (Roberts 2016).

Limits to Francis's radicalism

If Francis is in many ways radical, there are limits to how far he wants to go in changing the Church. He has stated emphatically that he will not open the question of allowing women to become priests ('Pope says women will not be ordained as priests' 2016), though he does seem open to married male priests (Gallagher 2017) and has improved the Vatican's relationship with the American nuns who had been under investigation in the previous pontificate (Goodstein 2015). There are other ways in which he can give women more power and authority in the Church, but this is one issue on which the 78-year-old pontiff is unlikely to be as radical or progressive as many Catholic women might hope. Moreover, although he stirred brief controversy when he announced in an interview that contraception could be considered the 'lesser of two evils' for women in countries where the Zika virus was prevalent (Romero and Yardley 2016), Francis emphasized in *Amoris laetitia* that natural family planning should still be promoted to Catholic couples (Francis 2016). He also continued to reject gay marriage and maintained the church's position that civil unions between gay couples were not equal to a marriage between a man and a woman (Francis 2016).

In a 2014 interview with *Corriere della Sera*, he was uncharacteristically defensive and aggressive on the paedophilia question. He insisted that the Catholic Church 'is perhaps the only public institution to have acted with transparency and responsibility' and added: 'No one has done more. Yet the Church is the only one to have been attacked' (Pullela 2014). His comments upset advocates of the abused – and many rank-and-file Catholics still angry about the scandal – and the pope has since toughened his approach (Yardley 2014). In 2014, he appointed an eight-member commission on the problem that included four women, one of whom was herself a victim of sexual abuse in Ireland (Lyman 2014). The commission also included Cardinal O'Malley, known for his efforts at transparency and compassion for victims in a Boston diocese that was badly demoralized by the scandal. Francis subsequently issued an apostolic letter, declaring that bishops can and should be removed from office for failing to act on sex abuse in their dioceses (Francis 2016). Francis now seems to understand far better than when he started how critical it is, for Catholics of all ideological dispositions, that he get this issue right.

Francis and Trump

The complexities presented by Francis's approach to the papacy are perhaps most clearly seen in his relationship with Donald Trump. In February 2016, Francis appeared to criticize Trump's campaign rhetoric on immigration, including the promised wall along the U.S.-Mexico border, declaring, 'A person who thinks only about building walls . . . is not a Christian' (Burke 2016). Trump then attacked Francis, saying the pope was 'disgraceful' for questioning his faith. Francis later clarified that he was not discussing specific candidates (Rappeport 2016), but he continued to speak out forcefully against the nativism that characterized Trump's candidacy, regularly underscoring the need to provide more economic and social opportunities for marginalized people. Just after Trump reiterated his promise to ban large groups of Muslims from entering the United States at the 2016 Republican National Convention, Francis rejected the link between terrorism and Islam, noting that all religions – including Catholicism – have 'a small fundamentalist group'. Instead, he said that rising economic inequality was to blame for violence among Islamic youth: 'Terrorism grows when there is no other option and when money is made a god' (Pullela 2016).

But the pope's willingness to engage with the issues of the 2016 campaign did not translate into shifts in the voting behavior of American Catholics. It appears that Donald Trump and Hillary Clinton roughly split the Catholic vote. The exit polling concluded that 52 per cent of Catholics voted for Trump, while 45 per cent cast their ballots for Hillary Clinton (Smith and Martinez 2016). A subsequent analysis conducted by Georgetown University's Center for Applied Research in the Apostolate of the data from the American National Election Studies estimated the split at 45 per cent for Trump versus 48 per cent for Clinton (O'Loughlin 2017). (The discrepancy seemed to arise principally over the issue of whether the exit polls had overstated Trump's share of the Latino vote.)

More significantly, the breakdown of the Catholic vote by ethnicity suggested that Catholics largely followed the preferences of their ethnic and racial group, suggesting that there was no particular 'Catholic difference' in the preferences of the faithful. White Catholics voted by almost exactly the same margin for Trump as all whites (56 per cent of white Catholics compared to 57 per cent of whites as a whole). Latino Catholics were only a bit more distinctive in their preferences. Clinton won 74 per cent of Latino Catholics compared with 66 per cent of all Latinos (although, again, there remains controversy over the accuracy of the Latino polling) ('Exit Polls' 2016; Krogstad and Lopez 2016).

Still, Francis brought his brand of Catholic populism into the conversation as a rival to Trump's (and the European far right's) language of xenophobia and nativism – to the point where multiple commentators dubbed him the 'anti-Trump' (Carroll 2017; Ivereigh 2017). And in his statement on the day Trump was inaugurated, Francis Day, he signalled that he would continue to speak out against actions that threatened refugees, immigrants and the poor, writing 'Under your leadership, may America's stature continue to be measured above all by its concern for the poor, the outcast and those in need who, like Lazarus, stand before our door' ('Pope Francis sends good wishes' 2017). Even when Trump and Francis met at the Vatican in May 2017, a meeting that was widely reported to have gone surprisingly well given their fraught history, Francis presented Trump with copies of *Laudato si*; *Amoris laetitia* and *Evangelii gaudium*, a tract condemning free-market economics (Green 2017).

Some US Catholic leaders were stung by Francis's not-so-subtle attacks on the Republican presidential candidate. Cardinal Burke went so far as to praise Trump after his victory, saying the new president 'will hold the defence of human life from conception . . . and put in place every action possible to fight abortion'. Burke added that he didn't think Trump 'will be inspired by hatred in his handling of the immigration issue' (McKenna 2016). In the meantime, progressive figures such as Cupich and McElroy continued to push back against Trump's views. And in a powerful rebuke to the Trump administration's first budget proposal, the US Conference of Catholics Bishops issued a statement in May 2017 arguing that '[s]harp increases in defence and immigration enforcement spending, coupled with simultaneous and severe reductions to non-defence discretionary spending, particularly to many domestic and international programmes that assist the most vulnerable, would be profoundly troubling' (Clarke 2017). If Francis has not yet brought about a sea change in the American Church, his appeals to economic justice and compassion for immigrants and refugees is finding a steadily more powerful echo from the Church's leadership.

Finishing what Pope John XXIII started

For many progressives of a certain age, the model Catholic pope is John XXIII, who called the Second Vatican Council that fundamentally altered the Church's stance towards human rights, religious freedom, toleration and democracy. John's two encyclicals, 'Mother and Teacher' (*Mater et Magistra*) on the subject of

'Christianity and Social Progress' and 'Peace on Earth' (*Pacem in Terris*) remain touchstones for more liberal Catholics. In one of the magazine's best-known one-liners, William F. Buckley Jr.'s *National Review* reflected conservative displeasure with the second document by declaring: 'Mater, si. Magistra, no' (Judis 1988).

Arguments over the impact of the council raged during the John Paul and Benedict years, with conservatives (notably Benedict) arguing that the 'spirit of the Council', a slogan much invoked by liberals, had wrongly superseded a kind of strict-constructionist reading of the council's documents (Wilkins 2010). Conservatives often spoke of 'reforming the reform'. Liberals saw a retreat from the openness John XXIII had championed, a misreading of its declarations, and an attempt by conservatives to roll back the council's changes by redefining its meaning.

Thus, one of Francis's most important signals: his decision to canonize both John Paul II and John XXIII simultaneously on 27 April 2014 (Yardley 2014). At one level, it was a deeply unifying act. Conservative Catholics – and many others – cheered swift sainthood for John Paul, while progressive Catholics were elated that an overly long process of elevating John to the same status finally reached its culmination. One for one side, one for the other was a good formula for harmony that the Church badly needs.

But more was going on than a quest for unity. Rapid sainthood for John Paul was already seen as inevitable, partly because of widespread devotion to him around the church and not simply in its conservative wing. But elevating both popes was the best way to signal support for the more progressive reading of the reforms of the Second Vatican Council. It also opened the way for the Church to affirm that John Paul's greatest achievements – his commitments to human rights, religious liberty and democracy, as well as a stern opposition to religious prejudice, including anti-Semitism and an emphasis on social justice and workers' rights – were all rooted in what John XXIII had started.

By lifting up John, Francis also reinforced the comparisons so many progressives have already made between his papacy and John's. Of the earlier pope, the current one once said: 'I see him with the eyes of my heart' (McElwee 2013). What might once have looked like wishful thinking on the part of progressive Catholics for their church's re-engagement with Pope John's purposes now seems to be nothing more – or less – than an accurate reading of where the new pope wants to lead.

Pope John once said: 'Distrustful souls see only darkness burdening the face of the earth. We prefer instead to reaffirm all our confidence in our Saviour who has not abandoned the world He has redeemed' (John XXXIII, quoted in Dionne 2009). Francis, who doesn't like sourpusses, seems to feel exactly the same way.

Notes

1   Parts of this chapter originally appeared in slightly different form in *The American Prospect*, Spring 2015, with the title 'A Radical Pope.' Thanks to the magazine for permission to reprint.

References

Allen, J. L. (2013) 'Right wing "generally not happy" with Francis, Chaput says', *National Catholic Reporter*, 23 July. Available from: www.ncronline.org/blogs/ncr-today/right-wing-generally-not-happy-francis-chaput-says [accessed 22 May 2017].

'Archbishop speaks about Supreme Court rulings on healthcare, gay marriage' (2015) *NBC News*, 29 June. Available from: www.nbcchicago.com/news/local/Archbishop-Cupich-Speaks-About-Supreme-Court-Rulings-on-Healthcare-Gay-Marriage-310529301.html [accessed 22 May 2017].

Benedict, XVI (2009) *Caritas in veritate*, Libreria Editrice Vaticana. Available from: http://w2.vatican.va/content/benedict-xvi/en/encyclicals/documents/hf_ben-xvi_enc_20090629_caritas-in-veritate.html [accessed 22 May 2017].

Bernardin, J. (1983) *A consistent ethic of life: An American Catholic dialogue*, 6 December. Available from: www.orbisbooks.com/chapters/978–1–57075–764–8.pdf [accessed 22 May 2017].

Boff, L. (2013) 'Pope Francis called to restore the Church', 15 March. Available from: http://iglesiadescalza.blogspot.it/2013/03/pope-francis-called-to-restore-church.html [accessed 22 May 2017].

Burke, D. (2013) 'Rush Limbaugh: Pope is preaching "pure Marxism"', *CNN*, 2 December. Available from: http://religion.blogs.cnn.com/2013/12/02/rush-limbaugh-vs-the-pope/ [accessed 22 May 2017].

Burke, D. (2016) 'Pope suggests Trump is "not Christian"', *CNN*, 18 February. Available from: www.cnn.com/2016/02/18/politics/pope-francis-trump-christian-wall/ [accessed 22 May 2017].

Carroll, J. (2017) 'Pope Francis is the anti-Trump', *New Yorker*, 1 February. Available from: www.newyorker.com/news/news-desk/pope-francis-is-the-anti-trump [accessed 22 May 2017].

Clarke, K. (2017) 'U.S. bishops and Trump administration diverge over budget priorities', *America*, 22 May. Available from: www.americamagazine.org/politics-society/2017/05/22/us-bishops-and-trump-administration-diverge-over-budget-priorities [accessed 13 June 2017].

Connor, J. (1980) 'A report from Romero's funeral', *America Magazine*, 26 April. Available from: www.americamagazine.org/issue/100/report-romeros-funeral [accessed 22 May 2017].

Dada, C. (2015) 'The beatification of Oscar Romero', *New Yorker*, 18 May. Available from: www.newyorker.com/news/news-desk/the-beatification-of-oscar-romero [accessed 22 May 2017].

Davis, L. (2013) 'Pope says he is not a Marxist, but defends criticism of capitalism', *The Guardian*, 15 December. Available from: www.theguardian.com/world/2013/dec/15/pope-francis-defends-criticism-of-capitalism-not-marxist [accessed 22 May 2017].

D'Emilio, F. (2016) 'Pope allows all priests to absolve grave sin of abortion', *Associated Press*, 21 November. Available from: https://apnews.com/8a9c47baf0764ae683ec20a618dd4c63/pope-francis-extends-special-permission-abortion [accessed 22 May 2017].

Dionne, E. J. (1984) 'Pope condemns "imperialistic monopoly"', *New York Times*, 18 September. Available from: www.nytimes.com/1984/09/18/world/the-pope-condemns-imperialistic-monopoly.html [accessed 22 May 2017].

Dionne, E. J. (2009) *Souled out: Reclaiming faith and politics after the religious right*, Princeton, NJ: Princeton University Press.

Dionne, E. J. (2014) Personal interview with Michael Sean Winters.

Dizikes, C. (2014) 'New archbishop praised for how he led in Spokane', *Chicago Tribune*, 22 September. Available from: www.chicagotribune.com/news/ct-cupich-leaving-spokane-met-20140921-story.html [accessed 22 May 2017].

Donadio, R. (2013) 'On gay priests, Pope Francis asks "Who am I to judge?"', *New York Times*, 29 July. Available from: www.nytimes.com/2013/07/30/world/europe/pope-francis-gay-priests.html [accessed 22 May 2017].

Douthat, R. (2014), 'The pope and the precipice', *New York Times*, 25 October. Available from: www.nytimes.com/2014/10/26/opinion/sunday/ross-douthat-the-pope-and-the-precipice.html [accessed 22 May 2017].

Douthat, R. (2016), 'The end of Catholic marriage', *New York Times*, 1 December. Available from: https://douthat.blogs.nytimes.com/2016/12/01/the-end-of-catholic-marriage/ [accessed 22 May 2017].

'Exit Polls' (2016) *CNN*, 23 November. Available from: www.cnn.com/election/results/exit-polls [accessed 14 June 2017].

Faggioli, M. (2014) 'The Italian job', *Commonweal*, 5 June. Available from: www.commonweal magazine.org/italian-job [accessed 22 May 2017].

Francis (2013) *Address of Pope Francis to the community of the pontifical ecclesiastical academy*, Libreria Editrice Vaticana. Available from: https://w2.vatican.va/content/francesco/en/speeches/2013/june/documents/papa-francesco_20130606_pontificia-accademia-ecclesiastica.html [accessed 22 May 2017].

Francis (2013) *Evangelii gaudium*, Libreria Editrice Vaticana. Available from: http://w2.vatican.va/content/francesco/en/apost_exhortations/documents/papa-francesco_esortazione-ap_20131124_evangelii-gaudium.html [accessed 22 May 2017].

Francis (2014) *As a Loving Mother*, Libreria Editrice Vaticana. Available from: https://w2.vatican.va/content/francesco/en/motu_proprio/documents/papa-francesco-motu-proprio_20160604_come-una-madre-amorevole.html [accessed 22 May 2017].

Francis (2014) *Presentation of the Christmas greetings to the Roman curia*, Libreria Editrice Vaticana. Available from: https://w2.vatican.va/content/francesco/en/speeches/2014/december/documents/papa-francesco_20141222_curia-romana.html [accessed 22 May 2017].

Francis (2014) *Regina caeli*, Libreria Editrice Vaticana. Available from: https://w2.vatican.va/content/francesco/en/angelus/2014/documents/papa-francesco_regina-coeli_20140608.html [accessed 21 May 2017].

Francis (2015) *Laudato si*, Libreria Editrice Vaticana. Available from: http://w2.vatican.va/content/francesco/en/encyclicals/documents/papa-francesco_20150524_enciclica-laudato-si.html [accessed 21 May 2017].

Francis (2016) *Amoris laeticia*, Libreria Editrice Vaticana. Available from: https://w2.vatican.va/content/francesco/en/apost_exhortations/documents/papa-francesco_esortazione-ap_20160319_amoris-laetitia.html [accessed 22 May 2017].

Francis (2017) *Address of his holiness Pope Francis to participants in the meeting 'Economy of Communion'*, Libreria Editrice Vaticana. Available from: https://w2.vatican.va/content/francesco/en/speeches/2017/february/documents/papa-francesco_20170204_focolari.html [accessed 21 May 2017].

Gallagher, D. (2017) 'Pope may allow married Catholic men as priests', *CNN*, 10 March. Available from: www.cnn.com/2017/03/10/europe/pope-married-men-priests/ [accessed 22 May 2017].

Gecewicz, C. (2017) 'U.S. Catholics, non-Catholics continue to view Pope Francis favorably', Pew Research Center, 18 January. Available from: www.pewresearch.org/fact-tank/2017/01/18/favorable-u-s-views-pope-francis/ [accessed 22 May 2017].

Gehring, J. (2015) *The Francis effect: A radical pope's challenge to the American Catholic Church*, New York: Rowman & Littlefield.

George, R. P. (2015) 'Four things to remember about the Pope's environment letter', *First Things*, 3 January. Available from: www.firstthings.com/blogs/firstthoughts/2015/01/four-things-to-remember-about-the-popes-environment-letter [accessed 22 May 2017].

Gerson, M. (2013) 'Pope Francis the troublemaker', *The Washington Post*, 23 September. Available from: www.washingtonpost.com/opinions/michael-gerson-pope-francis-the-troublemaker/2013/09/23/19084384–2481–11e3-b75d-5b7f66349852_story.html ?utm_term=.b0cd9390b2dc [accessed 21 May 2017].

Goodstein, L. (2015) 'Vatican ends battle with U.S. Catholic nuns' group', *New York Times*, 17 April. Available from: www.nytimes.com/2015/04/17/us/catholic-church-ends-takeover-of-leadership-conference-of-women-religious.html [accessed 22 May 2017].

Goodstein, L. (2016) 'Pope Francis names 17 new cardinals, including 3 Americans', *New York Times*, 9 October. Available from: www.nytimes.com/2016/10/10/world/europe/vatican-pope-francis-cardinals.html [accessed 22 May 2017].

Green, E. (2017), 'Pope Francis, Trump Whisperer?', *The Atlantic*, 24 May. Available from: www.theatlantic.com/international/archive/2017/05/pope-francis-trump/527916/ [13 June 2017].

Gutiérrez, G. (1971) *A theology of liberation: history, politics, and salvation*, New York: Orbis Books.

Hyer, M. (1983) 'Bernardin views prolife issues as "seamless garment"', *Washington Post*, 10 December. Available from: www.washingtonpost.com/archive/local/1983/12/10/bernardin-views-prolife-issues-as-seamless-garment/a361803f-c89b-47f2-a63d-d049175afb9e/?utm_term=.3a84349f471a [accessed 22 May 2017].

Ivereigh, A. (2014) *The great reformer: Francis and the making of a radical pope*, New York: Picador.

Ivereigh, A. (2017) 'As anti-*Amoris* critics cross into dissent, the Church must move on', *Crux Now*, 11 December. Available from: https://cruxnow.com/analysis/2016/12/11/anti-amoris-critics-cross-dissent-church-must-move/ [accessed 22 May 2017].

Ivereigh, A. (2017) 'Is the Pope the anti-Trump?', *New York Times*, 4 March. Available from: www.nytimes.com/2017/03/04/opinion/sunday/is-the-pope-the-anti-trump.html [accessed 22 May 2017].

Jones, R. and Cox, D. (2015) *The Francis effect? U.S. Catholic attitudes on Pope Francis, the Catholic church, and American politics*, PRRI, 25 August. Available from: www.prri.org/research/survey-the-francis-effect-u-s-catholic-attitudes-on-pope-francis-the-catholic-church-and-american-politics/ [accessed 22 May 2017].

Judis J. (1988) *William F. Buckley, Jr.: Patron saint of the conservatives*, New York: Simon & Schuster.

Kahn, J. (2015) 'Pope revamps scandal-wracked bank', *Bloomberg News*, 5 May. Available from: www.bloomberg.com/news/articles/2015–05–05/pope-francis-reforms-a-vatican-bank-steeped-in-dan-brown-intrigue [accessed 22 May 2017].

Krashesky, A. (2016) 'Blase Cupich elevated to cardinal by Pope Francis', *ABC News*, 19 November. Available from: http://abc7chicago.com/religion/blase-cupich-elevated-to-cardinal-by-pope-francis/1615497/ [accessed 22 May 2017].

Krogstad, J. M. and Lopez, M. H. (2016) 'Hillary Clinton won Latino vote but fell below 2012 support for Obama', *Pew*, 29 November. Available from: www.pewresearch.org/fact-tank/2016/11/29/hillary-clinton-wins-latino-vote-but-falls-below-2012-support-for-obama/ [accessed 14 June 2017].

Lyman, E. (2014) 'Pope appoints former victim to sex abuse commission', *USA Today*, 22 March. Available from: www.usatoday.com/story/news/world/2014/03/22/pope-francis-sex-abuse-commission/6731439/ [accessed 22 May 2017].

McElroy, R. (2017) 'Pope Francis makes addressing poverty essential', *America Magazine*, 8 October. Available from: www.americamagazine.org/church-poor?page=1 [accessed 22 May 2017].

McElwee, J. (2013) 'Pope Francis on John XXIII: "I see him with the eyes of my heart"', *National Catholic Reporter*, 2 April. Available from: www.ncronline.org/blogs/ncr-today/pope-francis-john-xxiii-i-see-him-eyes-my-heart [accessed 22 May 2017].

McElwee, J. (2013) 'Pope meets with liberation theology pioneer', *National Catholic Reporter*, 25 September. Available from: www.ncronline.org/news/theology/pope-meets-liberation-theology-pioneer [accessed 22 May 2017].

McKenna, J. (2016) 'Cardinal Raymond Burke: Trump will defend human life from conception', *Religion News Service*, 10 November. Available from: http://religionnews.com/2016/11/10/cardinal-raymond-burke-trump-will-defend-human-life-from-conception/ [22 May 2017].

Moore, S. (2015) 'Vatican's left turn would leave the poor even poorer', *Washington Times*, 4 January. Available from: www.washingtontimes.com/news/2015/jan/4/stephen-moore-pope-francis-misguided-policies-hurt/ [accessed 22 May 2017].

Morris-Young, A. and Morris-Young, D. (2016) 'San Diego diocesan synod seeks to put *Amoris Laeticia* into action', *National Catholic Reporter*, 31 October. Available from: www.ncronline.org/news/parish/san-diego-diocesan-synod-seeks-put-amoris-laetitia-action [accessed 22 May 2017].

National Conference of Catholic Bishops (1983) 'The challenge of peace: God's promise and our response', 3 May. Available from: www.usccb.org/upload/challenge-peace-gods-promise-our-response-1983.pdf [accessed 22 May 2017].

National Conference of Catholic Bishops (1986) 'Economic justice for all: Pastoral letter on Catholic social teaching and the U.S. Economy'. Available from: www.usccb.org/upload/economic_justice_for_all.pdf [accessed 22 May 2017].

Novak, M. (1984) 'The case against liberation theology', *New York Times*, 21 October. Available from: www.nytimes.com/1984/10/21/magazine/the-case-against-liberation-theology.html?pagewanted=all [accessed 22 May 2017].

O'Loughlin, M. J. (2017) 'New data suggests Clinton, not Trump, won Catholic vote', *America*, 6 April. Available from: www.americamagazine.org/politics-society/2017/04/06/new-data-suggest-clinton-not-trump-won-catholic-vote [accessed 14 June 2017].

Otis, J. (2013) 'In Argentina, the new Pope has many supporters, and a few critics', *NPR*, 14 March. Available from: www.npr.org/2013/03/14/174295530/in-argentina-the-new-pope-has-many-supporters-and-a-few-critics [accessed 22 May 2017].

Otterman, S. (2016) 'Coming to Newark archdiocese: A different kind of cardinal', *New York Times*, 22 December. Available from: www.nytimes.com/2016/12/22/nyregion/cardinal-joseph-w-tobin-archdiocese-newark.html [accessed 22 May 2017].

Paul II, J. (1981) *Laborem exercens*, Libreria Editrice Vaticana. Available from: http://w2.vatican.va/content/john-paul-ii/en/encyclicals/documents/hf_jp-ii_enc_14091981_laborem-exercens.html [accessed 22 May 2017].

Pentin, E. (2016) 'Four Cardinals formally ask for clarity on *Amoris Laetitia*', *National Catholic Register*, 14 November. Available from: www.ncregister.com/daily-news/four-cardinals-formally-ask-pope-for-clarity-on-amoris-laetitia [accessed 22 May 2017].

Peralta, E. (2013) 'In ritual, Pope Francis washes feet of inmates, young women', *NPR*, 28 March. Available from: www.npr.org/sections/thetwo-way/2013/03/28/175601237/in-ritual-pope-francis-washes-the-feet-of-young-inmates-women [accessed 22 May 2017].

Piqué, E. (2014) *Pope Francis: Life and revolution*, Chicago, IL: Loyola University Press.

Poggioli, S. (2013) 'Pope Francis: Even atheists can be redeemed', *NPR*, 29 May. Available from: www.npr.org/sections/parallels/2013/05/29/187009384/Pope-Francis-Even-Atheists-Can-Be-Redeemed [accessed 22 May 2017].

'Pope Benedict pledges to work for reconciliation and peace' (2005), *New York Times*, 27 April. Available from: www.nytimes.com/2005/04/27/world/europe/pope-benedict-xvi-pledges-to-work-for-reconciliation-and-peace.html [accessed 21 May 2017].

'Pope says women will not be ordained as priests' (2016), *New York Times*, 2 November. Available from: www.nytimes.com/video/world/europe/100000004743754/pope-says-women-will-not-be-ordained-as-priests.html [accessed 14 June 2017].

'Pope Francis sends good wishes to US President Donald Trump' (2017) *Vatican Radio*, 20 January. Available from: http://en.radiovaticana.va/news/2017/01/20/pope_francis_sends_good_wishes_to_us_president_donald_trump/1287205 [accessed 22 May 2017].

Pullela, P. (2014) 'I'm not a superman, Pope Francis says', *Reuters*, 5 March. Available from: www.reuters.com/article/us-pope-interview-idUSBREA2410Z20140306 [accessed 22 May 2017].

Pullela, P. (2016) 'Pope Francis says it's wrong to identify Islam with violence', *Reuters*, 1 August. Available from: www.reuters.com/article/us-pope-islam-idUSKCN10B0YO [accessed 22 May 2017].

Rappeport, A. (2016) 'Donald Trump calls Pope's criticism "disgraceful"', *New York Times*, 18 February. Available from: www.nytimes.com/politics/first-draft/2016/02/18/donald-trump-calls-popes-criticism-disgraceful/ [accessed 22 May 2017].

Roberts, T. (2016) 'Pope Francis appoints Archbishop Cupich to Congregation for Bishops', *National Catholic Reporter*, 7 July. Available from: www.ncronline.org/news/vatican/pope-francis-appoints-archbishop-cupich-congregation-bishops [accessed 14 June 2017].

Romero, S. and Yardley, J. (2016) 'Francis says contraception can be used to slow Zika', *New York Times*, 19 February. Available from: www.nytimes.com/2016/02/19/world/americas/francis-says-contraception-can-be-used-to-slow-zika.html [accessed 22 May 2017].

Smith, G. and Martinez, J. (2016) 'How the faithful voted: A preliminary 2016 analysis', Pew Research Center, 9 November. Available from: www.pewresearch.org/fact-tank/2016/11/09/how-the-faithful-voted-a-preliminary-2016-analysis/ [accessed 22 May 2017].

Spadaro, A. (2013) 'A big heart open to God: an interview with Pope Francis', *America Magazine*, 30 September. Available from: www.americamagazine.org/faith/2013/09/30/big-heart-open-god-interview-pope-francis [accessed 22 May 2017].

'The Pope: Journey from liberal to conservative' (2013), *BBC*, 12 February. Available from: www.bbc.com/news/magazine-21425105 [accessed 22 May 2017].

'Transcript of speech by San Diego Catholic bishop Robert McElroy to community organizers' (2017) *San Diego Union Tribune*, 22 February. Available from: www.sandiegouniontribune.com/news/religion/sd-me-mcelroy-speech-20170221-story.html [accessed 22 May 2017].

Walzer, M. (2005) *Politics and passion: Toward a more egalitarian liberalism*, New Haven, CT: Yale University Press.

Weigel, G. (2003) 'Moral clarity in a time of war', *First Things*. Available from: www.firstthings.com/article/2003/01/001-moral-clarity-in-a-time-of-war [accessed 22 May 2017].

Weigel, G. (2013) *Evangelical Catholicism: Deep reform in the 21st century*, New York: Basic Books.

West, K. (2004) 'Jesus Walks', *The College Dropout*, Roc-a-Fella.

Wilkins, J. (2010) 'Ratzinger at Vatican II', *Commonweal*, 31 May. Available from: www.commonwealmagazine.org/node/31907/31907 [accessed 22 May 2017].

Winters, M. S. (2013) 'Bishop Tobin "disappointed" with Francis', *National Catholic Reporter*, 13 September. Available from: www.ncronline.org/blogs/distinctly-catholic/bishop-tobin-disappointed-pope-francis [accessed 22 May 2017].

Yardley, J. (2014) 'Pope asks forgiveness from victims of sex abuse', *New York Times*, 7 July. Available from: www.nytimes.com/2014/07/08/world/europe/pope-francis-begs-forgiveness-of-victims-of-sex-abuse.html [accessed 22 May 2017].

Yardley, J. (2014) 'On historic day, John XXIII and John Paul II become Saints', *New York Times*, 27 April. Available from: www.nytimes.com/2014/04/28/world/europe/John-XXIII-and-John-Paul-II-become-saints-in-historic-canonizations.html?_r=0 [accessed 22 May 2017].

Yardley, J. and Horowitz, J. (2013) 'Pope Replaces Conservative U.S. Cardinal on Influential Vatican Committee', *The New York Times*, 13 December. Available from: www.nytimes.com/2013/12/17/world/europe/pope-replaces-conservative-us-cardinal-on-influential-vatican-committee.html?mcubz=1 [accessed 14 June 2017].

PART 2

Moral sentiments

5

MORE THAN ENOUGH

Contentment and the dominance of the economic sphere

Christine D. Pohl

Contentment is an awkward disposition, theological commitment and moral practice in light of the prevailing assumptions of modern capitalism. Nevertheless, many people continue to believe that contentment is at the heart of a fulfilling life. This tension has yielded a distinctive mix of pride and dismay over the combination of constant innovation, perpetual dissatisfaction and persistent inequality that dominates the American social scene. Few people would argue against the value of individual contentment in theory, but many fear that if it were widely cultivated, it would endanger economic innovation and social engagement.

Such ambivalence in relation to contentment is not new. Henry Ward Beecher identified a particularly American version of it in a sermon he delivered in 1871 to a meeting of the YMCA in Brooklyn:

> The idea of making a fortune is one which our American youths are particularly alive to. In other lands there is a pride of following the father's course, or there is contentment with the humble place where one is born. This is almost unknown among us. It is peculiarly American not to be satisfied with anything. Whatever we have gained is but that step by which we are prepared to take the next step. Enterprise, Progress – these are the American mottoes; and children are early taught to feel that they must better their condition. There is much in it. I do not know that it should be changed. Yet, there are incidental evils accompanying it.
>
> (Beecher 1995 [1871], pp. 305–306)

Nearly 150 years later, it appears that some of the 'incidental evils' that accompany perpetual dissatisfaction are catching up with us: people are stretched beyond their capacity by work expectations; the natural environment is suffering from generations of careless misuse; and individual dissatisfaction with particular personal circumstances seems widespread.

In addition, there is enormous economic benefit for those enterprises that respond to the latest version of individual discontent. Whether regarding the shape and performance of aging baby-boomer bodies, the scope of opportunities to find true love, or the condition of retirement portfolios, various remedies are offered for a fee. To increase their profitability, companies and their marketing firms cultivate envy, anxiety and covetousness.

Contentment and moderation are often associated with each other, and both were highly valued in many ancient cultures and societies. There is, however, little moderation in supersized meals, 24/7 work schedules, binge-watching television, extreme sports or the other expressions of excess which characterize contemporary society. In this culture, contentment is often associated, not with moderation, but with lack of drive, settling for second best and resignation to a set of less than desirable circumstances. To describe someone as 'content with his or her lot' is not usually intended as a compliment.

At the same time, discontent and immoderate lifestyles have left many people feeling overwhelmed. A substantial portion of the contemporary writing on 'enough' has been generated because people are overwhelmed by 'too much' – too much stuff, too much to do, too many demands. Today, as a result, there is a growing discontent with excess (along with a significant market for books and advice on how to reduce clutter, build tiny houses, organize time, etc.). While the United States has always had a robust market for self-help books, websites and programs on strategies to get ahead, today these are rivalled by a proliferation of resources on how to address the deep, nearly societal-wide longing for a more contented life. Paradoxically, meditation has blossomed into an industry in itself, approaching $1 billion in sales in 2015 (Wieczner 2016).

Current attention to contentment is coming from multiple sources. It is being addressed by mental health professionals and physicians concerned about the psychological and physical well-being of their patients, as well as by Christian leaders concerned about economic injustice, personal priorities, gender roles and family and finding rhythms of work and rest. Popular websites on contentment are also provided by writers from Eastern, especially Buddhist, perspectives – traditions in which contentment is a significant topic.[1] Few of the materials on contentment, however, address the deep internal tensions between individual well-being and market expectations beyond offering suggestions for choosing a simplified lifestyle, taking time to 'breathe' and to offer gratitude, or making small changes in one's immediate family.

In an effort to explore and address some of the challenges related to contentment and discontent in contemporary society, and particularly among followers of Christ, this chapter attempts to identify and untangle some of the complexities of contentment in relation to one sphere – the economic.[2] Much of my adult life has been spent preparing men and women for Christian ministry. In typical Christian ethics courses at the seminary level, the economy is always a factor and inequality and injustice are always concerns, but the topic of contentment is rarely addressed. So why focus on contentment, especially in the context of economic justice?

In part, this focus on contentment is a continuation of my work on the practices of hospitality and gratitude. It is also linked to my more recent interest in the importance of Sabbath-keeping, a biblical practice which recognizes the value of work and rest, trust and responsibility. None of these practices is primarily economic, and yet each is related to, and affected by, economic assumptions and activities. These practices interact in complex ways with the contemporary yearning for having more and having better, or doing more and doing better. Whether at the individual or institutional level, there is significant pressure for continual growth and better results: bigger churches, more effective ministries, a stronger bottom line, better bodies or fuller agendas. Furthermore, at the personal level, this often intersects with a nagging sense of entitlement. Individuals do not just want more or better, they often believe they deserve it. The restlessness and discontent that result are not only located out there 'in the world', they are very much inside the church and its related institutions.

A recovery of the disposition and practice of contentment, however, brings with it numerous risks and potential misunderstandings. Contentment is sometimes interpreted as apathy, passivity or quietude in the face of need or injustice. What are the understandings of contentment that have room for concerns about pursuing justice, encouraging innovation, and finding rhythms of work and rest? How might biblical and historical understandings of contentment help pastors lead congregations to think more responsibly about work, consumption, generosity and equality? In what ways can and does the Christian tradition shape concerns about contentment in relation to the economic sphere and inequality?

Critiques of contentment

People who worry about economic injustice, structural inequality and distributions of power are appropriately wary of discussions about contentment. Attention to contentment can be seen as a way to deflect energy from addressing injustice or from recognizing how one benefits from particular economic arrangements. It can be used to justify privilege and to help people acquiesce to their unjust circumstances.

In 1992, economist John Kenneth Galbraith offered a devastating critique of a 'culture of contentment' that led to complacency (Galbraith 1992). Concerned about a majority of citizens who were focused on their immediate personal comfort to the exclusion of their own long-term well-being, the needs of their less well-situated neighbors, and the necessities of the common good (e.g. maintaining a sound infrastructure), he wrote:

> Doing well, many wish to do better. Having enough, many wish for more. Being comfortable, many raise vigorous objection to that which invades comfort. What is important is that there is no self-doubt in their present situation. The future for the contented majority is thought effectively within their personal command.
>
> (Galbraith 1992, pp. 16–17)

Galbraith argued that certain social and economic doctrines, both ancient and modern, provide convenient justification for a posture of contentment that assumes that individuals who are comfortably situated deserve what they have, based on 'personal virtue, intelligence and effort'. This type of contentment allows people to avoid difficult long-term planning to address systemic issues. Galbraith further noted that central to an economics of contentment is a 'belief that it is in the nature of things and especially of economic life, that all works out for the best in the end. Nothing that happens in the short run is in conflict with longer-run well-being'. He explained that 'the specific instrument for ensuring benignity . . . is the market' (ibid., p. 18, pp. 51–52).

Galbraith's argument is complex and far-reaching, but serves here primarily to illustrate the ways in which contentment can easily be linked to self-satisfied complacency and wilfully ignorant optimism about the general direction of society. He maintained that this form of contentment is shaped by three viewpoints: a general commitment to limiting government in relation to the economy, a social justification for 'uninhibited pursuit and possession of wealth', and justification for 'a reduced sense of public responsibility for the poor' (ibid., p. 96). Such an understanding of contentment clearly puts it at odds with concerns about social responsibility and justice.

While Galbraith's 1992 critique focused on the corruption of contentment as complacency, a popular song by the British musicians, Queen, released just a few years earlier, seemingly rejected the idea of contentment altogether. Speaking to a generation coming of age in the 1980s, Queen's 'I Want It All' resonated with those who were driven by an intense dissatisfaction with their current station in life (Queen 1989). To be sure, Queen's hit played out in complicated ways around the globe, serving as a soundtrack for both night-club hedonism and the anti-apartheid movement; it's a testimony to the song's reflection of the cultural *zeitgeist* that it could take on different valences in various contexts. But the power of the song came from its expression of open-ended desire, demand and discontent. While it was anything but complacent, it offered little in terms of a way forward towards change. In the decades since Galbraith's essay and Queen's hit, people are generally more uncertain about the future, and the combination of complacency with the 'incidental evils' of ambition and greed seem to be taking their toll on those who are both well and poorly situated.

But are these sentiments – complacency or an insatiable quest for what is always just out of reach – our only options? Today, we are in desperate need of a rehabilitated conception of contentment that does not kill a zeal for justice and energy for change, but helps release it. Contentment, properly understood, allows space and freedom for individuals and communities to labor for justice, equality and creative innovation in the midst of significant social and economic problems.[3] Certainly, if people with economic advantages are satisfied with deep inequalities, they are choosing complacency in the face of persistent injustice. And if the privileged encourage the disadvantaged to be satisfied with their lot, contentment has become a tool for perpetuating injustice. That is not, however, the way the biblical texts or the Christian tradition have understood contentment. Contentment involves a much larger vision of the good that presses those with abundance to observe limits and sustains those lacking basic necessities in their struggle for justice and human dignity.

Christian understandings of contentment

Current dictionary definitions of contentment focus on being satisfied, or 'feeling or manifesting satisfaction with one's possessions, status or situation'. They also note the connection of contentment to limits in 'requirements, desires, and actions' (Merriam-Webster 2003). Ancient Christian understandings of contentment were more expansive and drew partially but critically on Stoic views which emphasized 'being sufficient in oneself', independent and complete.[4] This sufficiency was not self-focused or self-derived, however; for followers of Christ, it was linked to confidence in God's providential reign and care (Banks 1922).

Augustine and other writers in the Christian tradition helped to form an understanding of contentment that linked it to the right ordering of desire, wanting or longing for the right things, shaped by a *telos* which is true happiness in God. Discontent, then, involves misplaced confidence or trust, having the wrong focus or desire, and is fuelled by comparison, envy, covetousness and worry.

Contentment can also be understood by identifying what it is not. Contentment, in the Christian tradition, is not equivalent to stoic resignation or to denying a need for deliverance from trouble. It is not the same as enduring abuse or being careless about the well-being of others, nor is it complacency in the face of injustice. It is not the same as despair, sloth, carelessness or self-satisfaction. It is opposed to a constellation of vices that includes grumbling, envy, distraction, querulousness, covetousness and greed.

Because it does not preclude intentionality or effort, contentment should not be seen as located on a continuum between apathy and striving for excellence, nor between sloth and pressing on towards a goal. Biblical texts place it in opposition to worry, anxiety and fretfulness and in relation to trust. Whether there is or is not 'enough', and whether circumstances are good or bad, contentment is possible because it does not depend exclusively on the situation. Contentment is connected to virtues and practices that include gratitude, generosity, hospitality, peaceableness and patience. It is closely related to the practice of the Sabbath, with its emphasis on limits to work and on trust in God's provision.

A surprising number of writers in seventeenth-century England addressed the importance of contentment to the Christian life (e.g. Jeremiah Burroughs, Symon Patrick and Thomas Watson).[5] Their works were biblically and historically rooted, substantive, and focused primarily on the challenges and grace of trusting God in the midst of various forms of affliction: the loss of a child or business, difficult family relationships, betrayals by friends, loss of reputation or esteem and physical sufferings (Watson 2011 [1653], pp. 31–57). They emphasized the ordering, providential wisdom of God in a larger context of social, cultural, political and economic upheavals. They offered extended warnings about the dangers of a 'murmuring spirit' and a 'discontented heart'.

Attention to the importance of contentment seems to appear periodically. It is not necessarily related to explicitly economic circumstances, but it does come into focus when the larger socio-economic context is unsettled or when major cultural changes regarding roles and expectations are emerging. Given the current US experience of significant economic and cultural change – shifting gender roles, transitions from a manufacturing to service economy, and increased political polarization – it is not surprising to see a number of popular books taking up the topic.

Contentment and the economic sphere

Many current reflections on contentment and discontentment are, not surprisingly, related to economic circumstances or possessions. Even when the connection with the economic sphere is indirect (as it is in areas such as church life, sexuality, beauty and marriage), a pervasive market orientation shapes our evaluation of our circumstances. This market mind-set powerfully displaces contentment and is disturbingly evident when choices about vocation, church programs, and even life partners are assessed largely by their anticipated 'return on investment'.

An unbounded economy quickly becomes sovereign over all spheres and subtly reshapes many choices and opportunities. The situation is made more difficult by a work ethic that regularly pronounces that employees and companies will do 'whatever it takes' to get the job done and a marketing sector that continually invents new needs and tweaks new desires. Furthermore, the popular emphasis on moving 'from good to great' raises questions about what is enough; is it possible ever to be 'good enough'? Institutional and social pressures intersect with individual desires and leave persons feeling incomplete and often dissatisfied.

Associated with a market orientation that looks for the best deal or the strongest return on investment is the impulse 'to keep all options open'. Persons shaped by market values are hesitant about making choices or foreclosing alternatives given the possibility that something better might come along. This impulse assumes that having numerous alternatives is always better. Given human finiteness, however, a vast and continual array of choices can be overwhelming and disempowering. Contentment involves a voluntary embrace of certain limits or a willingness to live within certain limits that are externally imposed.

Discontent can also be fuelled by a lifestyle without any acknowledged *telos* or focus. Unfocused lives cannot rightly order anything and a diffuseness regarding desire can feed a sense of fretfulness, anxiety and dissatisfaction. To alleviate anxiety, persons sometimes pursue material goods and economic success because identifying fewer but more significant goods and desires seems complicated and less accessible.[6] But again, the power of the market is such that it manipulates and shapes desire towards the things it can provide, things that are almost always penultimate.

In the seventeenth and eighteenth centuries, arguments for increasing civic concord and well-being through focusing human avarice and ambition in the emerging economic sphere were powerful. This optimistic faith in the market as a mild or safe place for harnessing energy, ambition, effort and discontent (especially in place of the dangers of unfettered ambition within politics and the military) has yielded ambiguous consequences (Hirschman 1977). The innovative energy of the market has resulted in abundance for some and extraordinary improvements for many. But the market's harnessing of economic energy has not replaced political ambitions; it has instead sometimes made them deadlier. The language of war on the environment and the poor in relation to economic expansion is not farfetched. In addition, the supposedly safe and mild economic sphere has turned out to be a subtle sovereign over most areas of public and private life.

Are there understandings of contentment that could shape human interaction with a powerful and dominant economic sphere? The Christian tradition offers some insights. In contrast to Galbraith's view of contentment, which understands it as self-absorbed complacency, contentment can be understood as a spacious practice. Like gratitude, generosity, Sabbath and hospitality, contentment is a practice that makes room for larger concerns and focus beyond the self. By embracing limits, it opens up resources of time, money and creativity for pursuing more complete and sustainable visions of life together. An embrace of limits allows persons to say 'enough'; it also gives individuals, communities and institutions the freedom to claim completeness even when every bit of space, time and agenda has not been filled. In a paradoxical way, contentment and Sabbath are both related to limits such that voluntary acceptance of limits allows them to be spacious.

Sabbath and contentment

Sabbath and contentment, work and rest, limits and freedom are beautifully linked in Karl Barth's comments on the doctrine of creation.[7] In his discussion of Genesis 1 and of God's rest on the seventh day, Barth writes:

> The fact that God rested means quite simply, and significantly enough, that He did not continue His work of creation, i.e., that he was content with the creation of the world and man. He was satisfied to enter into this relationship with this reality distinct from Himself, to be the Creator of this creature, to find in these works of His Word the external sphere of His power and grace and the place of His revealed glory. A limit was revealed. God . . . had fixed it . . . and had now reached it.
>
> (Barth 1958, pp. 214–215)

Barth continues, 'a being is free only when it can determine and limit its activity'. God refrains 'from further activity on the seventh day' because God 'has found the object of His love and has no need of any further works'. With the creation of human beings, God ceased from the work of creation and 'halted at this boundary'. God 'was satisfied with what He had created and had found the object of His love' (ibid., pp. 214–217).

A recognition of limits and a sense of enough or completion links contentment and Sabbath. Barth describes God as content with creation; despite a capacity to continue creating, God did not need to make anything more. It was enough, and God rested. The Sabbath is a structure that inserts into our weeks and years a sense of enough: enough work, enough striving. Sabbath gives shape to time and work by imposing a predictable, defined limit on human effort. In resting, humans have a chance to see their work as good, but also to see it as limited.

What was practised by God in creation is evident also in God's work of redemption. The connections between contentment, Sabbath and trust in God are revealed in the distribution of the *manna*, described in Exodus 16. The children of Israel had been freed by God from unrelenting labor and miserable work that had no boundaries. In their desert wanderings, however, they found themselves without food and without the capacity to work for it. In this setting, the God of the Exodus also became their provider as long as they lived into a new rhythm of trust and effort. For six days of every week they gathered the freely provided food, and on the sixth day they were promised that there would be enough to last them through a seventh day set aside for rest. When they were unable to trust in the generosity of God to supply what they needed, their own efforts did not suffice. The nature of God's provision precluded hoarding. When they gathered more than they needed, it spoiled and served no purpose. Limits and provision are significantly linked in this story, as are rest, contentment and trust.

Laws on keeping the Sabbath in the Hebrew Bible recognized human limits and finitude. Violations and transgressions of Sabbath law were often associated with greed and economic oppression. In the laws concerning the sabbatical year (e.g. Leviticus 25:1–7; Deuteronomy 15:1–18), the land was allowed to rest, loans were cancelled, and slaves were freed. Freedom, restoration, limits and contentment once again were knit together in faithfulness to a trustworthy God. In the Jubilee (the grand Sabbath addressed in Leviticus 25), even destitution was to be cancelled, as those who had lost their land were able to reclaim it. Limits to acquisition of property and to inherited poverty were institutionalized.

Several fruitful lines of reflection on contentment emerge from ancient teachings on Sabbath. First, the Hebrew Bible materials recognize that contentment comes from a rhythm of work and rest. If either work or rest is unavailable, human beings suffer. Second, in the biblical tradition, contentment, as it is reflected in Sabbath rest, does not stand in opposition to intense creative effort. Sabbath events are brief but crucial rests in the midst of effort. Third, contentment and Sabbath allow human beings to express trust in God's care and provision in a way that work alone cannot. Fourth, respect for Sabbath involves acknowledging limits on how much the market can demand from human beings, and how much some human beings can benefit from the labor of others. Sabbath-keeping requires a voluntary imposition of limits. But Sabbath-keeping also reminds us that there is much more to rest than simply ceasing from work. It is spacious in that it opens up time to engage in activities other than work and, importantly, to be something other than a worker.

Like contentment, keeping Sabbath is not a framework for irresponsibility, nor is it a model for spiritually legitimated self-indulgence. It is a gift for all creation to be protected and cherished. Thus, it invites a reconsideration of how natural resources are used, the impact of business decisions on families, and the long-term implications of patterns of leisure and consumption.

Business models that run 24/7, stress constant improvement, demand more work from fewer employees and continually emphasize a better bottom line take a high toll on the people involved. Because it seems as if the company itself, rather than any particular individuals within it, is making the increasing demands, it is very difficult to address the discontent that is embodied in the institutional practices themselves. Institutions, even religious ones, that are tied to the market find institutional practices of Sabbath very difficult.

Although the standardization of 40-hour work weeks – a gift of early twentieth-century labor organizing – represent an acknowledgment of the human need for regular rest, work expectations that intrude into non-work time are now common, especially as facilitated by the constant connectedness available through technology. For those persons who need to work multiple jobs because they cannot find full-time employment, any kind of Sabbath experience is even more elusive. It is not surprising that discontent is common in these various circumstances. While for some people, life without rest or Sabbath is voluntary and tied to ambition, for others who cannot find sufficient work, the struggle to make ends meet leaves little room for rest and reflection, a critical practice for experiencing contentment.

Part of the reason that contentment is rare today is related to distorted understandings of rest and time. Sabbath rest was intended to regularly remind the people of God of their identity and priorities and provide a pause in the week's work. Today, when there is an occasional segment of time not defined by work, leisure can be quite frenzied or mindless. In addition, the widespread use of social media where the maintenance of a curated 'second self' is expected, and the importance of being connected – lest one miss out on something – contributes to an overall sense of being overwhelmingly busy and distracted. The frequent complaint about 'never having enough time' suggests how commonly time itself is viewed as a scarce resource to be consumed quickly.

In the biblical tradition, voluntary and regular acceptance of limits was not for the purpose of inhibiting growth and creativity, but for the purpose of recognizing human finiteness and potential. God's good purposes for creation, community and individuals involve a rhythm of work and rest; and the practice of the Sabbath in religious communities is a corporate expression of important elements of contentment.

Holy discontent

Importantly, contentment does not entail a denial of misery, injustice or evil. Among the faithful, prayers of petition and supplication that explicitly lay out complaints, fears and disappointments are common (e.g. Psalms 140–142). In addition, Hebrew prophets frequently express dissatisfaction and anger with oppression and idolatry among God's chosen people, suggesting that discontent can be the godly response to sin, injustice and oppression. There is, then, a place for what might be called 'holy discontent' within the biblical tradition and a clear recognition of the dangers of complacency in the face of evil.

But holy discontent is always shaped by trust and commitment to God's purposes. The psalmists and prophets cry out against injustice, expressing deep concern about what is wrong while simultaneously acknowledging that God will ultimately set things right. Contentment and holy discontent are significantly connected in the capacity to name evil and resist injustice without becoming overwhelmed by the enormity of the problem.

In Psalm 37, David repeats the phrase, 'do not fret' three times within a few verses: 'Do not fret because of the wicked, do not be envious of wrongdoers . . . do not fret over those who prosper in their way, over those who carry out evil devices . . . Do not fret – it leads only to evil'. This is possible because of confidence that God will act and God's justice will ultimately prevail. Those who trust in God will be able to pursue justice and righteousness, despite present difficulty, because of God's immediate help and future promises.

Holy discontent in the form of truthful speech about injustice and steady resistance to unjust circumstances is sometimes interpreted as ingratitude to God or a lack of trust in God's power. Yet in the biblical tradition, there is room for lament, prophetic anger and sharp criticism of complacency and wrongdoing. Trust in the generous and sustaining power of God makes it possible to seek justice and transformation without yielding to the temptation to employ the evil practices we are called to resist or lapsing into despair because the problems seem too large.

Learning contentment

In his letter to the Philippian church, the apostle Paul addresses contentment directly. While in prison and responding to the recent gift from the Philippian congregation, he explains:

> Not that I am referring to being in need; for I have learned to be content with whatever I have. I know what it is to have little, and I know what it is to have plenty. In any and all circumstances I have learned the secret of being well fed and of going hungry, of having plenty and of being in need. I can do all things through him who strengthens me.
>
> (Philippians 4:11–13)

Paul reports that he had *learned* to be content or self-sufficient in various circumstances. Later in the chapter he further explains, 'I am fully satisfied' (ibid., 18). He has learned to be self-sufficient while being deeply connected to community, and fully satisfied while still striving and pressing on towards the goal. Paul's contentment is anchored by Christ's supply but also by the concern and help of the community at Philippi. This contentment did not come naturally; it was learned and cultivated within circumstances of adversity and abundance.

Jesus' teaching in Luke 12:22–34 (also Matthew 6:25–34) is a central text for recognizing the connections among trust, anxiety and contentment in the Christian tradition.

> Therefore, I tell you, do not worry about your life, what you will eat, or about your body, what you will wear. For life is more than food, and the body more than clothing . . . And can any of you by worrying add a single hour to your span of life? If then you are not able to do so small a thing as that, why do you worry about the rest? . . . And do not keep striving for what you are to eat and what you are to drink, and do not keep worrying. For it is the nations of the world that strive after all these things, and your Father knows that you need them. Instead, strive for his kingdom, and these things will be given to you as well.

By trusting in God's benevolence and focusing on God's kingdom, a person can learn to live without anxiety. Freedom for contentment and from worry is not dependent on a denial of the needs every person has for food, clothing and shelter. Freedom comes from a confidence that in God's benevolent economy there is enough.

This has always been a difficult teaching. We are challenged by it at a number of levels, but those concerned about justice in the economic sphere wonder what it means when so many in the world struggle with poverty and disparities in economic resources are so extreme. For much of the Christian tradition, writers assumed that the problem was not with having an adequate supply of resources, but with distribution. Because everything comes from the hand of a generous God as a gift to creation, anything persons had beyond what they needed was not truly theirs, but given by God to be shared with others. If there was not enough, the problem was a human blockage in the conduits of God's provision and grace.[8]

While this perspective does not directly address issues of economic disparity and distribution, it does serve as a major challenge to people of faith to reconsider their own assumptions regarding contentment, sufficiency, resources, and ownership. Jesus' parable about the foolish man who built bigger barns to store his excess harvest remains an important warning against misunderstandings of both security and ownership. Experiencing unexpected abundance, the man chose to store rather than share his excess, only to lose everything because he misunderstood what was important and lasting (Luke 12:13–21).

Contentment and the allure of wealth

Several New Testament texts explicitly link concerns about contentment to the allure of wealth. The writer of Hebrews instructs the community, 'Keep your lives free from the love of money, and be content with what you have; for he has said,

"I will never leave you or forsake you'" (Hebrews 13:5). In his commentary on the passage, John Calvin (1979, p. 343) observes, 'It rarely happens that anything satisfies an avaricious man; but on the contrary they who are not content with a moderate portion, always seek more even when they enjoy the greatest affluence'. Covetousness, he explains, is rooted in mistrust. Calvin notes that Paul's capacity to learn contentment had emerged as he had 'set limits to his desire' (ibid.).

According to 1 Timothy 6, contentment is related to recognizing that no one brings anything into the world, nor can they take anything with them when they leave. Having the necessities of food and clothing in the interim is enough for contentment (1 Timothy 6:7–8)

> But those who want to be rich fall into temptation and are trapped by many senseless and harmful desires that plunge people into ruin and destruction. For the love of money is a root of all kinds of evil, and in their eagerness to be rich some have wandered from the faith and pierced themselves with many pains.
>
> (1 Timothy 6:9–10)

While much of the ancient Christian tradition regarded wealth as useful if rightly directed, the pursuit of wealth was generally viewed as dangerous and distracting.[9]

In the seventeenth and eighteenth centuries, economic assumptions and opportunities broadened and challenged this traditional Christian orientation towards wealth. The individual pursuit of wealth was viewed more positively, as a potentially significant contributor to both personal and communal well-being. Unlike many of his eighteenth-century contemporaries (including Samuel Johnson and Adam Smith), John Wesley continued to view the pursuit and accumulation of money as both problematic and risky. While valuing the increase in trade that provided jobs for many, he deplored some of the other effects of the changing economy, including its complex impact on Christian contentment.

For several reasons, John Wesley is a particularly interesting figure in discussions of contentment and the economic sphere. While he stood squarely within the Christian tradition's teaching on contentment and wealth, the larger social context within which he taught increasingly celebrated the pursuit of wealth and the value of dissatisfaction and restlessness. Wesley was deeply concerned about the spiritual, moral and social implications of Adam Smith's economic arguments that were gaining popular support in the late eighteenth century.

Wesley was convinced that certain trends in economic thinking and activity had enormous but ambiguous consequences for human beings both inside and outside the Methodist movement. Recognizing the opportunities that growth in the economy afforded, he was also very attentive to the social implications of newly acquired wealth. While strongly encouraging responsible labor and economic innovation, Wesley also preached and published numerous sermons on the danger of riches; these messages became increasingly frequent and intense towards the end of the eighteenth century.[10]

Because he worked among people who were vulnerable and from the lower socio-economic classes, the tensions among the values of economic improvement, social responsibility, and self-discipline quickly became apparent to him. Self-indulgence was frequently associated with an increase in wealth, and together he found that they consistently yielded a 'decrease' in grace, a concern he frequently raised. This decrease in grace, he wrote, was characterized by a wrong ordering of desire, a loss of love for God and neighbor, a sense of entitlement and particularly, a loss of zeal for works of piety and works of mercy (Wesley 1986, pp. 242–244; 1987, pp. 95–96).

Wesley also recognized that to guard their sense of contentment and their comfortable positions, those with substantial resources sometimes deliberately avoided knowing about the desperate circumstances of poor people in their same communities. He noted that they then pleaded their 'voluntary ignorance as an excuse for their hardness of heart' (Wesley 1986, pp. 387–388).

While rejoicing in what some today call 'redemptive lift' – the phenomenon of destitute persons turning to Christianity, learning self-discipline, and becoming more successful in the economic sphere – Wesley worried that many of his followers then became comfortable with their new wealth and status and were unwilling to live sacrificially or share their newly acquired resources with others. In addition, he found that they were increasingly drawn towards desiring finer things, pursued a higher social status, and fell into the trap of always wanting more. To him, this gain in wealth and loss of self-denial were causes of the 'inefficacy' of Christianity. It resulted in a loss of contentment and blindness to the needs of poorer neighbors. He grieved that the 'diligence and frugality' that were direct effects of Christian conversion ultimately undermined Christian faithfulness, *unless* the benefits were shared with others in need (Wesley 1987, pp. 91–96).

Wesley's notion of sufficiency, of having enough, can be understood through how he defined what it meant to be 'rich'. To be rich was having more than necessities and possibly conveniences. He also described being rich as having more than one used. While this is a flexible understanding of wealth, it significantly moderates excess while allowing some difference in possessions and resources.

For Wesley, the 'desire to be rich' or the pursuit of riches was a 'thing as expressly and clearly forbidden by our Lord as either adultery or murder'. 'Delighting' in money was unnatural, but there was also a more 'refined species of covetousness' which he described as a 'desire of having more' than what was needed or useful. He saw a close connection between unholy desires for wealth and 'every other unholy passion and temper'. He finally asked:

> Have those the largest share of content[ment] who have the largest possessions? . . . Is it not a common observation that the richest of men are in general the most discontented . . .? You have more substance; but have you more content[ment]? You know that in seeking happiness from riches you are only striving to drink out of empty cups. And let them be painted and gilded ever so finely, they are empty still.
>
> (Wesley 1986, pp. 232–241)

Wesley's struggle to both embrace and critique the changing economic conditions in eighteenth-century England was prescient. Unwilling to deny the benefits of a more productive and dominant economy, he was also unwilling to allow its social and human fallout to be ignored. The dangers he warned about, the complex inequalities he identified, and the ongoing difficulties with contentment he named have only increased in the subsequent centuries. He, more than many Christian writers and economic theorists, recognized that contentment, justice, inequality and economic practices were deeply intertwined.

If contentment is understood as connected to trust in God and rightly ordered desire, then it is relevant to persons across the economic spectrum. The 'allure of wealth', of always wanting more, is a challenge for most of us, whatever our economic status. Cultural emphases on the self-made person, pulling oneself up by one's bootstraps, and rags-to-riches stories have made individual striving for material success an important part of the American economic narrative.

Because contentment is compatible with a desire for human flourishing, the value of work and having sufficient resources, and the pursuit of justice, its importance is not limited to those who have already achieved a comfortable lifestyle. For those who struggle each day, the support of a community, trust in God and rightly ordered desires can shape an identity strong enough to sustain efforts to improve a difficult economic situation.

John Wesley's words on contentment and the danger of always wanting more were addressed to a mixed community but one that certainly included a large number of very poor parishioners. The beauty and life-giving quality of contentment is relevant to all followers of Christ. The expectations of social responsibility, self-discipline, and gaining resources to care for oneself, one's family and others are held in tension – but are not at odds – with contentment.

Concluding thoughts and implications

Renewed attention to contentment today is not surprising, given ongoing major changes in social life, roles and economic practices. This brief exploration of biblical resources and voices from the Christian tradition offers several insights into understandings of contentment that are relevant for contemporary concerns and challenges, especially within church communities. Because of the power of the market and marketing, a recovery of contentment will require very critical engagement with the assumptions that presently govern the economic sphere.

First, Christian communities could fruitfully explore the meaning of excellence, the kinds of growth that are most desirable, and questions about resource distribution and 'always wanting more'. A renewed emphasis on the importance of contentment need not be viewed as a threat to economic innovation, excellence, effort or creative activity, but it will involve a reordering of desires and priorities. It will also involve difficult wrestling with the power of the economic sphere to shape what counts as excellence, success and responsibility.

Second, a concept of contentment grounded in Christianity assumes trust in a loving God and connection with a community. Discussions about 'how much is enough' belong in community because contentment is generally learned and reinforced there. This is particularly important because discontent is fuelled by comparison and envy – vices most likely to appear in close relationships.

Third, congregations can model contentment while encouraging innovation and efforts at justice by embracing its spacious capacity. A recovery of the disposition and practice of contentment could unleash the enormous energy for good that is stored in churches. Contentment is a rich resource out of which people can work for the benefit of others. When those with economic advantages are satisfied to live with less than they can afford, there is freedom to use resources differently, to trust God more fully, and to share more generously.

Fourth, while recognizing that contentment does not support complacency or laziness, churches can explicitly link it to Sabbath-keeping and an acknowledgment of limits. This could apply to the structuring of staff expectations, committee work, programming and use of resources. Because the expectation of 'more' – more work, programming, finances, and growth is so strong – churches that choose a more life-sustaining pace for their employees and volunteers and use their resources in ways that make sure that their abundance is shared could speak a powerful word to the larger culture.

Fifth, teaching on contentment can create space for economic innovation and partnerships with those who have not benefited from the present economy. Moves in this direction are evident in efforts such as church-based mentoring programs, small business incubators and community gardens. When congregations recognize the importance of each person having a way to contribute to a community, they find or create opportunities for persons ordinarily excluded from the economic sphere to contribute to community in other ways.

Sixth, because competition generally precludes contentment, it is not always clear how religious institutions that are tied to the market can fully embrace or embody contentment. Voluntary organizations, religious schools and Christian healthcare providers often compete in the larger marketplace. Issues related to contentment and Sabbath are important and can challenge some of the management models that are adopted. Businesses and companies located fully in the economic sphere can still explore the implications of human well-being in terms of the importance of rest, work schedules, flex time, family leave, etc. A more careful and robust embrace of Sabbath-keeping at the institutional level could help work environments to become more humane. While requiring a different model from biblical understandings of Sabbath, attention to contentment and rest could prompt a challenge to corporate expectations that are overbearing.

And finally, a recovery of contentment can provide a sustainable basis from which to work on efforts at a more just economic order. Insights into the importance of contentment and Sabbath remind us that the life-giving rhythms of work and rest are important for every human being. Contentment remains an important and relevant practice in the twenty-first century in which we are faced with a variety of 'incidental evils' that accompany discontent, acquisitiveness and excess. In choosing to resist the impulse to always want or strive for more than we need, use, or even can enjoy, we imitate God who was willing to say enough on the sxith day of creation. Contentment is an expression of gratitude to a loving and generous God who gladly gives more than enough.

Notes

1 See, for example www.buddhisma2z.com/content.php?id=83; www.buddhanet.net/e-learning/qanda02.htm.
2 I am delighted to write this chapter in honor of Dr. Jon Gunnemann. His classes were central in shaping my understandings of ethics and society. His teaching and guidance while I was a Ph.D. student at Emory University laid the crucial groundwork for my ongoing interest in the intersections of ethics, theology, biblical studies, and social and economic theory. His generous willingness to mentor my dissertation on recovering the practice of hospitality has continued to bear significant fruit. It is a joy for me to follow in his footsteps and mentor additional generations of students. Two of my former students at Asbury Theological Seminary are now completing Ph.D. dissertations on related topics: Maria Russell Kenney has written on temperance and David Lilley is writing on Sabbath. I have benefited from their insights in reflecting on contentment.
3 Sidney Callahan (1988) argues that practicing patience while bearing systemic types of wrongs plays a similar role.
4 The ways in which early Christian understandings of contentment were similar to and different from Stoic views are important but beyond the scope of this paper. See, for example Augustine, *The City of God*, Book XIV.8.
5 See Burroughs (1964); Patrick (1858); Watson (2011).
6 In his findings from a recent longitudinal study of emerging adulthood, Christian Smith (2011) suggests that significant numbers of young adults are wary of ambition and envy but seem to float along in a lifestyle of consumption and distraction.
7 I am indebted to David Lilley for pointing out this passage.
8 This is particularly clear in John Wesley's interpretation of the tradition, and in his teaching on the distribution of resources. In his sermon, 'Causes of the Inefficacy of Christianity', Wesley (1987, p. 91) said to his parishioners, 'Many of your brethren, beloved of God, have not food to eat; they have not raiment to put on . . . And why are they thus distressed? Because *you* impiously, unjustly, and cruelly detain from them what your Master and theirs lodges in *your* hands on purpose to supply *their* wants'.
9 See, for example, Wheeler (1995, pp. 121–134).
10 These include: Sermon 28: 'Upon our Lord's Sermon on the Mount, VIII' (vol. 1); Sermon 50: 'The Use of Money', (vol. 2); Sermon 87: 'The Danger of Riches', Sermon 108: 'On Riches', (vol. 3); Sermon 122: 'Causes of the Inefficacy of Christianity', Sermon 131: 'The Danger of Increasing Riches', (vol. 4) in *The Works of John Wesley* (Wesley 1983–1987).

References

Banks, J. S. (1922) 'Contentment', in J. Hastings (ed.), *Dictionary of the apostolic church*, vol. 1, New York: Charles Scribner's Sons, pp. 244–245.
Barth, K. (1958) *Church dogmatics*, vol. 3, G. W. Bromiley and T. F. Torrance (eds), Edinburgh: T&T Clark.
Beecher, H. W. (1995 [1871]) 'A sermon to young men', in C. E. Fant and W. M. Pinson (eds), *A treasury of great preaching*, vol. 4, Dallas, TX: Word Publishing, pp. 305–306.

Burroughs, J. (1964 [1648]) *The rare jewel of Christian contentment*, London: Banner of Truth.

Callahan, S. (1988) *With all our heart and mind: The spiritual works of mercy in a psychological age*, New York: Crossroad.

Calvin, J. (1979) 'Commentaries on the epistle of Paul the apostle to the hebrews' in *Calvin's Commentaries*, vol. XXII, reprint edn, Grand Rapids, MI: Baker.

Escamilla, P. (2007) *Longing for enough in a culture of more*, Nashville, TN: Abingdon Press.

Galbraith, J. K. (1992) *The culture of contentment*, Boston, MA: Houghton Mifflin.

Hirschman, A. O. (1977) *The passions and the interests*, Princeton, NJ: Princeton University Press.

Patrick, S. (1858) *The works of Symon Patrick*, vol. IX, A. Taylor (ed.), Oxford: Oxford University Press.

Queen, (1989) 'I want it all', London: Parlophone.

Samson, W. (2009) *Enough: Contentment in an age of excess*, Colorado Springs, CO: David C. Cook.

Simon, A. (2003) *How much is enough: Hungering for God in an affluent culture*, Grand Rapids, MI: Baker.

Smith, C. (2011) *Lost in transition: The dark side of emerging adulthood*, Oxford: Oxford University Press.

Watson, T. (2011 [1653]) *The art of divine contentment*, reprint edn, Grand Rapids, MI: Soli Deo Gloria Publications.

Wesley, J. (1983–1987) *The works of John Wesley*, A. C. Outler (ed.), Nashville, TN: Abingdon Press.

Wieczner, J. (2016) 'Meditation has become a billion-dollar business', *Fortune* (March 12). Available at: http://fortune.com/2016/03/12/meditation-mindfulness-apps/ [accessed August 8, 2017].

Wheeler, S. E. (1995) *Wealth as peril and obligation*, Grand Rapids, MI: Wm. B. Eerdmans.

Wilson-Hargrove, J. (2009) *God's economy: Redefining the health and wealth gospel*, Grand Rapids, MI: Zondervan.

6

STRESS

Julie Meadows

I am trembling in an extended plank as the yoga instructor paces the studio, his voice lifted in full lecture mode. 'Stress is not bad!' he says, emphasizing each word. 'The only way to not experience stress . . . is to be dead. You can learn to endure stress. Here we induce stress on purpose, and we observe that it does not kill us'. On a different day, in a different studio, another lecture, this time on fear. 'There is absolutely no reason for a person in this country to be afraid', he tells us.

I am in yoga class because my endocrine system has shut down under the weight of a lifetime of prolonged, severe stress. There is so little cortisone in my system when it is finally tested that the doctor tells me he does not know how I am still standing. I am in constant pain; I wake every morning feeling as though I have been beaten in my sleep. I can barely bend enough to put on my own socks. Daily life feels like I am swimming through mercury or some other heavy, resistant liquid. My brain has stopped working; when I teach I am constantly having to work around the fact that when I reach for words they slip away from my grasp. For a while my symptoms track my mother-in-law's. She has Alzheimer's. I do not know if I will recover, or if this is my new reality. I do not know who I am. *Stress is not bad.*

In 1987, when President Ronald Reagan was busy cutting funding for housing programs, I spent Christmas with my family in a homeless shelter. The director was worried about how long the shelter would be able to stay open; it was full and had to limit stays to 2 weeks. For the entirety of my adult life, I have been narrowly escaping as social policies engineered to punish the least well off have been enacted one after another. *There is absolutely no reason for a person in this country to be afraid.*

The term *stress* has become ubiquitous, the constant descriptor for the lives of many Americans, and especially for women. We are told of its dangers and surrounded with techniques for 'managing' it. But the word means too many things.

Stress covers a range of conditions all the way from the benign and even pleasurable demands of interesting work or healthy exercise to demands that wreck the body and the mind, bringing about changes that will be passed on biologically to children and future generations. It includes both one's unnecessarily anxious response to busy life circumstances and one's appropriately anxious response to circumstances that threaten one's human survival. This is too much meaning for one word to bear.

For middle-class, working mothers, the people in my yoga class, *stress* is used in ways that refer to mental habits, to worrying. (Hence, its gendering: men's suffering is caused by external realities, women's by neurosis.) Women are constantly admonished that they must not allow the stress to increase to the point that it begins to do damage to their bodies; this is a failure of self-care. The response which women are invited to make is one of increasingly vigilant self-management. Women (like everything else) are urged to function like factories, increasing efficiencies and reducing waste. Ultra-efficiency holds the promise of happiness; banishing waste leads to the possibility of rest. If one works hard enough, *all the time*, then one deserves some 'down time'. The right to have a good life, a human life, is earned.

For poor women, *stress* means something very different. *Stress* is fear for one's basic animal survival. A more apt term might be *terror*. Terror as a constant, daily undercurrent to everything that you do. What reason is there for a person in this country to be afraid? Simply this: we have made clear, as a society, that we do not care whether you survive or not. We have made clear that if you need help, you should be punished. Terror's companion is shame: you are constantly reminded that you do not deserve better. No matter how hard you work, a good human life is not something you can earn.

In this chapter, I explore two women's descriptions of the stress in their lives. Both write about their experiences vividly and analyze them thoughtfully. Each one offers an important picture of the pressures that inequality creates in her day-to-day life. Brigid Schulte's book, *Overwhelmed: Work, love and play when no one has the time* (2014), narrates her search for solutions to 'the overwhelm' of her daily life as a professional woman and mother. She learns that the demands of professional work have expanded, so much so that more than one of the experts she consults claims that work has become a religion. At the same time, the 'cult of intensive motherhood' demands that more and more time and energy be devoted to raising one's children, perhaps as compensation for the fact that one is also working. No matter how hard she works, Schulte can't seem to meet the impossible standards of either realm. She wants time to 'work, love, and play' – time to be fully human – but this doesn't seem possible.

Linda Tirado's blog post, 'Why I make terrible decisions, or, poverty thoughts' (2013), offered a description of the kinds of conditions that poor people live with. Coping strategies that from the outside are often judged as imprudent or irrational are actually a rational response to these circumstances. Tirado's post went viral and led to the book, *Hand to mouth: Living in bootstrap America* (2014). In the book, Tirado describes her own reality of survival on low-wage work, making evident that the toll of this work is much more than financial. While being able to meet one's basic needs and live with some measure of security are clearly important – and way too elusive – Tirado eloquently captures the multiplicity of ways in which the poor are shamed, their self-esteem continually and purposefully assaulted. Tirado calls for the possibility of a 'basic maybe, but decent' life for all Americans.

Reading Tirado after Schulte helps reveal what the equivocation between different forms of 'stress' works to hide. We are not all in the same boat. In search of 'elusive' answers to her own discomfort with 'the time bind', Schulte will travel to Paris and Copenhagen, and all across the United States. She'll tell us that a group of highly successful women are 'pioneers, showing us all the way' (Schulte 2014, p. 261). Tirado describes her efforts to get through the day without punching someone as she tries to find and keep demeaning and underpaid jobs, move to decent affordable housing and negotiate maddening run-arounds from government agencies. Schulte embraces self-management techniques, including contemplative practices, which she offers as a solution for us all. But the problems Tirado describes will not be solved through meditation and learning how to live differently in time. Reading the two books together might help us resist optimistic but problematic solutions to the damage that inequality is doing in and to our lives.

We might also notice something that both authors share: a reluctance to engage politically, a backing away from the systemic problems that they have so carefully described in order to focus on individual choice. While Tirado's book is powerful, it, too, stays largely in the realm of appeal to individual readers ('rich people') to change their own behaviors. Both women minimize (or perhaps privatize) the problems they have worked so hard to illuminate, while guaranteeing that the 'we' of the two books will not intersect.

Stress and time

In *Overwhelmed*, Brigid Schulte narrates her search for solutions to 'the overwhelm', her experience of living a life that feels 'scattered, fragmented, and exhausted . . .' (2014, p. 4). For Schulte, the problem of stress is primarily a problem of time. Schulte describes her experience of time as torn up into little bits like confetti, and her desire to find some way to piece it back together again into longer, more continuous chunks. She names the fear, panic and dread she feels when it comes to time, and her own ongoing self-recrimination and feelings of inadequacy (ibid., pp. 12–13).

Schulte's narrative begins with her encounter with a pioneering time-management researcher, Dr. John Robinson. A single professional man, he has loads of free time, and tells her that she has 30 hours of leisure a week, she just doesn't realize it. If she doesn't *feel* like she has leisure that's her own fault. Her standards are too high. How clean does the house really need to be? It's also not something that Dr. Robinson can help her fix. 'I'm not a chronotherapist', he tells her (ibid., p. 18).

In response to Dr. Robinson's unlikely account, Schulte works to show that her own personal 'overwhelm' is part of a set of larger social shifts that place an increasing burden on everyone, but especially on working mothers. Schulte organizes babysitters for her children and heads to Paris for a conference of researchers who study time. The dimensions of 'the overwhelm' have names. 'Contaminated time' is the phenomenon of always having a mental to-do list scrolling through one's mind, so that mental work is constant, and even while working on one task, one is always also thinking of everything else that needs to be done (ibid., p. 27). 'Role overload' is having multiple, competing hats to wear and never feeling like you can adequately meet the responsibilities of any of them – and never, ever having what feels like true leisure time. And 'task density' refers to the importance of all the tasks one is trying to juggle, or how dire the consequences would be of dropping the ball (ibid., p. 25).

Schulte finds that 'the overwhelm' is getting worse for nearly everyone, but especially for Americans, and most of all for women. 'At the conference, researchers sought to unravel how the explosive speed and sheer quantity of information, and the rapid and mystifying shifts in the economy and politics, and the uncertainty about the future, are swamping everything' (ibid., p. 26). But the researchers are hopeful that they can somehow rehabilitate our experience of time.

> What the researchers in Paris said they hoped to discover were the keys to transforming the modern squeeze of endless, fractured work hours, frantic family time, and crappy bits of leisure time confetti into a blissful-sounding state they called . . . time serenity.
>
> (ibid., p. 28)

Although the hours Americans work have increased and technology has helped work permeate even non-work hours, other dimensions of 'the overwhelm' are cultural. Schulte explores two of these: the increasing cultural value placed on busyness, and the ongoing power of the stereotypical 'ideal worker'. Schulte learns that contemporary culture opposes work not to leisure, time for rest and play and hobbies and civic life, but to idleness, laziness and unimportance. 'Somewhere toward the end of the twentieth century, Ann Burnett and other researchers contend, busyness became not just a way of life, but *glamorous*. Now, they say, it's a sign of high social status' (ibid., p. 45). As one research subject put it, 'We assume that if people aren't always busy, then they must be lazy'. We *want* to be busy, so that we feel like we matter. Some researchers think that this cult of busyness is at the heart of people's experience of being overworked and overwhelmed. It's a choice we're making, they say, because it makes us feel valuable. But Schulte is pretty sure that her own experience of 'the overwhelm' is more than this, that it is not simply self-created.

For answers, Schulte turns to leisure researcher Ben Hunnicutt, who tells her that something more *is* going on. The de-valuing of leisure is the flip side of the outsized role that we have given to work. 'Work has become central in our lives', he tells her, 'answering the religious questions of "Who are you" and "How do you find meaning and purpose in your life?"' There is a cost to work becoming our religion, even beyond the singular loyalty and devotion that it allows our jobs to claim from us. Hunnicutt says that our lives are lessened by this misplaced faith: it crowds out the possibility of true meaning. 'Without time to reflect, to live fully present in the moment and face what is transcendent about our lives, Hunnicutt says, we are doomed to live in purposeless and banal busyness'. Worse still, as we run ourselves ragged, 'we starve the capacity we have to love' (ibid., p. 53). Busyness may be status-conferring, but it comes at a great cost.

The second cultural force Schulte identifies is the stereotype of the 'Ideal Worker'. The Ideal Worker devotes himself exclusively to the demands of his job, unfettered by family responsibilities or competing priorities of any kind. Consistent with Hunnicutt's claim that work has become a religion, many workplaces demand (and reward) demonstrations of complete devotion. They do this *for its own sake,* not because it actually improves the quality of anyone's work. In spite of research that shows that 'workers are more engaged, productive, and innovative when they have full lives at home and are refreshed with regular time off', the image of the Ideal Worker still holds sway (ibid., pp. 88–89). As Joan Williams tells Schulte,

> It's not about the rational weighing of evidence. We're talking about work as people's religion . . . If you're not giving your all, putting work ahead of family or any other obligation, then you are violating the work devotion ideal. You become suspect. Lazy. Undependable. A slacker.
>
> (ibid., p. 86)

Schulte recognizes this stereotype as being at the root of her ongoing feelings of inadequacy in the realm of work. She routinely works longer hours than she's being paid for; she works late at night and early in the morning. It's not that she's not good enough, she realizes. It's that the system is rigged: no one is ever good enough. 'With smartphones and Skype and e-mail and other fast-emerging technologies keeping us all tethered to work, the ideal worker is now expected to be on call and ready to roll all day, every day, all the time . . . No matter how much you do, how hard you work, how much you sacrifice, how devoted you are, you can never attain that ideal' (ibid., p. 95).

But some people can get closer to the ideal than others. The people who succeed and become supervisors and managers tend to be ideal workers, devoting themselves to work, gaining a sense of worth and purpose from their accomplishments, and with no family responsibilities or with a spouse who shoulders these. In turn, they help perpetuate the same expectations for their employees. Discussions of work-life balance, especially for women, are riddled with the language of 'choice'. But Schulte finds that the ability to choose is largely an illusion.

> With such rigid and work-devoted cultures, how much of a "choice" does any worker who wants a full life and a family have? If we have designed

workplaces around an expectation of work without end, if those workplaces expect all-out dedication of body, mind, and soul, then *no one*, male or female, has much of a choice. There is only one way to work to succeed or to survive: all the time.

(ibid., p. 76.)

This may be the most powerful paragraph in Schulte's book. If work has become a religion, it is one that serves a jealous and unforgiving god. What would we have to do to escape from its clutches, to have something like real choices about how much of ourselves and our lives to give to our employers? How might we go about finding different answers to questions like 'Who are you' and 'How do you find meaning and purpose in your life'? But Schulte's narrative doesn't press any further into these questions.

Schulte seems content with the reassurance that what she's experienced is not due to a personal failing or flaw. Expiated of guilt, she searches for ways to cope with the circumstances of her life. As she notes earlier, how people *feel* about stress seems to matter more than how much stress they're actually under. 'In other words, what we *think* about ourselves and our lives *is* our reality' (ibid., p. 61). In spite of all of her careful research about gender discrimination, alternative ways of structuring work and even her trip to Denmark to see a more equitable (and less work-obsessed) society in action, she concludes that these are problems that will take a long time to solve, and she simply can't wait (ibid., p. 261). So Schulte turns to self-management for ways to make time *feel* better. Although the concrete demands of the modern workplace are unforgiving and unsustainable, what matters most is our subjective experience of time.

Why isn't Schulte angrier? She's still optimistic that, at least for her, the problem of 'the overwhelm' has a solution. She starts to pinpoint the conflict at the heart of her own overwhelm: 'the fog of guilty ambivalence' that overshadows both her work and her mothering, and makes it difficult for her to choose between the multitude of competing tasks that she constantly faces. She looks for women who have overcome this ambivalence. She discovers the 'WoMoBiJos', the Working Mothers with Big Jobs. The WoMoBiJos manage to work fulfilling jobs and be 'good enough' parents. They make their own choices and they stand by them.

They were freed from the mire of ambivalence because the structures of their lives, like the best of the bright spots I'd found, fully supported them in work, love, and play. They all work in incredibly flexible work environments . . . They have worked their way into positions of authority, so their time is their own to control and is predictable . . . Their partners are, to greater and lesser extents, equitably sharing care of kids and domestic work. They automate, delegate, or drop everything else – shopping for groceries online, hiring help, or not caring if the house is less than perfect or if their husbands always make sandwiches for dinner. So none face the double time bind at home.

So, for at least some women, the possibility Schulte set out to find, a life that has room for work, love and play, seems to be a reality. They are still tired, but they are also 'able to embrace their lives with passion' (ibid., p. 261).

Schulte wonders whether what makes this possible is something that the WoMoBiJos all seem to have that she feels she lacks: confidence.

> More than anything, I was struck by how supremely confident the WoMo-BiJos are . . . I wondered, Was that it? Their confidence? Were they able to create these rich, complex, and full lives and live them wholeheartedly simply because they *believed* they could? And if that were the case, could the WoMoBiJos, instead of being just a small group of admirable women in enviable special circumstances, really be pioneers showing us all the way? If they could believe their way into living unambiguously, could others? Could I?
>
> (ibid., p. 261)

For Schulte these are rhetorical questions, of course; she sets out to develop the 'mind-set' for 'living unambiguously'. She hires Kathy Korman Frey, 'the Confidence Guardian'. The 'gospel' that Korman Frey 'has been preaching' is 'that what keeps so many women running ragged and out of time is that most have yet to develop the skill of confidence, or what she calls 'self-efficacy' (ibid., p 261) Korman Frey describes many of the same issues facing women that Schulte has researched in the rest of the book, but for Korman Frey, the root of these issues is a failure of self-development. 'I'm not saying it's not hard', Korman Frey tells Schulte, 'But I am saying it's like you're wearing the ruby slippers. You have the power. You've had it all along' (ibid., p. 262).

Maybe 'the overwhelm' *was* Schulte's fault, after all – she was missing a crucial skill, one that could help her piece time back together, and have something like a good life. She hires a coach, Terry Monaghan, to help her develop her own self-efficacy. Schulte shows us how Monaghan has helped a previous client, Liz Lucchesi, escape the overwhelm. First, Monaghan pressed Lucchesi to overcome ambivalence by defining her priorities. Then,

> Monaghan forced Lucchesi to take the most important pieces of her jigsaw puzzle and fix them on her calendar first. Everything else flowed around those big pieces. At work, as Lucchesi began to focus on doing what she really *liked*, her business grew and she was able to hire other people and delegate . . . She slept eight hours a night. She had time to play with her children and go to church. She'd become an active philanthropist in her community. She was running again and enjoying it, not just slogging through a workout. For fun, she was taking piano lessons and had just returned from a weekend camping trip . . . She was put on this earth to live a good life, she told me. And she finally felt that she was.
>
> (ibid., p. 264)

Although Schulte tends to use 'religious' to mean not open to rational persuasion, this sounds a lot like a conversion story. Everything follows from overcoming ambivalence, from knowing what you want. Success at work follows, and, in turn, you get to have a life, too. Lucchesi is able to live a good life – to work, love, play and even sleep – because she becomes an employer. By moving up in the system, she earns the ability to live a full human life.

Monaghan presses Schulte to address her main priorities first and ignore less important tasks. She teaches her to work in 'pulses', focused periods of time followed by intentional breaks. She encourages her to break free from 'contaminated time' by 'dumping' schedules and tasks and worries onto lists. But the most important thing that Schulte learns from Monaghan is to shed her feelings of inadequacy. 'Every human being has some flavour of "not enough"', Monaghan tells her. 'You can either be stopped by it, or simply notice it, like the weather' (ibid., p. 264).

Living a better life in time, Schulte finds, is a matter of developing the right skills.

> Time is still a struggle. I still work too much. I still don't sleep enough. I haven't made much progress on a family budget . . . But I am *learning*. Time *feels* better. Rather than ambivalence, what I feel most of the time is gratitude.
>
> (ibid., p. 271)

Schulte distinguishes time as regulated by the clock, *chronos* time, from time in which we are fully present, *kairos* time, a distinction she attributes to the Greeks. Her goal is to learn to live less of her life by chronos and more by kairos (ibid., p. 271). As the book closes, Schulte describes her experience at a mindfulness meditation retreat. If stress shrinks the brain, mindfulness expands it. 'The overwhelm never goes away', a neuroscientist studying meditation tells her, 'but you can change how you think about it: pausing and noticing it without judgment, not reacting to it' (ibid., p. 275).

If perception *is* reality, then Schulte's ability to reframe 'the overwhelm' as a subjective experience over which she has control *will* actually make time feel better. Instead of 'face time' and single-minded devotion, Schulte's new faith rewards clarity of purpose and self-efficacy. It feels better to overcome your ambivalence about the demands you face, and to pin the root cause of your unhappiness on a skill you lack (but can develop!) rather than a whole raft of societal choices that shrink the space professional mothers have for love and play. The personalization and interiorization of major social structural problems allows us to continue to believe that the world is basically just, and that some kind of providential force is working to help us get ahead. But this is precisely the problem: like the dictates of my yoga class, the plot of this book, while it may be therapeutic within the confines of pressurized middle-class life, encourages us to presume that we're all in the same boat. The liturgy of many classes where yoga is sold as therapy for stress follows the same pattern: work hard, earn rest. If success comes to the devoted, or, in the revised version, the self-efficacious, it's tempting to assume that the converse is also true. Like Schulte before her conversion, those who are not successful must be trapped by their own ambivalence, feelings of inadequacy and underdeveloped skills of self-efficacy. They're wearing the ruby slippers, too, they just don't know it.

Once beyond the fog of ambivalence and self-doubt, once freed from living in 'contaminated time', once freed from chronos to live in kairos, Schulte describes herself as having awakened. Her old habits still exert a pull, but she's trying to live differently in time, to be aware of, and find joy in, the present moment. Schulte's meditation teacher echoes this idea. 'Getting out of the overwhelm, she says, means waking up. Waking up to life. Waking up to the fact that it's fleeting'. Sustaining this 'waking up' isn't easy; we need support from other women who share our struggle. 'That's why there's power in finding like-minded communities . . . Because when you forget, I'll remind you that life is going to be over quickly and that this is an amazingly beautiful day' (ibid., p. 275). Who are we, and what are our lives for? Schulte quotes a line from one of Mary Oliver's poems: 'To pay attention, this is our endless and proper work'.

Stress and survival

What if you're not a WoMoBiJo and not likely to become one? What if you're a MoWoLi(ttle)Jo? What if you're sick or disabled or if you face prejudice against your race or your sexuality as well as your gender? What if you're unemployed or single or both? Where does the power of believing in yourself stop, and the power of concrete economic and social reality begin?

The post that went viral and turned Linda Tirado into a published author was called 'Why I make terrible decisions, or, poverty thoughts' (2013). It was her response to the question 'Why do poor people do things that seem so self-destructive?' In it she describes some of the realities of her life, and many poor people's lives, explaining that in the midst of *those* circumstances, decisions that may appear to be self-destructive are actually pretty rational. She explains:

> You have to understand that we know that we will never not feel tired. We will never feel hopeful. We will never get a vacation. Ever. We know that the very act of being poor guarantees that we will never not be poor.
>
> (Tirado 2013)

The post prompted an interesting – and expletive-filled – online discussion about poverty and inequality. While many working people's comments expressed gratitude to Tirado for articulating so much about their own struggles so clearly, there was also an outpouring of outrage.

The angry comments seize on some aspect of Tirado's post as evidence that she deserves whatever hardships she faces. The 'perception *is* reality' ideas that Schulte finds so helpful are furiously turned against Tirado. Although Tirado makes clear that she's answering a question, describing a set of circumstances (hers and others') under which what look like bad decisions might sometimes make sense, *not* saying that this is how *she* looks at things all the time, readers tear into her for her failure to be hopeful. With an attitude like that, of course she is poor – but then what's the point in whining about it? Some of the most virulent comments come from people who have 'escaped' poverty themselves. They seem to have the most at stake in defending the system as a meritocracy, insisting that Tirado is just not willing to work hard enough. Tirado stands by her original point: it's reasonable to learn not to hope for much when your hopes end up in disappointment over and over again. Some realities don't alter no matter how optimistic you try to be. When the world *isn't* going to magically align with your deepest desires and make them reality, it's more rational to be realistic than to be hopeful.

A second group of commenters pounces on Tirado's admission that she smokes, which for them reveals that she is stupid, and wasteful, and gross. Tirado patiently explains that, while smoking isn't good, it's the best option she has in her circumstances. Her life expectancy is 15 years shorter anyway, just because she is poor.

> So given that the statistics tell us that, and given that nicotine is both a stimulant and a mood enhancer, and given that smoking is still cheaper than antidepressants and the other associated medicines I do not take that do essentially what smoking does, it makes sense.

Beyond these rationalizations, Tirado reveals the struggle to be human in the midst of dehumanizing circumstances, asking, 'How long do you think you would last without something of your very own, a tiny luxury that is yours?' (Tirado 2013)

Some readers challenge Tirado's right to author such a piece by questioning the authenticity of her poverty. They scrutinize her online photos and search for her employment and educational histories. Her column is 'debunked' by someone who misreads the figures from a time when her salary was *so* low that they assumed the annual figure must be a monthly one. Her middle class upbringing complicates things; what qualifies you as 'really' poor? Did Tirado have a choice that other people did not? Did she screw up, in contrast to the poor who have been victims of tragedy of one sort or another? Isn't it disrespectful to put yourself in the same category as them if you don't deserve to be? Some of them misread the essay, shouting 'gotcha' when they find an inconsistency. If her life is really as she describes it (never mind that she says that she's not describing just her own life), how could she have a blog at all? And anyway, if she's capable of writing as well as she does, why doesn't she get herself a decent job?

It's mostly not poor people who are eager to de-authorize Tirado. Many of them are grateful to Tirado for making them feel less alone. And they're glad to see someone writing about poverty who's actually poor, instead of seeing yet another commentary from someone who does not know what their lives are like. It's people, Tirado thinks, for whom the cognitive dissonance of encountering an intelligent, articulate *and* poor person is too great to tolerate.

Tirado takes issue with one last group of respondents to her post. These people are not hateful, but solicitous. They just really want to help. They offer suggestions for how she can solve the problems she describes in her post. Your teeth are bad? Have you thought of a dental school? One even offers a numbered list of solutions to each and every problem in Tirado's essay. Tirado points out that the 'have you thought of . . .' questions are every bit as patronizing as the angry dismissive obscenities.

> I think that you are trying to be helpful, and I am not trying to be negative about that. But your post assumes that I have not already thought of the things that it took you only a few minutes to come up with, and I don't like having it even subconsciously inferred that I am abjectly stupid. I am not. I am just not one of the luckier ones. There are a lot of us with perfectly good brains that simply don't have much money.
>
> (Tirado 2013)

It seems to be genuinely difficult for readers who are not poor to accept that some-one might face a difficulty for which there is no obvious practicable solution. Over and over, she patiently explains that there are circumstances in her life that have simply not occurred to her readers, that problems that might easily be solved in *their* lives are not so tractable under the conditions of hers.

As is evident in her post, Tirado has a gift for not only describing the circum-stances of poverty – the low salaries and abusive supervisors and vulnerability to bad luck and the astonishingly dysfunctional social programs – but for pointing out how continually the poor are abused. This would be bad enough, but in addition there's the constant policing of attitudes, the expectation of gratitude and good cheer. Tirado wants 'rich people' (the upper 2/3 of Americans by income) to under-stand what this life is like. She wants us to pay attention to the impact of our lifestyles and our attitudes on the poor. She sets out to explain further in *Hand to mouth: Living in bootstrap America* (2014).

The conditions of low-wage work make organizing a life in the present, let alone any kind of planning for a future, impossible. Early in *Overwhelmed*, Schulte sheepishly admits that she doesn't have a family budget, because she has not found the time to create one. Clearly, her family is managing to stay afloat without one; by the end of the book she admits that it's still on her to-do list. Tirado doesn't have a budget, either: there's never enough money to cover everything, so what use would a budget be?

We have set the minimum wage at a level that makes living an orderly life impossible, and even that is not guaranteed. Low-wage jobs demand that workers be available all the time, while simultaneously paying them for as few hours as possible. Like budgeting, 'scheduling is impossible' (Tirado 2014, p. 19). And employers are under no obligation at all to their 'at will' employees.

> So, let's break this down: You're poor, so you desperately need whatever crappy job you can find, and the nature of that crappy job is that you can

be fired at any time. Meanwhile, your hours can be cut without notice, and there's no obligation on the part of your employer to provide you with severance regardless of why, how, or when they let you go.

(ibid., pp. 20–21)

The toll of unpredictable schedules and 'on call' hours has been well documented elsewhere, making it very clear that, if treating workers even less like human beings will increase profits, companies will do exactly that. While we're used to telling each other that there are trade-offs to every work situation, Tirado observes that low-wage workers give up everything, and gain nothing. '[I]n exchange for all the work that we're doing, and all our miserable work conditions, we're not allowed to demand anything in return. No sense of accomplishment, or respect from above, or job security. We are expected not to feel entitled to these things' (ibid., p. 25). If stress is, as one of Schulte's experts says, 'no more and no less than the inability to predict and control the forces that shape our lives' (Schulte 2014, p. 62), the poor live in a state of constant, inescapable stress.

The circumstances that cause the poor to lose jobs involve things like lack of transportation, conflicts with second jobs that you have to have because the first job pays so little and won't give you enough hours, or needing but not being allowed time off to take care of an injured spouse or a sick child. These are circumstances that would make it difficult for anyone to live a stable life. Because so many better-off Americans are used to having choices, Tirado faces the constant presumption that all the hardships she faces could be solved through choice-making, if only she were better at it. 'Because our lives seem so unstable, poor people are often seen as being basically incompetent at managing their lives. That is, it's assumed that we're not unstable because we're poor, but rather that we're poor because we're unstable' (Tirado 2014, pp. 132–133).

This reversal of cause and effect happens a lot. 'Having household pests isn't a result of a sloppy, irresponsible nature. It's a result of being broke', Tirado writes, after running through a litany of pests and the reasons why poor people can't avoid them.

> Roaches are nearly impossible to kill without repeated professional extermination treatments, and those ain't free . . . Flies are inevitable when there are holes in your screens during the summer and your AC sucks or is non-existent and you have to keep the windows open . . . If you live in an older building, you'll get mice somewhere in it.
>
> (ibid., pp. 162–163)

Tirado describes these conditions matter-of-factly. What makes her angry isn't the bugs or the mice, it's the 'insulting and priggish' attitude of wealthy people towards poor people.

Like their lives, poor people's houses tend to be messy. To keep a home bug-free and tidy, to keep a lawn mowed (and to seed and water it in the first place), takes money, and also time, and also some leftover energy. Tirado writes that

> . . . there's always a time crunch. There just aren't enough minutes in the
> day for me to earn enough money and keep up on life's details and clean
> my house and maintain my yard and have a marriage and hang out with my
> kids. So my husband and I rank those things in order of importance by
> visibility: Are we the only people who see or have to live with this? Yes?
> Then who cares?
>
> (ibid., p. 162)

So you live with all the things that don't get fixed or painted or tended or even
discarded because there just isn't money, or time, or energy, or all three. It's not
laziness, or shamelessness, it's actually the result of exactly the kind of ranking of
priorities that Schulte found so liberating, except that there's nobody to delegate
to and no money to hire a maid. It's a result, not a cause. It's what the life working
multiple part-time low-wage jobs looks like.

Adam Smith wrote that each society had its own standards regarding what a
person would need in order to be able to appear in public without shame. Smith's
example for his own society is a clean white shirt. This matters because anyone
lacking in those basic possessions, whatever they might be, is effectively prevented
from participating in society. It's probably not a surprise at this point to learn that
our society does not guarantee any such basic standard for our own poor. If anything, we're strongly invested in making sure that the poor experience as much
shame as possible. One aspect of 'self-efficacy' is the ability to choose how one
presents oneself to others and the ability to have that presentation reflect one's
own sense of self. For the poor, this is impossible. They know both that they cannot
present themselves as they would like and that they will be despised for failing to
do so. And, if they do manage to obtain something stylish, something that makes
them feel a little bit proud in public, they'll be laughed at, or criticized for wasting
money, or maybe even accused of theft.

Tirado writes about many different sources of shame, but one of the biggest
for her is her teeth. 'Dentistry is one of the things we are most lacking in. And
it's one of the most glaring marks of poverty. I watch the tooth-bleaching ads and
cringe, because I know exactly what I'm being pegged as. Incapable. Uneducated.
Oblivious' (ibid., p. 34). Tirado's teeth were damaged in a car accident; she lives
with jaw pain and headaches and the shame of knowing that her mouth is ugly.
But worse, for her, is that if she goes out in public, she must confront people's
assumption that she doesn't realize this or doesn't care. So she hides them. 'I spent
years learning to speak with my mouth closed, learning how to fake eat in public
when I couldn't avoid it . . . My teeth have become one of my most hated
obsessions' (ibid., pp. 38–39). 'Contaminated time' takes on a whole new meaning
when applied to the constant mental load Tirado's teeth extract. Tirado has her
own way of describing this.

> Being poor is something like always being followed around by violins
> making 'tense' movie music. You know that commercial where the band

Survivor follows a guy around playing 'Eye of the Tiger'? Yeah, it's like that, but the musicians are invisible and they're playing the shower scene from *Psycho*.

(ibid., p. 59.)

Tirado describes the toll her untreated teeth take on her relationships – she avoids smiling, avoids eating with other people and dislikes kissing, which interferes with intimacy with her husband. The impact of shame reverberates outward, isolating her.

When she's finally able to try to see a dentist, she runs straight into the judgements she's trying to escape.

I got in the chair at the office, and promptly listened to forty-five straight minutes of the most upsetting, judgmental lecture I'd ever received in my life. This woman, the dentist, decided that I must be on meth . . . Never mind that I had none of the other signs of being a meth addict; my skin, while not exactly in great shape, lacks the *huge fucking sores* you get while on meth . . . This dentist had made her decision, though, no matter what I said. She made a point of telling me that they didn't make dentures as discoloured as I'd need and that I'd have to get used to having everyone see how dark my teeth were in comparison with these shiny white front teeth I'd have on the right side . . . I have never in my life felt more attacked, more vulnerable, trashier than I did in that dentist's chair.

(ibid., pp. 35–36)

Two years later when the denture breaks, Tirado does not get a replacement. 'There is a shred of dignity that I will not let go of', she writes. 'I will not intentionally put myself in that situation again' (ibid.). This is only one example; the shaming of the poor is ubiquitous. You can be blamed and shamed for all sorts of things that you simply can't afford to take care of, even and especially when you're finally trying to take care of them.

Tirado's attempt to preserve some shred of dignity is partial at best: like other low-wage workers, she faces the constant admonition to smile. She resents the indignity of being required to act cheerful while simultaneously being deprived of anything that might actually be a cause for cheer. 'Our bodies hurt, our brains hurt, and our souls hurt. There's rarely anything to smile about' (ibid., p. 78). And, when your teeth are a source of deep shame and embarrassment, being forced to smile is a kind of torture.

Tirado describes a society bent on making sure that the poor know that they are not worth much. How much someone earns is a measure of their social worth. The money the poor are paid is not just inadequate to their basic needs, it communicates a message to them about how we value them. 'As I've pointed out already, a lot of adults are getting just pennies over the minimum wage – and I'd argue that your average adult does his job, however lowly, a damn sight better than most teenagers. And when you think about how insignificant a raise of even 50 cents above the minimum wage turns out to be, it's hard not to feel devalued … ' (ibid., p. 8).

But this, Tirado writes over and over again, is not the worst of it. You are required to perform a role that demands that you *be* less than a person, where every word you say is scripted (ibid., p. 17).

> All of our actions are carefully dictated to us. I assume this is because employers think we have monkey brains and are incapable of making decisions. This means that they're paying me to pretend I'm not me and also that I care about you.
>
> (ibid., p. 18)

And if you try to exercise 'self-efficacy'? You get fired. You're completely fungible anyway. Someone else can wear your polyester uniform shirt. The difference between what work offers to Tirado and to Schulte is huge. Tirado captures it well in a commentary on another dehumanizing aspect of many low-wage jobs.

> Some people have the luxury of asking themselves whether a job fulfils their career hopes and ambitions. I've got my own metric to gauge the fabulosity of a job: Does that job require me to keep my boss informed of the inner workings of my gastrointestinal system, or am I allowed to go to the bathroom at will? It's physically uncomfortable to hold it forever, and it sucks to stand by for the okay like a dog waiting for someone to open the door (ibid., p.18).

Like Schulte's discussion of work, her exploration of leisure and its importance takes on a whole new dimension when we see what it looks like in Tirado's life.

Although the poor do their best to help each other out in the constant barrage of crises ('We do shit like that a lot … We'd never survive otherwise' [ibid., p. 25]), there's little time or energy to forge social bonds. Networks and social groups (like the WoMoBiJo's) that help women in more stable situations find support and encouragement are not something poor women can easily establish or sustain.

> Being poor is isolating. You're constantly being rude to friends and family because you never have time to talk, never have time to hang out. Never have the money to do anything, not even to reciprocate a birthday present. You don't ever have anything new happening – no news to share unless you're getting married or having a baby.
>
> (ibid., p. 96)

Tirado writes about how difficult it is to feel like a person, because she is simply too tired to do any of the things that she enjoys, that make her feel like herself. She loves to read, but minimum-wage work leaves her too tired (ibid., p. 54). 'You lose the most interesting parts of yourself to the demands of survival', she writes (ibid., pp. 95–96). This is Hunnicutt's 'banal busyness', not as chosen, but as imposed. It's clear now what he meant when he wrote that 'it starves our capacity to love'.

'Rich people' feel they have to criticize almost every aspect of how poor people live their lives. Unless a poor person never makes any bad choices at all, she is not entitled to any sympathy. But, Tirado writes, rich people smoke, drink, have sex, have children and even make stupid life choices once in a while. Why do the poor get judged so harshly for doing so many of the same things that rich people do?

> Because if you're poor, rich people assume you're on welfare, or you're getting food stamps or some other social services. Once you take a penny from the government, the morality clause goes into effect, where you're never allowed to have anything that you might actually enjoy. It's the hair shirt of welfare.
>
> (ibid., p. 84)

Once activated, the 'morality clause' governs even the most intimate aspects of a poor person's life, from how they spend each penny (and each food stamp penny).

> Responsible poverty is an endless cycle of no. No, you can't have that. You can't do that, can't afford that, can't eat that, can't choose that. This is off-limits, and that is not for you, and this over here is meant for different kinds of people . . . To be told that you deserve nothing more than that, are entitled to nothing more, is enraging.
>
> (ibid., p. 77)

The morality clause proscribes both sex and children. Chapter 7 is titled, 'We do not have babies for welfare money'. Tirado explains that she loves her kids, and had them for basically the same reasons that rich people have theirs. But the attitude of doubt surrounding poor people's right to procreate means that their children can be, and are, taken away (ibid., p. 125). Poor people face hugely disparate consequences for doing the same things that rich people do.

> [T]he very same situations and behaviours are treated completely differently depending on how nice your stuff is. Kid gets into a fight at school? If he's black and poor, he's going to jail. If he's rich and white, he's going to military school.
>
> (ibid., p. 126)

Tirado explains that sex, too, is a human thing. And – thanks to a society bent on devaluing every other aspect of poor people's lives – it's one of few places left where they can find some affirmation. 'You have no idea how strong the pull to feel worthwhile is,' Tirado writes. 'It's more basic than food' (ibid., xviii).

While Schulte closes her book with the observation that 'what I feel most of the time is gratitude', Tirado explains how maddening it is to be told that gratitude is the only emotion she's supposed to publicly admit to having. '[W]e're told to keep smiling, and to be grateful for the chance to barely survive while being blamed for not succeeding. Whether or not that's actually true isn't even relevant; that's what if feels like. Unwinnable. Sisyphean' (Tirado 2014, p. 77). Tirado speculates that some of the angry reaction to her original post may have been because she failed (spectacularly) to speak in the publicly prescribed manner. As Tirado asks in response to 'opalcat's' particularly furious comment to 'Why I make bad choices', 'I would like to understand what you are really angry about. Is it that I am poor and insufficiently servile about it? Is it that you legitimately think that you are somehow morally superior? . . . Is it that you are uncomfortable with the idea that even if I have no money I am allowed to sometimes complain about life?' Once again, Tirado points out how little space this leaves for her to be a person, asking, '. . . what amount of money do you think gives me the right to be human?' (Tirado 2013)

Like Schulte, Tirado offers some solutions to the problems that she so tellingly depicts. She'd like to see employers pay fair wages and treat workers decently and go to jail when they break the law. She wants us to fix incompetent government bureaucracy, decide that everyone deserves to have enough food and decent housing, and treat people with respect. People are hungry, so 'Fucking feed people' (Tirado 2014, p. 114). It's not that complicated. What's shocking is how far we are from doing any better.

> We're so far behind the curve on these issues that we're having a public fight about whether or not the poor are too comfortable. (Hi, Paul Ryan!) It's not fucking pleasant to be poor. It's not a free ride, a gentle swing in the hammock. It's what's left when you've lost everything, when you're fighting to survive as opposed to fighting to get ahead.
>
> (ibid., p. 190)

What Tirado recommends amounts to political change, but she admits that she doesn't have much use for politics. Between obstacles to voting if you're poor and gerrymandering that means your vote won't make any difference, that game is pretty much rigged anyway (ibid., pp. 154–155). She closes the book with 'An open letter to rich people', in which she explains all the ways that the rich are making poor life choices.

Like Schulte, she calls for a kind of awakening. She calls for a change in the attitudes, not of the poor, but of the wealthy. She wants 'rich people' (that's probably us, readers!) to recognize that we've basically been behaving like assholes. Tirado calls upon 'rich people' to stop expecting the poor to participate in their own dehumanization, to stop asking them to be *grateful* for jobs in which they're treated like brainless and entirely fungible and disposable commodities. If there are unpleasant jobs that need doing, the least we can do is appreciate the people who do them.

Tirado's book is funny and shocking and interesting to read. But Tirado's appeal to rich people to *act* better hides the fact that she's also asking them to acknowledge certain realities. Real-world conditions matter, not just attitudes, and Tirado thinks rich people are maybe not all that good at logic or else irrationally attached to their favorite self-deceptions. She asks them to acknowledge that government support for the poor is not fundamentally different from government support for everyone else. 'I know it's a pipe dream, but maybe you guys can just admit that we all get shit (see entitlements, roads, tax credits, crop subsidies and fire departments) from the government and move on with your lives . . .' (Tirado 2014, p. 174). She asks them to 'stop asking us to pretend with you' that wages reflect the value of someone's work. 'For the love of God, please stop telling us that outrageous salaries are justified because some people are worth that much' (ibid., pp. 172–173). Stop despising the poor and the work they do. Accept some civic responsibility, which, Tirado says, is

> about whether or not you'd want to live in the nation you've created: if you were born tomorrow into the lower classes, would you be quite so sure that America is the land of opportunity? (See what I did there? That's *philosophy*. I am trying to speak in your language here, rich people.)
>
> (ibid., pp. 173–174)

And, Tirado asks, stop equating your experience with ours (ibid., p. 176).

Conclusion

If our lives are basically similar, and competence leads to success, then failure must be due to incompetence. The myth of the meritocracy dictates that the poor are poor because they are ignorant, immoral and/or trashy. The conviction that the poor are inferior and its converse, that if one is poor one must also be stupid and oblivious, is difficult to shake. The arrogance, the patronizing, the insults to basic competence have become habitual. What authorizes us, in the United States, to not only neglect the poor, but to despise them? When the myth of opportunity for all is so evidently false, why does it still stand as a foundation for dismissing the poor as lazy, stupid and as actively choosing to be poor when they could be otherwise? Why have we made poverty a status deserving of so much shaming?

The stress that Tirado describes is the constant worry that one might not be able to scrape together basic necessities – food, housing, heat – and the constant awareness of the real possibility of losing these, once found. It's the necessity of taking a job that is far below one's abilities, even though the pay is terrible and the hours are random. It's having burn scars on your arms from fryer grease (ibid., p.15). It's never having enough money and never, ever getting enough sleep. It's being continually blamed and shamed for what you don't have, being denied the possibility of a fully human life. It's knowing that the economy needs you but still treats you like you're worthless, less than a person. For Tirado, the stresses of being poor are magnified because they are despised by 'rich people'. Tirado writes, 'I am certain that you have stress, rich people. Nobody's life is perfect. I am equally certain that your stress and my stress are only similar in that they are called the same thing' (ibid., p. 180).

It matters whether we use words like 'stress' to cover over the differences between our lives. It matters whether 'stress' is a condition that we all share in similarly, or instead something that differs between contexts so much as to be almost unrecognizable. It matters whether we assume that our experience is similar to everyone else's, or we instead pause and try to describe what's happening more carefully, with greater justice. Schulte is not alone in her assumption that her life is typical of a category called 'working women'. Newspapers like the *Washington Post*, which she writes for, and the *New York Times*, which ran favorable reviews of her book, make this presumption daily in their journalism. There are columns about the poor, but the implied audience, the 'we' of this journalism, takes for granted the same sorts of things as Schulte herself. In her endorsement on the cover of *Overwhelmed*, Anne-Marie Slaughter writes that 'Every parent, every caregiver, every person who feels besieged by permanent busyness, must read this book' (Schulte 2014).

Schulte's authority to speak for (all) working women is not challenged, it's celebrated. While Tirado is attacked for writing about poverty, she's careful to make clear that her experience is *not* necessarily the same as anyone else's.

> Instead of attempting to point out how people who are different from me are in many ways far more disadvantaged that I have ever been in every instance I can think of (because that should be clear unless you have the peripheral vision of a racehorse), I will just say this: Here is how I have felt, *as me*: a relatively young person who is perceived as white, who is naturally sociable, who is intelligent and well-spoken, who was taught well and as a result love learning things, who is able to lift objects up to fifty pounds repeatedly. And many times, with all of this going for me, I still saw no hope. I cannot begin to imagine how much harder it is for someone who faces more discrimination than I have or who grew up without these basic tools that I am lucky enough to have. Keep that in mind too.
>
> (Tirado 2014, pp. xxiii–xxiv)

Schulte's assumption of representativeness hides life stresses other than 'the overwhelm', that might require solutions other than 'self-efficacy' or 'waking up'. But it also hides tremendous advantages that Schulte takes for granted. Schulte's book includes two women she identifies as 'African-American' (one of whom grew up in Ghana and came to the United States for medical school). Schulte describes their experiences as successful professional working women, but does not ask how their race might make any aspect of 'the overwhelm' more intense. Tirado's book includes African Americans, people who don't speak English, immigrants, people with disabilities, people who've been in prison – because her life includes all of these people. Not only Tirado's preoccupation with her teeth, but also the energy and attention that an African American woman must devote to negotiating prejudice, give a whole new meaning to 'contaminated time'. And doesn't 'task density', as an abstract descriptive term, presume that whatever the stakes might be of dropping one of those balls you're juggling, it's not going to cost you your house, or your children, or even your life? Can it even be applied to lives where these things are very real possibilities?

Linda Tirado is right to ask, 'What amount of money do you think gives me the right to be human?' As a response to a society which allows such a bar to exist – a threshold below which we treat people as less than human, and above which we recognize humanity and agency ('choice'), but turn social conditions into individual pathologies – Tirado's anger may be a more helpful response than Schulte's hopeful practicality. But each, in her own way, demands too little. Neither Tirado nor Schulte calls into question the right of our employment to confer human worth. And neither explores the possibility that some alternative source of value, perhaps more equitable, and less in need of being earned, might be a good thing. As Jon Gunnemann would ask, '*Whose* are we?'

We have structured our society so that thriving social bonds and time in life for rest and play and beauty are a luxury reserved for the elite few. Poverty is not just a lack of resources but the condition of having your ability to connect with other people ravaged, your body used up at work like any other 'natural resource', and your surroundings constantly remind you that you are not good enough for anything that is not old or broken or dirty. The professional class may be better off, but working 60 hours a week and raising children doesn't leave much time for anything else, even if one learns to live differently in time. While Tirado's situation is undoubtedly worse, Schulte's is still unduly hard. And as jobs within the professions become less secure, and the jobs themselves less autonomous, the stress of overload is likely to be joined by the stress of fear for all but the richest 'rich people'.

It's worth asking why both women turn systemic problems into personal or interpersonal ones, why both women appeal to morality but neither appeals to justice. It's a particularly interesting question in light of Schulte's recurring references to religion. While she seems to value the rhetorical power of these references more than their analytical potential/intellectual possibilities (I think she'd consider participation in organized religion a kind of hobby), she describes her own conversion from one salvific belief system, work as religion, to another one that we might call 'salvific self-management'.

Even more fascinating, while Tirado's only reference to religion also treats it as 'the same sort of thing as smoking – a soothing ritual that brings someone a moment of peace' (Tirado 2014, p. 83), her book describes a social world in which the Protestant work ethic has run amok, justifying the conversion of people into less-than-human 'resources'. This faith has a particularly perverse understanding of Providence. God/the market is believed to distribute financial rewards in perfect correspondence with desert; conversely, those who are not rewarded can be fairly assumed not to deserve. For Schulte's faith to work, it requires something similar – a magical sense that the world responds to our own confidence and clarity of purpose and rewards us with success. Contemplative practices are translated into therapeutic ones; meditation and yoga help us to be mindful, but mainly of ourselves. When she learns not to react to 'the overwhelm', she is reducing her own discomfort, but also guaranteeing that she will not try to address the systems that affect other people's lives even more destructively than her own.

'To pay attention, this is our endless and proper work', writes Mary Oliver, in the concluding line of a poem titled 'Yes! No!' It seems like a perfect slogan for meditation, and it's quoted often. But what Oliver proposes is not a supplemental activity. It is a way of life, one which, to follow, would require that we leave behind 'the overwhelm' for good. The work of paying attention is endless, and 'proper' in the sense that we belong to it: this is work that makes us more fully human as we do it. In the poem, the narrator is not contemplating herself, but is wandering in nature, imaginatively engaging each living thing that she encounters. For Oliver, long patient attending to the natural world is how we learn faith. This is not a faith that says that the world will respond to our desires or reward only those of us who are deserving. It's one that tells us *being* human – imagining, loving – is all that really matters.

Divorced from their religious context, commodified contemplative practices may really help us cope with difficult social circumstances – at least, those of us with the time and the money to access them. But, in the process of translation, they lose their ties to justice. In their religious context, attention is linked not just to compassion for one's self, but to justice for others. The distorted religions described by both Schulte and Tirado press for responses from people who follow a different faith. God is not aligned with capitalism and we are, each of us, beloved no matter how poorly – or how well – organized our lives are, no matter how little, or how much, money we have. The possibility of a fully human life is not something that we should have to earn, nor is it something that anyone should be allowed to take from us.

I have lived both Schulte's 'overwhelm' as a professional mother and Tirado's years of trying to hide the shame of crooked teeth by not smiling. A more humane society would find ways to protect both of their rights to live fully human lives, lives in which the work that one needs to survive isn't destructive of the family and community bonds, spiritual life, and time to experience beauty that one needs to be fully human.

References

Schulte, B. (2014) *Overwhelmed: Work, love, and play when no one has the time*, New York: Farrar, Strauss and Giroux.

Tirado, L. (2013) *Why I make terrible decisions, or, poverty thoughts*. Available from: http://killer martinis.kinja.com/why-i-make-terrible-decisions-or-poverty-thoughts-1450123558/all [accessed 27 December 2014].

Tirado, L. (2014) *Hand to mouth: Living in bootstrap America*, New York: G. P. Putnam's Sons.

7

RIOTS AND RIP-OFFS IN BALTIMORE

Towards a theology of hopelessness

Miguel A. De La Torre

Riots erupted following the funeral services for Freddie Gray, the 25-year-old Baltimore man who died in police custody on 19 April 2015. Cars were set on fire, stores were looted, buildings were vandalized and six police officers were seriously injured. The loudest voices were pleas for peace and condemnations of the riots. These views were offered especially by powerful people who saw the riots as disproportionate responses to the death of a single black man. Even President Barack Obama, who was not unaware of the historical injustices that fuelled the protests, slipped into this language. During a press conference, Obama condemned the violence on the streets of Baltimore:

> There's no excuse for the kind of violence that we saw yesterday. It is counterproductive. When individuals get crowbars and start prying open doors to loot, they're not protesting. They're not making a statement. They're stealing. When they burn down a building, they're committing arson. And they're destroying and undermining businesses and opportunities in their own communities. That robs jobs and opportunity from people in that area.
>
> (Bradner 2015)

The President went on to refer to the protestors as 'criminals and thugs who tore up' the city.

Reflecting on these events and wrestling with the anger I felt at these myopic responses, I found the words of civil rights activist César Chávez to be deeply resonant: 'I am not a nonviolent man. I am a violent man who is trying to be nonviolent' (Dalton 2003, p. 143). To be sure, the language and practice of nonviolence has been effective in a diverse array of past movements for justice, from Gandhi's struggle for Indian independence from British rule, to Martin Luther King, Jr.'s fight for civil rights in the American South, to Chavez's efforts to organizing farmworkers in California. But I worry that the language of non-violence is now failing us. I am concerned that calls for non-violence have become a tool for oppressors, for those who are incensed at protestors on our television screens but ignore powerful actors who move subtly and methodically enough to build their own violent acts into systemic practices and institutions. It's easy to talk about 'thugs' in response to endlessly looped cable news clips on a specific day, but we too often fail to apply such language to those acting like 'thugs' while carrying badges or those carrying out exploitative activities while wearing pinstriped banker's suits.

Baltimore's shattered windows are not just the immediate results of a few opportunists with crowbars, they are the long-term outcome of decades of unjust economic policies and practices. Institutional violence in Baltimore built ghettos where black neighbourhoods' tax monies are extracted for the benefit of play-grounds like Baltimore's Inner Harbour, which exists chiefly for the benefit of tourists and wealthy locals. And the shattered spinal cord of a poor black man who was arrested with no probable cause was not a standalone event but the spark that ignited this dry powder keg.

In entrenched settings of injustice like these, if we are to call for non-violence, we must address not only black rioters in the streets but also white-collar executives who exploit the poor. We must distinguish between the ongoing institutional violence of the oppressors – who often have a monopoly on the legal use of force – and the episodic violence of the oppressed, who usually are left with little recourse but to engage in illegal acts in the hopeless hope of being heard. Violence cannot be condemned only in the streets; it must also be condemned in boardrooms and legislative backrooms. And we must be honest about this: the actions of protestors pale in comparison to the history of economic exploitation experienced by Baltimore's black communities. And if we have to choose, shattered spinal cords and lives should be of greater concern than smashed windows.

The looting of Baltimore by Wells Fargo

The looting of the city by banks like Wells Fargo is more grievous than any looting done by protestors during the Baltimore disturbance over Freddie Gray. The predatory lending practices of Wells Fargo, focused primarily on African Americans and Latinxs, devastated inner cities like Baltimore as these financial institutions pursued short-term profits. In 2008, Eric Halperin, director of the Center for Responsible Lending, declared flatly, 'We've known that African Americans and Latinos are getting subprime loans while whites of the same credit profile are getting the lower-costs loans' (Morgenson 2008). Middle-class African American home-owners who qualified for safe traditional mortgages were routinely steered towards ruinous subprime mortgages. One Wells Fargo loan officer referred to the subprime mortgage applicants as 'mud people' and to the mortgages as 'ghetto loans' (ibid.). In 2006, Wells Fargo subprime mortgages charged an interest rate of at least three percentage points above the federal benchmark, charged higher financing costs and imposed prepayment penalties to prevent subprime customers from refinancing at a lower interest rate. When the housing bubble finally burst, most of those who took these subprime loans were left destitute. They were disproportionately people of colour (ibid.).

Beth Jacobson, the bank's top-producing subprime loan officer whose annual salary hit $700,000, admitted that Wells Fargo singled out African American customers in Baltimore and suburban Maryland – even seeking black clergy and churches as marketing avenues – for high-interest subprime mortgages (Powell 2009). A *New York Times* analysis revealed that among Wells Fargo borrowers with household incomes of more than $68,000, 2 per cent of whites held subprime loans compared to 16.1 per cent of African Americans (Morgenson 2008). In a different study that focused on 3,027 Wells Fargo loans issued in Baltimore between 2000 and 2008, African American borrowers living in predominately African American neighborhoods were charged higher rates and fared worse than whites at every point of the borrowing process. Over the life of a 30-year mortgage, African Americans in Baltimore paid $14,904 more ($15,948 for those living in African American neighborhoods) than their white counterparts (Editorial Board 2015).

Wells Fargo's race-based lending policies caused hundreds of African American homeowners to face foreclosure. It also caused broader damage to the neighborhoods where the foreclosures were concentrated. According to the City of Baltimore, more than half the properties foreclosed by Wells Fargo from 2005 to 2008 stood vacant a year after the Great Recession, and 71 per cent of these homes were located in predominantly black neighbourhoods. These foreclosures resulted in reduced tax revenues and increased costs for city services that amounted to tens of millions of dollars (Morgenson 2008). Abandoned houses not only hurt remaining homeowners by driving down housing values, but they also cost cities more as they attempted to ward off crimes like arson, prostitution and drug use. The chief solicitor for the Baltimore City Law Department, Suzanne Sangree, best explained the damage banks like Well Fargo inflicted upon neighborhoods of colour: 'This wave of foreclosures in minority neighborhoods really threatens to undermine the tremendous progress the city has made in developing distressed neighbourhoods and moving the city ahead economically' (ibid.).

The 2008 Great Recession, rooted in the mortgage crises, took a far greater toll on the wealth of African Americans and Latinxs than it did on whites. From 2005 to 2009, Latinxs experienced an inflation-adjusted median wealth decrease of 66 per cent and African Americans experienced a 53 per cent decrease, compared to just a 16 per cent decrease for whites. To make matters worse, about a third of African Americans (35 per cent) and Latinxs (31 per cent) had zero or a negative net worth, compared to 15 per cent of white households (Taylor *et al.* 2011, pp. 1–2). Before protestors took to the streets to loot, Wells Fargo had been exploiting these communities for about a decade (De La Torre 2014, pp. 167–168). When Freddie Gray was but a young teenager, Wells Fargo was contributing to the hopeless economic conditions in which he grew up.

McDonald's and the lack of living wage jobs

As manufacturing jobs plummeted and struggling neighbourhoods were hollowed out by the foreclosure debacle, Baltimore's predominately African American poor population faced another crisis: a lack of jobs paying anything near a living wage. In many crumbling neighborhoods, the only remaining local employment opportunities were minimum wage jobs at fast-food outlets such as McDonald's.

While some fast food giants have responded to pressure to improve wages, these efforts often amount more to gestures than to substantive reforms. Ten days before Freddie Gray was arrested, for example, McDonald's placed a full-page advertisement in *The New York Times* announcing that it would begin paying employees working in company-owned US restaurants 1 dollar per hour above local minimum wage requirements. Ninety thousand employees in 1,500 outlets were affected, and their pay was expected to rise by 2016 to about $10 per hour on average. Despite the hype, however, this action turned out to be largely symbolic, because nearly nine in ten of McDonald's employees (750,000 workers) are employed at locally-owned franchises, which were exempt from this mandate (Editorial Board 2015).

Even among those beneficiaries of the wage increase, $10 per hour equates to $20,800 per year. At this income level, a single parent with one child would be living just above the official 2015 poverty level of $15,930 (US Department of Health and Human Services 2015). But this doesn't mean a single parent working full-time at one of the McDonald's restaurants affected by the wage increase wouldn't be poor, because the official definition of poverty masks the true extent of poverty in the United States. This definition, which was outlined in the early 1960s, fails to consider the radical changes in cost of living since that time. Originally, the formula was based mainly on food consumption, which since then has proportionately become less expensive in relation to housing, health care, childcare and transportation (Blank 2008). These shifts have converted the original formula into near nonsensical numbers.

According to the 'Family Budget Calculator' provided by the Economic Policy Institute (2015), the budget for a single parent with one child to meet her family's basic needs is closer to $50,000 per year, more than twice the pay level McDonald's was proud to tout as evidence of wage reform. Through the waning years of the Obama administration, employees and labour groups placed pressure, through picketing and protests, on the fast-food behemoth for a base salary of $15 per hour. Even at this wage, a single parent working full time would only make $31,200, well below the level recommended by the Economic Policy Institute (2015). By contrast, McDonald's paid its incoming chief executive officer, Steve Easterbrook, $1.1 million in 2014 (McDonald's Corporation 2015).

Discontent with McDonald's wage policies was evidenced by living-wage protest rallies throughout the country just days after the Baltimore unrest following Freddie Gray's funeral in 2015 (Kearney 2015). While the media covered these two sets of protests as unrelated events, the Baltimore riots and the McDonald's protests are not unrelated. In cities like Baltimore, the failure of corporations like McDonald's to pay anything close to a living wage kept even many working families trapped in persistent poverty, fully aware that profits were being extracted from their communities to swell distant corporate coffers and executive pay packages. The fact that this extreme level of worker exploitation and inequality exists out in the open is a sign of just how frail our country's moral imagination and convictions have become. Franz Hinkelammert, the Latin American theologian, may have said it best: 'The existence of the poor attests to the existence of a Godless society, whether one explicitly believes in God or not' (Hinkelammert 1997, p. 27).

Do 'All Lives Matter'?

A black mother in Baltimore cries for the child who is no more. She cries for her child crucified in the name of profit and power. And it does not matter if her child died while in police custody or after a few decades of normalized institutional economic violence. Her tears are shed because she realizes that all lives are created for liberation – and yet black lives matter less in Baltimore than other lives.

The devaluing of lives with darker hues starts early for the children living in the poor Baltimore neighbourhoods where the disturbances took place. In our education system, an average of $1,200 less is spent per student in mostly racial minority school districts compared to mostly white school districts, a testimony to the decreased value of their lives. In neighbourhoods serving mostly students of colour, like Baltimore, the differences are even higher, closer to $2,000 per student (Ushomirsky and Williams 2015, p. 1). These results create a pernicious cycle of poorly educated students who become an under-skilled and ultimately underemployed work force.

And while cases like Freddie Gray's garner national media attention, and the deaths of police officers regularly make the news, too many bodies of colour that have been killed by police go unnoticed. We know how many police officers were killed in 2014: 126 (National Law Enforcement Officer's Memorial Fund 2017). We do not know how many black bodies died in the hands of the police, or how many brown bodies, or even how many civilians regardless of colour (Johnson 2014). But we know enough to know that the odds of being killed by the police are dramatically higher for non-whites than for whites (Buehler 2017).

Some lives are dismissed as thugs, playing on racial stereotypes, while other lives can depend on the structures of society to protect them, even in the wake of unquestionably thuggish behaviour caught on video. Some lives get funeral possessions and parades, while others are ignored and only acknowledged if communities take to the streets or if cell phone videos goes viral.

Even amid documented inequalities and injustices, many whites want to counter this black cry for justice by asserting that 'all lives matter'. This attempt reflects at best blindness and at worst a blatant reassertion of power, for the current social structures strongly testify to the value of white lives. If white Americans truly believed that all lives mattered and had eyes to see, they would have been on the frontlines dismantling the systems of power that disproportionately threatened black lives, long before Freddie Gray's life was ever taken.

But if whites are already protected by the current social status quo, what about other non-white lives? There is a dearth of attention to the oppression of Latinx lives as part of the Black Lives Matter movement. How then do Latinxs stand in solidarity with Black Lives Matter activists without ignoring the fact that brown lives are also devalued in ways that largely remain invisible? One is hard-pressed to find media coverage of the twenty-eight killings of undocumented immigrants by border patrol agents between 2010 and 2014 (Becker 2014). Unlike local and state police in Baltimore and elsewhere throughout the United States, where internal affairs agents can investigate potential crimes, the border patrol has no such internal function. The humanitarian organization No More Deaths has documented over 32,075 incidents of abuse during short-term border patrol detention (2011). Even those who elude mistreatment or capture face a serious risk of death because of harsh border policies and the hazards of crossing the desert. Every four days, five brown lives are lost attempting to enter the country (Santos and Zemansky 2013).

Undocumented lives matter, brown lives matter; but how do we make this case without taking away from the importance of black lives? Finding an answer to this question is vital. As long as communities of colour and other oppressed groups fail to build the necessary bridges among themselves, the social structures protecting white privilege will remain intact. Communities of colour are partially at fault for accepting a zero-sum mentality that assumes any advances made by blacks are at the expense of other marginalized communities. Like a four-leaf clover, our separate racially or ethnically distinct cul-de-sacs operate side by side with few of us ever venturing into the adjoining community. Solidarity may occur from time to time, but it usually happens with little long-lasting effects. More disturbing is when communities of colour are oblivious to how they are locked into structures that cause oppression to other communities of colour. How can we, with any integrity, criticize white Americans for not engaging in the liberation of our own community when we too seldom accompany our neighbours in the adjacent cul-de-sac?

Neither black lives nor brown lives will succeed in the crucial work of dismantling these racist and ethnic discriminatory institutionalized structures until brown folk march in places like Baltimore and black folk stand in solidarity at the border. Fighting with each other for the crumbs that fall from the master's table only reinforces our subservience and focuses our energies against those who should be our allies rather than our competitors. We must refuse to enter meaningless debates as to who has suffered more in this country. For if just one black or brown life is lost due to institutionalized violence, then that is one life too many. All lives reflect the image of the Creator of the universe and thus are sacred with infinite worth. 'Black Lives Matter' must continue. 'Brown Lives Matter' must develop. And 'All Lives Matter' should only be asserted as a statement that privileges, rather than discounts, these affirmations.

Rethinking the crucifixion

In the introduction, I mentioned my concern that a theology of non-violence has too often become complicit in perpetuating injustice by calling for non-violence on the part of the oppressed while ignoring the violence of the privileged. These appeals are generally grounded in a Christianity centered on a theology of the cross, which too often has functioned as a tool for privileged voices to call upon the oppressed to suffer passively, glorifying suffering itself as an end. In short, theologies of the cross can quickly devolve into efficient ideologies for reinforcing control over bodies of colour. For such reasons, this traditional understanding of crucifixion, along with the accompanying understanding of salvation it generates, should be rejected. Rather, the concept of crucifixion should be rehabilitated as a command to stand in solidarity with the least among us – all those who today continue to be nailed to the crosses of racism, classism, sexism and heterosexism.

What does it mean to invoke theological language to say that in America today, black and brown people are being crucified by systems of oppression and police violence? Or, to go further, to say that black and brown people are seemingly abandoned not only by Christians in positions of power who remain apathetic but also perhaps by God? Even those pursuing a more liberative interpretation of Scriptures have boldly declared God to be the God of the oppressed who incarnates Godself among the least of these. But human experience demands that we ask a more difficult question – whether God is in reality the God of the oppressors – without the imposition of an all-good God upon the text.

The Bible contains multiple passages that present us with a very disturbing picture of God's character, one that Christians too often systematically and purposely avoid. Reading these texts leads us to the troubling conclusion that God is the cause and author of all that is good – and all that is evil. The book of Isaiah describes God's darker side, when the Almighty proclaims: 'I am YHWH, and there is none to rival me. I form light and create darkness, make peace and create evil, I YHWH do all these things' (45:6–7). The prophet Amos reminds us, 'If there is evil in a city, has YHWH not done it?' (3:6). While Christian theologians typically find the idea of a God who is responsible for evil to be heterodox, the biblical record nonetheless describes God sending evil spirits to torment Saul (1 Sm. 18:10) and Jeroboam (1 Ki. 14:10). It is God who tempts Abraham to sacrifice his son Isaac (Gn. 22:1). This God of love and forgiveness calls for genocide (Judges 6:21); delights in smashing the heads of infants against rocks (Ps. 137:9); and wipes out innocent children who just happened to be the first-born without regard to their nursing mothers (Ex. 11:4–5). And this malevolent side of God cannot be explained away – as many Christian theologians do – with a supposed 'Old Testament' vs. 'New Testament', 'law' versus 'love' dichotomy. The New Testament depicts this Jesus of love as one day returning, leading an army, and with a sharp sword striking down the ungodly in such numbers that the birds of the air will gorge upon their rotting flesh (Rev. 19:11–21; De La Torre 2017, p. 79).

How can any reader of the biblical text ignore the violence attributed both to God and the Messiah, especially a violence directed against those who are not chosen in covenant or salvation for what often seem like capricious reasons? How can this bloodthirsty God be the God of the oppressed? Are the inquisitors, conquistadores, colonizers, slaveholders – and today's Christian apologists for unfettered capitalism and unjust social structures – being more faithful to God's biblical ways than the oppressed who attempt to humbly wait for a deliverance which probably never will arrive in their lifetime?

These concerns about suffering and ultimately about the questions it raises about the character of God have caused theologians no shortage of difficulty. In response, many Euro-Americans who follow Jesus rush past the crucifixion to the resurrection in order to explain the cross as a sign of hope, as a salvific symbol. These Christians do not dwell on the tragedy, the hopelessness, the failure or the powerlessness of the event. For them, there is redemption in Jesus' sufferings: atonement. But with this conception, the meaning of the cross shifts from tragedy to necessity. And salvation loses its footing in this world and slips into the next. We should resist this deeply-rooted part of Christian tradition and clearly declare that there is nothing redemptive about suffering. The bloody Christ, along with all bodies broken on the wheel of hatred and oppression, ought to repel, or even repulse.

This 'theology of atonement' was not always the norm. Anselm of Canterbury (1033?–1109) created the 'satisfaction theory' of atonement, reasoning that Jesus' death on the cross was necessary to satisfy God's anger about human sinfulness; specifically, Jesus served as a substitute for an undeserving humanity (Anselm, *Cur Deus Homo*, 2.6). Only a sinless God-as-human-being could gratify God's thirst for vengeance, make restitution and restore creation. In other words, in order to satisfy God's vanity, God's only begotten son had to be humiliated, tortured and brutally killed in place of the true object of God's wrath – us humans. God was placated by filicide. The problem with Anselm's 'satisfaction theory' is that it casts God as the ultimate oppressor who finds satisfaction through the domination, humiliation and pain of God's own child.

Maybe the opening theological question should not be 'Why did Jesus have to die?' – a position that already assumes a positive role for suffering – but rather: 'What do we do with the fact that the political and religious authorities arrested, tortured and killed him unjustly without God's intervention on his behalf?' If the tortured Jesus on a cross before complicit religious authorities, self-interested political forces and a silent God is the real human experience, then the theological work for today's crucified is to resignify the Jesus of the dominant Christian culture. Could Primo Levi, a Holocaust survivor, be right when he wonders whether Auschwitz has more reality than God? If crucifixion, rather than the goodness of humans or even God, is the historical norm, a substitutionary theory of atonement only aids and abets the violence that has brought so much human life to a brutal and torturous end (De La Torre 2017, p. 74).

For marginalized communities in Baltimore, the importance of the cross is not its redemptive power, for all aspects of Jesus' life are redemptive. The importance of Jesus' crucifixion is that this is the historical moment when Jesus chose solidarity with the world's marginalized, even unto death. Jesus chose solidarity with Freddie Gray. He invites his disciples to put their hands in his wounds to allow the reality of violence to sink in (Jn. 20:27). To touch the wounds of Jesus is to touch the wounds of Freddie Gray. Jesus becomes one with the crucified people of his time, as well as with all who are crucified today on the crosses of sexism, racism, ethnic discrimination, classism and heterosexism that secure the power and privilege of the few. Freddie Gray, along with all being 'crucified' today, suffered and died so the privileged can have life, and have life abundantly. For us to pick up our cross, deny ourselves – that is to deny our status and station – means that we, too, must find solidarity with Freddie Gray and all others of the world's crucified people. Jesus' solidarity with the world's so-called 'losers' and 'failures' leads us to become one with the God of the oppressed (De La Torre 2015, pp. 147–154).

Towards a theology of hopelessness

The logic of hope, as it is usually understood, is a project rooted in a Eurocentric characteristic of hyper-individualism; it is fundamentally egocentric. The bones of my compatriots may indeed be crushed into dust; but if only *I* survive, then *I* can bear witness to the power of hope in *my* life, the promises kept by *my* God. I can ignore the body count of those who did not endure. And in a twisted bit of logic, I credit my survival to my unwavering belief in hope, thus insinuating that those crushed might have also survived if they too had had sufficient faith, if only they would have named it and claimed it.

But hopelessness may paradoxically be a more appropriate theology for the oppressed. Properly understood, the act of deliberately choosing to embrace hopelessness is a decision to acknowledge the realities of oppressive social structure's triumph, not a destructive subjective disposition of the soul. While inevitable defeat and desperation are recognized, embracing these facts allows for a praxis of determination, opening a space for realistic action without metaphysical illusions.

A theology of hopelessness does not engender despair but perseverance. Hopelessness is a recognition that night is coming. Darkness may defeat us, may even consume us; nonetheless, the hopeless refuse to go silently into the night. In the desperation of the oncoming abyss, one may desire hope for its avoidance of reality. But a theology of hopelessness recognizes that it is a clear-eyed commitment to liberative principles – not a naïve hoping against hope – that defines our very humanity. We can speculate whether – on the rim of the void – God makes God's presence felt. But even if God remains deaf-and-dumb, even if we share in Jesus' forsakenness upon the cross, our angst makes our presence felt by God.

Sitting in the reality of desperation, one discovers that any semblance of hope can become a mechanism for creating obstacles, a power responsible for maintaining rather than challenging prevailing oppressive social structures. Rushing to hope deprives the disenfranchised of the chance to lament what is lost and what cannot be. Grief and lament are necessary, and should not be numbed with an opiate of hope. Hopelessness embraces lament, while hope short-circuits the struggle. As an ideology, hope whitewashes reality, preventing praxis from formulating. As a statement of unfounded belief, hope is as an illusion beyond critical examination, serving an important middle-class purpose, providing a quasi-religious contentment in the midst of oppression. All too often, hope becomes an excuse not to deal with the reality of injustice. To be hopeless is to be emboldened into necessary action in the present, even while knowing a different result is not dependent on us (for we are not the Saviour). Hopelessness thus saves us from burnout or giving up when just outcomes are not within reach (De La Torre 2017, pp. 140–141). Most importantly, a theology of hopelessness incubates the development of positive and liberative praxis, even when the situation is dire.

We continue the struggle for justice not because we hope we will win in the end; we struggle for justice for the sake of justice, regardless of the outcome. And we certainly do not struggle for justice in anticipation of some heavenly reward. There may or may not be a Heaven. We struggle for justice because we have no other choice, for the struggle defines our very humanity – or lack thereof (De La Torre 2017, pp. 140–143).

Western Christian theology, as the theology of the privileged, has too often devolved into a Pollyannaish theology of hope. Perhaps no verse in the Christian canon has done more mischief than Romans 8:38: 'All things work for the good of those who love God, and who has been called according to God's purpose'. But it is deeply problematic to construct a theological conception of hope around the idea that all things will work out for the best. History and personal experience shows that it seldom does. Good Christians with plenty of hope in God's protection die in horrible accidents, experience financial collapse and lose all that is dear – just like non-Christians. Bad things do happen – and happen often – to good people.

With Job, and all who suffer unjustly, we are forced to cry out to an apparent silent Heaven, 'Where then is my hope and who can perceive any hope for me?' (Jb. 17:15) I am not convinced, as was Martin Luther King, Jr., that 'the arc of the moral universe is long, but it bends towards justice' (King 1986, p. 52). Claiming a moral universe is an unprovable faith statement that seems to be contradicted by history's body count. The circumstances in Baltimore seem more representative of the historical norm, where many are born into crushing poverty and hopelessness in close proximity to a privileged few. The marginalized offer up their lives as living sacrifices so that an elite can be saved and live well.

I fear that philosopher Walter Benjamin's stark images might have been closer to understanding the unfolding of history. Reflecting on Paul Klee's painting *Angelus Novus*, which he owned, Benjamin noted, 'This is how one pictures the angel of history. His face is turned towards the past. Where we perceive a chain of events, he sees one single catastrophe which keeps piling wreckage upon wreckage and hurls it in front of his feet' (Benjamin 1968, p. 256). As Benjamin describes the scene, a storm is blowing from Paradise that has caught the Angelus Novus wings with such violence that the angel can no longer close his wings. 'The storm irresistibly propels him into the future to which his back is turned, while the pile of debris before him grows skywards. This storm is what we call progress' (ibid.). There is nothing inevitable about the passage of time, no teleology to history, only a piling up of catastrophe.

The dominant forms of hope that have been developed in Euro-American Christianity are ill-equipped to deal with such a vision. They depend on a counter-factual or otherworldly assertion that history ultimately ends with justice. But such a hope too often serves the interests of those in power by relativizing the demands of justice. For those struggling to survive on the streets of Baltimore, and indeed for most of humanity alive today, the likely ends of their histories are tragic. If something that might go by the name of hope exists, it feels more like the thin odds of winning the lottery than the abundance of divine providence.

But we who are familiar with marginalization are used to this. The oppressed of the world occupy the space of Holy Saturday, the day after Friday's crucifixion, the not-yet-before-the-resurrection of Easter Sunday. This is a space where the faint rumour of Sunday's Good News is drowned out by the continuing echoes of Friday's violence. In this space, hopelessness becomes the currency of used and abused people. Here, Sunday seems far away.

Where does hope exist for generation after generation of disenfranchisement? When hope is professed by those from the dominant culture, it smacks of an indivi-dualistic worldview that consciously or unconsciously blames the victims living on the underside of history for lacking sufficient hope. According to Jürgen Moltmann,

> in the promise of God [hope] can see a future also for the transient, the dying and the dead. That is why it can be said that the living without hope is like no longer living. Hell is hopelessness, and it is not for nothing that at the entrance to Dante's hell there stand the words: 'Abandon hope, all ye who enter here'.
>
> (Moltmann 1967, p. 32)

Moltmann, however, moves too quickly to condemn hopelessness in the present as the death of humanity, while pushing the grounds of hope into the next world.

A theology of hopelessness rejects any such easy fixes that may temporarily soothe the consciences of the privileged. All too often the fast-moving current of hope rushes past opportunities to listen and learn the lessons of hopelessness. To sit in the reality of Saturday is to discover that hope can become false when it serves as a mechanism for maintaining rather than challenging unjust social structures.

When I consider the hellish conditions under which black and brown bodies are forced to live, not just in parts of Baltimore but throughout the world, I simply lack the luxury or privilege to hopefully wait for God's future promise to material-ize. Too many dead and broken bodies obscure my view of the eschaton. Instead, I call for storming the very gates of Hell not at some future time, but now; even if said storming leads to some broken windows. Moltmann's theology of hope is a theology of optimism based on a God of process that grounds its hermeneutic in linear progressive thinking rooted in the Eurocentric modernity project. And, while such a hope may be comforting for middle-class Euro-American Christians whose mighty fortresses shield them from the Hell where desperation on the underside exists, it is too meagre for the disenfranchised (De La Torre 2017, pp. 136–137, p. 139).

In place of a passive theology of hope, I call for an active theology of hopelessness. One of the biggest misunderstandings of hopelessness is that it is equated with despair, which indeed entails disempowering traits such as inertia, depression, acquiescence and inaction. But a theology of hopelessness does not despair. Rather, hopelessness must be understood as a condition fuelled by desperation. When a people are desperate, they will do whatever it takes to change the situation because there is nothing is left to lose. The greatest heroes of history, those who have moved mountains for the cause of justice, have been those who, out of desperation, were driven to act. The Latin root for 'desperate' suggests a hopelessness that leads to action, at times reckless action, brought about by great urgency and anxiety. It was not hope that propelled people to protest on the streets of Baltimore, it was desperation.

Understood in this way, hopelessness is not disabling; rather, it is fertile ground in which a liberative praxis can grow, as the disenfranchised continue their struggle for justice regardless of the odds against them. It may be Saturday, but that's no justification to passively wait for Sunday. They continue the struggle, if not for themselves, then for their progeny (De La Torre 2017, pp. 139–140).

Moving forward

Baltimore is not the only city sitting on a powder keg that is just one body of colour away from igniting. If white America really wants to avoid violence, it must be as indignant about rampant police brutality and the sanctioned murder of dark bodies as it is about looting. White America must become incensed about racist banking practices and a minimum wage that falls far short of a living wage, trapping so many – including poor whites – in poverty.

A new theology, grounded in Holy Saturday rather than Easter, could give white Christian Americans new eyes to see. Given a new lens, privileged white Americans might just be able to see riots as a lurching liturgy of the hopeless and understand broken windows as lamentations of injustices and invocations of divine presence. And, most of all, they might feel a calling of the Spirit to reject the temptations of a passive theology of hope in favour of action in solidarity with the oppressed. Hopelessness becomes an act of courage to embrace reality and to act even when the odds are in favour of defeat. Only at this critical junction of desperation, rooted in the now, is there a possibility for revolutionary change. That change might impact the future in a positive way. Or it might make the future worse as newer forms of oppression manifest themselves. Because we cannot discern the future with any accuracy, and because new stages of liberation are always littered with unintended consequences, we can only and boldly engage in liberative praxis within the now and hope for the best.

Desperation becomes the means by which we work out our liberation – our salvation – in fear and trembling. But this liberation/salvation we work out is not some egocentric project; rather, what is being worked out is how we can stand in solidarity with hopeless people who are struggling for their liberation/salvation. To stand in solidarity with those facing genocide, pauperization and unmitigated hatred precludes any simplistic platitudes concerning hope. For hearts to weep and bleed, they must be broken upon the rocks of realism. Imposing hope upon the least of these from the safety of power and privilege is highly paternalistic. To stand in solidarity is to stand in the space of the hopelessness they share. We embrace hopelessness when we embrace the sufferers of the world. And in embracing them, we discover our own humanity and salvation, providing impetus to our praxis, for hopelessness is the precursor to resistance and revolution (De La Torre 2017, pp. 139–140).

Maybe some forms of violence, or at least threats of force, are inevitable for change to come for people who are oppressed. A theology of hopelessness offers us some tools to incorporate this truism into a religious worldview. I recall a conversation I once had in Mexico with a Zapatista rebel who told me that when he went to the government's bureaucracy to protest injustice he was told, 'Go away, you smelly Indian'. When he showed up the next day with a bandana covering his face and carrying a rifle, they took the time to listen to his complaints.

Some forms of violence, such as the destruction of property, when employed by the marginalized to overcome their own oppression, can in fact be understood as a kind of sacramental act – the burning buildings and cars becoming a makeshift altar, with smoke ascending into the heavens. Those living on the underside of society's power structures can rarely avoid wrestling with hopelessness. Those protesting in the streets of Baltimore (and the next cities that are poised to erupt) are faced with deciding in which violence they will participate. Will they remain quiet and do nothing, thus becoming complicit with the violence of a dominant culture protecting 'by any means necessary' the privileged spaces of Wells Fargo or McDonald's? Or, with nothing to lose, will they stand in solidarity with the oppressed, fighting against the powers and principalities of this world that bring disenfranchisement, dispossession and death into their communities?

But the oppressed are not the only people whose lives and souls are at stake. Although we should not equate the suffering of those who are disenfranchised with those who are privileged, those who are the beneficiaries of oppressive social structures are also victims of these structures. In the United States, white middle-class Christians are indoctrinated into believing they have a right to power and privilege, and they are trapped into living into this false ideal of superiority. While they may not know it, the privileged require the same liberation yearned for by the disenfranchised. Yes, liberation is for the abused of Baltimore's inner city who seek deliverance from death-dealing social structures that deny them their humanity. But liberation is also for their oppressors who work in the corporate offices of Wells Fargo and McDonald's. And liberation is also for those millions of comfortable white middle-class Christians, whose own humanity is eroded by their complicity with these same structures that protect their privileged lives at the expense of others.

References

Becker, A. (2014) 'Lawmaker calls for new investigations into border agent fatal shootings', *The Center for Investigative Reporting*, 12 September. Available from: www.revealnews. org/article-legacy/lawmaker-calls-for-new-investigations-into-border-agent-fatal-shootings/ [accessed October 3 2017].

Buehler, J. W. (2017) 'Racial/Ethnic Disparities in the Use of Lethal Force by US Police, 2010–2014', *The American Journal of Public Health*, 11 January.

Benjamin, W. (1968 [1940]) 'Theses on the philosophy of history', in H. Arendt, (ed.), *Illuminations*, H. Zohn (trans.), New York: Schocken Books, pp. 253–264.

Blank, R. M. (2008) 'Presidential address: how to improve poverty measurement in the United States', *Journal of Policy Analysis and Management*, 27(2):,233–254.

Bradner, E. (2015) *Obama: 'no excuse' for violence in Baltimore*, CNN, 28 April. Available from: www.cnn.com/2015/04/28/politics/obama-baltimore-violent-protests/index.html [accessed 3 October 2017].

Dalton, F. J. (2003) *The moral vision of César Chávez*, Maryknoll, NY: Orbis Books.

De La Torre, M. A. (2014) *Doing Christian ethics from the margins*, 2nd edn, Maryknoll, NY: Orbis Books.

De La Torre, M. A. (2015) *The politics of Jesus: A Hispanic political theology*, Lanham, MD: Rowman & Littlefield.

De La Torre, M. A. (2017) *Embracing hopelessness*, Minneapolis, MN: Fortress Press.

Economic Policy Institute (2015) '*Family budget calculator*', Washington, DC: Economic Policy Institute. Available from: www.epi.org/resources/budget/ [accessed 3 October 2017].

Editorial Board (2015) 'Racial penalties in Baltimore mortgages', *The New York Times*, 30 May. Available from: www.nytimes.com/2015/05/31/opinion/sunday/racial-penalties-in-baltimore-mortgages.html?_r=0.

Editorial Board (2015) 'McDonald's Minimum Raise', *The New York Times*, 03 April. Available from: www.nytimes.com/2015/04/04/opinion/mcdonalds-minimum-raise. html [accessed 3 October 2017].

Hinkelammert, F. J. (1997) 'Liberation theology in the economic and social context of Latin America', in D. Batstone, E. Mendieta, L. A. Lorentzen and D. N. Hopkins, (eds), *Liberation theologies, postmodernity, and the Americas*, London: Routledge, pp. 25–52.

Kearney, L. (2015) 'Protesters rally for higher U.S. fast-food wages, union rights', Reuters, 10 November. Available from: www.reuters.com/article/us-usa-wages-protests-idUSK CN0SZ1KB20151110 [accessed 3 October 2017].

King, M. L. Jr. (1986) *A testament of hope: The essential writings and speeches of Martin Luther King*, New York: HarperCollins.

McDonald's Corporation (2015) 'McDonald's reports fourth quarter and full year 2014 results', 23 January. Available from: http://news.mcdonalds.com/Corporate/Press-Releases/Financial-Release?xmlreleaseid=123060 [accessed 3 October 2017].

Moltmann, J. (1967) *Theology of hope: On the ground and the implications of a Christian eschatology*, J. W. Leitch (trans.), New York: Harper & Row Publishers.

Morgenson, G. (2008) 'Baltimore is suing bank over foreclosure crisis', *The New York Times*, 8 January. Available from: www.nytimes.com/2008/01/08/us/ 08baltimore.html [accessed 3 October 2017].

National Law Enforcement Officer's Memorial Fund (2017) 'Deaths, assaults, and injuries over the past decade (2007–2016)', 10 April. Available from: www.nleomf.org/facts/officer-fatalities-data/daifacts.html [accessed 3 October 2017].

No More Deaths (2011) *A culture of cruelty: abuse and impunity in short-term US border patrol custody*, Tucson, AZ: No More Deaths.

Powell, M. (2009) 'Banks accused of pushing mortgage deals on blacks', *The New York Times*, 6 June. Available from: www.nytimes.com/2009/06/07/us/07baltimore.html [accessed 3 October 2017].

Santos, F. and Zemansky, R. (2013) 'Arizona desert swallows migrants on riskier paths', *The New York Times*, 20 May. Available from: www.nytimes.com/2013/05/21 /us/immigrant-death-rate-rises-on-illegal-crossings.html [accessed 3 October 2017].

Taylor, P., Kochlar, R., Fry, R., Velasco, G. and Motel, S. (2011) *Wealth gaps rise to record highs between whites, blacks and Hispanics*, Washington, DC: Pew Research Center.

US Department of Health and Human Services (2015) '2015 poverty guidelines', 3 September. Available from: https://aspe.hhs.gov/2015-poverty-guidelines [accessed 3 October 2017].

Ushomirsky, N. and Williams, D. (2015) *Funding gaps 2015: Too many states still spend less on educating on students who need the most*, Washington, DC: The Education Trust.

PART 3

For the love of the world

8

WASTING HUMAN LIVES

Hyper-incarceration in the United States

Elizabeth M. Bounds

Regardless of any actual social or economic inequalities, the fundamental equality of persons continues to be a central American belief. As the beginning of the Declaration of Independence says: 'We hold these truths to be self-evident, that all men are created equal, that they are endowed by their Creator with certain unalienable Rights . . .' Of course, for those who first wrote and ratified the words, 'all' did not really refer to every human. It was assumed that all manner of human beings was not 'men' – women of course, but also those who were enslaved, and others. These exclusions were woven into all dimensions of the assumed world, from theology to economics.

Yet the claim of a universal equality has served as a powerful visionary force in US history. As Martin Luther King, Jr. put it, 'When the architects of our republic wrote the magnificent words of the Constitution and the Declaration of Independence, they were signing a promissory note to which every American was to fall heir' (1986, p. 217). Two centuries of political struggle over the 'hidden' inequalities behind this proclamation have enabled us finally to affirm, at least in the social consensus of law, that 'all men' actually includes women, African Americans, indigenous persons and gay and lesbian persons, among others. However, there has been one consistent exception to the affirmed equality of 'all men,' and that is those who are incarcerated because of a criminal conviction. The Thirteenth Amendment abolished slavery and involuntary servitude 'except as a punishment for crime whereof the party shall have been duly convicted'.[1] Although legal battles, especially in recent decades, have specified certain rights (such as religious freedom) for the incarcerated, these guarantees are seen as exceptions to an assumed basic deprivation of rights. An unquestioned understanding is that violation of the law requires, either for the good of society or for the balancing of justice, the rendering of certain persons as inferior or unequal citizens, ineligible for constitutional rights, legal protections and economic opportunities.

In recent decades, democratic theories of justice have engaged questions of political participation, rights, economic access and identity recognition as areas crucial to a good or decent social order. However, criminal justice and the justice of punishment are hardly ever considered as part of a basic theory of justice.[2] An exception is Michael Walzer, who points out, in his brief discussion of punishment in *Spheres of Justice*, that 'Punishment is a powerful stigma; it dishonors its victims' (1983, p. 29). In Walzer's view, punishment removes persons from membership and the common life, 'the primary good' that is distributed in society (Walzer 1983, p. 31). For Walzer, being a citizen in democratic society means participating in shared meanings and shared life. Citizenship is not merely possession of a passport but a form of inclusion and participation that is foundational for social identity and for the basic conditions of justice. As an example, segregation in the US South excluded African Americans from full participation as citizens because whites would not acknowledge their full dignity and equality. Segregation meant exclusion from processes that form one's self-respect based 'in the dignity of the position [i.e., citizenship] and the integrity of the person who holds it' (Walzer 1983, p. 274).

While Walzer believes in the necessity of punishment, he also believes that the loss of dignity inherent in punishment is dangerous. Punishment, he says, is a challenging enterprise where 'it is critically important that we find the right people . . . the deserving . . . We aim at an extraordinary and difficult precision' (Walzer 1983, p. 269). A just distribution of punishment is a negative good, one might say, allocated on the basis of desert. When we do not find that precision and misdistribute punishment, Walzer says, we deprive persons of the dignity and the respect of others which is the precondition to self-esteem and self-respect (1983, pp. 268–280). Dignity, says conflict theorist Donna Hicks, 'is a birthright . . . [w]e must treat others as if they matter, as if they are worthy of care and attention' (2011, p. 4). Protest of the violent and dehumanizing conditions of punishment as deprivation of dignity has been voiced by many incarcerated persons over the past centuries. Elliot Barkley, one of the leaders in the 1971 Attica Prison Riot/Uprising, wrote a manifesto claiming equality, saying

> We are Men! We are not beasts and do not intend to be beaten or driven as such. The entire prison populace has set forth to change forever the ruthless brutalisation and disregard for the lives of the prisoners here and throughout the United States.
>
> (Attica 2011)

In this chapter, I will use Walzer's concerns about punishment as a practice within a just democratic social order as an entry point to raising moral questions about how punishment in the United States acts as a mechanism of exclusion – particularly through incarceration – and generates political, social and economic inequality. First, I expand the scope of moral reflection to include the 'who', 'how', and especially the 'why' of punishment, noting how fundamental theological values are present in the 'why'. Then I will consider what could be termed the 'data of injustice', examining the actual 'who' and 'how' of US punishment practices. Finally, I will ask what these practices suggest about the real 'why' of punishment, drawing upon some contemporary theorists of US incarceration.

Unpacking just punishment

Walzer's concerns about the just use of punishment are critical in the wake of a period of extraordinary growth in the US criminal justice system. After World War II, there was an overall consensus on the rehabilitative purposes of punishment emphasizing psychological reasons for crime and giving therapeutic treatment to those convicted (Rotman 1995, pp. 168–71). However, since the 1970s, US politics has been dominated by demands for retributive law and order in response to crime. Those demands have not varied with the amount of actual crimes committed. While overall crime rates did increase fairly rapidly from the 1960s through the 1970s, they rose more slowly in the 1980s and have slowly declined or remained stable through today (Disaster Center 2015). However, fear of crime and criminals did not decline (Simon 2001). In the last few decades, politicians have known that they could generally appeal to constituents with a tough-on-crime stance – or risk being accused by political opponents of not being tough enough. Exponential increases in arrests and sentences on drug charges (particularly in relation to crack cocaine), loss of judicial discretion in sentencing, and legislative initiatives which mandated lengthy sentences for repeat offenders have all contributed to the current state of mass incarceration.[3] By 2008, 1 in 100 persons was involved in some way with the criminal justice system (The Pew Center on the States 2008). By the end of 2015, an estimated 2,173,800 people were incarcerated in the US (Kaeble and Glaze 2016).[4] The rate of imprisonment in the United States far outstrips not only that of its economic counterparts but of almost all countries in the world. It is impossible to believe that a system that includes such a large percentage of its population can possibly have the 'precision' Walzer names – and I will indeed show that it does not.

But there is a further issue about the justice of punishment that is not specifically raised by Walzer, but is inherent, I think, in his understanding of the centrality of membership. What is the purpose of punishment (the 'why' of punishment), and do the persons we punish (the 'who' of punishment) and forms by which we punish (the 'how' of punishment) realize these purposes? Walzer says that 'Punishment requires a specific judgment, a jury's verdict; and that suggests that we punish people only when they deserve to be punished' (Walzer 1983, p. 268). Desert is a central term for Walzer's notion of distributive justice because it enables a combination of a liberal universal acknowledgement of equality with a communitarian recognition of the real particularities of persons. Given the exclusionary stigma imposed by punishment, it is important to be sure that the judgment is deserved. The standard accounts of the purposes of punishment are retribution, deterrence, incapacitation and rehabilitation. Walzer's emphasis on the careful determination of desert and his negative example of preventive detention rules out deterrence as unjust.

His framework of punishment as a deserved response that involves the imposition of pain (the stigma of 'social disgrace') suggests a retributive approach. On first glance, Walzer's views on punishment align with the currently prevailing view of the purpose for punishment: giving people who break the law their just deserts. However, Walzer's deep sense of social community and the relational nature of membership prioritize connection over exclusion. His approach is probably closest to philosopher R.A. Duff's liberal communitarian view of punishment as 'the communication of deserved censure' where the communication must occur 'in the appropriate language of communal values' rather than the 'coercive language of deterrence' which '(re)creates a conception of 'us' and 'them' (Duff 2001, p. 30, pp. 83–84). Whoever the 'who' are, the forms of punishment need to remember that they are still part of 'us'.

Walzer's strong focus on the primary good of membership, especially in his discussion of the ways 'strangers' can access membership, may also give further clues or at least limits on the 'how' of punishment. He insists that 'every immigrant and every resident is a citizen too – or at least a potential citizen' (Walzer 1983, p. 52). Participation in a community without the access to the participatory rights of members of that community is intolerable, an unjust exercise of power. Political justice requires that

> the processes of self-determination . . . must be open, and equally open, to all those men and women who live within its territory . . . and are subject to local law . . . Men and women are either subject to the state's authority, or they are not, and if they are subject, they must be given a say, and ultimately an equal say, in what that authority does.
>
> (Walzer 1983, pp. 60–61)

The implication is, I believe, that while temporary lack of access to membership or inequality of membership is possible, any broader limitation on persons resident within one's society is inherently unjust.

Walzer's account of democratic community points to certain deep values of dignity, equal worth and recognition. These values can also be construed theologically from a Christian perspective. For example, Paul's metaphor of the body in First Corinthians points to relationality, since 'If one member suffers, all suffer together with it; if one member is honoured, all rejoice together with it' (1 Cor 12:26). And his insistence in Galatians, that 'In Christ, there is neither Jew nor Greek' (Gal 3:28) implies a sense of equal worth that was borne out by many practices of the earliest Christian communities. While these values can be and have been realized in exclusionary ways, for example dividing Christians from non-Christians, or suggesting that social relations were immaterial to Christian identity, they also have energized powerful claims for equality.

On the basis of Walzer's membership-based concerns about 'why' we punish, 'who' we imprison, and 'how' we punish, I will argue that our current prison-based punishment system is profoundly unjust. It breeds disrespect and wastes human lives, functioning as a powerful engine of ongoing political, social and economic inequality that excludes whole classes of persons from membership in our democratic social order. The values at its heart negate equality, respect and recognition in ways that should be deeply disturbing. To make this argument, I first review the 'who' of incarceration by highlighting some of the demographic realities of mass incarceration and the ways it reproduces and perpetuates race and class inequalities. I then turn to the 'how' of incarceration, showing how current processes include deprivation of rights and degradation, not only during the time served but even after a prisoner is purportedly 'free'. When this deprivation of rights is linked with the degrading experience of incarceration, we are left with a retributive system that permanently excludes members from society. Given this reality, I return to the 'why' of punishment in dialogue with some recent theories of mass imprisonment that link incarceration to broader structures of inequality.

A dangerous imprecision

Who we punish

A basic justification for punishment is the need to maintain and protect the order of society. However, the history of the United States is filled with examples where punishment has been only an exercise of coercive power, enabling certain citizens to preserve their power over against marginalized and disenfranchised citizens. Our societal problem is not simply how many persons we incarcerate but *which* persons we incarcerate and why. And there is no doubt that those more marginal in terms of race and class are disproportionately among those in prison. As sociologist Bruce Western (2006, p. xi) puts it, the current system 'is a story as much about race and poverty as it is about crime and deviance'.

The majority of prisoners in the United States are poor, poorly educated, and black or Latino. For example, in 2014, the Bureau of Justice Statistics reported that 35 per cent of state prisoners were white, 38 per cent were black, and 21 per cent were Hispanic. In twelve states, more than half of the prison population was African American. The Hispanic population in state prisons was as high as 61 per cent in New Mexico and 42 per cent in both Arizona and California. In an additional seven states, at least one in five inmates was Hispanic (Nellis 2016). Poverty and class are entwined in complex ways with race. Bruce Western's study of rates and reasons for imprisonment through the early 2000's concluded that '[c]lass inequality in imprisonment increased significantly' in the last decades of the twentieth century as increases in prison admission were concentrated among non-college men, regardless of race (Western 2006, pp. 75–76).[5] About 41 per cent of those incarcerated have never completed high school – in contrast to 18 per cent of the general population over eighteen (Harlow 2003). Poverty also lies behind the reality that an estimated 56 per cent of state prisoners are diagnosed on entry with a mental health disorder, often combined with substance addiction. Often these disorders have been undiagnosed or untreated because of the cost and difficulty of access to mental health care, including prescription drugs (Kim, Becker-Cohen and Serakos 2015).

In most states, researchers can identify a few impoverished inner city or suburban ZIP codes, primarily African American and/or Hispanic, which are the sending and receiving neighbourhoods for a significant portion of the state's prison population. For example, in Pennsylvania, taxpayers will spend over $40 million to imprison residents of neighbourhoods in a single ZIP code in Philadelphia, where 38 per cent of households have incomes under $25,000. In Shreveport, Louisiana, nearly 7 per cent of all working-age men living in the neighbourhoods of a single ZIP code were sent to prison in 2008. And in Austin, Texas, while the neighbourhoods in three of the city's 41 ZIP codes are home to only 3.5 per cent of the city's adult population, they receive over 17 per cent of people returning from Texas state prison each year (National Justice Atlas). Julio Medina, director of the Exodus re-entry programme, has said that when he first arrived at New York's Sing Sing prison for his sentence for drug crimes, he felt he was back home in his neighborhood, since there were so many men he knew that he could connect with building-by-building, street-by-street (Medina 2010, personal correspondence 26 October). Not surprisingly, these are neighbourhoods with low economic opportunities and poorly performing public schools, caught in cycles of poverty and violence.

How we punish

Prisons were developed in Europe and the United States starting in the late eighteenth century as enlightened institutions of penal reform that would replace public practices of physical punishment with processes of reformation occurring behind walls and locked doors. However, from the beginning, these intentions were generally overwhelmed by overcrowding and lack of funds, along with political contention. By the time of the passage of the Thirteenth Amendment in the mid-nineteenth century, even the most 'enlightened' prisons in the North were known to keep order through vicious flogging and irons. After the Civil War, reaction to immigration in the North and Reconstruction in the South meant a significant increase in policing and convictions. In the North, this increase was dealt with through some prison reform and more prison construction. In the South, the focus was on controlling African Americans, which occurred through convict labour rather than through building new prisons.[6]

Given these conditions, it is not surprising that for a century after the passage of the Thirteenth Amendment, there was no real legal concern about the nature of 'involuntary servitude' for those convicted of a crime. In the 1866 case *Pervear v. Massachusetts*, the Supreme Court of the United States ruled that prisoners had no constitutional rights, not even Eighth Amendment rights prohibiting 'cruel and unusual punishment' (*Pervear v. Massachusetts* (1867) 72 US 475). In 1871, the Virginia Supreme Court ruled that a prisoner was not covered by the state's bill of rights since he 'has, as a consequence of his crime, not only forfeited his liberty, but all his personal rights except those which the law in its humanity accords him. He is for the time being a slave of the state' (*Ruffin v. Commonwealth* (1871) 62 VA 790). For nearly 100 years, this hands-off doctrine meant that federal and state courts generally refused to hear cases involving the rights of prisoners or ruled on such cases in ways that denied any possibilities of rights.

In the 1960s, prisoners' rights claims began to gain some traction as part of broader movements such as civil rights and Black Power and through key Supreme Court decisions under Chief Justice Earl Warren. Throughout the 1960s and 1970s, legal battles, marked by moments of direct resistance such as the Attica Prison Uprising, built a framework for prisoners that included the right to practice religion, the right to access legal materials, and the rights to read, write and communicate with the outside world. However, as incarceration rates began to accelerate in the later 1970s, rights cases began to lose momentum. For example, when a prisoner sued over the destruction of his possessions in a 'shakedown' search (where possessions are torn apart and dumped on the floor), the Supreme Court made clear that Fourth Amendment rights against unreasonable searches 'did not apply within the prison cell' as security overrode any right to privacy (*Hudson v. Palmer* (1984) 468 US 517). In his dissent, Justice John Paul Stevens remarked that the court 'declares prisoners to be little more than chattel, a view I thought society had outgrown long ago' (cited in Whitman 2003, p. 177). In 1996, Congress passed the Prisoner Litigation Reform Act, which installed a series of restrictions on prisoner rights cases, limiting the capacity for prisoners to bring cases in terms of the scope of the litigation, preventing instigation of court-granted rights during appeal, and requiring exhaustion of all internal administrative remedies (Pollock 2013, pp. 150–174). Although the incarcerated do maintain positive rights to religious expression, health care and certain legal processes, along with negative rights to freedom from inhuman conditions and sexual harassment, the reality is often that there is little that can be done when rights are violated, especially in the face of arguments concerning security.[7]

With the loss of rights comes loss of personhood. The underlying experience of prisons is one of isolation, boredom and degradation with few opportunities for change or for preparation for a life after incarceration. Prisoners are well aware that by 'locking them up and throwing away the key' society has both condemned and forgotten them. As one inmate writes about prison, 'No one measures the justice and fairness of our system and the cracks we've fallen through are wide and deep' (George 2010, p. 148). The lack of possibility for re-gaining membership and participation is symbolized by the denial in 1993 of Pell Grant education funds to incarcerated people (Violent Crime Control and Law Enforcement Act of 1994; Higher Education Reauthorization Act of 1994). Education is, of course, a key vehicle for equality, and a key source of the skills and background for employment on release. With little access to education and a limited number of vocational programmes, it is not surprising that a majority of those re-entering the community post-incarceration struggle to find employment or hold only the most boring and degrading of jobs.[8]

The lack of economic opportunity is compounded by direct limitations on rights and participation experienced by the formerly incarcerated. When people are released, having 'served their time', they are generally not able to claim full membership in society since, as 'collateral consequences' of conviction, many rights are not immediately, or ever, restored. For example, only Vermont and Maine permit incarcerated persons to vote, and thirty-two states extend that ban to persons on probation or parole.[9] The Supreme Court in Iowa recently upheld a complete ban on voting rights for all convicted persons, which is also the case for all persons convicted of certain (generally violent) felonies in Nevada, Delaware and Tennessee. Arizona and Nevada permanently disenfranchise anyone with two or more convictions. In a few states, there are waiting periods after parole or probation are completed or voting is only possible after the state responds to an individual appeal for reinstatement to voting rights (Chung 2016).

Limitation of voting rights is not the only sign of inequality. As the title of an article in the American Bar Association's journal puts it, 'Ex-offenders face tens of thousands of legal restrictions, bias and limits on their rights'. These include challenges in obtaining employment, signing leases, accessing public housing, gaining professional licenses and obtaining identification such as driver's licenses (Laird 2013). Those re-entering face these explicit restrictions on top of the lack of previous access to education that many have suffered and the general stigma of a prison record that all endure. Thus, it is no surprise that studies have shown that over two-thirds of prisoners released in thirty states in 2005 were arrested for a new crime within 3 years of release from prison, and that three-quarters were arrested again within 5 years (Durose *et al.* 2014).

While such limitations on political rights and economic opportunities are troubling in their own right, the impact is magnified in the context of the particular ZIP code concentrations noted above. Districts in these ZIP codes may have a significant loss of voting residents which affects both political power and funding allocations so that few government resources are allocated to develop employment, schooling, etc. Incarceration becomes part of a cycle of inequality leaving certain groups and communities in the United States with little or no expectation of any economic or political opportunities. Many of these communities are African American so that, as Western (2006, p. 199) puts it, our system of imprisonment 'has subtracted from the gains of African American citizenship' in civil rights. Thus, we have a society in which a certain segment of the population – poor people, primarily of colour – are permanently disenfranchised as participating citizens since incarceration has exacerbated the limitations of living in contexts with little social capital, educational possibility, or job options.[10]

A return to the why of punishment

Having outlined the manner in which the 'who' and the 'how' of our current forms of punishment generate inequality, I want to return now to the 'why'. As I have noted, for several decades of the postwar years, the assumed purpose of punishment, at least in the North and Midwest, was rehabilitation.[11] While programs supporting this purpose were frequently absent or, when present, poorly executed, there was at least agreement on the underlying institutional goal. Even when paternalistically executed, the practice of rehabilitation implies 'an innate moral equality . . . that could be restored . . . through penal discipline' (Western 2006, p. 2). However, this agreement of purpose has in recent decades dissolved into a focus on retributive punishment and incapacitation or deterrence.

Many of the critics of the current US criminal justice system see its major purpose as maintaining a system of white supremacy and racism. Michele Alexander has powerfully argued that the War on Drugs under the Reagan administration was a 'new Jim Crow', that is, a new way of continuing the historical disenfranchisement of African Americans in response to the political and social gains of the Civil Rights movements. The current system of mass incarceration is, she writes, 'a set of structural arrangements that locks a racially distinct group into a subordinate political, social, and economic position, effectively creating a second-class citizenship'. While she acknowledges that the prison system is exclusionary by nature, she argues that 'as a white criminal you are not a *racial* outcast, though you may face many forms of social and economic exclusion.' Now, she says, 'the stigma of race has become the stigma of criminality' (Alexander 2010, pp. 180, 192, 14).

Alexander's argument about the ways our punishment system generates racial inequality does explain a large part of how the United States has approached punishment both in the past and the present. However, it does not, in my view, grasp entirely all of the dimensions of the history and reality of our prison system. For example, Alexander does not fully explain the presence of large numbers of incarcerated white people. The explanation she offers – that they are there to preserve the notion of the 'colour-blindness' of the system – lacks evidence and explanatory power. Other critics have woven a dimension of economic purpose into mass incarceration, pointing to the impact of global capitalism in which, as David Harvey puts it, the model of the worker globally now is 'the disposable worker' (2007, p. 171). This worker, Loïc Wacquant argues, is under the control of interlocking welfare and penal systems where 'the incipient "penalisation" of welfare match[es] the degraded "welfarisation" of the prison' (2010, p. 203). Acting as part of the neo-liberal state, the welfare and prison systems 'foster vastly different profiles and experiences of citizenship across the class and ethnic spectrum' which 'contravene the fundamental principle of equality of treatment by the state and routinely abridge the individual freedoms of the dispossessed . . . In short, the penalization of poverty splinters citizenship along class lines, saps civic trust at the bottom, and saws the degradation of republican tenets' (Wacquant 2010, p. 218).

Of course, racism has kept persons of colour over-represented among those US citizens who are poor. But class and race intertwine in complex ways to choke ideals of equality.[12] And here is where, in my view, the moral and theological issues underlying the purposes and effects of US punishment become clear. Hallmarks of a claim to equality are a concern for dignity and recognition connected to a concern for fairness, in light of which unfair treatment is experienced as an assault to a sense of self-worth and dignity. In *Harsh Justice*, James Whitman (2003) argues that, while European states evolved to a justice system using milder 'high status' treatment, the United States consistently chose harsher 'low status' treatment. In this context, Whitman argues, US citizens have generally chosen forms of formal equality – that is, processes that (at least in theory) treat all persons exactly alike with less reliance on discretion and mercy. He connects this difference to the fluidity of status in the United States which is, as Walzer says, 'a society of misters', where recognition is not based on a fixed class status but requires living in 'a world of hope, effort, and endless anxiety' (Whitman 2003; Walzer 1983, p. 254). Whitman ties the impulse towards degradation specifically to the status and treatment of African American persons who have indeed experienced the worst deprivation and punishment under policies of separate and unequal treatment throughout most of US history.

Whitman suggests that in the United States, the moral ideal of equality can only be lived out in an uncertain and punitive context, shaped by our particular history of class and race relations. In his argument, he points several times to the critical role of Christianity in the formation of US attitudes to punishment. The question of punishment was often not understood as a political question of status and treatment, but a moral-theological question of desert (Whitman 2003, pp. 189, 194, 201). Thus, the question of equal worth becomes a question of moral worth. The strong moralism of US culture has been shaped by a traditional Protestant Christian understanding that there is no worth or desert for humans apart from a grace offered through the redemptive suffering of Jesus Christ on the cross. Thus, background theological worldviews shaped a culture that stressed moving to redemption through suffering. Even though explicitly theological arguments disappeared from penal policy by the Civil War, the residue of moral-theological judgment exists in the ongoing assumption that the redemption of those convicted to crime demands degradation so that prisoners can 'understand every human being's degraded status before a God that governed the universe' (Graber 2014, p. 183).[13] The 'why' embedded deeply in our current justice system points not towards dignity, but degradation.

Conclusion

In the last decade, there has been a slow turning away from harsh and retributive forms of criminal justice, often because state legislatures have realized the costs of incarceration, both in terms of budgets and in terms of the prospects of those who, even after long sentences, do return to society. But without conscious effort to discuss the purposes of incarceration, our coercive powers, entwined with default understandings and fears, shape penal policy as engine of inequality. 'The distinctive new form and function of the prison today is a space of pure custody, a human warehouse, or even a kind of social waste management facility' (Simon 2001, p. 141).

Bryan Stevenson is the founder of the Equal Justice Initiative, which has defended numerous persons on death row in Alabama while calling both for criminal justice reform and a reckoning with the history of racial violence embedded in our justice system. In 2012, he gave a TED Talk entitled, 'We Need to Talk About an Injustice,' in which he said,

> We have a system of justice in this country that treats you much better if you're rich and guilty than if you're poor and innocent. Wealth, not culpability, shapes outcomes. And yet, we seem to be very comfortable. The politics of fear and anger have made us believe that these are problems that are not our problems. We've been disconnected . . . Because ultimately, our humanity depends on everyone's humanity . . . I've come to understand and to believe that each of us is more than the worst thing we've ever done . . . And because of that there's this basic human dignity that must be respected by law . . . .Ultimately, you judge the character of a society, not by how they treat their rich and the powerful and the privileged, but by how they treat the poor, the condemned, the incarcerated.
>
> (Stevenson 2012)

Underlying Stevenson's words is an appeal to 'we', the community of the United States. If this community is to be just, as Walzer realizes, all residents must be fully able to participate in political, social and economic life. Although punishment necessitates a period of non-participation, that exclusion must be distributed justly in terms of desert and must be, with few exceptions, temporary. Our current punishment system in the United States ensures that far too many of us, vulnerable through poverty and racism, are not now nor ever will be full and equal members.

Notes

1 The Thirteenth Amendment, ratified in 1865, abolished slavery, 'except as a punishment for crime whereof the party shall have been duly convicted'. The Civil Rights Act of 1866, along with the simultaneously developed the Fourteenth Amendment ratified in 1868, were the first federal laws defining citizenship and claiming equal protection under the law for all citizens. The major purpose of both was to afford some degree of civil protection for the recently emancipated slaves in the midst of strong opposition from white Southerners. Yet, in the Civil Rights Act, citizens were defined as persons born in the United States, except for 'untaxed Indians', 'persons subject to a foreign power', and those who were subject to 'punishment for a crime whereof the party shall have been duly convicted'. While the Fourteenth Amendment does not include these exclusions, there was a tacit understanding, named in subsequent court decisions, that the convicted had forfeited rights to citizenship (McLennan 2008, p. 141, p. 144).

2 Rawls, for example only mentions briefly that principles of responsibility governing punishment can be derived from his Basic Principle of Liberty (*Theory*, 254). Martha Nussbaum discusses questions of law in several works and discusses stigma and exclusion in *Hiding from Humanity: Disgust, Shame, and Law* but as questions of law and emotion, not of justice. It is also important to note that philosophical engagement with punishment and desert have not always been concerned with basic questions of a just social order. Commenting on this lacuna, Ted Honderich (2006, p. 204) writes, 'the theoreticians of punishment, very nearly all of them, and all of them until recently, have considered the

question of the justification of punishment without attending to the general question of the decent society'.

3 While each state had its own pattern of increases, the trends were captured in The Comprehensive Crime Control Act, passed in 1984 under President Reagan, and the Violent Crime Control Law Enforcement Act of 1994, signed by President Clinton. The 1984 Act created a commission to issue sentencing guidelines for federal crimes (ending judicial discretion), while the 1994 Act increased the number of federal crimes punishable by death, created a 'three strikes' provision, opened the door for juveniles to be tried as adults, and provided funding for building state prisons while ending access to Pell education funding by incarcerated persons. The Obama Administration worked to counter some of these harsh sentencing guidelines for low-level drug offenders and began a pilot programme of funds to certain correctional educational programmes. However, the current Attorney General, Jeff Sessions, has issued a memo ordering federal prosecutors to 'charge and pursue the most serious, readily provable offense', signaling a return to harsh drug sentencing (Dwyer 2017).

4 The 2015 number represents a decline from the 2008 Pew number of 2,319,258.

5 'Although prison rates are five times lower for whites than blacks . . . whites with only a high school education were more than twenty times more likely than their college-educated counterparts to go to prison' (Western 2006, pp. 75–76).

6 See, among others, McKelvey (1972), Ayers (1985), Morris and Rothman (1995), Christianson (1998), and Blackmon (2008).

7 As one prison medical expert remarked in response to the revelation of dangerously substandard medical care in Georgia by a physician who had falsified his employment history, 'Correctional systems receive little oversight in many areas, including medical . . . The only oversight we really have comes from the courts, with people suing, or the press' (Robbins 2015). For a summary of rights see http://civilrights.findlaw.com/other-constitutional-rights/rights-of-inmates.html.

8 Although overall national employment data for the formerly incarcerated/returning citizens can be difficult to obtain, a study of employment rates in 2014 suggested that overall for formerly incarcerated men their employment rate was 1.6–1.8 percentage points lower than the employment rates of US males. More tellingly, the study estimated a gap of 7.3–8.2 percentage points for men returning with less than a high school degree (Bucknor and Barber 2016, p. 13).

9 Probation is the supervisory monitoring of an offender based on conditions set by the courts; parole is a system of early release following imprisonment for a criminal conviction where the person is under regular supervision and must comply with a series of regulations concerning travel, etc. as determined by the relevant parole board.

10 Although I am talking about those who have been often termed the 'underclass', I do not use the terms, which I think tends to stigmatize and stereotype. For its use and description, see Wilson 1987. For a critique of the term, see Wacquant 2008.

11 The South and Southwest have a different story, particularly because African Americans were generally not considered fit for rehabilitation (for example see Wilkinson 2010).

12 Gender also threads through the intertwined strands of race and class, but I have chosen not to highlight this dimension here. Kimberle Crenshaw's initial definition of intersectionality provides the perfect metaphor for the complexity (and necessity) of these cross-cutting analyses: 'Consider an analogy to traffic in an intersection, coming and going in all four directions. Discrimination, like traffic through an intersection, may flow in one direction, and it may flow in another. If an accident happens in an intersection, it can be caused by cars traveling from any number of directions and, sometimes, from all of them. But it is not always easy to reconstruct an accident: Sometimes the skid marks and the injuries simply indicate that they occurred simultaneously, frustrating efforts to determine which driver caused the harm (Crenshaw 1989, p. 149).'

13 An example of the presence of this residue is the relatively large percentages of white US Protestants who still support the death penalty. According to the 2014 PRRI American

Values Survey 59 per cent of white evangelical Protestants and 52 per cent of white mainline Protestants support the death penalty, in contrast to 25 per cent support among black Protestants (Jones and Piacenza 2015).

References

Alexander, M. (2010) *The new Jim Crow: Mass incarceration in the age of colorblindness*, New York: New Society.

The Attica Liberation Faction (2011) 'The Attica Liberation Faction manifesto of demands', *Race & Class*, 53(2): pp. 28–35.

Ayers, E. (1985) *Vengeance and justice: Crime and punishment in the 19th century American South*, New York: Oxford University Press.

Blackmon, D. (2008) *Slavery by another name: The re-enslavement of black Americans from the Civil War to World War II*, New York: Doubleday.

Bucknor, C. and Barber, A. (2016) *The price we pay: Economic costs of barriers to employment for former prisoners and people convicted of felonies*, Center for Economic and Policy Research. Available from: http://cepr.net/publications/reports/the-price-we-pay-economic-costs-of-barriers-to-employment-for-former-prisoners-and-people-convicted-of-felonies [accessed 18 May 2017].

Christianson, S. (1998) *With liberty for some: 500 years of imprisonment in America*, Boston, MA: Northeastern.

Chung, J. (2016) *Felony disenfranchisement: A primer*, The Sentencing Project. Available from: www.sentencingproject.org/publications/felony-disenfranchisement-a-primer/ [accessed 15 February 2017].

Crenshaw, K. (1989) 'Demarginalizing the intersection of race and sex: A black feminist critique of antidiscrimination doctrine, feminist theory, and antiracist politics', *University of Chicago Legal Forum, 1989*(1): pp. 139–167.

Disaster Center (2015) *United States crime rates 1960–2015*. Available from: www.disastercenter.com/crime/uscrime.htm [accessed 26 June 2017].

Duff, R. A. (2001) *Punishment, communication, and community*, New York: Oxford University Press.

Durose, M. Cooper, A. and Snyder, A. (2014) *Recidivism of prisoners released in 30 states in 2005: Patterns from 2005 to 2010*, NCJ 24420, Washington, DC: US Department of Justice.

Dwyer, C. (2017) 'Sessions tells prosecutors to seek "most serious" charges, stricter sentences', NPR. Available from: www.npr.org/sections/thetwo-way/2017/05/12/528086525/sessions-tells-prosecutors-to-seek-most-serious-charges-stricter-sentences [accessed 14 May 2017].

George, E. (2010) *A woman doing life: Notes from a prison for women*, New York: Oxford University Press.

Graber, J. (2014) *The furnace of affliction: Prison and religions in antebellum America*, Chapel Hill, NC: University of North Carolina Press.

Harlow, C. W. (2003) *Education and correctional populations*, NCJ 195670, Bureau of Justice Statistics Special Report, Washington, DC: US Department of Justice.

Harvey, D. (2007) *A brief history of neo-liberalism*, New York: Oxford University Press.

Hicks, D. (2011) *Dignity: The essential role it plays in resolving conflict*, New Haven, CT: Yale University Press.

Honderich, T. (2006) *Punishment: the supposed justifications*, rev edn, Ann Arbor, MI: Polity Press.

Hudson v. Palmer (1984) 468 US 517.

Jones R. P. and Piacenza, J. (2015) *Support for death penalty by religious affiliation*, Public Religion Research Institute, Washington, DC. Available from: https://www.prri.org/spotlight/support-for-death-penalty-by-religious-affiliation/. [accessed 17 May 2017].

Kaeble, D. and Glaze, L. (2016) *Correctional populations in the US, 2015,* NCJ 250374, Washington, DC: US Department of Justice.

Kim, K., Becker-Cohen, M. and Serakos, M. (2015) *The processing and treatment of mentally ill persons in the criminal justice system*, Washington, DC: The Urban Justice Institute.

King, M. L. Jr. (1986) 'I have a dream', in J. Washington (ed.), *A testament of hope: The writings and speeches of Martin Luther King, Jr.*, New York: Harper and Row, pp. 217–220.

Laird, L. (2013) 'Ex-offenders face tens of thousands of legal restrictions, bias and limits on their rights', *ABA Journal*. Available from: www.abajournal.com/magazine/article/ex–offenders_face_tens_of_thousands_of_legal_restrictions [accessed 17 October 2015].

McKelvey, B. (1972) *American prisons: A history of good intentions*, Montclair, NJ: Patterson Smith.

McLennan, R. (2008) *The crisis of imprisonment: Protest, politics, and the making of the American penal state, 1776–1941*, New York: Cambridge University Press.

Morris, N. and Rothman, D. (eds) (1995) *The Oxford history of the prison*, New York: Oxford University Press.

National Justice Atlas of Sentencing and Corrections, Justice Mapping Center. Available from: www.justiceatlas.org/ [accessed 15 May 2017].

Nellis, A. (2016) *The color of justice: Racial and ethnic disparity in state prisons*, The Sentencing Project. Available from: www.sentencingproject.org/publications/color-of-justice-racial-and-ethnic-disparity-in-state-prisons/ [accessed 15 May 2017].

Pervear v. Massachusetts (1867) 72 US 475.

The Pew Center on the States 2008, *One in 100 behind bars in America 2008*, Pew Public Safety Performance Project, Washington, DC: The Pew Charitable Trusts.

Pollock, J. (2013) *Prisons and prison life: Costs and consequences*, 2nd edn, New York: Oxford University Press.

Robbins, D. (2015) 'Women's deaths add to concerns about Georgia prison doctor', *Atlanta Journal Constitution*, 17 July. Available from: http://investigations.myajc.com/prison-medicine/womens-deaths-add-concerns/ [accessed 31 December 15].

Rotman, E. (1995) 'The failure of reform: United States, 1865–1965', in N. Morris and D. Rothman (eds), *The Oxford history of the prison*, New York: Oxford University Press, pp. 151–177.

Ruffin v. Commonwealth (1871) 62 VA 790.

Simon, J. (2001) 'Fear and loathing in late modernity', *Punishment and Society*, 3(1): pp. 21–33.

Stevenson, B. (2012) 'We need to talk about an injustice', TED2012. Available from: www.ted.com/talks/bryan_stevenson_we_need_to_talk_about_an_injustice [accessed 1 November 16].

Wacquant, L. (2008) *Urban outcasts: A comparative sociology of advanced marginality*, Malden, MA: Polity Press.

Wacquant, L. (2010) 'Crafting the neoliberal state: Workfare, prisonfare, and social insecurity', *Sociological Forum*, 25(2): pp. 197–220.

Walzer, M. (1983) *Spheres of justice: A defense of pluralism and equality*, New York: Basic Books.

Western, B. (2006) *Punishment and inequality in America*, New York: Russell Sage Foundation.

Whitman, J. (2003) *Harsh justice: Criminal punishment and the widening divide between America and Europe*, New York: Oxford University Press.

Wilkinson, R. (2010) *Texas tough: The rise of American's prison empire*, New York: Metropolitan Press/Henry Holt.

Wilson, W. J. (1987) *The truly disadvantaged: The inner city, the underclass, and public policy*, Chicago, IL: University of Chicago Press.

9

CHALLENGING A NEW FRONTIER OF MARKET MORALITY

The case of sweatshop economics

Keri Day

Sweatshops have found support in some surprising places in recent decades. In 2000, Nicholas Kristof, a columnist for the *New York Times* who often advocates for liberal causes, wrote an essay that offered 'Two cheers for sweatshops' (Kristof and WuDunn 2000). In the essay, Kristof defends sweatshops as a viable route out of poverty for impoverished persons in Two-Thirds World nations. The article received scant attention. It wasn't until 2009, when Kristof wrote another essay in the *Times* defending sweatshops ('Where sweatshops are a dream') that his ideas ignited a wider public debate (Kristof 2009). In both articles, Kristof rejects the idea that sweatshops should be interpreted as exploitative and ethically wrong. He asserts that sweatshops are often charitable responses to complex, contradictory national contexts where individuals experience forms of chronic poverty. Liberal economist and fellow *Times* columnist Paul Krugman, who has spent considerable time critiquing the inequalities of global markets, affirmed Kristof's claim about the positive effects of sweatshops in global contexts that afforded poor people very few opportunities for survival, arguing that sweatshops move millions of workers from abject poverty to something still awful but qualitatively better (Krugman 2013). As Kristof and Krugman show, arguments for sweatshops in poor countries are not limited to political and economic conservatives.

Over the last decade, more and more proponents of 'sweatshop economics' have made the topic an important emerging discourse in the field of economics. Benjamin Powell's *Out of poverty: Sweatshops in the global economy* (2014) has been perhaps the most prominent manifesto in support of sweatshop economics. Powell and other proponents are attempting to bridge the gap between market and morals by offering a new brand of 'market morality' that would acknowledge the import-ance of ethical norms in market processes. Sweatshop economists such as Powell are not justifying their support of sweatshops based on claims of economic efficiency alone. Rather, these economists are also attempting to privilege moral and ethical arguments in defending sweatshops around the world. They claim that their economic argument *is* a moral argument.

This chapter explores and challenges this brand of market morality. It argues against both more conservative free-market economists such as Benjamin Powell and Matt Zwolinski (2007) and more politically liberal economists like Kristof and Krugman, who argue that sweatshops are morally defensible as forms of enlightened compassion within global communities ravaged by chronic poverty. I first review the key economic arguments of sweatshop theorists like Powell who maintain that economic claims for the support of sweatshops are also proper moral concerns. I next explore these theorists' more explicitly ethical and moral arguments, which I understand as a new kind of market morality. I then probe underneath this brand of market morality by discussing and critiquing its particular 'religious' assumptions about the meaning of human life, such as its secular *telos* of material abundance. Finally, I propose that critics of sweatshop economics might rethink their 'moral entry points' when participating in the sweatshop debate.

A moral claim beyond efficiency

Sweatshop economists stress that their claims are something more than amoral arguments about economic efficiency. They insist that their economic arguments for sweatshops reflect moral concerns. These economists want to distinguish themselves from other economists who understand themselves as decoupling economic matters from morality. Instead, sweatshop economists contend that economic efficiency and growth are important *moral* concerns. Economic efficiency, for these theorists, gets reframed as a moral and ethical goal that promotes human thriving. American economist Benjamin Powell provides one of the most important examples of this line of thinking in his recent book, *Out of poverty* (2014).

Powell's claims in defence of sweatshops are undergirded by assumptions that sweatshops lead to greater economic efficiency and growth over the long term – dynamics that, he argues, have moral significance. Powell maintains that sweatshops have an effect that Western advocacy groups often fail to consider: sweatshops actually may provide a considerably better employment option for poor people in developing nations, an option that would be denied if sweatshops were not present. Powell suggests that sweatshops often emerge in parts of the world where chronic poverty and squalid conditions present *no* options for the poor. Although sweatshops are seen as economically exploitative by Western standards, he insists that such jobs actually provide a way for the global poor to earn wages that would not otherwise be possible within their national contexts (Powell 2014, pp. 25–45).

Powell provides a vivid example of the employment options that millions of Two-Thirds World workers often confront. A poor woman in Bangladesh finds herself mired in chronic poverty, caring for her two children. She is faced with three options for work: the agricultural sector, the informal economy as a domestic servant, or some kind of sex work. What these three options have in common is very low pay. And one might argue that the third option further assaults her human dignity. She is locked within a national economy that keeps her perpetually trapped in chronic poverty. Her prospects for work that can bring her out of chronic poverty remain dismal (Powell 2014, pp. 26–30).

However, Powell insists, sweatshop employment provides a unique opportunity for her within her national economic context. While sweatshop employment does not pay high wages by the standards of Europe or the United States, it pays well in relation to the other actual prospects for a woman in the Two-Thirds World. A Bangladeshi woman, for instance, is presented with the opportunity to fare somewhat better through sweatshop employment than she could through any of her other options. Powell's argument, then, is that when a poor woman in a developing nation is able to make $23 per month from working in sweatshops rather than $8 per month (or less) from working in the informal domestic sector, sweatshop employment offers her a significantly better option (Powell 2007, pp. 28–32).

It is important to note that Powell wants to make an ethical distinction between crude, exploitative sweatshops that should *never* be defended and sweatshops that adhere to basic human rights. Powell remarks that sweatshops that coerce persons to work in inhumane conditions should not be supported. In Powell's view, these inhumane conditions would include forcing workers to work long hours of overtime, forcing labourers to meet production quotas despite the possibility of physical injuries, and coercing workers to acquiesce to psychological abuse while working (Powell 2014, pp. 65–67). For Powell, sweatshops that engage in these practices should never be defended because they violate the key foundational principle upon which markets flourish: the right to choice among workers. Instead, the kind of sweatshops Powell envisions being supported are those that honour the basic human rights of workers and offer a choice for workers that competes with and wins over other employment options they face within their developing national economies. Although Powell might seek to grant agency to those who work in sweatshops, I will problematize later in the chapter why his account of choice might be too limiting and even intellectually dishonest.

Economists such as Powell argue that the economic legitimacy of sweatshops must be evaluated from within the national economies in which they are situated rather than assessed by Western standards for fair wages. For example, multinational corporations pay above average wages in Indonesia when those wages are compared to other ways of making a living in the country. Powell contends that this is the relevant measure, that wages and conditions must be evaluated from within Two-Thirds World economies in order to grasp the real opportunities such jobs provide for these workers.

The more liberal Paul Krugman makes a similar case, asserting that sweatshops 'move hundreds of millions of people from abject poverty to something still awful but nonetheless significantly better . . . [so] the growth of sweatshop employment is tremendous good news for the world's poor' (Krugman 2013). In this statement, Krugman wants to emphasize that sweatshop employment is good news for the global poor when considered within their own national economies, which offer them no better options. Western standards of employment should not be applied to employment standards in developing countries. Powell and Krugman want to insist on a contextual hermeneutic for evaluating sweatshop employment. Any economic benefits of sweatshops that might emerge in regions like Southeast Asia and Eastern Europe cannot be compared to the economic contexts of more post-industrial regions like North America and Western Europe. A one-size-fits all argument about sweatshops doesn't work. These economists instead contend that we must think *contextually* about the virtues of humane sweatshops against the backdrop of a developing nation's political economy.

Sweatshop economists such as Powell and Krugman also argue that the support of sweatshops provide long-term economic growth in developing nations. These economists have a specific interpretation of economic history. For them, sweatshops have been central to most industrialized nations' economic growth over the long term. These economists operate with the assumption that poverty is an *a priori* condition that is addressed through industrial processes. Specifically, Powell maintains that arrangements like sweatshops played essential roles in the history of Western economic development (Powell 2014, pp. 15–22). Most Western nations were unable to develop the capital needed to become wealthy nations without the historical presence of sweatshops. The free operation of market forces – even with sometimes painful consequences – helped move Western countries to higher standards of living. While these economists concede that there might be moral complexities associated with sweatshops, they nevertheless believe that they are 'necessary evils' or 'lesser evils' for developing nations to move towards industrialization, wealth and growth in the long-term. This is the path most developed nations followed in the past and it is the path that today's developing nations should also follow to share in the rising standard of living that comes with economic growth.

As a result, Powell argues that Western anti-sweatshop activists actually harm sweatshop labourers when boycotting factories. For example, he notes that when anti-sweatshop activists demand living wages, it leads to potential widespread unemployment, as multi-national corporations feel the only way to remain profitable and pay living wages is to scale down on labourers or take their company to new shores. Because higher wages eat into profit margins, demands to increase wages produce higher rates of unemployment. Anti-sweatshop activists do not suggest ways for wages to increase without causing unemployment. For Powell, this issue isn't merely about economic efficiency or profitability. This issue is an ethical concern as it leads to the unemployment of workers who have extremely poor choices, throwing them back into chronic cycles of deprivation and poverty. Powell wants to maintain that activists have a very strong moral reason to consider how their activism works against the welfare of those workers they purport to advocate for (Powell 2014, p. 20).

When anti-sweatshop activists begin to call upon First World citizens to boycott such corporations, it potentially forces such corporations to take their business to another country or raise their costs to comply with international labour standards. Both of these corporate actions produce one thing: the probability of jobs being cut for poor workers, which forces them back towards other working options that are even more deleterious. Actions to boycott do not automatically lead to the welfare of poor workers, Powell argues. Instead, these activists' actions work *against* the welfare of such workers. Powell believes that anti-sweatshop activists refuse to acknowledge this internal inconsistency in their own moral arguments.

Powell suspects that anti-sweatshop activists overlook this inconsistency due to the nature of their moral reasoning. The problem is that their moral reasoning is primarily deontological. He states, 'Objections to sweatshops grounded in concepts of coercion and exploitation are perhaps most at home within a deontological system of ethics' (Powell and Zwolinski 2011, p. 250). A deontological system of ethics articulates morality in terms of duty, assessing the rightness or wrongness of an action in itself, with only secondary attention paid to the consequences of the action or the character of the actor. Deontological ethics tend to evaluate morality based on universal rules of right or wrong. If an action is wrong in one time or place, it is always wrong. Within this deontological framework, many critics of sweatshops maintain that no matter what contextual factors are present, sweatshops violate the human dignity of persons and are therefore unequivocally unethical. This deontological approach requires that sweatshops are ethically inappropriate and morally wrong across time, space and place. Because such moral reasoning holds that sweatshops are universally wrong, such activists are unable to consider contextual factors that may enable one to evaluate sweatshops in different ways within different national economies. This mode of moral reasoning, Powell argues, does not allow opponents of sweatshops to see the *limits* of their ethical arguments.

The market alone? Interpreting economic history and the role of social policies

Not all economists accept Powell's free-market account of economic history or his low estimation of the ability of social policies to correct economic problems. Within his account of economic history, Powell assumes that poverty is 'natural' and a 'pre-existing' condition. But is this assumption correct? A number of scholars in post-colonial studies, such as Amartya Sen (2000) and Dipesh Chakrabarty (2002), have challenged this assumption by demonstrating that chronic poverty and disparity over the last several centuries have been produced and exacerbated within colonial and neocolonial matrices of capitalist power. So much chronic poverty that is experienced in Two-Thirds World countries is due to the historical legacies of colonialism in which African, Asian, Caribbean and South and Central American countries' resources and lands were conquered and exploited for capitalist gain by nations in the West. Economists such as Daron Acemoglu, Simon Johnson and James Robinson (2002) provide a compelling argument on how British and French colonial legacies affect the resources and institutional settings for future economic development in African countries. Due to colonial legacies, extreme shortages of natural resources and capital have created a severe crisis of deprivation in these nations, intense deprivation that was not present during precolonial eras. These economists also maintain that over the last 500 years, there has been a 'reversal of fortunes', in which non-European nations who were once quite wealthy experienced a reversal of fortunes due to plundering and conquest by European nations, which have now become quite wealthy after rising from centuries of poverty (Acemoglu, Johnson and Robinson 2002).

These colonial histories are exacerbated by new forms of neocolonial slavery in which global economic policies are instituted by the West to further exploit 'under-developed' nations. A number of scholars have documented how supranational economic institutions such as the International Monetary Fund (IMF) and the World Bank keep poor nations in debt and, as a result, in service to Western economic interests (Peet 2009; Harvey 2010). Consider the debt vulnerability that many Two-Thirds World nations endure through globalizing processes. Argentina is an example of how poor countries are encouraged to 'develop' through market forces. In 1991, Argentina was offered an IMF loan package with a commitment that the nation would implement free market models. This loan was to serve as 'transitional funding' on the way to greater economic freedom through free markets. The aggregate impact of the loans and the presence of multinational corporations led to cuts in doctors' and teachers' salaries, education spending and health coverage (such as decreases in social security payments). Moreover, the domestic economy took a tremendous hit as multinational corporations put local businesses out of work, leading to massive poverty rates. In order to foster recovery, in 2004 the Argentine government staged an aggressive plan to improve tax collection among the wealthy and allocated large sums towards social welfare, although it was cautious about its expenditures. The economy began to improve, making Argentina a case study that belies Powell's basic assumptions about how countries develop economically. There is not just one path to development; there are alternatives to free-market models that rely on the presence of sweatshops producing goods primarily for multinational corporations (Conway 2004).

Because unjust systemic relations have produced poverty and economic inequality, another account of economic development has been offered. Economists such as Sen (2000) and Simon Kuznets (1955), for instance, argue that economic development has also happened because of social policies, not just unregulated market forces. Such economists also maintain that sweatshops do not 'naturally' disappear because of development but only after concerted social and political action. These economists have written at length about how organized labour has produced innovation and closed the gap of inequality generated by market forces. Sen, for instance, maintains that in the developed world, the sweatshop phase was not extinguished by market-led forces alone but by economic growth combined with the very kind of social action, or enlightened collective choice, that defenders of sweatshops are currently arguing against. I infer from these economists that Powell's interpretation of economic history distorts the historical record of how nations increase wealth and how sweatshops begin to be replaced by better-paying and more humane options. Economic development and the improvement of employment opportunities are not due to market forces alone but also to social policies that use regulations to correct the ill effects of markets.

These effects include the production of gross inequality. French economist Thomas Piketty's landmark *Capital in the twenty first century* (2014) offers sustained evidence that the share of income and wealth going to those at the very top has risen sharply over the last several decades, returning the world to patterns of inequality that prevailed prior to World War I. For Piketty, the most effective strategies to combat the production of poverty through concentrated wealth have not depended on market mechanisms alone. Rather, combating the economic inequality out of which poverty is (re)produced has involved expanding the terms of public and political debate about the causes of poverty and possible solutions in order to institute policy reform in ensuring that inequality was addressed and remedied (Piketty 2014, pp. 200–245).

Even economists like Simon Kuznets (like Sen, a winner of the Nobel Prize) would find Powell's story of market-led social progress questionable. Kuznets has done much to inspire economists' faith in the power of capitalist development to reduce inequality. He argues that after initially increasing capital in a country, inequality would diminish through the combined effect of economic growth *and* social legislation. For Kuznets, social legislation is as essential as market forces to the sustainability of economic growth and human flourishing. For instance, in a well-known *American Economic Review* article from 1955, Kuznets writes that

> In democratic societies the growing political power of the urban lower-income groups led to a variety of protective and supporting legislation, much of it aimed to counteract the worst effects of rapid industrialization and urbanization and to support the claims of the broad masses for more adequate shares of the growing income of the country.
>
> (Kuznets 1955, p. 17)

Kuznets acknowledges the inequitable effects of capitalism associated with industrialization and urbanization around the world, which necessitated *social policies* to address the economic vulnerability and loss that some groups encountered.

More recent research not only contradicts Powell's theory of economic history but also challenges his claim that sweatshops often have good working conditions. Christopher Blattman and Stefan Dercon (2017) recently wrote about factories in Ethiopia and whether such factories have been the 'better options' that Powell's argument requires. Blattman and Dercon discovered that many who got an industrial job in these factories soon changed their minds. The majority quit within the first several months. Serious injuries and disabilities were doubled for those who took factory jobs. These Ethiopian workers ended up going back to agriculture (the family farm) or selling goods in the market, earning as much money as they did in the factories with better working conditions. This recent research conducted in Ethiopia (a country at the beginning of the industrial process) throws into question many of Powell's basic assumptions about 'humane sweatshops' as an enlightened, compassionate alternative to other forms of employment in Two-Thirds nations (Blattman and Dercon 2017).

Powell's argument also relies on an understanding of worker 'choice' that is inadequate and misleading. His concept of choice does not sufficiently reveal what is at stake for Two-Thirds World workers. Choice is not merely a concept that names personal decisions. Choice is also a category that reveals structural realities. Choice must be seen as both enabled and hindered by systems and structures. Choice does not stand apart from systems but is inextricably linked to social and economic structures. Two-Thirds World workers certainly choose, but choice here is understood in a very limited way. These workers have often been made so desperate by systemic conditions that choice cannot be understood in its fullest democratic sense. Sociologists refer to this constraint of choice as one dimension of the 'structural violence' of unemployment (Galtung 1969, p. 176). Powell generally acknowledges these workers' desperate conditions but refuses to link these conditions to his understanding of choice. One might argue that these workers feel forced into sweatshop employment as their desperate circumstances do not allow them to *fairly choose* from competing options. They are trapped and must take the best situation available to them. This is a far cry from the kind of 'choice' that Powell's argument requires to argue specifically for the morality of sweatshops.

A new kind of market morality and its religious dimensions

Although I have offered critical responses to proponents of sweatshop economics, this new kind of market morality persists because of its moral and religious claims. A major moral claim that Powell makes is that consequentialism is the best form of ethical reasoning in discussing the legitimacy of sweatshops. He contends that we need a consequentialist approach in order to consider multiple end goals when morally evaluating the role of sweatshops in nations. A consequentialist moral approach is not simply utilitarian in nature; rather, this approach considers multiple goods and end goals that enable human flourishing. A consequentialist moral framework, for Powell, allows one to assess the morality of sweatshops based on the outcomes or consequences sweatshops produce. As already discussed, Powell suggests that sweatshops actually offer better options within developing nations that are mired in poverty. In Powell's ethnographic study, workers in sweatshops commented on how sweatshops keep them from being forced into working for extremely low wages in the agricultural sector or the informal economy (Powell 2014). Powell also argues that sweatshops help developing nations accumulate the capital needed to begin the process of industrialization that leads to long-term economic growth. This type of moral reasoning considers multiple goods that potentially lead to flourishing over the long-term for workers and the nations in which they live. This ethical approach then evaluates sweatshops in light of the possibilities, contradictions and complexities they generate.

The major religious claim Powell makes is his identification of capitalist progress and material abundance as 'ultimate concerns'. Powell assumes a *telos* of progress and material abundance when he argues that sweatshops will inevitably generate the kind of long-term economic growth in developing nations that has happened in industrialized nations. This *telos* is accepted uncritically in the sense that it is seen as absolute, inevitable and even *sacred* within capitalist economies. The *telos* of market progress is venerated and worshipped as 'true' and 'good'. It is hard for advocates of sweatshops to entertain the possibility that long-term economic growth and even material abundance may not lead to human flourishing and happiness in the fullest sense. The belief in the absolute goodness of economic growth is the foundation of sweatshop economics and its market morality. And it, too, is something like a religious conviction.

There is no better example of the uncritical acceptance of this sacred *telos* of material abundance than in arguments that the 'creative destruction' of poverty, job losses, ruined companies, vanishing industries and more are all justified as part of economic growth and renewal. In *Capitalism, socialism and democracy*, Austrian economist Joseph Schumpeter contends that there is a paradox to capitalist progress which inevitably involves acknowledging the fact that some people's lives will be worse off (in the short-term or perhaps forever) in order to create new industries and economic opportunities that generate greater profit and economic wealth (Schumpeter 2010, p. 65). For Schumpeter, capitalism naturally destroys previous economic orders (old companies, industries, jobs and whole ways of life) in order to reconfigure old orders into new economic orders marked by the emergence of new companies and industries that are more efficient and profitable, expanding economic wealth and growth. Although Schumpeter argues that creative destruction paradoxically leads to the failure of capitalism itself, neo-liberal economists such as Milton Friedman (1962) and Friedrich Hayek (1944) argue that creative destruction ultimately enables economic growth and sustainability within free market capitalism. By attempting to 'soften' such creative destruction through government regulation, market economists insist that capitalism will be robbed of its efficacy in producing unprecedented wealth and economic growth. Hence, the 'march towards progress' involves a 'creative' destructive force, which is not ultimately negative, for it enables global capitalism to become more efficient (and so more profitable). These are not just religious beliefs. They are theodicies.

The free-market idea of creative destruction sees the deleterious forces of capitalism ultimately as 'creative goods'. Powell and others certainly see sweatshops as part of the process of 'creative destruction'. While marked by lower wages and working conditions compared to the West, sweatshops participate in the generation of capital in order to inaugurate higher levels of economic well-being. Sweatshops also bring foreign investment into developing nations, which is critical for enlarging the economy. As a result, sweatshops might be interpreted as instruments of creative destruction that ensure economic stability over the long-term. For Powell, this is the moral contradiction of sweatshops: they are not the most preferable sites of employment, but they are necessary for nations to move from chronic poverty to an economy that delivers greater wellbeing for its citizens.

Interestingly, Powell never explores how this assumption might be wrong. He treats this assumption as a dogma and as an unalterable *a priori* principle. One could argue that Powell and other advocates overestimate the idea that sweatshops inevitably generate the march towards economic progress and material abundance in poor countries. Sweatshops have been present in parts of Asia, South America and Africa for a long time. Yet many nations in these areas have not necessarily experienced economic development in the ways that free market logic assumes. And, as I argued earlier in this chapter, when they have experienced growth, it has not necessarily been due to sweatshops and other manifestations of an unregulated free market. Rather, what growth has occurred has been due to a mixture of market forces and social policies. This is what advocates of sweatshops miss in their religious zeal to defend sweatshops as inevitably moving poor economies towards progress and abundance.

In addition, the effects of capitalism in human history have often been catastrophic, not simply 'creative'. They have involved depths of destructiveness that cannot reasonably be caught up in any narrative of justification. And those depths often persist, even in fully developed economies. The religious assumptions that undergird sweatshop economics can render invisible the human carnage and large-scale devastation that has resulted from Western economic systems left unchecked. The deepening economic inequality present even among 'developed' nations such as the United States shows one dimension of this destruction. Poverty is still experienced at high levels in the United States and around the world, despite the presence of markets.

Yet, from a teleological perspective, could the 'religious' worldview that Powell and other proponents offer be defended as a kind of advocacy for human dignity within complex economic contexts rather than simply a rationale used to objectify workers for the sake of market profitability? I think this is an important question. This question about the sacredness of human dignity and human choice is important for Powell. Within poor economies, poor workers are often called upon to exercise their agency and dignity within unfavourable conditions. At the heart of Powell's focus on human choice is a larger teleological question about human dignity, which might be construed more broadly as a religious question about human meaning and flourishing. In other words, one might contend that Powell's notion of 'ultimate concern' includes taking into account how poor workers of the Global South exercise agency and dignity within imperfect conditions.

Certainly, I am ascribing a religious character to the arguments of sweatshop defenders, recognizing that I understand their arguments to be religious in a broad sense of the term. I think this is an important observation, however, as scholars of theology and religion might not discern the moral and religious nature of Powell's arguments. Many theologians and religious scholars assume that Powell and other economists are simply making *economic* arguments, void of moral or religious content. On one level, they are indeed making economic arguments. Yet, these arguments are grounded in a much broader sacred worldview about the meaning of life and our place in the universe as moral agents. And it is at this level that theologians and scholars of religious studies can make their most important contributions to discussions of the ethics of sweatshops.

By entering into this conversation on sweatshop economics, theologians and religionists can contribute, in nuanced ways, to the moral dimensions of this debate. They might question why Powell and others do not substantively consider power relations in the construction of sweatshops around the world. They might acknowledge the complexities of Two-Thirds World poverty that make sweatshop employment an attractive option to some workers yet fail to question why these 'complexities' exist in the first place. Historical colonial legacies and structural inequities continue to intensify and exacerbate situations in which sweatshops are present. Theological and religious scholars might, in more nuanced ways, debunk the narrative of progress that informs the case that Powell makes. They might question the identification of material abundance and economic growth with well-being and happiness for citizens (it remains interesting that the United States, a wealthy, 'developed' nation, is one of the most unhappy and highly medicated countries in the world). These are not just questions of economics, but of religion, of *faith*. Scholars of theology and religion can bring their particular expertise to bear in arguing against the religious worldview that undergirds moral defences of sweatshop economics.

Reinventing moral 'entry points' into the sweatshop debates

With these insights in mind, critics of the new market morality must reinvent how they enter into the moral debate on sweatshops. In much of the rhetoric and activism of anti-sweatshop groups, there is a dismissal of the kind of questions Powell (and other defenders of sweatshop economics) raise. In order to provide more nuanced moral and theological arguments against sweatshops, critics must detail the limits of the claims that sweatshop economics rest upon. I would like to focus on three potential weaknesses of Powell's arguments. Critics of this new market morality might enter into the sweatshop debate by points like these three.

First, theological and religious scholars might challenge whether consequentialist reasoning is the most appropriate moral theory in assessing sweatshops. Powell certainly believes that consequentialism is the best form of ethical reasoning that considers how to achieve multiple moral ends and outcomes. Consequentialism avoids one kind of universal claim when making moral decisions (i.e. condemning sweatshops as always morally unethical across time, space and place). However, there are a number of ethical and religious traditions that provide other forms of moral reasoning that are as appropriate or even better than consequentialism.

For instance, Christian theologies have for centuries stressed the significance of virtues for moral reasoning (Herdt 2012; Gregory 2010) – sometimes above or against the significance of consequences. For virtue ethics, what is commended as morally right is not simply what achieves some particular set of external outcomes. Rather, virtue ethics considers how our actions cultivate moral character and virtue within the moral agent. Virtue ethics does not first ask what is the right action (universal rule) or desired outcome. Instead, virtue ethics asks what kind of community and individuals we aspire to *be*. The question of 'who we aspire to be' is important, as it emphasizes an ethics of neighbour care that is not necessarily oriented towards the ends of market logic. Virtue ethics maintains that only virtuous agents can act in virtuous or ethical ways. The emphasis is on how we develop ourselves as moral agents first before we are able to discern what is fitting and morally right. Virtue ethics moral theory asks: How should I live? What is the good life? How does this good life extend to social values?

A virtue ethics framework reveals some of the most acute limits of sweatshop economics. While sweatshop economics addresses consequentialist considerations such as increasing GDP and offering a wage that allows a poor worker to survive, it nevertheless situates moral value and moral formation within a logic of exchange. For instance, Powell argues against laws that would ban sexual harassment against women within sweatshops. He does not see sexual harassment as *morally* problematic enough to engender laws for the protection of vulnerable women. Instead, Powell speaks about sexual harassment in economic terms, as he sees this as one reason why poor female workers may opt to quit a sweatshop job in favour of another job. This move would hurt the bottom line of the corporation where the female employee quit. He argues that 'Laws that effectively eliminate sexual harassment would lower wages', because they would reduce the risk of women leaving the jobs and so the price they have to be paid to stay in them (Powell 2014, p. 69). He also argues that legislating against sexual harassment would hinder multinational corporations from maximizing profits, as such laws discourage companies from investing in countries with these laws (Powell 2014, p. 69). He believes that the threat of a female worker quitting is enough to potentially curb or limit sexual harassment in corporations. In contrast to a virtue ethics framework, Powell's consequentialism does not seem concerned with the ethical implications of his argument: sweatshop economics does not prioritize agents who are morally shaped by trust, mutuality and respect. Instead, such values are optional and subsidiary to the bottom line of profits and a narrow account of economic well-being. In other words, the 'utility' of such laws is in direct relationship to how well these laws can meet market goals.

Virtue ethics foregrounds a different kind of *value*. Powell sees the value of workers according to a logic of exchange. In terms of the worker, he is using an instrumental type of value. But there are different types of value other than instrumental value. I would maintain the intrinsic value of workers as ends in themselves, rather than workers as an instrumental value towards the ends of market profit. The question 'Who do we aspire to *be* as moral agents?' within virtue ethics is about how we assess the value of human beings as moral agents.

Virtue ethics substantively considers the intrinsic value of the worker and therefore the importance of ethical standards such as laws and codes against sexual harassment, as we must also cultivate societal contexts in which individuals experience care, safety, trust and respect. Workers are not just to be used instrumentally towards market goals, even if profits would be hypothetically higher through ignoring important laws. There are a plethora of examples of how multinational corporations associated with sweatshops displace millions of poor persons around the world in order to exploit land and natural resources (Roy 2015). These inhumane actions are morally legitimate within Powell's consequentialist line of reasoning because he does not see workers and people of the Global South as having intrinsic value and as ends apart from the market. Acknowledging workers as ends in themselves rather than means to other ends – even the end of their own 'improvement' – matters to the moral argument about sweatshops. Powell completely ignores this crucial issue.

A second limit theologians and religious studies scholars might foreground is the internal inconsistency within Powell's own moral reasoning. Powell argues against deontological claims that are applied to every culture and context. But he is making just this kind of claim about the efficacy of markets. For him, free market principles can be universally applied within any developing national context. No matter what economic circumstances developing countries might face, Powell treats market forces as rules that simply need to be used in order to experience inevitable economic growth. As a result, this market ideology provides no room to explore the limits of market logic in poor nations. Although Powell wants to jettison universalizing logics when speaking of sweatshops, he operates with this logic in order to legitimize the existence of sweatshops.

I think lifting up this internal inconsistency is crucial. This observation leads to an important question: what might it mean to assess sweatshops in less ideological and more empirical ways, acknowledging the ways in which some factories may contribute to poor people's survival without assuming that sweatshops are necessary in the universal and inevitable march towards progress? Powell operates with universalizing claims about the efficacy of sweatshops because he leaves unquestioned the belief that markets secure the march towards economic progress for poor nations. However, liberationist theologies have done well in questioning such uncritical market logic, demonstrating the failure of the free-market's promise of progress. Black liberation, womanist and postcolonial theologies have mapped how markets have been detrimental to people of colour around the world (Day 2012).

Finally, while Powell's market morality provides analysis of the present complexities associated with sweatshops, it doesn't provide a blueprint of a future beyond what we possess now. This is an important point because Powell's arguments foreclose the power of imagination in relation to global economics. Moral imagination matters to how we think about our future as human beings. What do we lose by simply acquiescing to the logic that sweatshops are the cure to poverty? Powell claims that economic options outside of free market logic are 'utopian'. However, the idea that articulating preferable futures or 'utopias' is naïve and unrealistic undercuts the power of *any* moral argument, as we need visions of better worlds by which to measure our present social realities. Sweatshop economics operates with an 'either/or' logic in which sweatshops are seen as the realistic alternative over against 'economic utopias', which are seen as the unrealistic and irresponsible alternative. However, it's not a zero-sum game. Moral imagination allows one to hold these two polarities in tension, refusing to allow one to cancel the other out.

Economists Amartya Sen and Joseph Stiglitz have written at length about how we might employ moral imagination in relation to global economics. Sen developed the 'capability approach', which redefines the idea of economic development. For Sen, economic development is not merely about increasing GDP, since increasing economic wealth in a nation may not lead to greater well-being for the entire population. Social, political and economic barriers and inequities may impede such wealth from being shared by all. Sen describes development as 'human development', which is based upon what each person is capable of doing and *being*. The poor not only need to possess central capabilities such as adequate economic resources to secure shelter, food, medical care and more, but also need to have cultural resources such as freedom and social respect to actualize themselves as free persons. In the case of sweatshops, Sen might be ambivalent about justifying sweatshops on *moral* grounds, as they do not provide economic and cultural capabilities for the poor to flourish in this fuller sense.

This idea of self-actualization is an important *moral* question, and it requires us to ask how economic arrangements might enable poor people not only to survive but also to thrive. Powell might make a case for how sweatshops may help the poor to survive in certain parts of the world, but he fails to prove that sweatshops enable the poor to *thrive*. His claim that sweatshops enable poor workers to climb 'out of poverty' mistakes survival for thriving. I have written at length about the concept of thriving, which offers sustainable economic and cultural resources that allow the poor to live beyond the bare minimum (Day 2015). Moreover, the idea that sweatshops enable the poor to climb out of poverty is inconclusive and intellectually dishonest when it presents itself as certain. This claim is undermined by the cycles of deprivation that plague poor countries around the globe, disproportionately affecting women and children. However, Powell doesn't allow for us to imagine how we might think outside of the 'sweatshop box'. His profound lack of imagination prevents more robust conversations on how we might foster self-actualization and thriving through economic arrangements. In fact, his universalizing assumption that sweatshops are essential to economic growth closes this kind of imaginative thinking down before it can begin.

The goal of self-actualization requires that we exercise moral imagination about what social worlds might be possible out of which to thrive. The real and ideal can be held together, even if this relationship is one of tension and ambiguity. This question of being or self-actualization provides an opportunity for religious and theological perspectives. For example, Christian theologies are invested in questions of self-actualization and flourishing, as I have somewhat already discussed. Virtue ethics is concerned with empowering moral agents to cultivate themselves in order to flourish as a community. Moral imagination is a key ingredient to interpreting and embodying the good life. Moreover, Christian feminist theologians have written at length about the need for moral imagination in how we think about our political and socio-economic spheres, as this imaginative action is central to human liberation (Brubaker 1994; Jarl 2000). Without these imaginative acts, the oppressed will remain locked within inequitable structures.

The three limits I have raised merely begin a conversation about how defenders of this new market morality can be challenged. These three limits of sweatshop economics point to the need for critics to have more nuanced, complex and imaginative arguments in light of sweatshop defenders' claims. We need to speak of hope and a new vision of global economy. We must join this conversation in new and fresh ways.

References

Acemoglu, D., Johnson, S. and Robinson, J. (2002) 'Reversal of fortune: Geography and institutions in the making of the modern world income distribution', *Quarterly Journal of Economics*, 117(4): 1231–1294.

Blattman, C. and Dercon, S. (2017) 'Everything we knew about sweatshops was wrong', *New York Times*, 27 April. Available from: www.nytimes.com/2017/04/27/opinion/do-sweatshops-lift-workers-out-of-poverty.html?_r=0 [accessed 27 April 2017].

Brubaker, P. (1994) *Women don't count: The challenge of women's poverty to Christian ethics*, Oxford: Oxford University Press

Chakrabarty, D. (2002) *Habitations of modernity: Essays in the wake of subaltern studies*, Chicago, IL: University of Chicago Press.

Conway, E. (2004) 'IMF admits mistakes in Argentina crisis', *The Telegraph*, 30 July. Available from: www.telegraph.co.uk/finance/2891368/IMF-admits-mistakes-in-Argentina-crisis.html [accessed 15 May 2017].

Day, K. (2012) *Unfinished business: Black women, the black church, and the struggle to thrive in America*, Maryknoll, NY: Orbis Books.

Day, K. (2015) *Religious resistance to neoliberalism: Womanist and black feminist perspectives*, New York: Palgrave MacMillan.

Friedman, M. (1962) *Capitalism and freedom*, Chicago, IL: University of Chicago Press.

Galtung, J. (1969) 'Violence, peace, and peace research', *Journal of Peace Research*, 6(3): 167–191.

Gregory, E. (2010) *Politics and the order of love: An Augustinian ethic of democratic citizenship*, Chicago, IL: University of Chicago Press.

Harvey, D. (2010) *The enigma of capital and the crisis of capitalism*, Oxford: Oxford University Press.

Hayek, F. (1944) *The road to serfdom: Texts and documents*, London: Routledge.

Herdt, J. (2012) *Putting on virtue: The legacy of the splendid vices*, Chicago, IL: University of Chicago Press.

Jarl, A. (2000) *Women and economic justice: Ethics in feminist liberation theology and feminist economics*, Philadelphia, PA: Coronet Books.

Kristof, N. (2009) 'Where sweatshops are a dream', *New York Times*, 14 January. Available from: www.nytimes.com/2009/01/15/opinion/15kristof.html [accessed 5 October 2017].

Kristof, N. and WuDunn, C. (2000) 'Two cheers for sweatshops', *New York Times Magazine*, 24 September. Available from: www.nytimes.com/2000/09/24/magazine/two-cheers-for-sweatshops.html [accessed 5 October 2017].

Krugman, P. (2013), 'Safer sweatshops', *New York Times*, 8 July. Available from: http://krugman.blogs.nytimes.com/2013/07/08/safer-sweatshops/ [accessed 5 October 2017].

Kuznets, S. (1955) 'Economic growth and income inequality', *The American Economic Review*, 45(1): 1–28.

Peet, R. (2009) *The unholy trinity: The IMF, the World Bank, and WTO*, New York: Zed Books.

Piketty, T. (2014) *Capital in the twenty-first century*, Boston, MA: Belknap Press.

Powell, B. (2007) *Making poor nations rich: Entrepreneurship and the process of economic development*, Stanford, CA: Stanford Economic and Finance.

Powell, B. (2014) *Out of poverty: Sweatshops in the global economy*, Cambridge, MA: Cambridge University Press.

Powell, B. and Zwolinski, M. (2011) 'The ethical and economic case against sweatshop labor: a critical assessment', *Journal of Business Ethics, 107*(4): 449–472. Available from: Springer Science + Business Media, www.benjaminwpowell.com/scholarly-publications/journal-articles/powell-and-zwolinski-the-ethical-and-economic-case-against-sweatshop-labor.pdf [accessed 5 October 2017].

Roy, A. (2015) *Field notes on democracy: Listening to grasshoppers*, Chicago, IL: Haymarket Books.

Schumpeter, J. (2010) *Capitalism, socialism, and democracy*, New York: Routledge.

Sen, A. (2000) *Development as freedom*, New York: Anchor Books.

Zwolinski, M. (2007) 'Sweatshops, choice, and exploitation', *Business Ethics Quarterly, 17*(4): 689–727.

10

WAGE AGAINST THE MACHINE

Wage activism, worker justice and disruptive
Jesus in the age of advanced capitalism

C. Melissa Snarr

'There are two kinds of power: organized money and organized people'. In the
world of faith-based community organizing (FBCO), this mantra undergirds a theory
of politics and political change.[1] Whether an organization is a direct inheritor of
Saul Alinsky or not, organizers emblazon his declaration on slides and explicate it
as part of trainings in church basements across the United States (Alinsky 1989).
Yet in these Alinsky-influenced traditions, not all forms of organized people are
equal. FBCOs continually question advocacy and mobilizing models that focus
primarily on elite leadership, temporary activation, or narrow self-interest. Con-
vincing a politician to introduce a bill, gathering folks for a rally, or even achieving
a desired outcome for one constituency does not necessarily define success. In this
view, the renewal of democracy and ongoing attention to real community needs
is sustained only by continued development of place-based relationships that build
grass-roots leaders who seek to solve community problems themselves through political action. Federations of local institutions – such as congregations, schools, unions
and local non-profits – provide stable vehicles for building these relationships and
constructing a 'common-life politics' (Bretherton 2014, p. 133). Without this work,
even seemingly coordinated people can be easily absorbed by state or market
apparatuses and surrender their political power. To avoid this, many a FBCO meeting involves asking three pragmatic questions: (a) Is an issue winnable? (b) Does
it build power? and (c) Does it develop leaders?

Whether or not one adopts the FBCO model, these three questions press us to
understand and strategize, in an age of widening economic inequality, towards forms
of resistance that build long-term political and economic power for non-elites. These
questions are particularly important because, as theorists of advanced capitalism
note, the rampant expansion and intertwining of both economic markets and the
nation state has resulted in a depoliticizing conversion of citizens to consumers and
clients. Here, I do not mean depoliticization as the loosening of political party

identification, but rather as the undervaluing and undermining of non-elite people's power to develop, contest and resist the norms and practices governing the distribution of resources in their communities (Elliott 2009, p. 250). Robust democratic contestation and contention is replaced by a technocratic approach to expert management of markets and public policy.

As a result of this depoliticization, even 'activism' can devolve into coordinated requests for better compensatory measures from the state (e.g. increases in food stamps, unemployment and earned income tax credits) rather than vigorous moral discussions and actions that reconstruct the practices and assumptions of our current political economy. Thus, the coordinated power of the state and corporations in advanced capitalism poses challenges for activists, both in mobilizing resistance and moving towards real economic justice and transformation. As the state's legitimacy increasingly relies on mitigating the deleterious effects of capitalism, while also supporting its expansion, activists must be careful not to get caught in the cycle of small compensatory gestures that ultimately do not address the grave inequalities in our political economy.

In this chapter, I draw on fieldwork in religiously informed worker justice movements to identify lessons from the creative activism of religious actors and organizations for economic justice in advanced capitalism. Carefully observing their work brings greater depth to theoretical reflections on the current political economy and also helps those of us in the Christian tradition reinvigorate a strain of resistance that has long resided in our faith communities. Taking seriously the challenges of advanced capitalism, I describe and affirm wage activism that does at least three things: (1) reclaims citizenry while resisting clientism; (2) builds bridges to counter interest-group isolation and (3) pluralizes politics to challenge political monism. I also contend that this activism draws, both explicitly and implicitly, on a key interpretive strain of the Christian tradition that reclaims Jesus and the Christian gospel as rejecting empire-based patron–client dynamics in favor of a discipleship where non-elites become co-creators of a more equitable community. Through this kind of transformed imaginary and practice, we may be able to find leverage for change even in ubiquitous advanced capitalism.

Religion and early wage activism in the United States

But first, we are helped by remembering how the changing dynamics of capitalism have birthed and also constrained various forms of wage activism and how religion has been intertwined with this activism. The first wave of minimum wage/living wage activism and legislation in the United States at the turn of the twentieth century relied heavily on religious themes, resources and activists. With the rise of the Industrial Revolution came the decline of independent craftspeople and the consolidation of workers into a system of differentiated labor with hourly wages. New industrial forms also produced enormous suffering and frustration for wage earners who could no longer provide for their families and thus reluctantly sent their wives and young children into the mills and factories (Glickman 1999).

At the turn of the nineteenth century, industrial workers themselves began to criticize the Gilded Age alignment of capitalists and the church and began to articulate a 'social gospel' even before prominent ministers and theologians such as Walter Rauschenbusch championed their cause (Carter 2015, p. 5). As historian Heath Carter documents, these labor reformers began to argue explicitly against 'great chain of being' arguments that claimed everyone was assigned by God to a particular position in society and that respect for this divine ordering enabled peace and relative prosperity for all (ibid., p. 39). Aligning themselves with the growing labour movement, these workers rejected the patronage model of wealthy industrialists who funded prominent churches and charities while claiming divine ordering or blaming workers themselves for their own poverty (e.g. because of excessive drinking, laziness, etc.). In one of his blistering labour newsletter editorials, Andrew Cameron opined, 'Poverty exists because those who sow do not reap; because the toiler does not receive a just and equitable proportion of the wealth which he produces' (ibid., p. 39).

Cameron and many other labor activists also connected this criticism of the political economy with the mission of Christ. After the conviction of the Haymarket anarchists in 1886, letters to the editor flooded Chicago's labor papers claiming that just as Jesus, the carpenter, had attempted to reform the world and had been nailed to the cross for it, the Haymarket Seven were also 'martyrs for the cause of the laboring classes' (ibid., p. 74). While certainly there were labor activists who rejected any religious association, the birth of the Progressive Era entailed a great struggle within many Christian churches about how they would understand and practice the gospel in relation to the working class.

In many ways, worker justice activists were calling their denominations and churches to reclaim a legacy of resistance that could be traced back to the early Christian community's resistance to the Roman Empire, particularly in its challenge to the patronage system. As contemporary biblical scholars attest, social and political relationships in the Roman Empire were constructed through a patron–client system where wealthy patrons, seeking honor, prestige and service, took on less powerful clients for whom the patron would provide things like legal and economic protection (Saller 2002). Defined by inequitable but reciprocal relationships between two parties, patrons and clients connected through key brokers. In an agrarian society with almost no middle class, the majority peasant class bore the burden of supporting the upper classes and the state while wealth was concentrated in few hands (Crossan 1991, p. 43). As contemporary scholar John Dominic Crossan argues, rather than replicating the patron–client system of the Roman Empire, Jesus and the early church rejected this paradigm by preaching and enacting a 'brokerless Kingdom' (ibid., p. 225). The open table fellowship of Jesus and his advocacy for a 'kingdom of nobodies' undid hierarchies among female and male, poor and rich, and Gentile and Jew (ibid., p. 262). Although the worker activists at the turn of the twentieth century were no longer in an agrarian economic system, they were reclaiming this historical Jesus who rejected the inequitable patronage system that sustained the political economy.

Decades of this kind of activism laid the foundation for a 'pro-labor faith' that animated many Christian churches eventually to become 'crucial players in the New Deal coalition' (Carter 2015, p. 179). By the time Franklin Delano Roosevelt introduced minimum wage legislation in 1938, prominent religious voices like Harry Ward and, particularly, Father John Ryan, had already laid out sophisticated Christian ethical arguments for the necessity of a 'sustenance wage' or 'family wage' and joined labor activists like Samuel Gompers in calling for national changes (Ryan 1996, p. 115).

Changing capitalism and the revival of wage activism

Religious persons and institutions were also influential in the rise of the second major living wage movement in the United States (Snarr 2011). Birthed in the mid-1990s from a FBCO coalition of black congregations in Baltimore, Baltimoreans United in Leadership Development (BUILD) led the first successful grassroots campaign for a municipal living wage ordinance. This was an ordinance that required all direct and contracted city employees to be paid a wage that would elevate a family of four above the federal poverty line. Much like labor and religious leaders at the turn of the century, BUILD members founded the campaign on grassroots insights into the plight of workers. Specifically, congregants and their pastors noticed more people who were working full-time were seeking food and rental assistance at their churches. These workers' wages simply could not match their most basic needs.

But unlike the living wage activists of old, BUILD's research into the source of these low wage jobs led the activists directly into one of the shifting dynamics of 'advanced' capitalism: the state, as an increasing protagonist of economic investment, was also the source of this new working poverty. For as capitalism developed, the state itself became a primary driver of economic development as businesses became reliant on state interventions and contracts that had little relation to the 'free market'. We saw this unfolding in downtown redevelopment strategies across the United States during the 1980s and 1990s. Federally funded 'urban renewal' programs under President Reagan initially offered interest-free grants for private redevelopment in urban areas, but after these programs ceased in 1987, municipalities began to embrace varied forms of tax incentives, bonds and subsidies to private companies willing to redevelop blighted downtown areas (Luce 2004a, p. 19).

Many cities, like Baltimore, focused much of their funds on creating new tourist destinations that would provide initial jobs through construction, ongoing employment through the hospitality/service industries and an expanded tax base. But like so many other cities, even after extending nearly 2 billion dollars in subsidies for downtown redevelopment in the late 1980s, the poverty rate in Baltimore continued to climb, and full-time workers were showing up at church charities (Levine 1987). Seeing this contradiction in their city, these religious activists pursued the first phase of their FBCO organizing model – developing research action teams – and identified a key source of the problem: the city itself was undermining wage rates by supporting low-bid government contracts, tax abatements and other subsidies to private firms that paid workers at or barely above minimum wage. The city was also outsourcing government jobs such as janitorial and food service positions, which had been unionized and received higher wages, to external low-wage employment agencies. Although Baltimore politicians bragged about the new jobs created by urban renewal, these new jobs were, on the whole, low-wage with few benefits. The cycle of working poverty had been deepened in Baltimore by the city itself.

In 1993, clergy and laity involved in BUILD attacked this contradiction when they joined forces with the federal and state employees' union, AFSCME, to create a 'Social Compact' campaign during the city's $165 million bond drive to renovate the Baltimore convention center. With clergy in collars and stoles and parishioners joining union members in singing hymns such as 'We Shall Not Be Moved', this new coalition demanded, in press conferences and council meetings, that any development funded by public subsidies had to offer quality jobs that included training and higher wages. Eventually this campaign expanded to demand that all businesses with city contracts pay their workers a 'living wage'. Within this new framing, the coalition highlighted the fact that the federal minimum wage was now a poverty wage and workers needed a *living* wage, not just minimum wage, to sustain a family with dignity.

As I have written previously, scholars analyzing Baltimore's living wage campaign concluded that religious activism was key to the campaign's success (Fine 2001; Figart 2004; Snarr 2011). Union leaders and clergy stood side by side in the campaign; the religiously grounded moral voice of BUILD and its broad-based network of congregational support were vital for the coalition. In fact, when a local newspaper reporter aggressively questioned a BUILD activist about his involvement in the labor and religion alliance, hinting he might be 'a union puppet', the activist declared emphatically, 'It is the church's traditional role, its prophetic calling [and] if anyone has any problems with it, let them take it up with our chief organizer, Jesus Christ' (Fine 2001, p. 65). Activists explicitly claimed the historical Jesus who disrupted empire and dominant power as the cornerstone of their activism.

By December of 1994, BUILD's and AFSCME's religion-labor alliance not only passed a municipal living wage ordinance in Baltimore but also laid the foundation for the emergence of a national living wage movement, which eventually spread to over 200 cities and countries across the nation over the next two decades. While the late-twentieth-century movement certainly shared a family resemblance to its early-twentieth-century sibling, the changing nature of capitalism also changed the kind of activism required. By the end of the century, activists no longer primarily appealed to the state for intervention in external market dynamics. Rather, BUILD and the new living wage movement had to confront the state as itself a propagator of economic markets and inequality.

From wage activism to worker justice movements

In paying close attention to this shift in activism over the course of the century, the living wage movement helps us see the complex realities of advanced capitalism while also providing insight into the opportunities and temptations of current wage activism. In order to build non-elite moral and political agency, the best of this movement reminds us to avoid activism that minimizes participation in governance, encourages narrow interest-group politics, settles for a singular conception of the political sphere, accepts the dominant narrative about the natural order of the political economy and domesticates the disruptive nature of the gospel. This is important because certain forms of wage activism could just serve to cover capitalism's contradictions with demands for what amount to short-term compensatory measures. Instead, wage activism is best embedded in a broader worker justice movement that seeks to reclaim citizenry, build bridges, pluralize the political, shift frames and include a more radical (as in 'going to the root') theology. This is not easy activism but it is the expansive organizing necessary to challenge the ubiquitous reality of advanced capitalism and its adverse effects on non-elite workers.

Exposing advanced capitalism

As the Baltimore case and the larger municipal living wage movement demonstrate, the realities of capitalism have shifted significantly over the last century. Critical theorists name this new phase of the political economy 'advanced' capitalism because it is constituted by an increased concentration of power in multi-national corporations alongside the emergence of state intervention to stabilize business cycles and compensate citizens for the most painful consequences of capitalist markets. In this arrangement, the state benefits from taxes provided by the economy, helps tame volatile business cycles through fiscal, investment and trade policies, and manages the 'dysfunctional secondary effects' of private production on citizens through things like unemployment benefits, food stamps and wage floors (Rhoads 2010, pp. 106–108). The proper management of this balance – by the state – which blunts the conflicts between capital and labor – is crucial in maintaining the state's legitimacy (Habermas 1975).

In this system, large business interests coordinate with each other and the state in order to regulate the market, concentrate power and wealth and then compensate an electorate adequately enough to avoid class conflict and legitimation crises. The invisibility of this symbiotic dance between the state and the economy produces the illusion of the free market in advanced capitalism. Religious leaders in FBCO coalitions regularly disrupt this illusion and challenge the small compensatory measures of the state that do little for non-elites while mostly protecting the state from a legitimation crisis. As Arnie Graf, the East Coast director of the Industrial Areas Foundation (the larger FBCO network to which BUILD belongs), explains, 'We came to realize that we could not subsidize our way out of the crisis. And why did we need so much subsidy? Why do people who are working every day need this subsidy in order to send their kids to school or buy a home? We had to get to the root of it. We had to deal with people's work and wages' (Fine 2001, p. 64). Through this kind of analysis, the living wage movement exposes some of the contradictions of advanced capitalism and attempts to mount a challenge to it.

Reclaiming citizenry

But to do this work, FCBOs also have to counter the power of advanced capitalism to erode citizenship by socializing us into primary identities of consumer (in the ✓ economy) and client (of the state). Reclaiming more robust citizenship for non-elites requires resisting this clientism, a model of narrow political engagement that consists of the 'proffering of material goods in return for electoral support' (Stokes 2009, p. 605). The more powerful politician thus becomes the patron of the less powerful citizen-as-client in material exchange for their vote. In a patron-client relationship, the client is never invited into the governance structure itself, except by a vote, and their only real protest is the withholding of that vote.

What is dominant in clientism is organized money, which is strategically deployed to ensure mass loyalty from passive clients. Sadly, while loyalty to the state is often encouraged (e.g. through nationalism or general political ideology), ongoing conscientization and participation in fulsome governance is not. Critical theorist Jürgen Habermas contends this is necessary because 'genuine participation of citizens in the processes of political will-formation . . ., that is substantive democracy, would bring to consciousness the contradiction between administratively socialized production and the continued private appropriation and use of surplus value' (Habermas 1975, p. 36). Thus, citizenry becomes increasingly passive as voters enjoy the 'right to withhold acclamation' (e.g. 'vote the bums out') but possess very little influence on the particulars of political administration (ibid., p. 37).

Even the state's compensations for seeming economic misfortunes often expand the regulatory role of the state in people's lives and thus transform their identities. Heightened monitoring by the state ensues, particularly for those enrolled in means-tested anti-poverty programs: 'Do you have any drug charges? Who resides in your house? What groceries do you purchase? Are you working in the underground economy?' This disciplinary surveillance can undo the agency of citizens, turning them into clients or, ultimately, wards of the state. Monitored lives make protest even more difficult.

Because so many low-wage workers in the United States are recent refugees or immigrants (many undocumented), invoking citizenship as essential to resistance to advanced capitalism may seem like a limiting approach. But I invoke this term purposely to challenge its narrow application. As political theologian Luke Bretherton helpfully notes, we can think of citizenship in at least five major ways. Citizenship can be conceived as a legal status, as a mode of participation in a legitimating system that determines who can and how one might govern, as membership in an imagined community, as a performance of a political vision and as a form of collective political and moral rationality (Bretherton 2014, pp. 4–5). While popular definitions of citizenship often focus solely on the legal status and legitimating/voting dimensions, we are better served by a broader understanding of citizenship that emphasizes the ongoing navigation of our common lives and common fates. As Bretherton states, citizenship is not just about 'possessing a set of rights but about having the capacity and virtues necessary to relate to and act with others in diverse ways and settings' (ibid., p. 5). Viewed this way, then, not having the correct legal status does not foreclose 'responsibility for and contribut[ion] to the life together and commonwealth of where [people] live' (ibid.).

BUILD's religious activists understood the importance of resisting clientism and embracing this more robust understanding of citizenship. They sought to build alternative identity and power in advanced capitalism, both by strengthening their membership training internally and joining forces with labor unions to pass, even before the start of the living wage campaign, a 'right to organize' ordinance that would void any city contracts for companies who fired workers for organizing (Quigley 2001). This alternative frame was clearly declared at the launch of the new low-wage worker organization, Solidarity, which was sponsored by the religion-labor alliance. Rev. Vernon Dobson, a local Baptist minister and civil rights leader, stated with prophetic passion their refusal to acquiesce to state and corporate dominance: 'The church is going to protect these workers. I have a message for employers – people who are upset because they don't want to pay workers more money . . . who don't want workers to organize. You keep your hands off these people because they are children of God' (Fine 2001, p. 67). In proclaiming their status as children of God and protection by the church, Rev. Dobson established an alternative identity and entity that would challenge the reduction of non-elites to their 'proper' places in the social order; he would reclaim more fulsome citizenship.

The claiming of this ground enables religious activists to ask pointed questions of experts representing state and corporate interests who argued that redevelopment policies would eventually build a larger tax base, bring new residents and thus increase wages for everyone. Living wage activists asked, 'When would that be? Who is really benefitting from revitalization, and in what proportions?' By actually asking these questions – and constructing their own answers – BUILD declared that the analysis of everyday persons mattered. Ultimately, BUILD's grassroots research drove a counter-narrative to official state discourse by focusing on *who* was sacrificing (mostly Black and Latina women) and interrogating the *kind* of growth really occurring.

Lessons from the wage activism movement underscore the importance of depth and quality in worker organizing. While activists may celebrate quick legislative victories won without extensive grassroots efforts, political scientist Stephanie Luce's study of 52 municipal living wage campaigns shows that the strongest ordinance implementation – the key to real change – coincided with a depth of organizing related to the original passage of the legislation (2004b). For example, even after the policy victory in passing a living wage law, Baltimore activists noticed that its implementation was weak. In response, they called upon the Solidarity Sponsoring

Committee, the low-wage workers' rights organization formed during the campaign. They utilized this organization to send members out to bus yards to see whether workers were receiving their wages. Finding discrepancies, they began a massive complaint filing process with the Wage Commission (Luce 2005, p. 87). The Hotel Employees and Restaurant Employees' (HERE) union soon followed and forced Aramark to pay back wages (ibid.). In other cities, like Boston, community organizations fought for accountability in the form of permanent seats on living wage advisory committees.

This depth of organizing begins to transform wage activism into a worker justice movement and also has resonance in the birth of 'worker centers' across the nation, which have been heavily sponsored by religiously informed organizations such as Interfaith Worker Justice (IWJ). As former IWJ director Kim Bobo describes them, 'worker centers are community-based and community-led organizations that create a safe space where workers can organize and build power' (Bobo and Pabellon 2016, p. 4). While these centers provide practical services such as English-language courses and wage theft clinics, they also place, as labor studies scholar Janice Fine notes, 'enormous emphasis on leadership development and democratic decision-making' (Fine 2005, p. 4). In so doing, they not only ensure that workers themselves guide the centers, but also that workers become leaders in their communities.

As Fine documents, most worker centers consider membership a privilege that must be earned through educational workshops and trainings that 'emphasize the development of critical thinking skills that workers can apply to all aspects of their public lives' (ibid.). In these worker centers, members do not just become more effective clients of the state (ensuring they receive proper benefits and legal protection), they are also trained – and then train each other – to challenge anti-immigrant legislation, fight for better working conditions, advocate for their families' healthcare and run community organizations that enhance their neighborhoods. Governance is taught and practiced in a manner that makes even highly vulnerable workers less controlled and depoliticized by state apparatuses. In this manner, those with fragile legal status teach the whole community much about a citizenship that resists the over-determinative power of the state and market.

While theological self-consciousness about this work is certainly not ubiquitous among these worker justice activists, trainings through IWJ and the Industrial Areas Foundation regularly remind Christian activists in worker justice movements that they are carrying on an organizing legacy inspired and embodied by Jesus's example (Bobo 1986; Chambers 2003). In Jesus, they see a 'chief organizer' who relied on relationships across common divides to identify new leaders, invited them into the risk of change, and trained them in the spirit and skills to build a new vision of community. Or as biblical scholar Halvor Moxnes explains, in Jesus we see someone who transformed old models of patronage and clientism and instead built a community grounded in egalitarian standing and an alternative negotiation of resources (Moxnes 1991).

Discipleship, rather than patronage, is the center of this community. In this community, the disciples, or in Greek the 'ones who learn' (Rausch 2003, p. 70), eventually are given 'the power and authority over all demons and to cure diseases, and [Jesus sends] them out to proclaim the kingdom of God and to heal' (Luke 9:1). Certainly, there is radical choice and risk involved, but the invitation is into new forms of relationship and community. And unlike patron-client relationships, where one never moves into leadership, the disciples become co-creators of the new kingdom. Jesus's invitation to take up the cross and follow him involves the constitution of a community where leaders are cultivated, power is distributed and new forms of kinship disrupt the dominant political economy.

Building bridges

This kind of leadership development also points us to the crucial bridge-building that must occur in worker justice movements in order to expand the power base of non-elites. Without connections across sectors, ethnicities and religions, wage activism can become a form of group clientism or interest group isolation that ultimately leaves low-wage workers even more vulnerable. Building power requires seeing and fighting for interconnections so that overall systems change rather than merely shifting some short-term compensatory measures from one group to another.

The need for this bridging work emerges most obviously in the pitting of African American and Latinx workers against each other in low-wage worker settings. This strategy is used so thoroughly that worker centers regularly undertake explicit black-brown solidarity education and action to counter interest-group isolation. In Mississippi, a poultry workers' alliance conducts educational circles where African American workers are asked to share what the legacy of the Civil Rights Movement means to them, while Latinx workers describe why they immigrated to the United States (Snarr 2011). In Tennessee, an IWJ-sponsored Latinx worker center has co-hosted, with a primarily black organizing institution, a film series on black history; over the past several years, worker center leaders also participated in Black Lives Matter marches and linked concerns about police brutality with unfair immigration enforcement.

While black-brown solidarity is becoming an important mainstay of wage activism, ongoing shifts in the demographics of refugees and immigrants are also pressing organizers to recognize the importance of intentional solidarity between people of different faiths. In the United States, foreign-born workers are not only more likely to be employed in low-wage jobs, but also to reflect the growing religious diversity of the United States (Pew Forum 2008).[2]

These immigrants and refugees are vulnerable both economically and culturally, and in ways that can intertwine maliciously. As legal scholar Khaled A. Beydoun notes, Muslim Americans are often viewed through a classless lens that renders their economic conditions invisible (Beydoun 2016, p. 1464). He continues,

> [The] incompatible caricaturing of indigent Americans and Muslim Americans facilitates the erasure of indigent Muslim Americans from both scholarly and advocacy interventions and consequently leaves their distinct

struggle ignored and unmitigated. This erasure has never been more dangerous than it is today – the vulnerability of indigent Muslim Americans to 'racialized poverty', 'Islamaphobia', and 'countering violent extremism' (CVE) policing is at an all-time high (and on the uptick).

(ibid., p. 1465)

While Muslims certainly are distributed across the economic spectrum, according to the Pew Research Center, 40 per cent of US Muslims have household incomes of less than $30,000 per year, compared to 32 per cent of the general population, which places these households solidly in the category of the working poor (Diament 2017). They also are more likely than the general population to be underemployed (29 per cent vs. 12 per cent, respectively) (ibid.). And even though many Muslim immigrants are professionals – and these tend to be the face of interfaith and Muslim activism in the United States – Muslim immigrants overall are actually 'disproportionately employed in personal transportation . . . and the food-processing industry', which leaves them vulnerable to considerable worker exploitation and with little access to labor unions (Adler *et al.* 2014, p. 37). These immigrants also intersect with native-born African American Muslims who populate the stratum of Muslim working poverty that is rarely discussed in the United States.

Even when these mostly immigrant populations begin to claim their agency, we see concomitant increases in anti-refugee and anti-Muslim legislation. Strict anti-immigrant legislation in Tennessee, for instance, has resulted in a decline of undocumented Latinxs working in poultry processing plants. This gap in the labor force provided an opening for the employment of Somali refugees, many of whom take these low-wage, low-skill, accessible jobs in order to fulfil the federal Refugee Act's requirement to be actively job-seeking and take the first 'reasonable' job offer.[3] Despite their legal and economic vulnerability, these Somali workers joined the Retail, Wholesale and Department Store Union and won the first-ever contractual recognition of a Muslim holiday in a US labor agreement (Cornfield 2014). But backlash to these Muslim workers' presence and increased power led state representatives from the area to author and pass the 'Refugee Absorptive Capacity Act', which, along with extensive reporting and meeting requirements, ultimately allows local governments to request a moratorium on any new resettlement by the Tennessee Office of Refugees (Mosely 2015).

With continued immigration of persons from Somalia, Egypt, Kurdistan and Iraq, Tennessee has become a national testing ground for both anti-refugee and anti-Muslim legislation, including proposals to impose criminal penalties for following Sharia, remove mentions of Islam from textbooks, and require refugee agencies to reimburse public schools for the cost of refugee education. Fortunately, most of these extreme proposals have been held up in legislative committees, but the intertwining of economic and cultural/religious repression threatens to dampen the political agency of these immigrant and refugee workers. In this environment, unions, worker centers and immigrant and refugee rights groups are expanding their vision and organizing practices by hiring Muslim staff, reaching out to local imams, showing up for each other's legislative fights, and educating the public on the links among union suppression, anti-refugee/anti-Muslim legislation and racism.

While focusing on low-wage workers could be perceived as a form of interest group politics, paying attention to the complexity of workers' lives invites wage activists to draw lines of connection among worker struggles as well as legislative battles around immigration, worker rights, and religious freedom. In this manner, wage activists are building a worker justice movement by countering the more isolating tendencies of clientism and consumerism and bridging towards enhanced understandings of citizenship that focus on longer-term political power.

Pluralizing the political

In this bridge-building, we can also see an important move towards pluralizing politics. One of the dangers of advanced capitalism's consolidation of capital and expansion of the state is the atrophying of political associations that discern and act without the state's sanction. Contemporary politics is too often understood to entail merely engaging the legislative and administrative roles of the state, with a focus on electing officials and developing policy. But this narrow approach to political struggle, or what might be philosophically called political monism, produces a political vision and practice that short-circuits the power of organized people in civil society and limits their range of engagement. Certainly, the state has crucial responsibilities, but much political work can be done in civil society to address economic problems and cultivate moral and political accountabilities.

Take, for example the creative actions of worker centers seeking to recover wages from local businesses. In Nashville, Tennessee, Worker's Dignity Project members utilized street theatre during 7:30 am 'wake-up calls' to increase pressure on managers at a hotel in the downtown tourist district. The group won $13,000 in unpaid wages as well as an overall increase in wages and benefits, resulting in an increase of approximately $120,000 per year across all thirty workers (Worker's Dignity 2015). Their Just Hospitality campaign expanded throughout the following year by coupling wage theft recovery actions with demands for company policy changes such as a 'Cleaning Workers' Bill of Rights'. While these claims could have been pressed through a lengthy state agency process, these workers, often undocumented, drew on the power of their member organization and allies within the community to make their presence known and exercise their political power within the economic marketplace.

In other Just Hospitality campaigns, religious symbolism and clergy action have been more explicit. In Los Angeles, Clergy & Laity United for Economic Justice (CLUE) delivered bitter herbs to hotels that refused to sign union contracts and milk and honey to those who did (Snarr 2011). They also held preach-ins in hotel restaurants where – over a cup of coffee – collared clergy would suddenly rise to give 2–3 minute homilies about worker dignity and religious foundations for fair wages and unionization. Rather than becoming reliant on the state as the only vehicle for justice and equity, wage activists point to the importance of mediating institutions for honing and enforcing moral norms about the political economy (ibid.). This self-proclaimed 'faith-rooted organizing' does not seek to secularize their activism, proclaiming an effort to connect people's dreams of justice with God's dreams of shalom justice, but they also do not contain their practices to dominant definitions of political spaces (Salvatierra and Heltzel 2014). They sacralize and encompass a pluralized politics that will not be contained or secularized by corporate interests or the state.

While government action will always be necessary to achieve broad economic change, community associations are vital in forming persons into their collective political power while also identifying the multiple sites for its deployment. The work of common life politics does not and cannot unfold solely through the nation-state. Wage activists, at their best, invite us to recognize the necessity of varied sites of political contestation and political association and to expand our political imagination both ritually and spatially.

Shifting frames

Ultimately this kind of organizing challenges the dominant frames of advanced capitalism, with its claim that decisions about our shared economic life are the domain of an insider conversation between governments and multi-national corporations. Wage activists ask pointed questions about why profits from productivity find their way increasingly in the hands of upper-level management and CEOs. They demystify 'free market' ideologies by uncovering government subsidies to businesses, whether directly through tax abatements or indirectly through government provision of food stamps and healthcare to underpaid workers. The national 'Let Justice Roll' (Amos 5:24) faith and community coalition argued that 'a job should keep you out of poverty, not in it' and set a foundational frame for the living wage movement that was later picked up by presidential candidate Bernie Sanders (Let Justice Roll: Living Wage Campaign 2011; Sanders 2013). Religious activists have also highlighted the cycle of working poverty through protesting at Walmart, striking at fast-food restaurants, and taking creative actions like BUILD did in placing giant price tags on downtown business offices that juxtaposed the amount of government subsidies with the salary of the company's CEO and the wages of its lowest paid workers (Snarr 2011).

With a broad, moral engagement with an unjust status quo, wage activists invoke stark contrasts between principles such as fairness and the fruits of hard work and the reality of the crushing inequalities produced by capitalist markets. These activists also trace the concrete choices made by business and state leaders that produce these inequalities, thereby disallowing the myth of market wages to dominate. For example taxi driver alliances in several cities (often led by recent immigrants and refugees) have challenged the management fees that taxi companies charge, the wage structure of these companies, and the government's practice of flooding the market by issuing too many operating permits. The National Taxi Driver's Alliance, now a union associated with the AFL-CIO, is working at the federal level to reclassify drivers as direct employees entitled to healthcare and bargaining rights rather than independent contractors (Gaus 2011). In many ways, taxi driver alliances' research on the low wages of cabbies unveils the elaborate coordination of government and businesses in advanced capitalism and the consolidation of capital and political power into fewer hands.

This tracing and challenging of the alliances of money and power in advanced capitalism is essential to disrupting the anti-democratic tendencies of our current political economy. Connecting this analysis to larger discussions of corporate welfare, progressive tax structures and employee governance may begin to shift the conversation about citizen control of the markets. But there is also a lingering danger in some wage activism that frames 'living wages' as a way for workers to be 'independent' from the state and not reliant on government subsidies for their lives. Wage activism has relied regularly on strategic arguments about the ultimate 'cost of low wages' and the 'double tax burden' on taxpayers who fund subsidies for companies paying poverty wages and then again for means-tested poverty programs (Sklar and Sherry 2005, p. 35). While these arguments are effective in the short-term for persuading more fiscally conservative stakeholders, the coexistent emphasis on workers not being 'dependent on government funds' ultimately undermines a larger worker justice movement (Snarr 2011). For if anything holds true in advanced capitalism, it is the fact that all parts of our social, political and economic system are deeply intertwined. Justice is not found in a mythic independence from the state but arises from an expanded sense of citizenship that claims power in relation to the political economy by uncovering our interdependencies and ensuring they are more equitable and more deeply democratic. Pandering to the trope of independence feeds a dangerous myth that any of us are free from the formations and regulations of the state (e.g. roads, water and mortgage tax breaks) while simultaneously obscuring the ways our work lives are constructed by the alliances of the political economy no matter our wage scale (e.g. healthcare, family leave and bargaining rights).

Again, wage activism is at its best when it feeds a worker justice movement that helps us see these patterns more clearly and understand our power in relation to them rather than vaunting a frame of independence from government. Certainly, higher wage floors can facilitate some undoing of clientism through the reduction of poverty surveillance, but decrying dependence is not the same as claiming citizenship. We are all dependent on each other and the government for the structure of our lives; the quality of those interdependent relationships is what is at stake – not the mere fact of their existence. Understanding our interdependence ultimately enables us to identify multiple levers of influence and a wider sense of our power for change.

Worker justice and gospel discipleship

The ubiquitous character of advanced capitalism is such that finding avenues of resistance and wellsprings of hope is not easy. In many ways, we are in – as many scholars have noted – a new age of Empire. This new Empire is defined not by military control of foreign territories but by the global collaboration, control and consolidation of capital by wealthy nation-states (such as the United States), multinational corporations and international institutions like the World Trade Organization and International Monetary Fund (Hardt and Negri 2001). The breadth of this imperialism is daunting, as is the increase of economic inequality and atrophying of non-elite power that accompanies it.

But when the best of wage activism begins to build a larger worker justice movement through reclaiming citizenry (resisting clientism), building bridges (rejecting interest-group isolation), pluralizing politics (defying political monism) and shifting frames (demystifying ideologies), we begin to see hope for resisting this new Empire. Christian activists within these movements, whether at the turn of the nineteenth or twentieth centuries, also revive a long-standing tradition of seeing Jesus as challenging rather than acquiescing to the terms of Empire. Whether through their conception of the historical Jesus as a 'martyr for the for the cause of the laboring classes', their 'chief organizer', or the One who transforms a patron-client system and gives all the disciples – including us – the power to be co-creators of a 'kingdom of nobodies', these activists remind us that in the midst of unjust structures, God does not just want better compensatory state actions; God desires changed relationships of compassion and justice. We will need a robust community to realize this vision – a community willing to train and sustain non-elite leaders for a different kind of citizenship – and, fortunately, we have the theological and activist resources to make it possible. Thank God.

Notes

1 Wood, Partridge and Fulton (2011) provide a thorough overview of the current state of the field and the four major faith-based community organizing networks in the United States, although they call these networks 'Institution-Based Community Organizing'. About 88 per cent of the institutions in these networks are religious congregations and the public meetings are infused with religious ritual and language.

2 Muslims currently account for 0.9 per cent of the US population, while Hindus constitute 0.6 per cent of the public. More than two-thirds of each group are foreign born (Public Religion Research Institute 2017).

3 As the federal Office of Refugee Resettlement noted in their report to Congress in 2013, 'the Refugee Act of 1980 and the Refugee Assistance amendments enacted in 1982 and 1986 stress the achievement of employment and economic self-sufficiency by refugees as soon as possible after their arrival in the United States' (2014, p. 90). Refugees without dependents have only 8 months to find a job before all Refugee Cash Assistance (RCA) and Refugee Medical Assistance (RMA) ends ('The Refugee Act' 2012). Families with dependents who fall beneath a minimum asset level additionally receive cash assistance through Temporary Assistance to Needy Families and Medicaid. But all refugees between the ages of 18 and 64 must actively seek employment in order to receive cash assistance and are contractually obligated to accept the first reasonable job offered. Once a refugee is employed, RCA terminates immediately, regardless of the wage rate or anticipated permanence of the job. In practice, many refugees are hired as seasonal or temporary workers. This federal emphasis on immediate, indiscriminate job placement for some of the most vulnerable persons in our society (many seeking asylum from war-

torn countries and considerable persecution), alongside short-term, minimal levels of cash and medical assistance, funnels most refugees into working poverty with almost no political or economic power.

References

Adler, L., Tapia, M. and Turner, L (eds) (2014) *Mobilizing against inequality: Unions, immigrant workers, and the crisis of capitalism*, Ithaca, NY: ILR Press.

Alinsky, S. D. (1989) *Rules for radicals: A practical primer for realistic radicals*, New York: Vintage.

Beydoun, K. (2016) 'Between indigence, Islamophobia, and erasure: Poor and Muslim in "War on Terror" America', *California Law Review*, *104*(6): 1463–1502.

Bobo, K. A. (1986) *Lives matter: A handbook for Christian organizing*, Kansas City, MO: Sheed & Ward.

Bobo, K. and Pabellon, M. C. (2016) *The worker center handbook: A practical guide to starting and building the new labor movement*, Ithaca, NY: ILR Press.

Bretherton, L. (2014) *Resurrecting democracy: Faith, citizenship, and the politics of a common life*, New York: Cambridge University Press.

Carter, H. W. (2015) *Union made: Working people and the rise of social Christianity in Chicago*, New York: Oxford University Press.

Chambers, E. T. (2003) *Roots for radicals: Organizing for power, action, and justice*, New York: Bloomsbury Academic.

Cornfield, D. (2014) *Union role in Muslim immigrant worker incorporation: The case of Somali workers in Middle Tennessee*, Case Study: Cornell University Worker Institute. Available from: www.ilr.cornell.edu/sites/ilr.cornell.edu/files/Tennessee-Taxi-and-Poultry-Workers-Case-Study.pdf [accessed 15 May 2017].

Crossan, J. D. (1991) *The historical Jesus: The life of a Mediterranean Jew*, San Francisco, CA: HarperSanFrancisco.

Diament, J. (2017) '*American Muslims are concerned—but satisfied with their lives*', Washington, DC: Pew Research Center. Available at: www.pewresearch.org/fact-tank/2017/07/26/american-muslims-are-concerned-but-also-satisfied-with-their-lives/ [accessed 10 August 2017].

Elliott, C. (2009) 'The day democracy died: The depoliticizing effects of democratic development', *Alternatives: Global, Local, Political*, *34*(3): 249–274.

Figart, D. (2004) *Living wage movements: Global perspectives*, London: Routledge.

Fine, J. (2001) 'Community unionism in Baltimore and Stamford: Beyond the politics of particularism', *Working USA*, *4*(3): 59–85.

Fine, J. (2005) *Worker centers: Organizing communities at the edge of the dream*, Washington, DC: Economic Policy Institute.

Gaus, M. (2011) 'Taxi workers become a union—officially', Labor Notes, 20 October. Available from: http://labornotes.org/blogs/2011/10/taxi-workers-become-union%E2%80%94 officially [accessed 6 October 2015].

Glickman, D. (1999) *A living wage: American workers and the making of consumer society*, Ithaca, NY: Cornell University Press.

Habermas, J. (1975) *Legitimation crisis*, Boston: Beacon Press.

Hardt, M. and Negri, A. (2001), *Empire*, Cambridge, MA: Harvard University Press.

Let Justice Roll: Living Wage Campaign [online] (2011). Available from: http://ljrdev.mayfirst.org/ [accessed 15 May 2016].

Levine, M. V. (1987) 'Downtown redevelopment as an urban growth strategy: A critical reappraisal of the Baltimore renaissance', *Journal of Urban Affairs*, *9*(2): 103–123.

Luce, S. (2004a) *Fighting for a Living Wage*, Ithaca, NY: Cornell University Press.

Luce, S. (2004b) 'What happens after laws pass? Implementing and monitoring living wage ordinances', *Perspectives on Work*, 8(1): 37–39.

Luce, S. (2005) 'Keeping living wages alive', *New Labor Forum*, 14(1): 84–94.

Mosely, B. (2011) 'Tracy refugee bill attacked by rights group', *Shelbyville Times-Gazette*, 3 July. Available from: www.t-g.com/story/1741393.html [accessed 5 Oct 2015].

Moxnes, H. (1991) 'Patron-client relations and the new community in Luke-Acts', in J. H. Neyrey (ed.), *The social world of Luke Acts: Models for interpretation*, Peabody, MA: Hendrickson, pp. 241–268.

Public Religion Research Institute (PRRI) (2017) The American Values Atlas. Available at: http://ava.prri.org/#religious/2016/States/religion/m/national [accessed 11August 2017].

Quigley, W. P. (2001) 'The living wage movement', *BLUEPRINT for Social Justice*, 54(9).

Rausch, T. (2013) *Who is Jesus? An introduction to Christology*, Collegeville, MN: Liturgical Press.

Rhoads, J. K. (2010) *Critical issues in social theory*, University Park, PA: Penn State University Press.

Ryan, J. A. (1996) *Economic justice: Selections from distributive justice and a living wage*, Louisville, KY: Westminster John Knox Press.

Saller, R. P. (2002) *Personal patronage under the early empire*, Cambridge, MA: Cambridge University Press.

Salvatierra, R.A. and Heltzel, P. (2014) *Faith-rooted organizing: Mobilizing the church in service to the world*, Downers Grove, IL: IVP Books.

Sanders, B. [SenSanders] (2013) 'A job should lift workers out of poverty, not keep them in it. #minimumwage', Twitter post, 9 November. Available from: https://twitter.com/SenSanders/status/399314775483482112 [accessed 15 May 2017].

Sklar, H. and Sherry, P. (2005) *A just minimum wage: Good for workers, business and our future*, Cincinnati: Friendship Press.

Snarr, C. M. (2011) *All you that labor: Religion and ethics in the living wage movement*, New York: NYU Press.

Stokes, S. (2009) 'Political Clientelism' in C. Boix and S. Stokes (eds), *The Oxford handbook of comparative politics*, New York: Oxford University Press, pp. 604–627.

Wood, R. L., Partridge, K. and Fulton, B. (2011) 'Building bridges, building power: Developments in institution-based community organizing', New York: Interfaith Funders.

Worker's Dignity (2017) 'Just hospitality program', Available from: www.workersdignity.org/about/ [accessed 3 October 2017].

11

SPEAK UP, JUDGE RIGHTEOUSLY, STAND WITH THE POOR

The Jewish imperative for economic justice

Jonah Dov Pesner

Over 100 years ago, on 25 March 1911, a fire broke out in New York City's Asch Building on the corner of Greene Street and Washington Place, off Washington Square (Sione 2011).[1] One of the most infamous industrial disasters in American history, the Triangle Shirtwaist factory fire killed 146 and injured many more. The fire's cause is not known for certain, but its deadliness can be largely attributed to the owners, who locked the factory doors to prevent workers from taking breaks. The Triangle Shirtwaist Company was an anti-union business and had been the site of protest against unfair conditions just a couple years before the fire. The fire has a special place in the story of American Jews. The owners of the factory, Isaac Harris and Max Blank, were successful Jewish businessmen. But the victims were also Jewish – mainly young women under the age of 23. This event is widely remembered because workers and unions leveraged the tragedy to bring about fundamental changes in American labour laws. And in its wake, Jewish immigrants became central to the labour movement, fighting alongside others to secure safer, more humane workplaces and for economic justice more broadly.

Of course, the Jewish commitment to economic justice originated long before 1911. In fact, concern for economic justice is central to the Jewish tradition and can be traced back to biblical stories and the earliest laws of our ancestors. Even when they differ about specific policies, most Jews of twenty-first century America care about a fair and just economic system, in part because it has been a recurring theme throughout both the narrative and legal frameworks of Jewish tradition. Whether owners or workers, most have empathy with those who struggle under the weight of inequality. Polls of the Jewish community consistently affirm how central social justice (including economic justice) is as an organizing principle of Jewish identity. For example, when asked which qualities are most important to their Jewish identity, significantly more American Jews cite a commitment to social equality than cite support for Israel or even religious observance (Jones and Cox

2012). And both individually and through their denominational activism, Jews remain disproportionately involved in many causes for social justice in American life.

Over the sweep of Jewish history, interpretations of the foundational narratives and laws of the Jewish people have reflected a deep and abiding concern and identification with oppressed people in various forms, with frequent references to 'the widow', 'the orphan', 'the stranger', and 'the poor'. In the Passover *seder,* the ritual meal during which Jews across the world retell the story of the Exodus, we read the instruction that 'in each generation, every person is obligated to see himself or herself as though he or she personally came forth from Egypt'. In this moment, Jews are taught not only to recall God's power of redemption, but to internalize the experience of oppression and in turn feel empathy.

Indeed, many verses in the Bible that establish specific laws to care for the needy are justified by referencing the experience of having been slaves in Egypt. The Jewish experience of slavery in Egypt serves as a 'master story' of economic injustice and oppression, in which Israelite enslaved workers are then brought to freedom. Jews are commanded to re-experience slavery and the Exodus each year not just as a ritualistic exercise, but also as a way of renewing our commitment to creating the world as we believe it should be: free of enslavement, oppression and injustice. Throughout history, rabbis and others have applied the lessons of this narrative and the commandments regarding economic justice to the economic challenges of their own day. Every generation invokes the lessons of the past to write their own chapter that weaves together sacred narratives and moral conclusions about concrete economic realities.

Ultimately, these texts – ancient and more recent – tell a story of a religion founded not only on the belief that every human being is obligated to care for others, but also that society itself must be organized in such a way as to provide economic justice for all inhabitants. We see this illustrated in the biblical commandment to care for the poor, the widow, the orphan; in early societal rules and norms setting aside the corner of the fields for the poor and the hungry; the equitable provision of social benefits to the stranger and the citizen; and in God's establishment of the sabbatical and Jubilee years, when fields are left to rest and debts are forgiven. We see it in the rabbinic effort, during the Talmudic period, to create one of the world's first social welfare systems. We see it in the array of charitable and communal social welfare institutions that were the norm in the 1400-year history of the self-governing Jewish communities of the medieval Christian and Muslim worlds – many of which continued even into the modern period in some areas of Eastern Europe, right up to the Holocaust. And we see it in contemporary Judaism's contributions to economic justice in democratic societies.

'You were strangers': principles of economic justice in the Bible

The contract revealed in the covenantal experience of Sinai creates the legal foundation for the historic Jewish commitment to economic justice. These laws are set down in that part of the Bible referred to as 'the Torah' (encompassing the first five books of the Bible: Genesis, Exodus, Leviticus, Numbers and Deuteronomy). The most frequently repeated commandment in the Torah addresses how we should treat the stranger. Deuteronomy teaches that '[God] upholds the cause of the fatherless and the widow, and befriends the stranger, providing food and clothing. – You too must befriend the stranger, for you were strangers in the land of Egypt' (Deuteronomy 10:18–19).[2] The text specifically names the three categories of 'orphans, widows, and strangers' because they were among the most economically vulnerable in their tribal, patriarchal society. These disadvantaged groups would have faced terrible difficulty providing for themselves or finding their place in the community. Furthermore, these commands are reinforced by reminding the Israelites of their own challenging experience of being strangers in Egypt.

Deuteronomy specifically establishes an individual commitment to the poor: 'There will never cease to be needy ones in your land, which is why I command you: open your hand to the poor and needy kin in your land' (Deuteronomy 15: 11). The text recognizes the persistent reality of poverty. But the writers of the Torah (and later, the prophets and rabbis) are unsatisfied with merely creating an individual obligation to help the poor. The Torah builds on the individual requirement for just behaviour by establishing societal mechanisms that protect the most vulnerable. An important example is the biblical injunction to treat workers fairly:

> You shall not abuse a needy and destitute labourer, whether a fellow Israelite or a stranger in one of the communities of your land. You must pay out the wages due on the same day, before the sun sets, for the worker is needy and urgently depends on it; else a cry to the Eternal will be issued against you and you will incur guilt (Deuteronomy 24:14–15).

The instruction to pay workers immediately and to treat them with dignity is a foundational obligation for all Jewish employers and an example of how societal norms and protocols that uphold economic justice are established through Jewish sacred texts.

The Torah also expresses this pattern of societal norms through its agricultural rules. During the biblical era, agriculture was the primary economic activity, and God's commandments offered an approach to agriculture that was intended to help all people, whether landowners or not. We read:

> When you reap the harvest of your land, you shall not reap all the way to the edges of your field, or gather the gleanings of your harvest. You shall not pick your vineyard bare, or gather the fallen fruit of your vineyard; you shall leave them for the poor and the stranger: I the Eternal am your God (Leviticus 19:9–10).

The Torah creates a system for ensuring that all people – not just landowners – benefit from the fruits of God's creation.

The commandment in Leviticus goes so far as to obligate the farmer to engage in two forms of providing for the poor: first, to intentionally leave the *pe'ah*, ('corner' or 'edge') for the gleaners who will come to gather; and second, to leave behind the *leket* (that which is dropped or left behind inadvertently) during the harvest. Later the text adds a third element: 'When you reap your harvest in your field and overlook a sheaf in the field, do not turn back to get it, it shall go to the stranger, the fatherless, and the widow – in order that the Eternal your God may bless you in all your undertakings' (Deuteronomy 24:19). The bottom line? The ancient farmer was obligated to share intentionally some portion of the harvest with those in need and to share the inevitable leftovers with them as well. Taken in total, these agricultural rules require that production involves giving away a portion of one's yield to the poor, a precursor to later taxation systems that redistributed goods to help meet the basic needs of the poor.

In addition to these rules, the *yovel*, or jubilee, and the *shmita*, or sabbatical, are two more practices intended to create a system of economic justice. The *shmita* is a biblical law that says that after 6 years of working the land, in 'the seventh [year] you shall let it rest and lie fallow. Let the needy among your people eat of it' (Exodus 23:11). Producers are told to take an entire year off from harvesting anything and to let the poor eat from their fields during that time, thus establishing a principle of economic fairness within the production process. Similar to the harvest rules, the *shmita* ensures that poor people will benefit and places a limit on the short-term enrichment of landowners. The *shmita* rule also requires that all debts be forgiven after 7 years. This requirement provided a safety mechanism for the poor and heavily indebted by ensuring that loans did not become an endless burden.[3]

In addition to the *shmita* occurring every 7 years, the *yovel* is a special year observed every 50 years (or after every 7 *shmita* years). The *yovel* is an even more radical version of the *shmita*, as it includes all the requirements of *shmita*, plus a requirement for land property to revert to its original owner. This in biblical times functioned as a 'reset' button to prevent inequality in wealth from persisting across generations, as well as ensuring that the property (mostly land in this case) remained with a family that is part of the tribe to which God had originally assigned it. While agriculture has not continued as the primary economic activity throughout Jewish history, this principle provides a basis for many of our values related to economic fairness. It simultaneously recognizes the importance of entrepreneurism and the need for regulations to mitigate extreme inequality.

In summary, the injunctions contained in the Torah articulate the Jewish commitment to economic justice by laying out (1) the duty to help others; (2) the special responsibility to help the most vulnerable and (3) the establishment of communal and societal norms and systems that imply a collective responsibility to help people in need. The commandments envision a world in which human action works alongside Divine redemption to achieve justice.

Following the five books of the Torah, the next section of the Hebrew Bible begins with the historical books of Samuel and Kings and then records the writings of the Prophets. This order functions to emphasize the prophetic understanding of the laws of the Torah. In contrast, in most Christian versions of the Bible, the prophets come at the end, after what are called the 'wisdom writings' (e.g. Psalms, Proverbs, Ecclesiastes, Ruth, etc.), thus emphasizing the role of the prophets as a precursor to the New Testament. But this Christian arrangement importantly breaks the connection between the Torah law and the prophets in the Hebrew texts.

Spanning several centuries, the prophets played the role of God's messenger of severe criticism during historical periods characterized by corruption, inequity and injustice. While most of the prophetic condemnation focused on issues of idolatry, ritual abuses, general corruption, and sexual immorality, the theme of failure to care for the poor and vulnerable runs powerfully though most of the prophets' writings – particularly Isaiah, Amos, Jeremiah and Micah.

The prophet Isaiah was among the boldest in reminding the people of Israel of their obligations to God's commandments. He railed against the hypocrisy of following ritual observance while disobeying ethical rules and showing indifference to human suffering. His ideas are echoed often in Jewish liturgy and given prominence by the rabbis in assigning this text to be read on Yom Kippur, the holiest day of the Jewish year when Jews are required to fast and reflect deeply on their own conduct over the last year:

> Do you call that a fast, a day when the Lord is favourable? No, this is the fast I desire: To unlock fetters of wickedness, and untie the cords of the yoke; to let the oppressed go free; to break off every yoke. It is to share your bread with the hungry, and to take the wretched poor into your home; when you see the naked, to clothe them. And not to ignore your own kin. Then shall your light burst through like the dawn and your healing spring up quickly. Your Vindicator shall march before you, the Presence of the Lord shall be your rear guard. Then, when you call, the Lord will answer; When you cry, God will say: Here I am.

Such prophetic criticism affirmed that the responsibility to prevent and address economic inequality and suffering lies in human hands. In the Torah, God's commandments were delivered to the Israelites, and they were asked to accept the commandments as a dimension of the covenantal relationship. By the time of the prophets, the people were already expected to know God's teachings and were harshly condemned for not following them. Isaiah reassured the people that when they do justly and restore the covenant by clothing the naked, feeding the hungry and providing shelter to those in need, God will respond by saying '*Hineini*', 'Here I Am'. God's response parallels the cry of *hineini* uttered both by Abraham and Moses in responding to God's call.

The prophetic tradition also addresses societal and governmental responsibility for the Torah's demand for justice. The prophet Amos identified unfair economic systems as a key root of injustice:

> Assuredly, because you impose a tax on the poor and exact from them a
> levy of grain, you have built houses of hewn stone but you shall not live in
> them; you have planted delightful vineyards, but shall not drink their wine
> (Amos 5:10–12).

Amos's prophesy addresses people who not only did not heed the Bible's agricultural rules, but actually reversed them by taking grain away from the people
who were supposed to benefit from biblical rules. Isaiah's prophesies cry out against
those in power who violated biblical agriculture rules ensuring that the poor received
what they needed:

> The Lord stands up to plead a cause, and rises to champion peoples. The
> Lord will bring this charge against the elders and officers of God's people:
> 'It is you who have devoured the vineyard, that which was robbed from the
> poor is in your houses. How dare you crush My people, and grind the faces
> of the poor', says my Lord God of Hosts (Isaiah 3:13–15).

Amos and Isaiah represent the prophetic voice that rejected the authority of powerful leaders who failed to help the most vulnerable. As outlined by Isaiah, 'A throne
shall be established in goodness in the tent of David, and on it shall sit in faithfulness a ruler devoted to justice and zealous for equity' (Isaiah 16:5). The prophets
demanded rulers who created collective good instead of benefitting themselves
and a wealthy few. Central to the vision of the prophets are kings who governed
with a commitment to economic justice and the dignity of all people.

The third section of the Bible, *Ketuvim*, or 'Writings', is a collection of narrative,
poetry, prayer and verses of wisdom that includes Proverbs and Psalms. Here too
are eloquent and consistent calls for protection of the weak and the vulnerable.
The book of Proverbs argues that 'Those who withhold what is due to the poor
affront their Maker; those who show pity for the needy honour God' (Proverbs
14:31). Proverbs records the injunction that serves as the title of this chapter,
demanding that the reader 'speak up, judge righteously, champion the poor and
the needy' (Proverbs 31:9).

The Psalms, written in the language of praise for God, also highlight the issue
of economic fairness: 'My mouth shall sing much praise to the Lord; I will acclaim
God in the midst of a throng, because God stands at the right hand of the needy,
to save [them] from those who would condemn them' (Psalms 109:30–31). The
psalms also affirm the biblical teaching that those who help the needy will
themselves benefit: 'Happy are those who [consider the poor]; in bad times may
the Lord keep them from harm' (Psalms 41:2–4).

Ketuvim also contains several narratives embodying the themes discussed above,
including the Book of Ruth, which tells the story of a poor Moabite widow who
travels with her Jewish mother-in-law, Naomi, back to the land of Judah. Although
she is not Jewish, she throws in her lot with her mother-in-law. In Judah, Ruth

utilizes the right to glean in the fields, which is where she meets a new husband, Boaz. The story of Ruth is a beautiful story that suggests that the themes of concern for the vulnerable (widows), the agricultural rules for helping the hungry, and the obligations to provide for the stranger were more than abstract rules and were enacted in concrete social settings. Moreover, this narrative suggests that caring for the poor may have unforeseen society-wide benefits. The story of Ruth ends in near fairy-tale fashion with a discussion of Ruth's lineage, explaining that a descendent of Boaz and Ruth's union is King David himself. And according to rabbinic commentaries on the Bible, the Messiah will come out of the line of David.

'In every generation': rabbinic interpretations of the economic justice imperative

Ketuvim is a helpful bridge from the prophetic books, in which the prophets amplified God's demands on the people to pursue social and economic justice, to the post-biblical rabbinic period, in which scholars (often referred to just as 'the rabbis') explicated those demands in detail, interpreting and applying the laws to evolving historical contexts and changing economic, social and religious conditions. The Talmud collects rabbinic wisdom over seven centuries, including the earliest attempts by rabbis to apply the Bible's laws after the destruction of the Temple in 70 CE, both inside and outside ancient Israel. Much more than just a legal text, the Talmud is far from one-sided or rigid, containing many rabbinic disagreements that help establish the Jewish respect for both the complexity of concrete situations and dissenting opinions. In commenting on the differing interpretations of the biblical rules, the Talmud observes famously: 'These and these are the words of the living God' (BT Eruvin 13b).

As discussed earlier, the rabbis often turned to the story of the Exodus as a master narrative of Judaism in the form of the Passover *haggadah*, the script for the annual ritual of celebrating and even re-enacting the ancient experience of moving from slavery to liberation. At one liturgical highpoint, the *haggadah* instructs the leader to throw open the door to the home and proclaim: 'This [*matzah*] is the bread of affliction, which we ate when we were slaves and became free; let all who are hungry come and eat!' In many communities, this was treated as a literal commandment.

The entire Passover *seder* experience was developed over time by the rabbis and aimed to fulfil their requirement that 'in every generation, all people are bound to regard themselves as though they personally had gone forth from Egypt' (BT Pesachim 116b). The requirement to re-tell the story every year was the rabbis' interpretation of the biblical injunction: 'And you shall explain to your child on that day, "It is because of what the Eternal did for me that I went free from Egypt"' (Exodus 13:8). As a result, the *seder* ritual has had an abiding impact on the Jewish psyche. Generations of Jews throughout the centuries have identified with the oppressed of their own era because of the performative power of the *seder*, with its many references back to the Jewish experience of slavery and redemption.

A recurring theme in the Talmudic text is that a system of economic justice should function in a way to protect the dignity of every person. This is why the Talmud taught that 'even a poor person who is sustained from charity must also perform charity' (BT Gittin 7b). According to the rabbis, the obligation reminds us that charity is not simply about redistributing wealth for maximum efficiency, but that every person shares the responsibility to fulfil the *mitzvah* of giving *tzedakah* (a Jewish term for charity that is perhaps more accurately translated as 'righteousness'). This conception of charity served to break down the wall between givers and receivers. Rabbinic literature also wrestles with other challenging questions provoked by the biblical text noting the persistence of poverty: 'If your God loves the poor, why does God not support them?' The Talmud teaches that individuals must heed God's call to assist the poor, so that 'through them we will be saved from the judgment of Gehonnim [hell]' (BT, Bava Batra 10a). Here, the rabbis are affirming the importance of human agency in protecting the most vulnerable. The righteous act of giving not only saves the poor person, it also saves the donor, who would have been judged severely for failing to fulfil the obligation.

The rabbis of the Talmudic era were concerned with paying close attention to the precise needs of each individual. While the Talmud's primary focus was on the most vulnerable – 'the orphan, widow, and stranger' – the rabbis also recognized that poverty comes in many forms and requires diverse responses. Leviticus Rabbah explains:

> It is not written 'Happy are those who giveth to the poor' but 'Happy are those who considereth the poor', which signifies: Consider closely how to benefit them. R. Jonah, when he saw a person of respectable family who had lost his money and was ashamed to take charity, used to go to him and say to him, 'As I heard that you have come into an inheritance somewhere abroad, I offer you this article, and when you are in better circumstances you will give it back to me'. At the same time, when he gave it to him he would say to him: 'I have given it to you as a gift'.
>
> (Leviticus Rabbah 34:1–2)

In this passage, Rabbi Jonah's offer of a loan that might also be a gift is a skilful example of preserving human dignity while tailoring assistance to the particular circumstances of someone in need.

The Talmud also established many rules that enshrine the collective responsibility for economic justice. If in the Bible it was not clear who ensured that the corner of the field was set aside for the poor, that *tzedakah* was paid, and that the widow and the orphan were cared for, by Talmudic times, the rabbis called for an array of social welfare funds and institutions paid for and run by the community (Tamari 1986). In later centuries, these grew into a broad network of social welfare institutions paid for by community enforced taxes and *tzedakah*. The Talmud outlined specific communal funds required for a self-governing Jewish community: a food distribution fund – the *tamhuy* – that gave food to members of the community and strangers alike, a burial fund, a clothing fund, the *kupah* – the general welfare given to eligible recipients every Friday – and a dowry fund for to assist orphan girls in getting married. It also delimited a public-school system to which all boys, rich and poor alike, were entitled to go.

Historians differ on how aspirational and how realized the call for these funds was, as well as on the question of which were run by Jewish governing entities as opposed to charity-supported 'societies' during Talmudic and medieval times. Nonetheless, there are numerous examples of communities implementing one or more of them. Orphanages, housing for the elderly, communal funds to ransom captives, interest-free loan societies and inns for travelers have all existed within Jewish communities for centuries.

Jewish tradition also views financially assisting poor people who become ill as among its highest priorities (Shulchan Aruch, Yoreh Deah 249:16). In medieval Rome, there were periods when the Gemulut Hasidim supplied free medical care for the poor (Shulvas 1973). In Spain, there were, for Jews and Christians alike, examples of full-blown public health systems where state-paid doctors visited every citizen. As A. A. Neuman wrote in his authoritative *The Jews in Spain*:

> The physician, on assuming the duties of his office to which he was generally appointed for a term of years, made a medical examination of every person in the territory under his jurisdiction and then gave everyone advice according to his findings, in the light of his knowledge of the science of medicine and as G-d inspired him. He treated the poor in the public hospital. He was obliged to visit every sick person three times a month.
>
> (Neuman 1942)

Some of these social welfare systems lasted in Central and Eastern European communities into the twentieth century, until the Holocaust destroyed them (Zborowski and Herzog 1956).

In many Jewish communities, interest-free loan systems continue to be used to help move needy people and small businesses towards self-sufficiency. The Hebrew Free Loan Society, founded in 1892 in New York, assists individuals and families – primarily Jews – facing difficult circumstances, and attempts to 'foster economic independence while preserving the dignity of the individual' (Hebrew Free Loan Society 2017). Similar programmes exist in modern-day Israel, serving Ethiopian, Russian and other immigrants seeking assistance in their new home (Israel Free Loan Association 2014).

The Talmud called not just for provisions for the poor and needy but for extensive intervention in and regulation of market economies. The Talmud regulated business and communal life in pursuit of environmental protection, including controlling the placement of polluting industries and ensuring a *migrash*, a belt of green, around cities. The Talmud similarly strengthened the biblical obligation to treat workers fairly: 'Those who withhold employees' wages are as though they deprived them of their lives' (BT, Bava Metzia 112a). In addition to the relationship between workers and employers, the Talmud emphasized the importance of landlords giving tenants sufficient notice of eviction so they could find new housing, particularly in times with harsh weather or limited housing markets (BT, Bava Metzia 101b). The rule of *ona'ah,* that sales needed to be within one-sixth of the fair market value, was a rejection of the Roman *caveat emptor,* the 'buyer beware' mentality of that same era (Shulchan Aruch, Hosen Misphat 22:72). And while economic realities resulted in the *ona'ah* rule becoming increasingly restricted over the centuries, it has always applied to essentials such as food and medicine. For example Maimonides and Joseph Caro (author of the authoritative *Shulchan Aruch,* a sixteenth century compilation of Jewish law) 'ruled in their codes that imposing such price controls on basic commodities was part of the obligation of rabbinic courts' (Tamari 1986).

The Talmud requires all people to give a certain portion of their money to collective services. Some forms of charity and taxes required similar percentage payments by rich and poor. However, some later rabbis advocated for a progressive taxation system, including the thirteenth century Spanish Talmudist Rabbi Shlomo ben Adret (Responsa Rashba cited in Yanklowitz 2014). Similarly, for certain types of assistance, the Mishnah established income levels that determined eligibility to receive communal social services (Mishnah Pe'ah 8), just as today we use means testing to determine eligibility for a number of government support programmes. In doing so, we are told by the Talmud to assume good intentions by the beneficiaries (BT Ketubot 68a).

While many of these injunctions applied only to self-governing Jewish communities, Jewish law emphasizes that fair economic treatment of one another is not limited to activity between Jews. For example, in a majority Jewish community,

> We support the poor of the gentiles along with the poor of Israel, and visit the sick of the gentiles along with the sick of Israel, and bury the poor of the gentiles along with the dead of Israel, in the interest of peace.
>
> (BT Gittin 61a)

In the view of the Talmud, the primary justification for generosity to non-Jews is 'the interest of peace'. This seemed to recognize that stability and peace would not be possible in a community unless all enjoyed the community government's protection and support when they were in need.

Perhaps the most widely cited Jewish teachings in the post-Talmudic era about one's economic responsibility to others came from the medieval Jewish scholar Moses Maimonides. Maimonides represents a Judaism that was enmeshed in the broader non-Jewish world. He was a rabbi, an authoritative commentator on the Bible and the Talmud, one of the most influential legal scholars in Jewish history, as well as a skilled physician, astronomer and philosopher who learned from and influenced Muslim and Arab scholars. He was born in Spain, lived across North Africa during his life, and wrote commentaries on the Talmud that remain significant until to this day. One teaching still widely cited is the ladder of *tzedakah,* which he created to rank different approaches to giving charity. They are listed below, in ascending order of value:

8 When donations are given grudgingly.

7 When one gives less than he should, but does so cheerfully.

6 When one gives directly to the poor upon being asked.

5 When one gives directly to the poor without being asked.

4 Donations when the recipient is aware of the donor's identity, but the donor still doesn't know the specific identity of the recipient.

3 Donations when the donor is aware to whom the charity is being given, but the recipient is unaware of the source.

2 Giving assistance in such a way that the giver and recipient are unknown to each other. Communal funds, administered by responsible people are also in this category.

1 The highest form of charity is to help sustain a person before they become impoverished by offering a substantial gift in a dignified manner, or by extending a suitable loan, or by helping them find employment or establish themselves in business so as to make it unnecessary for them to become dependent on others (Jewish Virtual Library, citing Hayim 1991).

Maimonides' ladder combines several principles we have discussed when evaluating best practices for helping the poor. The dignity of people is a key priority, which is why the relationship between beneficiaries and recipients is so important. Elsewhere he writes: 'If a poor person asks you for money and you have nothing to give him, placate him with words. It is forbidden to rebuke him or to raise your voice at him because his heart is broken and crushed' (Maimonides, Mishneh Torah, 'Gifts to the Poor', 10:5). He also advances the notion that helping someone achieve self-sufficiency is the greatest form of helping someone in need, a principle rooted in the biblical text.

Maimonides also affirmed the vital role of communal funds to empower the poor. He wrote, 'We have never seen nor heard of a Jewish community that does not have a [fund] for charity' (Touger n.d.) and went into detail about the two most commonly established funds: the *kuppah* and *tamhuy*. In terms of the *kuppah*, Maimonides explained that collectors were to take 'from each person what is appropriate for him to give and the assessment made upon him. They then allocate the money from Friday to Friday, giving each poor person sufficient food for seven days' (Touger n.d.). Funds were delivered on Fridays, demonstrating how a very material act of providing money can be integrated with religious life, since Jewish custom suggests that Shabbat evening (Friday night) meals should be as special as the family can afford.

The system operated as a welfare system based on wealth redistribution from those with more money to those with less. The *tamhuy* was designed to ensure that all people had sufficient food, for which 'collectors [were] appointed to fetch bread and foodstuffs from every courtyard, as well as fruit products or money, from anyone who donates for the needs of the moment', and was done daily. Rabbi Moses Alshich, a renowned preacher and biblical commentator writing 400 years after Maimonides, reminded his readers: 'Do not think that you are giving to the poor from your own possession, or that I [God] despised the poor by not giving them as I gave you. For the poor is My child, as you are, and the poor's share is in your grain' (Balinsky n.d.).

Enlightenment and diaspora, mysticism and rationalism in modern Judaism

In the early eighteenth century, Hasidism emerged as a major movement based on mystical strands of Judaism and marked by joyous prayer, singing and sometimes dancing. This movement emphasized new wisdom narratives, a number of which reaffirmed the centrality of economic justice in Judaism.

Many Hasidic stories discuss the prophet Elijah, who is said to be a harbinger of the coming of the Messiah. They frequently use the motif in which Elijah arrives in the form of a beggar to see how he will be treated and to assess if the world is worthy of being redeemed. Such stories artfully fuse the hope for the coming of Elijah (and ultimate salvation for the world) with acts of hospitality and compassion. For centuries and until today, Jews open the door twice during the Passover *seder*: once to ask all who are hungry to come and eat and a second to welcome Elijah into our homes. Judaism has understood that the world can only be redeemed from suffering, oppression and injustice when human beings act to help one another.

The contemporary story 'Elijah the Prophet in Minsk' demonstrates how Hasidism creatively leveraged a new narrative to explicate Judaism's age-old commitment to economic justice. Its author, Yitzhak Buxbaum, is a modern-day storyteller who utilizes mystical narrative to convey Jewish principles in works like *The Light and Fire of the Baal Shem Tov*. In this particular story, a man goes to the founder of Hasidism, the Baal Shem Tov, and tells him he wants to see Elijah:

> 'It's simple', said the Baal Shem. 'I'll tell you what to do. Get two boxes and fill one with food and the other with children's clothes. Then, before Rosh Hashanah, travel to Minsk. On the outskirts of town, right before where the forest begins, is a dilapidated house. Find that house, but don't knock on the door immediately; stand there for a while and listen. Then, shortly before candle-lighting time at sunset, knock on the door and ask for hospitality.
>
> The [man] went home and told his wife he would be away for the holiday. 'How can you leave your family?' she said. 'The children want their father to take them to the synagogue!' He told her, 'I have a once-in-a-lifetime chance to see Elijah the Prophet!'
>
> So he went and did as the Baal Shem Tov told him. He filled the parcels with food and clothing and went to Minsk, where he found the broken-down house at the edge of town. He arrived shortly before evening and

stood in front of the door, listening. Inside, he heard children crying, 'Mommy, we're hungry. And it's [the holiday] and we don't even have decent clothes to wear!' He heard the mother answer, 'Children, trust in God. He'll send Elijah the Prophet to bring you everything you need!'

Then the [man] knocked on the door. When the woman opened it, he asked if he could stay with them for the holiday. 'How can I welcome you when I don't have any food in the house?' she said. 'Don't worry', he said, 'I have enough food for all of us'. He came in, opened the box, gave the children the food, and they ate. Then he opened the other box and the children all took clothes for themselves: this one a shirt, that one a jacket, the other one a hat. He was there for two days, waiting to see Elijah the Prophet. He did not even sleep. How could he sleep? How often do you get a chance to see Elijah the Prophet? But he saw no one.

(Buxbaum n.d.)

As the story develops, the man eventually comes to recognize the point of Baal Shem Tov's assignment – that by meeting the needs of the poor, he himself became the embodiment of Elijah in the world. Hasidism's emphasis on storytelling helped infuse Judaism with a new and important spirit that was still committed to the centuries-old obligations to assist the most vulnerable.

Jews faced substantial questions in the post-Enlightenment world, particularly as millions migrated to the United States, about how their beliefs and practices fit into larger institutions that were beginning to accept Jews. The historic opportunity for integration and assimilation influenced their approaches to creating economic justice. Debra Kaplan and Adam Teller, professors of Jewish history, explain:

Since participation in the Jewish community and its institutions became voluntary [after the Enlightenment], poor relief could no longer be mandated as part of communal taxation. Nonetheless, social expectations and norms continued to serve as factors 'obligating' donors to help the Jewish poor (Kaplan and Teller 2013).

Jews remained committed to helping those within their own community, even as their community itself was beginning to shift.

Mass Jewish immigration to the United States, primarily between 1880 and 1920, happened prior to many of the federal poverty programmes we know today. Many Jewish immigrants came to the United States with little or no money, and some with no connection to family or friends in the country. It is in this environment that many Jewish communal funds in the United States emerged. Organizations like the Hebrew Immigrant Aid Society, Jewish federations, Jewish family services and a broad range of local Jewish social services agencies were started in the early decades of the twentieth century to meet the social service needs of these growing immigrant communities and, in general, of other communities in need – Jewish and non-Jewish alike. Additionally, hospitals, educational institutions, Jewish food pantries, interest free loan programmes and housing services all sought to help American Jews struggling to find their way in the land of opportunity. Many of these institutions served non-Jews as well. These institutions also existed because Jews faced exclusion in much of American life – whether in universities, hospitals, or even country clubs. Supplementing these efforts in communities throughout America, local synagogue social action committees arose, mobilizing volunteer efforts of congregants in an array of social service activities. During the twentieth century, these social service institutions served countless Americans in need and were mainstays of American Jewish life.

The traditional Jewish theological imperative for economic justice was, in some regards, strengthened during the Enlightenment period. Enlightenment philosophers argued that ethics was the most rational and scientific part of religion. The faith traditions that emerged in this context elevated social justice to a centerpiece of religious expression. Out of this intellectual milieu arose the Social Gospel strands of Christianity as well as the emphasis on the prophetic tradition in American Judaism. In the synthesis of traditional Jewish beliefs with the general Jewish embrace of rationalism, the Reform movement (my own stream) – along with Reconstructionist, Conservative and Orthodox Judaism – strengthened their emphasis on social justice issues as an expression of authentic Judaism.

The 1885 Pittsburgh Platform, a seminal early statement of dogma and principles for the Reform Movement in the United States, provides a clear illustration of this emphasis on economic justice among early Jewish immigrants:

> In full accordance with the spirit of the Mosaic legislation, which strives to regulate the relations between rich and poor, we deem it our duty to participate in the great task of modern times, to solve, on the basis of justice and righteousness, the problems presented by the contrasts and evils of the present organization of society
> (Central Conference of American Rabbis 2004).

The platform made it clear that charity alone was insufficient to realize a Jewish vision of economic justice. Further, it clarified that Jewish principles entailed moral responsibilities beyond the boundaries of Jewish community and extended to the organization of the entire society in which Jews lived.

'To solve, on the basis of justice and righteousness': ancient principles and contemporary practice

The arc of Jewish history and the theology of Jewish tradition suggests that modern American Jews must engage and support whatever structures are necessary to create a society that is economically just. For centuries, Jews (when not barred from doing so) have engaged in the political process, and their understanding of the moral principles of their religious tradition have served to inspire their strategies and priorities in addressing the special challenges the world faces. The 1999 Pittsburgh Platform, a modern commitment to the principles laid out in the original Pittsburgh Platform over 100 years before, affirmed the pursuit of economic justice: 'We are obligated to pursue *tzedek*, justice and righteousness, and to narrow the gap between the affluent and the poor' (Central Conference of American Rabbis 2004).

As the policy positions of the Reform Jewish Movement (the largest segment of American Jewry) and the Jewish Council on Public Affairs (the largest coalition of local and national Jewish agencies engaged in community relations work, which includes all major denominations in Jewish life) indicate, Jewish organizations today feel compelled to speak out on a wide range of contemporary domestic and foreign policy economic justice issues. A sampling of 2017 resolution topics underlines these commitments: international debt relief; predatory lending policies; government responsibility to ensure all people have the health services they need; a higher minimum wage; affordable housing and an end to homelessness through federal housing funds; and a paid family leave insurance programme (Jewish Council on Public Affairs 2017 and Union for Reform Judaism 2017).

Similarly, the newly formed Jewish Social Justice Roundtable, a network of fifty-seven national and local Jewish organizations, represents the centrality of social justice in Jewish life. These organizations have a variety of missions and approaches, but are unified by their belief that working for a more just world is at the heart of being Jewish. The diversity of this roundtable demonstrates how modern Jews grapple with pressing religious, social and political issues.

When I was a congregational rabbi in Boston, Massachusetts, my congregation, Temple Israel of Boston, was an active member of the Greater Boston Interfaith Organization. As a community of more than fifty churches, synagogues, mosques and other institutions, we worked together on a variety of economic justice issues on a state level, including affordable housing, living wages and public education. There were far more synagogues as a percentage of our coalition than there were Jews as a proportion of the greater population. At the peak of our power, the organized faith community succeeded in pressuring a Republican governor, Democratic legislature, health care providers and insurers, as well as unions and the Chamber of Commerce to support a health reform bill that led to high-quality, affordable care for hundreds of thousands of people and became the model for national reform. Later, thousands of Reform Jews would join people of faith across the country as the Religious Action Center played a key role in various coalitions to win passage of the Affordable Care Act. This is but one story of the Jewish commitment to work across lines of difference to shape a more economically equitable nation.

As the Director of the Religious Action of Reform Judaism, which was founded over 50 years ago in 1961, I oversee the social justice agenda of the Reform Movement, and work to shape policies and programmes of the secular government. Linking back to the Bible and a long chain of tradition, we still explicitly understand our work as reflecting God's call to protect and defend the widow, the orphan and the stranger. The American Jewish experience of the twenty-first century offers new challenges to the tradition of economic justice. Many American Jews, for example have achieved economic prosperity and no longer personally need to benefit from programmes designed to help people in poverty. Yet our compulsion to create economic justice in America does not derive from self-interest but from our memory of slavery in Egypt and our religious and moral obligations. American Jews who remain committed to economic justice understand that America has offered a home to Jews: a place that has afforded us more rights, freedoms and opportunities than we have known in any other land. The First Amendment to the US Constitution guarantees our ability to exercise our prophetic voice to speak truth to power, and protects our right to build communities that reflect our millennia-old social justice traditions, including seeking economic fairness. And with that freedom and increased security comes greater responsibility.

It is not surprising that the celebration of the Passover *seder* is the most commonly observed religious ceremony in American Jewish life. In the annual retelling of the Passover story, as every generation is charged to see itself anew as sharing in the Exodus from Egypt, we are reminded that just as the Jews of biblical times wandered for 40 years through the desert to reach the Promised Land, American Jews also wander to achieve God's vision here. As with all communities, there is diversity within the American Jewish community, and there are certainly some Jewish Americans, both past and present, whose decisions seem less guided by these principles. However, the narrative of the Exodus nonetheless remains an organizing principle of Jewish identity, and its lessons continue to undergird the policy agenda of the wider Jewish community. Whether we are honouring the legacy of those who died trapped in the stairwells of a New York City factory, marching in the streets of Selma, or advocating in the halls of Congress, American Jews are called by the voices of our tradition to fulfil the visions of the prophets. Immersed in ancient texts that call for both individual action and just social organization, and animated by centuries of experiencing both oppression and liberation, the Jewish community remains committed to the idea that the moral and religious measure of a society is ultimately what it does for the marginalized, the vulnerable and the poor.

Notes

1   This chapter could not have been written without the extraordinary efforts of two distinguished colleagues to whom I am most grateful. Nathan Bennett contributed much more than the research; he was a thought-partner at every stage, helping craft the arguments, structure, and rhetoric itself. His attention to detail was remarkable. Ambassador David Saperstein is my rabbi in every way; his significant editorial effort was invaluable, and his lifelong effort to lead the Jewish community's commitment to pursue economic justice for all people inspired the chapter, and inspires our ongoing work every day.

2   Primary texts have been adapted by the writer for gender-neutral language following the pattern of Plaut, G., general editor and Stein, D. general editor of revised edition, *The Torah, A Modern Commentary*, 2005 Revised Edition, Union for Reform Judaism, New York.

3   Eventually, however, the imposition of debt cancellation resulted in lenders withholding loans as the seventh year approached – a serious problem for the poor who needed loans more frequently to help them survive through difficult economic periods. This led Rabbi Hillel in the 1st century BCE to develop to a technical bypass of the rule in the early Talmudic period in order to protect the poor (Babylonian Talmud Gittin 34b-37b). These events highlight both the human temptation to circumvent just treatment of the poor out of self-interest and also the need for periodic reform to respond to changing conditions. Hillel's example demonstrates also the importance of leadership in keeping the original intentions of laws in view.

References

Balinsky, R. (n.d.) *The Alshich (Rabbi Moshe Alshich) On Leviticus* 19:9–10. Available from: www.on1foot.org/text/alshich-rabbi-moshe-alshich-leviticus-199–10 [accessed 18 April 2017].

Buxbaum, Y. (n.d.) *Elijah the Prophet in Minsk*, Chabad.org. Available from: www.chabad.org/library/article_cdo/aid/388664/jewish/Elijah-the-Prophet-in-Minsk.htm [accessed 13 July 2017].

Central Conference of American Rabbis (2004) *A Statement of Principles for Reform Judaism*, Central Conference of American Rabbis. Available from: https://ccarnet.org/rabbis-speak/platforms/statement-principles-reform-judaism/ [accessed 13 July 2017].

Central Conference of American Rabbis (2004) 'The Pittsburgh Platform'—1885', Central Conference of American Rabbis. Available from: https://ccarnet.org/rabbis-speak/platforms/declaration-principles/ [accessed 13 July 2017].

Epstein, I (ed.) (1938) *The Talmud*, London: The Soncino Press.

Hayim, D. (1991) *To be a Jew: A guide to Jewish observance in contemporary life*, New York: Basic Books.

Hebrew English Tanakh (1999) D. E. S. Stein (trans.), 2nd edn, Philadelphia, PA: Jewish Publication Society.

Hebrew Free Loan Society (2017) *About*. Available from: http://hfls.org/about/ [accessed 17 July 2017].

Israel Free Loan Association (2014) *IFLA's History Page*, The Israel Free Loan Association. Available from: www.israelfreeloan.org.il/en/about-ifla/iflas-history/ [accessed 20 July 2017].

Jewish Council on Public Affairs, 20 March (2017) *Policy Compendium*. Available from: http://jewishpublicaffairs.org/wp-content/uploads/sites/10/2015/09/Policy-Compedium-2017.pdf [accessed 9 July 2017].

Jones, R. and Cox A. (2012) *Chosen for what? Jewish values in 2012*, Washington, DC: Public Religion Research Institute. Available from: www.prri.org/research/jewish-values-in-2012/ [accessed 21 July 2017].

Kaplan, D. and Teller A. (2013) *An Introduction to Jewish Philanthropy*, E Jewish Philanthropy. Available from: http://ejewishphilanthropy.com/an-introduction-to-jewish-philanthropy/ [accessed 5 June 2017].

Maimonides M. (n.d.) *Mishneh Torah Sefer Zeraim Matnot Aniyim, Chapter 9*, E. Touger (trans.), Chabad.org. Available from: www.chabad.org/library/article_cdo/aid/986710/jewish/Matnot-Aniyim-Chapter-9.htm [Accessed 13 July 2017].

Maimonides M. (n.d.) *Mishneh Torah Sefer Zeraim Matnot Aniyim, Chapter 10*, E. Touger (trans.), Sefaria: A Living Library of Jewish Texts. Available from: www.sefaria.org/Mishneh_Torah,_Gifts_to_the_Poor.9–10?lang=bi [accessed 6 November 2017].

Midrash Rabbah Leviticus (1983) (trans.) H. Freedman and M. Simon, New York: The Soncino Press.

Newman, A. A. (1942) *The Jews in Spain: Their social, political and cultural life during the Middle Ages*, Philadelphia, PA: The Jewish Publication Society of America.

Roth, C. (1946) *The history of the Jews of Italy*, Philadelphia, PA: The Jewish Publication Society of America.

Shulvass, M. (1973) *The Jews in the world of the Renaissance*, Chicago, IL: Spertus College of Judaica Press.

Sione, P. (2016) *The 1911 Triangle Factory fire, January 2011*, New York: The ILR School of Cornell University. Available from: https://trianglefire.ilr.cornell.edu/index.html [accessed 10 July 2017].

Tamari, M. (1986) '*With all your possessions': Jewish ethics and economic life*, New York: The Free Press.

Union for Reform Judaism (2017) *Resolutions*. Available from: https://urj.org/what-we-believe/resolutions/resolutions-search?sortby=newest [accessed 13 July 2017].

Yanklowitz, S. (2014) *The soul of Jewish social justice*, Jerusalem: Urim Publications.

Zborowksi, M. and Herzog, E. (1952) *Life is with people*, New York: Schocken Books.

PART 4

Public theology and the common good

12

AMERICA, LAND OF THE FREE AND HOME OF THE POOR

Inequality as a way of life

Darryl M. Trimiew

America reluctantly accepts inequality as an ineradicable part of life. It is acknowledged as a moral affront, but not one that demands serious and immediate action (Newport 2015). Like death, it is understood as problematic but inevitable. And like death, inequality is neither celebrated nor condemned; it is accepted. Yet unlike death, inequality – in particular, economic inequality – can be ameliorated. I argue that America's failure to make ongoing and serious efforts to alleviate poverty and inequality is one of our primary moral and spiritual problems.[1] Unaddressed, it will ultimately lead to our demise.

In this chapter, I wish to explore why we, as a nation, do not take stronger steps to decrease inequality. I highlight four factors in particular: first, our narrow focus on protecting equality of opportunity through a focus on negative rights; second, our commitment to the myth of meritocracy; third, our justification of the status quo by means of scapegoating and blaming; and finally, our lack of a sense of solidarity and commitment to a common good. These issues explain why inequality, like poverty, will be with us always – not because they are inevitable features of life together, but because of particular values we hold and choices we make.

This work grows out of my career of theological and ethical analysis of American economic life and the moral arguments and narratives that give meaning, purpose and self-respect to many lives even as they allow inequality to persist. My thesis is that core moral, economic and theological justifications of our way of life simultaneously promote some positive corporate identities and assign blame to victims of economic policies. Our ongoing commitment to these cultural narratives raises our tolerance for economic inequality and makes it difficult to address the problem with public policy initiatives. Employing the concept of 'sub-rosa morality', I conclude that our current morality acts more like a justification of unequal economic outcomes than a spur for minimizing inequality. Sub-rosa morality is a morality of self-deception. Practitioners insist that all should uphold one point of view while simultaneously taking actions and making policies that contradict their explicit utterance and that result in the continuation of the situation they have declared to be immoral. It is different from Orwellian 'doublespeak' in the sense that the speakers are not consciously aware that they are contradicting themselves by what they are actually doing. It is more like a form of moral schizophrenia. Making real changes is difficult, but the first rule for digging your way out of a hole is to stop digging. We can stop digging by critically examining the actual results of our policies and then abandoning policies and approaches that justify a status quo that is widely perceived to be problematic. Doing so would do more than just reduce inequality. It would also help us create better and less self-deceptive identities.

Equal opportunity and a narrow focus on negative rights

Inequality is preserved in part by our society's commitment to guaranteeing equality of opportunity and refusing to examine equality of outcomes. Illumined by a focus on opportunity, unequal outcomes are seen as something like natural disasters: we might do our best to deal with them, but we assume that we cannot eliminate them.

Promoting the pursuit of life, liberty and happiness is not oriented towards particular substantive outcomes. Prevailing American moral visions maintain that individuals should be neither hindered nor unduly helped. We should be free to pursue social goods, but not to have them given to us. We have few 'natural rights', and those that we do have, as H. L. A. Hart (1955) has argued, are rights to liberty. Such rights to freedom or liberty enjoy wide support. Most Americans would agree that they should be protected by state action – but only when they are construed as *negative* rights rather than *positive* rights. Negative rights are rights that require the government to protect individuals from being interfered with by others. For example, our First Amendment right to freedom of speech requires our government to stop censors (including government itself) from interfering with us, but not to force anyone who is unwilling to listen to us to, in fact, listen. Negative rights require the government to restrain action, not to supply social goods. This commitment to freedom rather than sustainability or equality gives us few resources for discussing what constitutes inequality, and even fewer for thinking about how to cope with inequalities of starting points and outcomes.

Positive rights to particular social goods, on the other hand, could help us think more clearly about inequality. But an emphasis on positive rights runs against the grain of our prevailing morality. For example, the positive rights – including the right to work, the right to social security, the right to an adequate standard of living and the right to health – enumerated in the Covenant for Social Cultural and Economic Rights (hereafter referred to as the Covenant) have attracted little public support (United Nations General Assembly 1966). President Jimmy Carter broke with this tradition and as president signed the Covenant in 1977. For this treaty to be in force in America, however, it has to be ratified by Congress. Though decades have passed, it has yet to be ratified. There is almost no prospect that it will be. Carter was defeated by Ronald Reagan, whose Assistant Secretary of State Ernest W. Lefever vigorously rejected the Covenant and branded Carter's efforts as wrongheaded and against American values. For the Reagan administration, positive economic rights looked like claims that obliged government to be larger and more intrusive – and so, in their view, to interfere with individuals' responsibilities to provide for themselves and their dependents. One supporter of this form of conservatism, Michael Novak, called Carter's approach an attempt to create a servile state (Novak 1985). In previous works, I have argued that any society that recognizes human rights is wrong not to include economic rights among those basic human rights. Along with scholars like David Hollenbach and Henry Shue, I have argued for the compelling nature of economic rights and therefore the desirability of ratifying the covenant (Trimiew 1997). While our arguments seem to have won wide support among academics, they have not created change in the political sphere. Even now, the American public has not openly and widely considered the question of economic rights. No hue and cry for the ratification of the Covenant – or anything like it – has yet arisen. Thus, these academic debates were intellectually valuable but utterly insufficient for generating public support for ratifying the Covenant or some other statement of positive economic rights. They did not lead to the passage of anything like the array of legislation that it would take to fulfil such a statement. Such enabling legislation would provide for goods like a right to work, a right to a living wage and a right to other benefits that would make it easier for poor people to sustain themselves in a reasonable fashion and perhaps improve their economic standing and thereby reduce the inequality between themselves and wealthier Americans. If such legislation has been passed in a few local jurisdictions, there is little movement towards it on a national level.

Carter's vision of economic rights was rejected by Reagan in both foreign and domestic policymaking. The rugged individualism of the Reagan ethos not only rejected the idea that economic rights are human rights but also rejected the duty of government to intervene on behalf of the poor. This rejection was built on two important and interlocking assertions. First, Reagan's supporters argued that poverty was created not by bad economic policy, but rather by the bad morality of the poor. This determination was presented as fact-finding, but it is better described as victim-blaming. Citing Census Bureau statistics, Michael Novak (1986) writes that 83 per cent of poor people did not work full-time year-round in 1988, that 93 per cent of poor people did not graduate from high-school, and that more than half of poor households were families headed by women. Novak concludes that the Census Bureau figures show that most poverty in America results from bad behavior in relation to work, education and marriage. A second assumption flows from the first. Novak argues that good government should restrain itself from intervening on behalf of the poor because such intervention cripples the poor by engendering in them irresponsibility, laziness and dependency – qualities that only make their poverty worse (Novak 1986).

Reagan famously railed against those he called 'welfare queens' and used this image to undermine the so-called War on Poverty initiated by the Johnson administration. In Reagan's view, the poor did not need 'intervention' from the government; they simply needed to be left alone. They could only improve their lot by pulling on their own bootstraps without interference from a state that did them more harm than good. In this presumptively better world, poverty and inequality are problems generated primarily by immoral and irresponsible citizens, not by an oppressive capitalist economy proceeding with some combination of benign neglect and active support from the state. Public policy must, in this scenario, promote the common good by letting the invisible hand of the market make distributions without significant restraints and certainly without public policy intervention.

The myth of meritocracy

Reagan's emphasis on negative rights as a means of securing equality of opportunity fit closely with a second important element of America's sub-rosa morality: meritocracy. *The Oxford Companion to Philosophy* notes with regard to meritocracy that:

> A meritocracy requires equality of opportunity and some form of central planning; it must prohibit egalitarian levelling as well as any form of nepotism or hereditary aristocracy.
>
> (Honderich 1995)

In short, whether it is recognized or not, meritocracy requires, among other things, a strict prohibition of egalitarian levelling or interference. Good government must, by this definition, inhibit if not prohibit public policy that is directly interventionist in the meritocratic mission of America. Inequality might not be celebrated any more than illness or death, but it must not be addressed in ways that suggest that meritocracy is either unfair or insufficient to promote life, liberty and the pursuit of happiness. Meritocracy's confidence in just reward for hard work and talent was crystallized early on by Adam Smith, the father of modern economics:

> In all the middling and inferior professions, real and solid professional abilities, joined to prudent, just, firm, and temperate conduct can very seldom fail of success. Abilities will even sometimes prevail where the conduct is by no means correct.
>
> (cited in Trimiew 1997, p. 155)

Smith's conclusion is most easily seen in Reaganism, but it has been extended by more recent presidents. As Keri Day (2013) explained in a recent essay, government has bifurcated its responses to the poor with the institution of faith-based initiatives. In a move that looks like a perverse negative of the Wisdom of Solomon, George H. W. Bush split the poverty/inequality baby by having government trim welfare support to the poor at the same time he assigned the responsibility for helping the poor to religious and/or community organizations. With this move, the Bush administration was insulated from charges that it was doing nothing to address poverty. At the same time, religious organizations were opened up to new criticism along just these lines – particularly if the outcomes of their programs were not positive. However, the real villain in this scenario, the real causative agent for dysfunctionality and poverty, was declared to be the poor themselves. Indeed, the putative cause for poverty was assigned to the poor – and not just any poor people, but to the 'immoral' or 'depraved' poor (Trimiew 1997). As I have noted elsewhere and as Day updates, the phenomenon of female-headed households mired in poverty is characterized by the neoconservatives as the cause of poverty when it should rather be seen as a consequence of poverty. This decision to blame poor people for their poverty is both wrong and deeply rooted, extending from Republicans like Reagan and both Bushes to Democrats like Bill Clinton (Day 2013). This sleight of hand is assisted and abetted now also by Black conservatives such as Glenn Loury. As I have previously argued, the blaming of poverty on the 'depraved' poor completely misses the reality of widespread poverty among the 'virtuous' poor – those two-headed households with parents working two or more jobs (Trimiew 1997). Blaming the character of the poor for their poverty also fits neatly with systematic disinvestment by the state. For if the real problem is one of character, then private and religious organizations are best equipped to address the problem and government should only lend a partial and indirect hand.

If such arguments are not to be relegated to the dubious category of being faith statements of the problematic kind – the kind that does not depend on and cannot be refuted by empirical evidence – then they must, at some point, yield better results or outcomes. Time has demonstrated, however, that since these new welfare reforms have been instituted, both inequality and extreme poverty have increased (Floyd *et al.* 2017). The evidence suggests that programs to improve character do not in fact reduce poverty. Yet the opposite conclusions have been reached by many policymakers. William Julius Wilson's analysis of the association between female-headed households and poverty as arising primarily from a manifestation of bad economic and political policy – rather than bad individual character – is simply ignored (Wilson 1987). These secular and empirically verifiable explanations are widely rejected because they do not support the prevailing narrative that hardworking and virtuous individuals in a free market society always have freedom of opportunity to succeed economically. It is simply assumed that smart, hard work will inevitably yield positive outcomes that better individuals and therefore also reduce inequality. The corollary to this belief is also assumed: if people are poor, it must be because they are not smart enough or do not work hard enough. The narratives have such a hold on our political imaginations that mere facts cannot overturn them.

The pervasiveness of these myths of meritocracy lead many Americans, even those who detest inequality, to remain apathetic in the face of its expansion. For if poverty is caused primarily by bad morality, then it cannot be fixed by good public policy. Further, if the poor are the primary causes of their poverty and are poor because they are 'bad', then perhaps they 'deserve' their poverty. (This is, of course a kind of restatement, in a negative sense, of the logic of meritocracy.)[2] This cluster of views has the power to legitimate policy proposals like the ones in the platform of Jeb Bush, one of the candidates for the Republican nomination for President in 2016. Bush asserted that if more Americans would work harder in longer weeks, they would have more money and poverty would be reduced (Tuohy 2015).[3] This position still has cachet in many circles. While it is true that lazy people are sometimes poor it does not inevitably follow that all poverty is generated by laziness. Part of the reason that this discussion has not been settled has to be attributed to the weakness of counterarguments.

Let us return, for example, to the Carter administration, which supported economic rights and had a generalized support for New Deal/Great Society programs. In spite of this support, neither Carter nor his administration argued vigorously for the ratification of the Covenant. Carter's one-term presidency afforded him little time or opportunity to further the cause. But he did very little with the opportunities he had, seeming to rest on the laurels of having signed the document. Even that signing depended on the fact that he did not specifically and directly link it to making changes in domestic policy. In not specifically calling attention to the possible impact of the Covenant, he minimized public opposition to it. In not having it ratified, however, it remains, at least for Americans, an orphaned treaty. It has no standing here. But most of the rest of the modern, wealthy West has endorsed it. And that same West has many economic rights that America does not. The right to single-payer healthcare which the Covenant supports and which is supported by other human rights treaties cannot be accomplished by America – at least not currently. Instead, Barack Obama adapted Mitt Romney's state healthcare plan that allows the government to underwrite some of the market's cost for healthcare rather than taking primary responsibility for providing basic healthcare for its citizens. In doing so, it still placed the onus of bettering oneself squarely on the back of citizens. With the elections of 2016, even these incremental gains are eroding. Such timidity continues to reign in politics and public policy primarily because this approach does not challenge the meritocratic assumptions that have such a deep hold on America's collective imagination. Those assumptions reject interventionist policies that might mitigate inequality as heavy-handed interventions that restrain individual liberty. From this point of view, single-payer systems such as those in Canada, Great Britain and elsewhere are morally wrong-headed and act to rob the virtuous citizenry of meeting their own needs by their own moral economic efforts.

Yet what is the value and meaning of meritocracy as an organizing principle if, over a long period of time, public policy's devotion to its priority generates consistently bad outcomes and increasing inequality (DeSilver 2013)? At what point does such a notion lose its plausibility, its traction (Weissmann 2012)? At what point do inequality and widespread poverty become so intense that they produce a 'legitimation crisis' that relegates belief in the meritocracy to the dustbins of history?[4]

Such questions are quite difficult because meritocracy as a concept has both explanatory power and moral resonance. Specifically, meritocracy rejects every kind of *political* inequality. It argues especially against any trace of hereditary aristocracy in a form of government. The Fourteenth and Fifteenth Amendments to the Constitution, for example, were designed to remove legal impediments to civic participation previously excluded groups and promote equal opportunity for life, liberty and the pursuit of happiness. But commitment to this kind of basic, political equality has long been compatible, in American minds, with tolerance for vast inequality of economic outcomes. This country has already experienced the Great Depression and the recent recession without rethinking the value of meritocracy. Given the relative accomplishments of the meritocratic ideal, what more will it take to stir popular support for real action to alleviate inequality?

Perhaps an answer can be inferred by government action with reference to past catastrophes. The Great Depression and its horrors were at least partially addressed by Roosevelt's New Deal. The horrors of Jim Crow and poverty were at least partially addressed by Johnson's Great Society. These public policy programs made America a better society – that is less unequal. Thus, American history would suggest that growing inequality will only be addressed when life appears to be intolerable – or, perhaps, when its high priests trumpet its merits too loudly and too long.

Let us consider a recent historical example – Mitt Romney's 47 per cent theory. Romney said,

> There are 47 per cent of the people who will vote for the president no matter what . . . who are dependent upon government, who believe that they are victims . . . These are people who pay no income tax . . . And so my job is not to worry about those people. I'll never convince them that they should take personal responsibility and care for their lives.
>
> (MoJo News Team 2012)

Romney scrambled to explain his comments, but his running mate had a surprisingly similar message. Paul Ryan said,

> Right now about 60 per cent of the American people get more benefits in dollar value from the federal government than they pay back in taxes . . . So we're going to a majority of takers versus makers in America and that will be tough to come back from that. They'll be dependent on the government for their livelihoods [rather] than themselves.
>
> (Craw and Carter 2012)

The trope performed by Romney and Ryan depended on an assumption that America has always had makers and takers. Makers were virtuous members of society who had not only bettered themselves by means of hard work, but also had, as a side effect, generated jobs and wealth and opportunities for others. These paragons of virtue had made America great and would do so again, if not hampered by the state. Yet what Romney and Ryan also asserted was that America's decline could also be linked to a decline in the number of makers and an increase in the numbers of takers. These latter-day minions were those overly dependent upon the 'servile state' whose social welfare programs had made them economically weak and irresponsible. Accordingly, Romney and Ryan argued that good government and good public policy should reject cries for more hand-outs and entitlements and instead require poor people to be more productive in their efforts and more accountable for social goods distributed to them. Romney and Ryan's argument drew on deep currents of meritocratic conviction. Yet it failed to get them elected and could perhaps even be interpreted as a factor in their defeat.

Romney and Ryan's talk of makers and takers did not win a majority of voters, but it would be premature to proclaim the end of the meritocratic ideal in America. What Americans rejected were the broad strokes with which Romney and Ryan defined the 'takers' to get to 47 per cent. A total of 47 per cent of Americans as blameworthy takers depended on the inclusion of many people who would argue that their 'merit' should exempt them from this category. Most seniors in America are on Social Security, whether they need it or not. Many are reliant on Medicare. Many others are disabled and reliant upon Social Security disability payments. Other government interventions such as veterans' benefits are also highly popular and regarded as 'righteous entitlements'. To characterize Americans like these as 'takers' – just one step away from moochers or deadbeats – was political suicide for Romney. These 'takers' do not see themselves as non-meritorious and therefore their being scapegoated was highly offensive. It grated against many Americans' understanding of themselves as 'makers' and undercut their ability to define 'takers' as other people – and primarily people receiving unemployment or welfare benefits. The importance of this move should not be understated. The meaning of many people's lives is tied up with the possibility of America as a place to live out a gospel of success (cf. Betsworth 1990).

Yet here we find the trap of our current social relations and distributions. The entitlement programs criticized by Romney and Ryan are desperately needed in America. Over time they have come to be seen more and more as rights. To take them away is an acknowledgment that the political and economic ship of state is foundering on the rocks. And, increasingly, new interventions are becoming justified social goods or 'rights'. For example, as more Americans have access to healthcare because of the implementation of the Affordable Care Act and expanded Medicaid, coupled with the factor of the slowdown in the rising costs of healthcare services, arguments for healthcare acquired solely by meritocracy – that is by getting a job with good benefits – begin to look increasingly unpersuasive. This conclusion is not based on any poll, but is evidenced by the enormous difficulties that a Republican-controlled Congress in coordination with a Republican president has had with repealing and replacing the Affordable Care Act.

What is most remarkable is the resilience of the ideology of meritocracy in the face of real-world developments. If the Affordable Care Act ends up surviving, it will be because it was found to help people who are believed to deserve help.

If, on the other hand, it is undone, it will be because it got tagged with the fault of giving the money of 'makers' to 'takers' who did not deserve it. And if it fails to generate any good outcomes at all, its failure will not be blamed on state actions to undermine it, but on bad moral agents who are so incorrigible that they simply cannot be helped by any kind of government program. Prior explanations have long been successful in finding non-meritorious agents to blame, and we have no reason to think the pattern will not be repeated.

Scapegoating and blaming as a foundational aspect of bad public policy formation

Most discussions of inequality overlook the subtle dynamics of blame in managing the perception of the seriousness and extent of systemic failure. Theories of blame can help to illumine the ways these dynamics play out. The dynamics of blaming help explain both moral failure and bad subsequent social justice outcomes. At their most general level, theories of blame make reference to human frailty. It is easy to account for moral failure by pointing out the obvious: all people, at some time, do wrong. Human sinfulness therefore is an authentic and effective cause and source of moral failure and immorality in general. This very general explanation has long been available and useful in accounting for moral failure and is no doubt a trust-worthy partial explanation. But such explanation has few details and few practical consequences. When blaming theory begins to get more specific, though, its explan-atory power begins to expand.

When moral systems identify groups or individuals to blame for moral failure rather than simply falling back on general human peccability, they often achieve something more than mere maintenance of theoretical coherence. Singling out or scapegoating particular groups promises to account for the reality of systemic moral failure by identifying a source of peccability that can be localized. This localization insulates both the larger system and humanity as a whole from criticism. Such scapegoating makes analysis of actual cause and effect more difficult. It also blurs the lines that define who is and who is not a member of a given community.

How is this so? Scapegoating accounts of blame are very dynamic. As they explain moral failure, they simultaneously outline what it means to be a member of any given moral body. The scapegoat simultaneously defines the problem, identifies the causes of the problem and absolves the blamers of responsibility for the problem. The blamers' identity is therefore always connected in a dynamic way with that of the scapegoat. The more the problem and its foundational cause(s) can be attributed to those blamed, the less scrutiny needs to be focused on the functioning of the public policy itself.[5] Blaming justifies both the inclusion of good moral members and the exclusion of bad moral members, or, perhaps more accurately put, it obscures the reality of systems of first- and second-class membership within one moral system. It thereby obscures the detection of double standards that ordinarily would be unacceptable. And, as we will discuss hereafter, the processes of scapegoating and the punishment of scapegoats can also help in the moral revitalization of the scapegoating community and their idea of morality and adequate levels of equality. Indeed, as we will demonstrate hereafter, sometimes this secondary blaming function works best when it operates on an unconscious level in the minds of moral apologists rather than at a fully conscious level. That is, it often works best in what I have called a sub-rosa manner. Then the very act of scapegoating as scapegoating escapes detection by its carriers and creators and eventually comes to be seen by them as external to themselves – as facts outside of their creative control – as natural realities that must be acceded to as if they were part of the natural world, or perhaps as acts of God.

Ta-Nahesi Coates writes of this phenomenon in discussing American racism:

> Americans believe in the reality of 'race' as a defined, indubitable feature of the natural world. Racism—the need to ascribe bone-deep features to people and then to humiliate, reduce, and destroy them—inevitably follows from this inalterable condition. In this way, racism is rendered as the innocent daughter of Mother Nature, and one is left to deplore the Middle Passage or the Trail of Tears the way one deplores an earthquake, a tornado, or any other phenomenon that can be cast as beyond the handiwork of men.
>
> (Coates 2015, p. 7)

In this form of blaming, the powerful do not understand themselves as personally involved in blaming scapegoats. They rather understand themselves as moral detectives who are simply excavating and analyzing data before declaring what should be self-evident: that bad outcomes are due to the failures of the scapegoats themselves. Of course, those blamed sometimes do generate some of their own problems. The generalization of these discrete events into universal laws makes it morally palatable to blame victims of social injustice for their suffering. This achievement is of no small value in facilitating the continuation of inequality without engendering self-detection, self-criticism, concern for others and genuine repentance and reform. For if inequality is caused by bad people, then systems of social justice are not themselves faulty and the beneficiaries of such systems can believe that their success is due solely to their meritorious efforts. Failures are due solely to the actions of 'loafers'. Therefore, a tolerable measure of justice can be achieved with the employ of some form of Rawlsian difference principle without radically changing the system. If the system is not broken it need not be fixed. Meritocracy and blaming go hand and hand, lifting some up while simultaneously justifying the lack of success of others. Together they offer a complete account of inequality that does not depend on a critical examination of the morality of distributions, opportunities, or relationships.

Moral values and narratives in tension

Americans do not like inequality. Yet American disdain for inequality is never absolute. Moreover, this dislike is seldom attached to the formation of public policy that will make a lasting difference, particularly when such policy challenges the reigning cultural narrative of meritocracy – the story of hard work leading to success. Thus, Americans are both unhappy with inequality and simultaneously in opposition to making many changes in public policy that would decrease inequality – such as making a statement about positive economic rights or even directly redistributing wealth (Matthews 2015). This result is due in part to the sub-rosa dynamics of meritocratic ideals and the still-present practice of scapegoating. Most Americans want to believe that most successful and advantaged people have attained their positions solely or primarily by meritocratic effort. God's blessings, the exploitation of others and sheer luck have all been wrongfully excluded as contributing to the creation of wealth by means of the cover story of the gospel of success – and it is that self-deception that makes the successful feel so worthy (Betsworth 1990). Yet the gospel of success is false. Our actual reality, denied by many of us, is that our middle class is shrinking and will continue to shrink, regardless of the characters of individuals (Weissmann 2012). Furthermore, the buying power of wages has been shrinking for over 30 years (DeSilver 2014).

The logic of positive economic rights would allow the poor to sue for governmental redress, but in doing so, would challenge the efficacy of meritocracy. It would also require government intervention such as the formation of a national jobs office to assist all in getting better jobs – an approach championed by William Julius Wilson (1987). These changes would involve telling a newer and truer story, one that calls into question the accuracy of the story of success and the moral superiority of the wealthy and strivers to wealth and success. This truer story is that we are all created in the image of God, all subject to the whims of the market and the fickleness of fate, all in need basic human goods, and all morally ambiguous. Acceptance of this new story does not guarantee a groundswell for the ratification of the Covenant. However, this new story could certainly build public support for additional governmental interventions that, while falling short of the demands of the Covenant, might in themselves decrease the growing inequality in America.[6]

The truth is not that there is nothing that can be done. Rather, the truth is that, at least at the present, we cannot handle the truth that there are *some* things that can be done. This is why, for example the passage of legislation for a living wage at a national level meets with so much opposition. Too many Americans would rather believe that the poor deserve their poverty, as long as they can feel secure in their own dwindling success. As long as most Americans do not understand the limits of meritocracy and laissez-faire capitalism, the political will to wage a war on poverty and inequality will elude us. Where there is no will, there will be no way.

One might hope that we will not need another Great Depression to come to our senses. But I am not hopeful. My pessimism grows out of recognition of the deep resistance to expansion of social safety nets like those advanced by democratic socialist progressives such as Bernie Sanders.[7] His platform was widely dismissed, even by Democrats, as being unrealistic or inappropriate. A sea change in our understanding of ourselves and the mission of America will precede any successful efforts to contain or ameliorate inequality. Such deep change seems unlikely because it would require greater honesty and self-criticism. The economic struggles anticipated in the coming years might lead more people to display more of these qualities. But the opposite reaction seems even more likely, as people become risk-averse, grasping, selfish and eager to differentiate themselves from an undeserving mass of 'takers'. Yet, this chapter is not a prophecy predicting the future as much as it is a prophetic judgment on our present and our past. Perhaps before the next economic catastrophe, people will understand, accept and promote older notions of covenant and common good (Bellah 1975). At least, that is my hope.

Conclusion: gross inequality's negation of the common good

Clearly, the mere presence of some inequality does not in the West constitute a moral problem. John Rawls's classic text, *A Theory of Justice*, distils part of what he understands as our moral consensus into what he calls the difference principle. This principle holds that policy changes can produce inequality so long as they provide a net benefit for the least well off members of society (Rawls 1971, p. 15). This principle has not been instituted into American law or public policy, but it makes explicit a deep national sense that public policy should benefit not just the advantaged but also the least advantaged. It also makes clear our willingness, as a society, to live with the gross inequalities that are already in place. In other words, with Rawls we are at once committed to disliking inequality and *uncommitted* to serious projects of redistribution or systems of reparation that could begin to undo gross inequality.[8]

The difference principle alone obscures some of the moral problems with inequality. But a notion of the common good can begin to reveal them more truthfully. The term 'common good' has a long and honorable history in the West. As Klaus Bosselmann, Ron Engel, and Prue Taylor write, 'The "common good" is that in which all the members share, and not merely a collection of the goods of its individual members' (2008, p. 57). 'The common good' is a more religious concept than meritocracy, and in America it has often been associated with the concept of covenant – usually a biblical covenant (Bellah 1975). Covenant is grounded in the notion that all members are bound to each other in mutuality in terms of both responsibilities and at least some form of privileges, rights and benefits. In other words, covenant mandates a social connectedness in some type of organic solidarity – though not necessarily absolute economic equality.

All understandings of covenant and the common good assume that the distribution of benefits and burdens are justifiable only in an overarching conception of community. What has been most problematic in America has been the moral integrity of its self-conception of community. Our undeniable history is that America was founded on the realization of conquest, imperialism and slavery. As such, all of the people who have lived in territorial America were not automatically included as full members within the community. Surviving First Nations people have survived as a people precisely because they were neither included within the community nor killed by members of it.

Thus, the question that has been wrestled with in every generation of 'Americans' is just who are truly members of the covenant of the common good and what is their place and function within it. Even with the elimination of slavery, there has been no automatic instantiation of full covenanted citizenship. Charles Mills, an African American philosopher, notes just how degraded historically the status of oppressed peoples in America has been. He writes:

> But as we will see in greater detail later on, the color-coded morality of the Racial Contract restricts the possession of this natural freedom and equality of *white* men. By virtue of their complete nonrecognition, or at best inadequate, myopic recognition, of the duties of natural law, non-whites are appropriately relegated to a lower rung on the moral ladder (the Great Chain of Being). They are designated as born unfree and unequal. A partitioned social ontology is therefore created, a universe divided between persons and racial sub-persons, *Untermenschen*, who may variously be black, red, brown, yellow—slaves, aborigines, colonial populations—but who are collectively appropriately known as 'subject races'.
>
> (Mills 1997, pp. 16–17)

For those whose ancestors were held by law and custom in subjugation, meritocracy, linked to economic success, has been held out by the powerful as a carrot to them to encourage both their striving for success and their existential toleration of gross inequalities.[9] Yet, if inequality is substantial, growing in ways that show no sign of ending, meritocracy (as in a strident Protestant work ethic) must inevitably move from being seen as an empowering myth to being seen as a mythic fantasy – by the oppressed and, eventually, by the empowered.

In this scenario, as previously discussed, meritocracy's power to justify current distributions and present and future public policy formation fails. America then has an explicit 'legitimation crisis' not unlike that which proved so problematic in the old Soviet Socialist Republic (Habermas 1975). And this disillusionment and demoralization need not be limited to excluded and oppressed minorities but can also undermine traditional 'white' majorities. Indeed, these dynamics seem to be contributing to the growing opioid epidemic in white Rust Belt communities. In a country as wealthy as America, gross inequality coupled with our history suggests that none of the legal removals of slavery and ameliorations of Jim Crow laws have been effective in creating an America in which non-whites have actually achieved the status of full personhood. As such, do non-whites have full membership in a covenanted common good-oriented society? Meritocracy which can inspire all to strive to escape poverty is morally justifiable only so long as it does not prevent governmental interventions to fight inequality in situations in which gross inequality prevails. Gross inequality, accordingly, makes it morally impossible to hold to a preference for the primacy of meritocracy over government intervention.

This is true, even in a society like America in which equality of opportunity, rather than equality of outcome, has been the goal. Our current American preference for meritocracy ensures the continuation of our current immoral implementation of a common good that does not include all citizens on equal terms. It rather functions to sacralize the status quo. As long as this understanding of merit prevails, then – just as Jesus said – the poor will be with us always. And America will remain the land of the free and the home of the poor.

Notes

1 Of course, during crises such as the Great Depression or the War on Poverty, inequality or suffering gets so far out of hand that to preserve some sort of normal life, a 'war' on inequality or poverty is declared – at least for a while.

2 More Hispanic/Latino and black people live in poverty even when working; around 10 per cent of Hispanic/Latino and black workers live in poverty, compared with about 5 per cent and 4 per cent of white and Asian workers, respectively. The situation is worst for black working women, more than 11 per cent of whom live below the poverty line (income less than $21,756 for a family of four in 2009). This suggests that wages are too low to ensure an adequate standard of living. See the fact sheet of the Center for Economic and Social Rights (2010).

3 'My aspirations for the country, and I believe we can achieve it, is for 4 per cent growth as far as the eye can see', Bush said. 'Which means we have to be a lot more productive. Workforce participation has to rise from its all-time modern lows. It means that people need to work longer hours and through their productivity gain more income for their families. That's the only way we are going to get out of this rut that we're in' (Tuohy 2015).

4 For a full statement on a legitimation crisis, see Jürgen Habermas (1975).

5 Betsworth (1990, pp. 77–78) writes, 'While want and need are inevitable, the gospel of success attributes their cause to the character of the person who suffers them, not to God, as did Winthrop, or to the social situation, as did later reformers. Indigence is the punishment the universe metes out to the person of poor character, who will not train himself or herself in the virtues of industry and efficiency. The steady attack on the character of the poor also served to fuel the racism directed against blacks, Native Americans and Mexican Americans. Those groups that suffered from discrimination also suffered the most from poverty. To racists, poverty was but a further sign of the degradation of despised groups'.

6 One such intervention might be the implementation of a single-payer system of healthcare.

7 Sanders (2015) is blunt on the issue of inequality, writing: 'The reality is that for the past 40 years, Wall Street and the billionaire class has rigged the rules to redistribute wealth and income to the wealthiest and most powerful people of this country. This campaign is sending a message to the billionaire class: 'you can't have it all'. You can't get huge tax breaks while children in this country go hungry. You can't continue sending our jobs to China while millions are looking for work. You can't hide your profits in the Cayman Islands and other tax havens, while there are massive unmet needs on every corner of this nation. Your greed has got to end. You cannot take advantage of all the benefits of America, if you refuse to accept your responsibilities as Americans'.

8 See my critique of Rawls on this point, following the lead of Christian Bay (Trimiew 1997, p. 163).

9 President Andrew Johnson clearly expressed this testing of African American rights after the Civil War. Historian Carol Anderson, author of *White Rage*, writes about this issue as follows: 'The Civil Rights Bill of 1866 also came under attack by the president. In vetoing the proposed legislation, Johnson raised several telling objections. He argued that blacks had to earn their citizenship, reminding Congress that African Americans had just

emerged from slavery and, therefore, "should pass through a certain probation . . . before attaining the coveted prize". There was to be no born-on-American-soil-lottery, he intoned; instead, they had to "give evidence of their fitness to receive and to exercise the rights of citizens". For Johnson, nearly 250 years of unpaid toil to build one of the wealthiest nations on earth did not earn citizenship' (Anderson 2016, p. 30).

References

Allen, J. L. (1990) *Love & conflict: A covenantal model of Christian ethics*, 3rd edn, Nashville, TN: Abingdon Press.

Anderson, C. (2016) *White rage: The unspoken truth of our racial divide*, New York: Bloomsbury.

Bellah, R. N. (1975) *The broken covenant: American civil religion in time of trial*, New York: Seabury Press.

Betsworth, R. G. (1990) *Social ethics: An examination of American moral traditions*, Louisville, KY: Westminster John Knox.

Bosselmann, K., Engel R. and Taylor, P. (2008). *Governance for stability: Issues, challenges, successes*, IUCN Environmental Policy and Law Paper No. 70, Gland, Switzerland: International Union for Conservation of Nature and Natural Resources.

Card, D. and Krueger, A. B. (2000) 'Minimum wages and employment: A case study of the fast-food industry in New Jersey and Pennsylvania', *The American Economic Review, 90*(5): 1397–1420.

Center for Economic and Social Rights (2010) *Fact sheet no. 11: United States of America*, New York: Center for Economic and Social Rights. Available from: www.cesr.org/sites/default/files/USA_Web_final_0.pdf [accessed 28 December 2015].

Coates, T. (2015) *Between the world and me*, New York: Spiegel & Grau.

Covert, B. (2012) 'Clinton touts welfare reform. Here's how it failed', *The Nation*, 6 September. Available from: www.thenation.com/article/clinton-touts-welfare-reform-heres-how-it-failed/ [accessed 15 May 2017].

Craw, B. and Carter, Z. (2012) 'Paul Ryan: 60 percent of Americans are "takers," not "makers"', *HuffPost Politics*, 5 October. Available from: www.huffingtonpost.com/2012/10/05/paul-ryan-60-percent-of-a_n_1943073.html [accessed 28 December 2015].

Day, K. (2013) 'Saving black America? A womanist analysis of faith based initiatives', *Journal of the Society of Christian Ethics, 33*(1): 63–81.

DeSilver, D. (2013) 'U.S. income inequality, on rise for decades, is now highest since 1928', Pew Research Center, 5 December. Available from: www.pewresearch.org/fact-tank/2013/12/05/u-s-income-inequality-on-rise-for-decades-is-now-highest-since-1928/ [accessed 28 December 2015].

DeSilver, D. (2014) 'For most workers, real wages have barely budged for decades', Pew Research Center, 9 October. Available from: www.pewresearch.org/fact-tank/2014/10/09/ for-most-workers-real-wages-have-barely-budged-for-decades/ [accessed 28 December 2015].

Ellison, C. D (2015) 'Inequality is the new affirmative action—for white people', *The Root*, 23 July. Available from: www.theroot.com/inequality-is-the-new-affirmative-action-for-white-peop-1790860600 [accessed 27 December 2015].

Epps, G. (2015), 'Is affirmative action finished?' *The Atlantic*, 10 December. Available from: www.theatlantic.com/politics/archive/2015/12/when-can-race-be-a-college-admissions-factor/419808/ [accessed 18 December 2015].

Floyd, I., Pavetti, D. and Schott, L. (2017), *TANF reaching few poor families*, Washington, DC: Center on Budget and Policy Priorities. Available from: www.cbpp.org/research/family-income-support/tanf-reaching-few-poor-families [accessed 8 June 2017].

Habermas, J. (1975) *Legitimation crisis*, Boston, MA: Beacon Press.

Hart, H. L. A. (1955) 'Are there any natural rights?', *Philosophical Review*, *64*(2): 175–191.

Honderich, T. (ed.), (1995) *The Oxford companion to philosophy*, New York: Oxford University Press.

Johnson, L. B. (1966) 'Commencement address at Howard University: "To fulfill these rights"', in L. B. Johnson, *Public papers of the presidents of the United States 1965*, vol. 2, Washington DC: Government Printing Office, pp. 635–640.

Matthews, C. (2015) *4 things you didn't (but should) know about economic inequality*, Fortune, 11 June. Available from: http://fortune.com/2015/06/11/income-inequality/ [accessed 28 December 2015].

Mills, C. W. (1997) *The racial contract*, Ithaca, NY: Cornell University Press.

MoJo News Team (2012) 'Full transcript of the Mitt Romney secret video', *Mother Jones*, 19 September. Available from: www.motherjones.com/politics/2012/09/full-transcript-mitt-romney-secret-video/#47percent [accessed 28 December 2015].

Newport, F. (2015) *Americans continue to say US wealth distribution is unfair*, Gallup. Available from: www.gallup.com/poll/182987/americans-continue-say-wealth-distribution-unfair.aspx [accessed 17 December 2015].

Novak, M. (1985) 'Economic rights: The servile state', *Catholicism in Crisis*, *3* (October): 8–15.

Novak, M. (1986) 'Free persons and the common good', *Crisis*, *4* (October): 11–19.

Piccard, A. (2010) 'The United States' failure to ratify the international covenant on economic, social and cultural rights: Must the poor be always with us?', *The Scholar: St. Mary's Law Review on Minority Issues*, *13*(2): 213–272.

Rawls, J. (1971) *A theory of justice*, Cambridge, MA: Belknap Press.

Sanders, B. (2015) *Issues: Income and wealth inequality*, Burlington, VT: Friends of Bernie Sanders. Available from: https://berniesanders.com/issues/income-and-wealth-inequality/ [accessed 17 December 2015].

Trimiew, D. (1997) *God bless the child that's got its own: The economic rights debate,* Atlanta, GA: Scholar's Press.

Trimiew, D. (2001) 'Sub-rosa morality: An account of moral failure', *American Baptist Quarterly*, *20*(2): 191–212.

Tuohy, D. (2015) 'Jeb Bush: "We've got to start solving problems"', *New Hampshire Union Leader*, 8 July. Available from: www.unionleader.com/article/20150709 /NEWS0605/150709206&template=mobileart#sthash.mHgyqiFp.dpuf [accessed 15 May 2017].

United Nations General Assembly (1966) *International covenant on economic, social and cultural rights*, GA Res 2200A (XXI), United Nations, *Treaty Series*, vol. 933, pp. 3–106.

Walzer, M. (1983) *Spheres of justice: A defense of pluralism and equality*, New York: Basic Books.

Weissmann, J. (2012) 'U.S. income inequality: It's worse today than it was in 1774: Even if you count slaves', *The Atlantic*, 19 September. Available from: www.theatlantic.com/business/archive/2012/09/us-income-inequality-its-worse-today-than-it-was-in-1774/262537/ [accessed 28 December 2015].

Wilson, W. J. (1987) *The truly disadvantaged: The inner city, the underclass, and public policy*, Chicago, IL: University of Chicago Press.

13

THE INTEGRITY OF THE CHURCH IN A DIVIDED SOCIETY

Steven M. Tipton

Many American churches have sought to respond faithfully to problems of inequality.[1] Understanding and evaluating those responses pushes us to the most basic questions about the place of religion in a free, self-governing society such as the United States. Mainline Protestant ideals of the public church lift up its voice as a prophetic witness and conscientious advocate in the moral argument of public life, seeking to guide law and policy to serve justice and fulfil the common good. Many conservative evangelical voices, by contrast, call faithful individuals to volunteer as Good Samaritans and entrepreneurs to help their neighbors face-to-face and so help change America for the better – one heart, soul and conscience at a time. What stymies univocal efforts to address inequality in the United States today is not simply the conflicting play of political interests and ideologies, it is an argument between contrary ideals of faith in public and the good of government, even when it comes down to the ground of particular problems of economic hardship and actual prospects for progress and prosperity. This contest of moral meaning and practice unfolds within the peculiar yet essential ambiguity of the American polity, both as a cultural constellation of shared meanings and a social order of institutionally structured relationships and practical activities.

Are we a republic in recognizable relation to classical or Calvinist republics, dependent for our integrity upon a sense of civic virtue and the mores of republican citizenship? Or are we a liberal constitutional state, governed through the coordination of individuals' conflicting interests and equal rights? The American answer, in short, is that we have sought to be both; to enjoy civic and liberal freedoms alike; to retain the moral integrity and binding public spirit of a republic in the political structure of a liberal constitutional state, with its stress on voluntarism and personal sovereignty.[2] In so doing, we have lived with profound tensions. Overriding concern for self-interest is the very definition of the corruption of republican virtue, which must check free choice even as it guides free conscience through a sense of mutual responsibility and duty (Bellah 1980, p. 8). Yet from the beginning, American society has been a mixture of republican and liberal political ideals and arrangements, not a pure type of either one.

We are both a religiously resonant republic that depends on the participation of public-spirited citizens for its shared self-government and a liberal constitutional state that pledges to protect the individual rights of self-interested citizens who pursue wealth and knowledge through free markets for economic and intellectual exchange (Bellah *et al.* 1991, pp. 111–144, pp. 179–219; Bellah *et al.* 1996, pp. 27–54). The liberal tradition of public philosophy in America conceives persons as independent selves, 'unencumbered' by moral or civic ties they have not chosen.[3] Freedom consists of the very capacity of such persons to choose their own values and ends. The rival republican tradition conceives freedom as the fruit of sharing in self-government whose public-spirited character is cultivated by these very practices of deliberating together over common goods and sharing responsibility for the destiny of the political community.

Each tradition poses key questions of public life within a distinctive logic of moral argument. How can citizens become capable of self-government, ask republicans, then seek the social conditions and political arrangements needed to promote the civic virtue self-government requires and the liberty it breeds? Liberals, on the other hand, first ask how government should treat its citizens, then seek the principles and procedures of justice needed to treat persons fairly and equally as they pursue their own ends and interests. Fair procedures take priority over particular moral ends posed as public goods. Individual rights function as moral trump cards, played to ensure the state's neutrality among competing conceptions of the good life, in order to respect persons as selves free to choose their own ends.

Part of the fundamental bias of modern liberal theorists of religion and politics – and their communitarian critics – is their common reliance on over-simplified consensus models of culture and community to grasp the nature of moral unity within social diversity. But what holds us together as a polity and a people is not some comprehensive cultural agreement conceived as a value-consensus, or as a value-free arrangement of rules and rights to coordinate our disparate interests and ideals across seamless subcultural communities. Rather, what holds us together is the coherence of our moral disagreement within an ongoing cultural conversation that embraces multiple moral traditions, languages and practices in the interrelation of their social settings (Tipton 1986, pp. 167–171). Through this process come into being the 'semi-covenants', the 'conditional absolutes' and the situationally shared and varied 'ought-tos', as the historian Martin Marty calls them, which critically rework and balance our social order across institutional spheres (Marty, 1990, pp. 9–10). This argument does not go on among moral communities that are each organically fused together around shared values and myths that they socialize into their members. The moral argument of public life goes on within each one of us and among us all, because all of us share a common culture woven of contrasting moral traditions which themselves embody continuities of conflict over how we ought to live together. And all of us lead lives that span the different social institutions and practices to which these traditions ring more or less true – more or less arguably true – including a polity that is at once a religiously resonant republic and a liberal constitutional democracy. Any serious reckoning with inequality will need to unfold as part of this morally multi-vocal and contested conversation.

Inequality and the good of government

Americans have always wanted to do better and become better. They have sought to get ahead and make something of themselves by hard work and self-discipline in an open society, and to make their society itself a freer and fairer place. At the same time, the milk of human kindness has nursed Americans fed on freedom, and washed their wounds of anger and loss at the unequal fortunes they find in a land of equal opportunity. In both respects, communities of faith have played a central part in shaping our character as a people and ordering the public institutions we inhabit. Amid clashing 2016 campaign calls to 'make American great again' and 'begin a political revolution to transform our country', Americans continue to look to religious beliefs and institutions for answers to what ails us (Bellah *et al.* 1991, pp. 111–144, pp. 179–219). Among those perceived ills, the politics of economic inequality and social difference have taken moral form over the past generation in a now-familiar question: 'Why do those who work hard and play by the rules fail to find the rewards they deserve?' This moral quandary is a social analogue to the questions of classical theodicy. The 'religious' dimension to the question is not imported from outside, but inheres in it. The question spans the broad middle class, the citizens whose votes and interests make up most of our electorate. It touches the prayers and troubles the consciences of the faithful who fill most of the pews in congregations of every tradition.

With democratic ideals declared triumphant after a half-century of Cold War, Americans have since found themselves deeply divided over the meaning and prospect of our own democracy in practice. 'What good is government?' they wonder, if it is unable to fix the things that have somehow gone wrong with our society in the experience of many 'middle Americans'.[4] They have felt the fabric of their lives and communities loosening around them, not only when they think of healthcare, decent schooling, or deepening divides of income and opportunity as social problems, but when they worry about the future of their own wages and jobs, their families and children. Many of these doubts and fears arose from threats to the expanding prosperity, social security and public provision most Americans have enjoyed since World War II. Between 1947 and 1973 the middle class doubled in size and real household income, as income grew more quickly at the bottom than at the top of the society. Since then, income has grown more quickly at the top than at the bottom, while it has sagged in the middle. This has made our prosperity much less equally shared than a generation ago. It has left our rates of poverty about the same and increased extreme poverty, even though the economy has grown steadily in size and productivity.[5]

The US economy has more than doubled in size since 1980, in fact, lifting national average wages by 60 per cent to $64,500 in 2014. But the top tenth of earners took $7 out of every $10 gained, leaving the bottom half of all earners flat for three decades at about $16,000 in real wages on average before taxes and transfers. The bottom half collapsed from earning 20 per cent of all national income in 1980 to only 12 per cent in 2014, while the top 1 per cent shot up from earning 11 per cent of the total in 1980 to 20 per cent in 2014. They tripled their yearly income from $428,200 in 1980 to $1,307,800 in 2014, jumping from 27 times as much take-home pay to 81 times as much as a typical earner on the bottom half of the income ladder. In the top half, except for the top tenth, middle-class earners lost about five and a half points in their share of all national income since 1980. In the top tenth, except for the top 1 per cent, upper-middle class earners gained about three points in their share of the total since 1980. By 2015, families in the bottom 99 per cent of households had recovered only about two-thirds of their losses in the Great Recession. Job growth outpaced wage growth in a slow, uneven recovery, so more people were working but many still struggled to get by. They numbered one-third of all households surveyed by the Federal Reserve; half said they could not cover an emergency expense of $400 without borrowing or selling something (Piketty *et al.* 2016).[6]

Why so? Economic downturns over the past generation have bred 'jobless recoveries', as output rebounds but good jobs and wages do not. Led by 'superstar firms' that concentrate sales in major industries and minimize midlevel jobs, employers have improved productivity and profits by investing in technology and cutting payrolls. Large-scale automation of routine handwork and headwork by robotics, computers and information technology hollows out the middle of the job market. Only one in four Americans works in a routine job today, compared to one in three in 1985, and our factories now produce twice as much with one-third fewer workers. Recent losses in manufacturing jobs stem mainly from greater productivity, not greater imports. Employment that involves performing a limited set of repetitive tasks by rote and rule has dropped by a third since 1990, mostly within 1-year windows in recessions. Firms fire but do not rehire, while consolidating and moving manufacturing jobs overseas in a global economy based on greater international trade, cheaper labor and more mobile capital. Machines replace manpower to take on the routine administrative tasks of sorting, counting and filing once done by secretaries and bank tellers as well as the routine manual tasks of making and growing things done by factory machine operators and farm laborers. Jobs decline in both pink-collar clerical and administrative positions (two of three held by women), and in blue-collar production, craft, and operating occupations (five of six held by men) at the core of the middle class (Siu and Jaimovich 2015; Hicks and Devaraj 2015, pp. 5–6).[7]

Wages lag and participation in the labor force shrinks for the less educated, particularly blue-collar males displaced from manufacturing jobs into service occupations such as janitorial and protective services. Employment in these low-wage service occupations has grown since the 1980s, along with highly paid bright-collar professional, technical and managerial occupations, especially 'STEMpathy' jobs that require science, technology, engineering and math skills along with empathic interpersonal communication. At the same time, contingent workers in outsourced, subcontracted jobs on call in the 'on-demand economy' have mushroomed to nearly one in six US jobs today, widening wage inequality and the ranks of the working poor while cutting down on pensions, unions, insurance and workplace regulations. This polarization of jobs at the top and bottom, with the hollowing out of routine jobs in the middle, has led to greater economic inequality in a 'two-tiered society' that reflects not only structural changes in technology and global markets. It also reflects a weakening of the nation's equalizing institutions – strong unions, public schools, trade regulation, public provision, progressive taxation and public investment in infrastructure – backed by bipartisan law-making to check the most extreme market outcomes and ensure that citizens benefit fairly from economic growth through democratic self-government (Reich 1995; Levy 1998, pp. 3–4; Furman *et al.* 2016, pp. 13–14).[8]

Over the last three decades, government taxes and transfers have done little to redistribute income overall, or raise income for working-age Americans on the bottom half of the income ladder in the face of massive shifts to the top in *pre-tax* income distribution. Almost all the meagre growth in *post-tax* income for the bottom 50 per cent since 1980 has come to the elderly from Medicare and Medicaid, and almost all of that has gone to meet the rising cost of healthcare. Not by taxes and transfers alone can we curb economic inequality and hardship, policy analysts conclude, without distributing more equally the primary assets of human capital, financial capital and collective bargaining (Piketty, *et al.* 2016, pp. 16–22, pp. 25–32).

In 2011, corporate profits after taxes jumped to a record 80-year high of 10.3 per cent of the overall size of the economy, and wages fell to a record 80-year low of 43.7 per cent of GDP. At the same time, corporate taxes fell to 21 per cent of corporate profits, a new low since World War II and one-third lower than the 1960–2010 average of 34 per cent. Personal taxes dropped below 14 per cent of total personal income, well below the 50-year average of 15.5 per cent. Why have wages lagged so far behind rising productivity and record corporate profits? Automation, information technology, and offshoring more routine jobs played parts in this wrenching drama since the 1970s. But much of the credit goes to corporations radically reallocating their earnings away from wages and reinvestment over the past 20 years to buy back their stock on the open market to pump up the price of shares and hike their dividends to maximize 'shareholder value' and inflate executive compensation driven by stock-based pay. From 2003 through 2012, for example, S&P 500 companies used more than half of their earnings to buy back their own stock and an additional third to pay dividends, leaving less than a tenth to raise wages or improve jobs for workers. At the same time, CEO compensation ballooned to $30.3 million on average (Bureau of Economic Analysis, US Department of Commerce, reported in Norris 2011; Lazonick 2014).

After years of flat wages and jobless recovery before the Great Recession and an uneven rebound from it, a more comprehensive new poverty measure in 2011 showed one in six Americans living below the poverty line, and more than one in four living in or near poverty. By 2015, this 'supplemental' measure showed that the poverty rate had improved to one in seven Americans living below the poverty line. That was still more than before the Great Recession, when one in eight Americans fell below the official poverty line in 2007. In 2015, moreover, nearly one in four Americans remained in or near poverty at less than 50 per cent above the poverty line of $24,250 by the official poverty measure, while almost one in three remained poor or near-poor by the supplemental measure (US Census Bureau 2011, 2016).[9]

Among the world's thirty advanced national economies the US ranked last in equality of wages and non-wage compensation in 2017, and twenty-ninth of thirty in the effect of taxes and transfers to reduce inequality of market income. It ranked twenty-fifth in social protection, and twenty-third on the 'inclusive development index' used by the World Economic Forum to measure how well economic growth translates into social inclusion (World Economic Forum 2017, p. 16). Deepening inequality in the United States over the past generation clearly stems not only from technological change, market dynamics and economic globalization, but also from political choices in making public policy and remaking public institutions. In particular it stems from 'the retreat of institutions developed during the New Deal and World War II', concludes economist Emmanuel Saez,

> such as progressive tax policies, powerful unions, corporate provision of health and retirement benefits, and changing social norms regarding pay inequality. We need to decide as a society whether this increase in income inequality is efficient and acceptable and, if not, what mix of institutional and tax reforms should be developed to counter it.
>
> (Saez 2016, p. 5)

For all the complexity of economic causes and effects in this story of deepening inequality and persisting poverty, it is nonetheless important to understand it as a moral drama with unsettling civic implications for how we pose and answer questions of what's fair, who deserves what, and who is responsible for making things right at what cost. This is particularly true as our society grows more segregated by income into different neighborhoods, suburbs and schools, modes of transportation and places of work and play. Only 40 per cent of Americans live today in middle-income neighborhoods, compared to 65 per cent in 1970. More than one-third of American families now live in areas of either affluence or poverty, up from just one-sixth in 1970, with the affluent rising from 7 per cent to 16 per cent of all families (Reardon and Bischoff 2011, 2014, 2016). Has this narrowed the everyday interaction of affluent Americans with those worse off and deepened differences between their ways of life? Has it shrunk their reservoir of mutual empathy, and blurred the vision of their mutual understanding when it comes to common concerns, for example over fair wages and taxes, or adequate provision for pensions and healthcare, education and employment?

Far fewer children escape poverty, or move onward and upward through school and work, in metro areas of America more segregated by income and race, with lower local taxes and weaker public schools, fewer married parents, looser social networks and spottier involvement in congregations and civic groups. By the time she turns 3 years old, a child born into a low-income home has heard 30 million fewer words than a child from a well-off family, a deficit that usually compounds over time in unequal schools (Chetty *et al.* 2014a, 2014b).[10] Historic economic shifts that hollow out middle-class jobs are creating larger-scale inequalities between cities and regions themselves, as dramatized by 2016 voting cleavages between blue coastal cities and red plains strapped by rustbelts with the largest losses of college graduates as well as industrial jobs. Yet even as 2016 voting patterns retraced the rustbelt epidemic of 'deaths of despair' among less educated white Americans suffering economic hardship, African Americans could still expect to live 4 years less, on average, than their white counterparts, to face jobless rates twice as high, and endure wage gaps a third wider than a generation ago (Berube 2012; Shearer *et al.* 2016).[11]

High inequality and low mobility threaten 'middle-class America's basic bargain – that if you work hard, you have a chance to get ahead' and leave poverty behind, declared President Barack Obama a year after his re-election. The defining challenge of our time is making sure 'our economy works for every working American'. Failing to meet it poses 'a fundamental threat to the American Dream, our way of life, and what we stand for around the globe', Obama warned, by diverting progress, fraying families and undermining faith in the good of government and free enterprise alike (Obama 2013, pp.1–3). On the other hand, charged the Tea Party movement, the Club for Growth, and GOP fiscal conservatives, the welfare socialism of tax-and-spend big government reduces half of Americans to dependency. It unfairly entitles them to take what workers earn by vainly trying to do good with other people's money. It strangles job-creation with red tape, and handcuffs free enterprise with needless taxes, rules and healthcare insurance subsidies.[12]

Americans can argue over changes in law and public policy that follow from such critiques, or dismiss their logic. Recent polls show us doing both. Two-thirds of Americans agree that the gap between the rich and everyone else has grown over the past decade, and they likewise agree that government should act to reduce this gap, although this majority includes 90 per cent of Democrats but only 45 per cent of Republicans. Eight-in-ten Americans agree that the government should act to reduce poverty. How? Three-quarters of Democrats favor raising taxes on the wealthy and corporations to help the poor, since most Democrats believe that government aid does more good than harm because people can't get out of poverty until their basic needs are met. Six in ten Republicans favor cutting taxes to encourage investment and economic growth, since most Republicans believe that government aid to the poor does more harm than good by making people too dependent on government. Only one-third of Americans remain convinced that some people are rich because they worked harder, and some are poor because they did not work hard enough. By contrast, half believe that the rich have had more advantages than others, and the poor have been held back by circumstances beyond their control. Predictable differences in income and party identification bear on these views. Yet across both these dividing lines, six in ten Americans in 2014 believed that the economic system in this country unfairly favors the wealthy *and* that most people who want to get ahead can make it if they're willing to work hard (Pew Research Center 2014). By Election Day in 2016, however, three-quarters voters agreed that 'the American economy is rigged to advantage the rich and powerful', and that 'America needs a strong leader to take the country back from the rich and powerful' (Kahn 2016).[13]

The glare of the 2016 Presidential revealed the political impact of wide gaps in social experience and moral judgment between the educated upper middle class in the top fifth of American households and those in the middle, with the poor isolated at the bottom and working families struggling to stay afloat (Edsall 2016; Reardon and Bischoff 2016; Smeeding 2016, pp. 255–295). Driven by greater income inequality, these gaps further separate rungs of the social ladder defined by residence, household formation, schooling, occupation and pension, health and stress levels, tied together more tightly in turn as dimensions of social advantage.[14] Voters making $100,000 or more split their votes for President in 2016, as in 2008 and 2012, instead of favoring Republican candidates by two-to-one as they did in the 1980s. By contrast, Donald Trump won white voters without a college degree and making less than $30,000 a year by a margin of 62–30 per cent in 2016, compared to Mitt Romney's narrow win by 52–45 per cent in 2012, as almost one-quarter of Obama's white, working-class supporters in 2012 defected in 2016 (Edison Research 2016).[15]

The influx of more affluent, educated voters into the Democratic Party helped replace the white working-class voters who switched to the GOP over the past generation. But it also helped distract Democrats from responding to working-class concerns in tandem with organized labor. Less affluent but well-educated, culturally liberal and independent younger white voters in the 2016 Democratic primaries proved readiest to answer the call from Senator Bernie Sanders to make a 'political revolution' by hiking taxes on the rich and raising wages for workers, breaking up big banks and spending much more on the social safety net, job creation, healthcare and student aid. Older white voters with less income, education and job prospects, meanwhile, proved readiest in the GOP primaries to answer Mr. Trump's call to 'make America great again' by bringing back manufacturing jobs and prosperity for the deserving, protecting Social Security and Medicare for the working class, pinching programs for the poor, cutting taxes for the rich and fencing out immigrants and imports. Economic populism and nationalism in response to deepening social divisions resounded across political parties and ideologies, however at odds were their audiences and angles of approach, to decide the 2016 election. At the same time, this partisan combat reflected the gaping distance between those at the top and bottom of the social ladder. It underscored the need for greater moral coherence and political cohesion to engage the problems of the poor, help struggling workers and serve the good of the country as a whole (Pew Research Center 2016a; Williams 2016; Porter 2017).[16]

Citizens need not be equal in income and education to engage in self-government. But democratic citizens of different backgrounds, unequal resources and diverse social positions must share a common life and decide in common how they want and need to live together, if government of and by the people is to endure. Otherwise it threatens to tilt towards the most powerful and divide the body politic through bitter protest, mistrust and withdrawal driven by anger and despair, if ordinary citizens find themselves in a society so unequal that no matter how hard they work, they cannot make ends meet, buy a home, pay for college, or save for retirement. Democracy thrives only if it sees to the universal distribution of hope as well as rights, and gives to all its citizens a representative voice as well as a fair slice of the economic pie (Sandel 2012, p. 203; Delbanco 1999, p. 67).

Religious faith and moral argument in public

In an era of continuing prosperity, deepening inequality and persisting poverty, two aspects of our religious life have come to the fore. Most obvious is the spirit of charity, compassion and neighbor-love with which communities of faith have responded to care for the neediest, particularly where public aid has ebbed. Many mainline Protestant churches have multiplied their effort by 4–6 times what it was two decades ago, relying on public sources for some 30 per cent of their funding yet contributing plenty of money, time and helping hands of their own.[17] Less obvious, but no less profound in its religious dimensions. is the peculiar moral spirit Americans bring to the struggle to understand why some prosper and others suffer social and economic trials, and how we ought to face up to the problems posed by both outcomes. For all of our supposed value conflicts and social differences, Americans have been remarkably alike in holding themselves individually responsible for their worldly success or misfortune. More than 70 per cent of Americans believe that people can get out of poverty on their own, while 60 per cent of Europeans think the poor are trapped there, although the poor are equally mobile in both places. Most Americans think those who remain poor deserve to be poor, since they are too weak-willed or just too lazy to pull themselves out of poverty, while most Europeans believe 'luck or stuck, not pluck' explains why people are rich or poor (Alesina and Glaeser 2004; Moore 2005, pp. 14–16).

Other industrialized nations have undergone much the same sort of global economic jolts as the United States over the past generation, but none of them show comparable gaps between the best-off and worst-off. Though many of them accept more joblessness and slower economic growth than we do, they also pay higher taxes and tolerate far less poverty, neither stigmatizing the jobless nor excluding them from other forms of social participation. Indeed, European governments define poverty in terms of income inequality and seek to eliminate it by decreasing such inequality. The United States defines a 'poverty line' in terms of the cost of a good diet adjusted against the consumer price index, and seeks to end poverty by raising people above this line (Alesina and Glaeser 2004).[18]

When faced with worldly failure, why do Americans commonly find so much fault with themselves and so little with the world? The distinctive cultural values that lead us to do so have roots in 'ascetic Protestantism' and in secular strains of individualism that are formative in our history and still influential in our shared self-understanding. We value independence, self-reliance and autonomy as intrinsic virtues, not merely as means to win success or invite romance in a competitive society. We commonly think of society as a free association of individuals who account for themselves and look after their own interests, thereby advancing the prosperity of all in a fair and thriving marketplace. And in private life we believe one should enjoy a circle of freely chosen friends and family.

At once utilitarian and self-expressive, these convictions yield a kind of 'first moral language' in which Americans tend to think about their lives in ways that can inspire great individual effort and achievement yet leave us blind to our essential interdependence and unmoved by our need to share responsibility for the commonweal (Bellah *et al.* 1996, p. 20, p. 242, p. 334). In the name of defending individual liberty against arbitrary state authority these convictions also anchor the restricted jurisdiction and decentralized arrangement of American political institutions at city, county, state and federal levels. This arrangement makes it difficult to reduce poverty by sharing wealth across a diverse society, especially across racial lines linked to residential segregation by economic class.[19]

By contrast, the chief social role of America's Jewish and Christian communities of faith can be seen in this light as embodying biblical visions of life in their everyday practices and relationships as well as voicing them in public.[20] Contrary to models of social exchange and contract embodied by the market and the welfare state, religious congregations characteristically call for forms of covenantal fellowship and self-giving communion comparable to the political friendship and mutual recognition among citizens a classical republic praises. Especially in times of social crisis and renewal, religious communities in America have joined biblical and civic ideals in distinctive fashion to stress the common moral aims and responsibilities of our lives together as citizens. Yet these efforts fix no civil-religious consensus in cultural concrete. They draw no moral blueprint for public discourse. Instead, they inform the moral argument of public life that many voices unfold within and across traditions, understood as continuities of conflict over how we ought to live.

Thus, this argument includes religious voices raised to give traditionally strong reasons to hedge against public participation in the larger society. God helps those who help themselves, after all, and God saves souls from a sinful world. Involvement in the body politic pales before the ideal body of a church whose members will care for one another in separated-out communities of the saved. Similarly, anti-federalist strands of our republicanism, like Jefferson's 'small republic' of yeoman farmers, inspire aversion to a society centered around big cities, big business and big government alike. So it is that we can learn much but not everything we need to know about conflicting religious visions of a good society by conceiving them as ideological calls to arms in culture wars waged by Weberian class-carriers on opposing sides or as dysfunctional divisions in a civil-religious consensus that threaten to break the Durkheimian template of social authority. We need a more layered, multivocal account of cultural pluralism, and a more dialectical, interactive analysis of moral disagreement in public. Only in this way can we explore alternative lines of interpretation to the strategically streamlined path of legitimation used to survey the familiar functionalist relationship of religion to political authority.

More diverse communities of faith across the denominational spectrum have found their voices in a more democratized argument of public life within a more densely organized, decentered and contested polity populated by a larger, more educated and religiously representative middle class. In the coherence of its conflicts, this cultural conversation bears the singular imprint of state-centered changes in our polity. The state has extended more rights to its citizens generally, and more diversified social rights to more differentiated status-occupants, for example women, children, homeowners, minorities, professionals and the elderly (Meyer 1987; Boli 1987). Expanded rights more powerfully require reciprocal responsibilities and obligations to respect them. An enlarged, diversified demand for public moral justification finds expression in expanding claims to rights and entitlements, and counterclaims against them. It echoes in calls for broader civic membership and participation. But it also helps make public participation more competitive and unequal, pushing the less resourceful and advantaged to the edge of the polity. It spurs broader recognition of the public consequences of apparently private actions and decisions. But it also creates more occasions for disappointment with public failure to remedy the harm of these consequences.

The effective meaning of all claims to human rights rests, however implicitly, on deeper ideals of human nature and a good society that ground justice in telic visions of the dignity and goodness of persons and the social relations that bind them. In America, these ideals are inextricably rooted in the moral syntax of religious and civic traditions that churches, synagogues, temples and mosques have long cultivated. So the modern state's expansion and diversification of rights have made greater demands for moral coherence on the polity in its efforts to argue out the public good and realize it in policy. Yet these same processes of expansion and diversification have posed sharper difficulties for defining the public good by simple reference to congruent interest-calculation among similarly aligned social classes or broad moral consensus among similarly situated subcultural communities. New forms of religion in public have arisen and clashed in response to these state-centered changes.

Tensions between public-church and religious-lobby models of religion in public have gained force from the confluence between changing patterns of religious and political participation in recent decades. Lower and less solid participation in mainline Protestant churches since the 1960s, notably by educated young adults joining the ranks of 'unchurched believers' in the name of personal autonomy, has weakened the web of denominational loyalties and confessional commitments in mainline Protestantism in the last generation. Evangelical and Catholic churches are seeing declines of their own, which emerged later but are likewise concentrated among young adults without spouses, children, or conservative political convictions (Hout and Fischer 2014; Wuthnow 1991, 2007). Meanwhile, more educated and elite Americans have led the way in withdrawing from the kinds of civic associations and political organizations that have long built bridges between more and less privileged citizens, and between national leaders and local groups. They have moved away from face-to-face membership in veterans and fraternal groups, community clubs and women's associations, charitable and reform societies such as the PTA, Elks and American Legion. They have moved towards mailing-list membership in single-issue political associations and advocacy groups such as the AARP and ACLU, and participation in socially narrowed professional guilds and special-interest groups.

Broader voluntary associations have flourished in tandem with electoral democracy and pervasive domestic activity by the Federal government in American history, the sociologist Theda Skocpol argues, by uniting citizens for shared public purposes across local communities, states and the nation as a whole. The chief problem in our civic life today, she judges, is 'the weakening of such encompassing national associations and a breakdown of two-way relationships between leaders and actual groups of citizens' (Skocpol 1997, p. 1; ibid. 1999). This 'missing middle' is likewise missing from the recent rise of national advocacy groups devoted to single issues and narrow constituencies, along with the proliferation of headquarters for professional guilds and trade associations, think tanks and lobbies in the expanding 'imperial capital' of Washington, DC. Sharp, class-bound declines in almost every form of civic voluntarism show up in the broad surveys and interviews analysed by Sidney Verba (1995) and his colleagues in *Voice and Equality*. Meaningful democratic participation, they conclude, requires that the voices of citizens in politics be

> clear, loud, and equal: clear so that public officials know what citizens want and need, loud so that officials have an incentive to pay attention to what they hear; and equal so that the democratic ideal of equal responsiveness to the preferences and interests of all is not violated.
>
> (Verba *et al.* 1995, p. 509)

Their analysis of voluntary activity in American politics suggests that 'the public's voice is often loud, sometimes clear, but rarely equal'. Although the worldly means and ends of politics cannot come first or last for communities of faith that recognize 'our kingdom is not of this world', religious institutions can and do exert a vital counter-influence to such skewed declines in public participation and membership in American society. For all their voluntarist fluidity, membership and attendance in the mainline churches have stabilized over the past decade, after declining by about one-sixth from their baby-boom highs in the 1950s (Hout *et al.* 2001). These churches continue to 'play an unusual role in the American participatory system', as Verba and his colleagues observe, 'by providing opportunities for the development of civic skills to those who would otherwise be resource-poor' (Verba *et al.* 1995, p. 18). American society is exceptional in 'how often Americans go to church – with the result that the mobilizing function often performed elsewhere by unions and labor or social democratic parties is more likely to be performed by religious institutions' (Verba *et al.* 1995, p. 19, pp. 518–521). Communities of faith nurture democratic citizenship by serving as schools of civic virtue, not only civic skills. Such virtue is of particular importance for those who are otherwise left disadvantaged, excluded or unschooled as citizens.[21]

Religious communities are among the *least* class-divided communities of moral discourse, reflection and inspiration in American society. They are almost alone in reminding Americans of the moral implications of the greater inequalities that divide them from two-thirds of humankind around the world. Compared to the major political parties or the biggest religious lobbies, that holds true for the mainline churches despite the greater individual voluntarism of religious affiliation, and the increased internal polarization of denominational memberships along class and cultural lines of liberal-versus-conservative opinion drawn by age and education in particular. Compared to their declining participation in other forms of civic voluntarism, more Americans across the broad middle class continue to fill church pews, notably in large 'moderate' Protestant denominations such as the United Methodist Church and in the Catholic Church. That may make these churches more morally divided or equivocal on some issues, but in the longer run it makes their moral struggles all the more significant for the society as a whole. Within a denser, more diversified polity in response to an expanded state and realigned political parties, their struggles over love and justice unfold in a social landscape all of us inhabit. And all of us have a real stake in the course and outcome of this moral drama for the way we live.

It may seem paradoxical if not perilous that, in seeking to embody the ideal of the Church universal, the mainline churches in America must wrestle with the particulars of social class and risk the dangers of economistic idolatry as well as political faction. But the universal community of creation and redemption, which the Church signifies and serves, calls our attention to the particularity of human suffering and need in order to name sin and proclaim grace. To be the Church, not only the denominations of mostly middle-class Americans, the churches must tell the larger truth of human interdependence and shared responsibility. They must keep trying to live out this truth in exemplary ways that can reach into the fearful hearts of the righteous who have earned everything they have, and reach out beyond our economically segregated neighborhoods and national boundaries to embrace those who have so much less of everything except infinite value in the eyes of God.

Only thus can the mainline American churches escape the irony of the American state at the dawn of the twenty-first century, and instead engage it critically. For more than a century the regulatory reach and administrative sway of our state have grown on the moral strength of its almost religious aspiration to do social good, to enlarge human rights and realize human potential among all its citizens as partakers in the good life of the modern middle class. However stunning its failures to achieve these ends fully, the strength of its partial triumph since the New Deal has given us a middle-class majority torn between voting their conscience and their interests in the name of the public interest. Unsure how to distinguish the two, they are eager to affirm for everyone their relatively meritocratic experience of schooling and work, and to mark off by respectable moral measures those more or less deserving of personal aid.

Especially for middle-class Americans, we cannot forgo the civic promise of religious efforts to enlarge public conscience and cast clearer light on the commonweal. For those who 'work hard and play by the rules' still bring to the pews of the mainline churches the burden of both their moral confusions and their faithful convictions. As members of this middle-class majority now question their shifting social rewards and responsibilities amid diverging fortunes and diminished dreams, high societal stakes rest in the moral balance of their counterposed yet interwoven visions of a world worth living in and working for. As the majority of the richest and most powerful nation in the world, the outcome of their choices entwines the fate of peoples everywhere.

Public churches and the public sphere

Between modern market economies and administrative states lies a broad social realm, stretching from the family, local churches and clubs to the political parties and associations that surround official government. Since the early modern era in the West, a public realm *between* market economies and states has commonly been identified as 'civil society', a political community inhabited by democratic citizens.[22] Paying critical attention to civil society makes clear that neither market nor state is an autonomous moral realm of interests and exchanges or rights and duties. Neither is justifiable or even comprehensible in its own terms abstracted from social life as a whole. Neither makes sense apart from expression in terms of the living traditions of moral narrative, dialogue and argument within communities of discourse, beginning with their dramatic rites and stories of good persons, practices and relationships within the ways of life a coherent social order nurtures.

Within this conception of civil society and the polity, religion takes on a very different shape from the authoritarian advocate of absolute principles or divinely revealed commands modern liberals fear, or the source of legitimation and moral glue for the social order modern communitarians extol. Instead religion in public becomes a crucial questioner. It is an interlocutor of states apparently all too certain of their progressive programs and procedural formulae for distributive justice, and markets all too oblivious to injuries worked by their rationality and efficiency (Weintraub 1997, pp. 7–13, pp. 34–38; Casanova 1994, pp. 57–58). Precisely because religious faith respects no *moral* boundaries in facing up to human goodness, evil and suffering – even when church and state are legally separated institutions, each governed by its own members – communities of faith are ideally suited to question the state's *moral* authority to draw the 'private-public' boundary lines that separate institutions as different realms of moral understanding and discourse. In a democracy that is for citizens to decide, again and again, without privileging the moral perspectives of either state or church. That can and should be so because democratic citizens actually do their deciding as different sorts of believers and non-believers, workers, students, neighbors and family members; not as abstracted, unsocialized political beings.[23] They do it through pitching in or pulling away from efforts decided more or less in common. They do it through engaging or following public dialogue about ordering our lives together in practice, not only about making policy, passing laws, or backing candidates and parties.

The Reformation gave rise to more or less radical movements that emerged from the structure of the larger Christian church as 'a church within the church', an exemplary *ecclesiola in ecclesia*, seeking to engage the church at large in dramatically counterpointed conversation, and revise its overall articulation as a truly catholic concilium (Niebuhr 1929, p. 282; Troeltsch 1960). Evangelical and reformed churches conceived themselves as models of civic and political order in the early modern West. In America today, the descendants of both Reformation and Counter-Reformation impulses link denominations organized as voluntary associations within a free society to the historic institution of the Christian church at large. This genuinely Catholic church, organizationally counterfactual yet institutionally conceivable, is itself a concilium of smaller publics and counter publics (evangelical, liberal, liberationist, fundamentalist, feminist, pentecostal, traditionalist, Americanist and more) within and across denominations. Together this conciliar communion of communions, bound by their ongoing argument as well as their worship and fellowship, constitutes a prototypical 'super public' counterposed to official government yet conversable with it. It is a moral interlocutor of states which citizens can serve well only by being faithful to God before country.[24]

Only by recognizing its own interculturally inclusive 'polycentric' nature, conversely, can a truly Catholic church embody the word of God and the spirit of Christ in public dialogue in the world today, by contrast to a monocentric church reinforced against the modern world as 'a dictatorship of relativism' (Habermas 2002, pp. 129–138).[25] For we inhabit a public sphere itself indebted to biblical forms of covenantal communal fellowship no less than the Socratic reciprocity of unforced dialogue between full citizens of a polis. The universalistic, egalitarian moral spirit of modern democracy, human rights and the sovereignty of individual conscience is 'the direct legacy of the Judaic ethic of justice and the Christian ethic of love', as Jürgen Habermas puts it (ibid., p. 149). This legacy remains vital to respecting yet transcending the Eurocentric cultural-political limitations of an enlightenment universalism whose religious roots are still inseparable from its practical authority to proclaim the dignity of all human beings as true subjects, and to protect cultural pluralism from drifting into moral relativism (ibid., p. 136, pp. 149–150). The Christian church must sustain this legacy to enable us to meet the challenges of a post-national polity to judge and reform today's economically fragmented, unfairly stratified and unpacified world of global commerce, communication and coercion in the direction of a just and peaceful global civilization to come. But the church must also sustain its reflexive and self-critical awareness through historically conscious dialogue with other world religions, with the dialectical thinking of Western philosophy since the Reformation, with the scepticism of modern science and with the quasi-scientific pragmatism of modern commonsense (ibid., pp. 149–150).

The distinctive stance of churchly engagement towards the larger society in all its diversity gives rise to a recognition that criteria of justice will vary with the kinds of relationships to which persons belong and the kinds of activities – working, parenting, governing – in which they take part in different social institutions. Just recognition and reward of others will vary, for example, according to the relative merit of professional work, the absolute need for parental love and the equality of democratic votes. But this churchly stance rests on a faith in the moral coherence and integrity of goods distinguished by social spheres such as the family, market and polity, yet unified as human virtues in the interdependent lives of persons acting, feeling and relating together across these spheres in society as a whole. It also rests on a faith that this coherence and integrity can be expressed in exemplary stories of how and why persons so act and feel in relation to God. We can come to know stories of creation, sin, grace and redemption so truthfully, for example, that no Americans today can witness the suffering of their hungry and homeless neighbors, fail to respond, and go on calling themselves chosen people of God *or* good citizens of a commonwealth.[26]

Given the wholeness of Creation and its human stewardship in biblical terms that ground the church's self-understanding, the church finds itself entrusted by God with the whole of society, not only the whole of its members' social lives. The church carries no ultimate responsibility to or for the state, its policies or programs. But it is more ultimately responsible than any other given institution for the moral conduct and character of the society as a whole, for its immediate texture and deepest coherence. Raising the matter of such societal responsibility by religious institutions may sound like claims of moral absolutism asserted on highly contested public ground, and subject to fierce rebuttal in defense of church-state separation and civil liberties. Yet in a curious sense that amounts to little more than commonsense in a differentiated society, such common ground is more often simply ignored than contested. Communities of faith compose virtually the only modern American institution that cares to accept such responsibility, or indeed that can even recognize its form and grasp its meaning. It should be granted that the welfare state extends rules, rights and programs into almost every social institution. But its mind is almost always elsewhere, as it were, divided or distracted by a thousand disparate social issues and jurisdictional concerns. It is preoccupied by its own bureaucratic career and political prospects, and only fitfully aware of its progressive calling, if not downright doubtful that its programmatic interests really represent the society's common good.

The church certainly does not claim legal or governmental authority over the society, nor in any conventional sense over its members' lives in a denominational society, in which churches, synagogues, temples and mosques are voluntary associations. Nor does it conventionally 'represent' the society, its politically excluded members, or even the faithful themselves to the state as if they were its political constituents. Instead what the churches and the public church they embody seek to do is to remain mindful of the society as a whole, its moral needs and its viewpoints otherwise unmet by the state, especially as such recognition is essential to care for the whole of humankind, human nature and Creation itself. The church persists in reminding the state that society as a whole continues to exist and calls for full recognition of its common good, not only recognition of specific social groups and the goods they affirm to be essential for their own survival or social membership (Taylor 1992, pp. 25–73).

No less significant, the public church seeks to enlarge the public that underlies and informs the state in a democratic society by helping to interarticulate the smaller 'publics', especially those with relatively few resources of money, power and influence that enable them to demand to be heard and heeded by government, the major political parties, or mass social movements. It seeks to do so in forms that interrelate these publics dialogically and offer them more than a foot in the door, a voicing of demands, or even a vote. Rather the public church, as one god-parent of a democratic 'superpublic' or public-at-large outside the state, seeks to bring publics into conversation and argument with one another. It seeks to enable their members to exchange good reasons in mulling over issues and deciding policies. It also seeks to inspire them to persuade others by the good example of living out their ideals and practicing what they preach. But it seeks, too, to awaken them to grasp and better intuit the differences in experience, social situation and convictions that shape their reasoning, in order to clarify and open up the terms of their disagreement even when they cannot compromise or as yet find common ground.

If the state is impartial and its justice is blind in the course of due process, the church is always on the side of the whole of human society and the whole of God's creation. It is always trying to see the big picture, hear the whole story and discern the justice of the entire social order. It begins and ends with the essence of justice as a virtue incarnated in faithful persons who love and feed their neighbor. It insists on the duty and aim of nation-states of the world to do likewise, even if it is not inherent in their self-defined interests or character to do so.

While the state, then, may see churches as no different in nature from any other voluntary association, nongovernmental organization, public-interest group, political constituency, or lobby, the church sees itself embodying the rest of society and the whole of society. It finds itself insisting on the primacy of the society before the state. As such, its political reality in a democratic republic rests in the polity per se, not in its relationship to the state. There the church is one voice among many. But it is a presence that seeks to set a good example in public by trying to listen more than any of the others to the many, to weave together their voices, and center their conversation around the goods human beings need to live well enough to become good, including the goods of public participation and social membership as goods in themselves (Hollenbach 1988, pp. 82–83). As such, the church continues to play an essential role in ongoing efforts to respond to inequality of every kind within the moral community of society seen as a whole.

Notes

1 This chapter is adapted from Tipton (2007, pp. 48–65, pp. 405–421), with the generous permission of the publisher, the University of Chicago Press.
2 Here and below, see Tipton (1990); Bellah *et al.* (1996, pp. vii–xxxv); Bellah (1980); and Taylor (1990b).
3 Cf. Sandel (1998, pp. 4–19ff).
4 Cf. Gans (1988, pp. 23–42); Phillips (1993) and Sandel (1998, pp. 329–333).
5 Net productivity rose 73.4 per cent in 1973–2015 and average hourly pay grew 11.1 per cent, compared to 96.7 per cent productivity growth and 91.3 per cent pay growth in 1948–1973, reports the Economic Policy Institute (2016). In 1947–1973 US income grew 31 per cent more slowly in the top quintile than in the bottom quintile, while in 1973–2000 income grew 55 per cent more quickly in the top quintile than in the bottom, report Mishel *et al.* (2005).
6 Cf. Saez (2016); Saez and Zucman (2015); Bricker *et al.* (2016); and Board of Governors of the Federal Reserve System (2016, pp. 1–3).
7 See Autor (2010); Pew Research Center (2016b); Cheremukhin (2014); Acemoglu and Restrepo (2017); Autor *et al.* (2017); and Song *et al.* (2015).
8 On STEMpathy jobs and industrial jobs lost to microchips instead of Mexicans, see Friedman (2016) and Deming (2015). On the rise of the on-demand economy, see Katz and Krueger (2016).
9 See US Census Bureau (2016), 'Table 3. Percentage of People by Ratio of Income/ Resources to Poverty Threshold', showing 22.6 per cent of Americans under 150 per cent of the poverty line in 2015 by the official measure and 30.6 per cent by the supplemental poverty measure.
10 On a '30 million word gap' between 3-year old children from low-income and high-income families, linked to the 'achievement gap' in elementary education via differential language acquisition in early childhood brain development, see Hart and Risley (1995).
11 See Monnat (2016); Case and Deaton (2015); and colour-coded data on longevity, joblessness and wages in Arias (2015, p. 5); Wilson and Rodgers (2016, pp. 4, 21).
12 Cf. Club for Growth, 'Our Philosophy: Prosperity and Opportunity through Economic Freedom,' 2012, in behalf of 'pro-growth tax policy, fiscally conservative spending, federal death tax repeal, expanding trade freedom, reform[ing] Social Security with personal retirement accounts, medical malpractice and tort reform, regulatory reform and deregulation and educational choice,' at www.clubforgrowth.org/philosophy.
13 Kahn (2016) reports agreement with these two statements by 72 and 75 per cent respectively of 10,604 voters with ballots already cast.
14 Here and below see Edsall (2016); Reeves (2015); Board of Governors of the Federal Reserve System (2016, pp. 1–3); and Whitmore *et al.* (2016).
15 Hillary Clinton won Obama's 2012 white working-class supporters by a margin of only 78 per cent to 18 per cent over Donald Trump, with 10 per cent voting for a third-party candidate, according to the Cooperative Congressional Election Study, reported Nate Cohn (2017).
16 Cf. Senator Bernie Sanders, 'Bernie's Announcement', May 26, 2015, at https://bernie sanders.com/bernies-announcement/; and Donald Trump, 'Donald Trump's Presidential Announcement Speech', at www.time.com/3923128/donald-trump-announcement-speech/ [accessed 15 May 2017].
17 Mainline Protestant congregations have sustained relatively high rates of civic engagement and social service, compared to other Protestants and, to a lesser extent, Catholics, with

the significant exception of specifically political activity, according to Chaves *et al.* (2002, pp. 108–128).

18 Since 1964, the US has defined poverty by adjusting the cost of a standard diet against the consumer price index and multiplying by three, since Americans on average spend one third of their income after taxes on food, to draw a poverty line (of $24,250 for a family of four in 2015) across the country, from Manhattan to Mississippi. Cf. Boushey *et al.* (2001), for variable standards of poverty in relation to median income and the actual cost of living in specific areas, which typically double the official US poverty line, upping it by 3–4 times in costly metropolitan areas such as Boston and San Francisco.

19 Alesina and Glaeser (2004) attributes half the difference between US and European redistribution policies to deliberately constructed differences in their political systems, and half to racial diversity. The greater the racial diversity of individual US states, the less those states spend on redistributive welfare. The greater the racial, ethnic, linguistic and religious homogeneity among European nations, the more generous their welfare policies and the stronger the socialist political parties that support them. Among Americans opposition to redistribution correlates more strongly with Caucasian racial identity than with income, gender, place of residence or any other social factor. See Moore (2005, pp. 15–16).

20 Here and below I draw on Bellah *et al.* (1996, pp. vii–xxxix).

21 See Wood (2002) and Wuthnow (2002).

22 See Walzer (1991) and Taylor (1990a). This section is indebted throughout to Weintraub (1997) and Casanova (1994), especially Chapter 2.

23 See Tipton (1986); also Perry (1988, pp. 82–90).

24 Cf. Marty (1981, pp. 16–22).

25 See especially Habermas (2002, pp. 135–137) on 'the polycentric world Church'. See J. B. Metz (1987, pp. 93–115). Cf. Cardinal Joseph Ratzinger, 'Homily at the Mass for the Election of the Roman Pontiff,' Vatican City, April 18, 2005, in defense of 'a clear faith, based on the Creed of the Church' to withstand modern multiplication of ideological and sectarian 'error' and modern establishment of egoistic relativism.

26 See, for example Vorspan and Saperstein (1992, ch. 1, 15). Cf. John Boli (1987, pp. 143–44).

References

Acemoglu, D. and Restrepo, P. (2017) *'Robots and jobs: Evidence from US Labor Markets'*, March, NBER Working Paper no. 23285, Cambridge, MA: National Bureau of Economic Research.

Alesina, A. and Glaeser, E. L. (2004) *Fighting poverty in the US and Europe: A world of difference*, New York: Oxford University Press.

Arias, E. (2015) 'United States life tables, 2011', *National Vital Statistics Reports*, 64(11), Hyattsville, MD: National Center for Health Statistics.

Autor, D. (2010) 'The polarization of job opportunities in the U.S. labor market', April, Center for American Progress and the Hamilton Project, Washington, DC: The Brookings Institution. Available from: www.brookings.edu/wp-content/uploads/2016/06/04_jobs_autor.pdf [accessed 15 May 2017].

Autor, D., Dorn, D., Katz, L. F., Patterson, C. and Van Reenen, J. (2017) *'Concentrating on the fall of the labor state'*, January, NBER Working Paper no. 23108, Cambridge, MA: National Bureau of Economic Research.

Bellah, R. (1980) 'Religion and the legitimation of the American republic', in R. Bellah and P. E. Hammond, *Varieties of civil religion*, San Francisco, CA: Harper and Row, pp. 3–23.

Bellah, R., Madsen, R., Sullivan W. M., Swidler, A. and Tipton, S. M. (1991) *The good society*, New York: Alfred Knopf.

Bellah, R., Madsen, R., Sullivan W. M., Swidler, A. and Tipton, S. M. (1996) *Habits of the heart: Individualism and commitment in American life*, 2nd edn, Berkley, CA: University of California Press.

Berube, A. (2012) 'Where the grads are: Degree attainment in metro areas', 31 May, Washington, DC: The Brookings Institution. Available from: www.brookings.edu/blog/the-avenue/2012/05/31/where-the-grads-are-degree-attainment-in-metro-areas/ [accessed 15 May 2017].

Board of Governors of the Federal Reserve System (2016) 'Report on the economic well-being of U.S. households in 2015', May, Washington, DC: Federal Reserve Board. Available from: www.federalreserve.gov/2015-report-economic-well-being-us-households-201605.pdf [accessed 15 May 2017].

Boli, J. (1987) 'Human rights of state expansion? Cross-national definitions of constitutional rights, 1870–1970', in G. M. Thomas, J. Meyer, F. Ramirez and J. Boli (eds), *Institutional structure: Constituting state, society and the individual*, Beverly Hills, CA: Sage, pp. 133–149.

Boushey, H., Brocht, C., Gundersen, B. and Bernstein, J. (2001) *Hardships in America: The real story of working families*, Washington, DC: Economic Policy Institute.

Bricker, J., Henriques, A. M., Krimmel, J. A. and Sabelhaus, J. E. (2016) 'Measuring income and wealth at the top using administrative and survey data', Brookings Papers on Economic Activity, BPEA Conference Draft, March 10–11, 2016. Washington, DC: The Brookings Institution. Available from: www.brookings.edu/wpcontent/uploads/2016/03/bricker textspring16bpea.pdf [accessed 6 November 2017].

Bureau of Labor Statistics (2016) 'The employment situation – October 2016', USDL-16–2095, Washington, DC: U.S. Department of Labor.

Casanova, J. (1994) *Public religions in the modern world*, Chicago, IL: University of Chicago Press.

Case, A. and Deaton, A. (2015) 'Rising morbidity and mortality in midlife among white non-hispanic Americans in the 21st century', *Proceedings of the National Academy of the Sciences of the United States of America, 112*(49): 15078–15083.

Chaves, M., Giesel, H. M. and Tsitsos, W. (2002) 'Religious variations in public presence: Evidence from the national congregations study', in R. Wuthnow and J. H. Evans (eds), *The quiet hand of God: Faith-based activism and the public role of mainline Protestantism*, Berkeley, CA: University of California Press, pp. 108–128.

Cheremukhin, A. (2014) 'Middle-skill jobs lost in U.S. market polarization', *DallasFed, 9*(5): 1–4.

Chetty, R., Hendren, N., Kline, P. and Saez, E. (2014a) 'Where is the land of opportunity? The geography of intergenerational mobility in the US', January, NBER Working Paper no. 19843, Cambridge, MA: National Bureau of Economic Research.

Chetty, R., Hendren, N., Kline, P., Saez, E. and Turner, N. (2014b) 'Is the United States still a land of opportunity? Recent trends in intergenerational mobility', January, NBER Working Paper no. 19844, Cambridge, MA: National Bureau of Economic Research.

Cohn, N. (2017) 'Turnout was not driver of Clinton's defeat', *New York Times*, 28 March, p. A17.

Delbanco, A. (1999) *The real American dream: A mediation on hope*, Cambridge, MA: Harvard University Press.

Deming, D. J. (2015) 'The growing importance of social skills in the labor market', August, NBER Working Paper no. 21473, Cambridge, MA: National Bureau of Economic Research.

Economic Policy Institute (2016) 'The productivity-pay gap', August, Washington, DC: Economic Policy Institute.

Edison Research (2016) 'Election 2016: exit polls,' *New York Times*, 8 November. Available from: www.nytimes.com/interactive/2016/11/08/us/politics/election-exit-polls.html [accessed 15 May 2017].

Edsall, T. B. (2016) 'How the other fifth lives', *New York Times*, 27 April.

Friedman, T (2016), 'Trump voters, just hear me out', *New York Times*, 2 November, p. A23.

Furman, J., Holdren, J. P., Munoz, C., Smith, M. and Zients, J. (2016) *'Artificial intelligence, automation, and the economy'*, December, Washington, DC: Executive Office of the President.

Gans, H. J. (1988) *Middle American individualism: The future of liberal democracy*, New York: Free Press.

Habermas, J. (2002) *Religion and rationality: Essays on reason, god, and modernity*, E. Medieta (ed.), Cambridge, MA: The MIT Press.

Hart, B. and Risley, T. R. (1995) *Meaningful differences in the everyday experience of young American children*, Baltimore, MD: Brookes Publishing.

Hicks, M. J. and Devaraj, S. (2015) *'The myth and reality of manufacturing in America'*, June, Ball State University: Center for Business and Economic Research. Available from: http://conexus.cberdata.org/files/MfgReality.pdf [accessed 15 May 2017].

Hollenbach, D. (1988) *Justice, peace, and human rights: American Catholic social ethics in a pluralistic world*, New York: Crossroad.

Hout, M. and Fischer, C. S. (2014) 'Why more Americans have no religious preference: Political backlash and generational succession, 1987–2012', *Sociological Science*, *1*(24): 423–447.

Hout, M., Greeley, A. and Wilde, M. (2001) 'The demographic imperative in religious change in the U.S.', *American Journal of Sociology*, *107*(2): 468–500.

Kahn, C. (2016) *'U.S. voters want leader to end advantage of rich and powerful'*, 8 November, Washington, DC: Reuters/Ipsos Poll.

Katz, L. F., and Krueger, A. B. (2016) 'The rise and nature of alternative work arrangements in the United States, 1995–2015', September, NBER Working Paper no. 22667, Cambridge, MA: National Bureau of Economic Research.

Lazonick, W. (2014) 'Profits without prosperity', *Harvard Business Review*, *92*(9): 46–55.

Levy, F. (1998) *The new dollars and dreams: American incomes and economic change*, New York: Russell Sage Foundation.

Marty, M. (1981) *The public church: Mainline, Evangelical, Catholic*, New York: Crossroad.

Marty, M. (1990) 'On a medial moraine: Religious dimensions of American constitutionalism', *Emory Law Journal*, *39*(1): 9–20.

Metz, J. B. (1987) 'Im Aufbruch zu einer kulturell polyzentrishen Weltkirche', in F. X. Kaufmann and J. B. Metz (eds), *Zukunftsfähigkeit*, Freiburg, Germany: Herder, pp. 93–115.

Meyer, J. W. (1987) 'Self and life course: institutionalization and its effects', in G. M. Thomas, J. Meyer, F. Ramirez and J. Boli (eds), *Institutional structure: Constituting state, society and the individual*, Beverly Hills, CA: Sage, pp. 242–260.

Mishel, L., Bernstein, J. and Allegretto, S. (2005) *The state of working America*, Ithaca, NY: Cornell University Press.

Monnat, S. M. (2016) 'Deaths of despair and support for Trump in the 2016 presidential election', 4 December, Penn State University Research Brief. Available from: http://aese.psu.edu/directory/smm67/Election16.pdf [accessed 15 May 2017].

Moore, J. (2005) 'Upwardly immobile', *Harvard Magazine*, *107*(January-February): 14–16.

Niebuhr, H. R. (1929) *The social sources of denominationalism*, New York: Henry Holt.

Norris, F. (2011) 'For business, golden days; for workers, the dross', *New York Times*, 26 November, p. B3.

Obama, B. (2013) 'Remarks by the president on economic mobility,' 4 December, Washington, DC: The White House. Available from: https://obamawhitehouse.archives.gov/the-press-office/2013/12/04/remarks-president-economic-mobility [accessed 15 May 2017].

Perry, M. J. (1988) *Morality, politics, and law: A bicentennial essay*, New York: Oxford University Press.

Pew Research Center (2014) *Most see inequality growing, but partisans differ over solutions*, Washington, DC: The Pew Charitable Trusts.

Pew Research Center (2016a) *The public's policy priorities for 2016*, Washington, DC: The Pew Charitable Trusts.

Pew Research Center (2016b) *The state of American jobs*, Washington, DC: The Pew Charitable Trusts.

Phillips, K. (1993) *Boiling point: Republicans, Democrats, and the decline of middle-class prosperity*, New York: Random House.

Piketty, T., Saez, E. and Zucman, G. (2016) 'Distributional national accounts: Methods and estimates for the United States', December, NBER Working Paper no. 22945, Cambridge, MA: National Bureau of Economic Research.

Porter, E. (2017) 'A budget reflecting resentments', *New York Times*, 8 March, pp. B1, B6.

Reardon, S. F. and Bischoff, K. (2011) 'Income inequality and income segregation', *American Journal of Sociology, 116*(4): 1092–1153.

Reardon, S. F. and Bischoff, K. (2014) 'Residential segregation by income, 1970–2009', in J. Logan, (ed.), *Diversity and disparities: America enters a new century*, New York: Russell Sage Foundation, pp. 208–223.

Reardon, S. F. and Bischoff, K. (2016) 'The continuing increase in income segregation, 2007–2012', Stanford, CA: Stanford Center for Education Policy Analysis. Available from: http://cepa.stanford.edu/content/continuing-increase-income-segregation-2007–2012 [accessed 15 May 2017].

Reeves, R. (2015) '*The dangerous separation of the American upper middle class*', 3 September, Washington, DC: The Brookings Institution. Available from: www.brookings.edu/research/the-dangerous-separation-of-the-american-upper-middle-class/ [accessed 15 May 2017].

Reich, R. (1995) '*The revolt of the anxious class*', 22 November, Washington, DC: Democratic Leadership Council.

Saez, E. (2016) 'Striking it richer: The evolution of top incomes in the United States', 30 June, Berkeley, CA: University of California. Available from: https://eml.berkeley.edu/~saez/saez -UStopincomes-2015.pdf [accessed 15 May 2017].

Saez, E. and Zucman, G. (2014) '*Wealth inequality in the United States since 1913: Evidence from capitalized income tax data*', October, NBER Working Paper no. 20625, Cambridge, MA: National Bureau of Economic Research.

Sandel, M. (1998) *Democracy's discontent: America in search of a public philosophy*, Cambridge, MA: Harvard University Press.

Sandel, M. (2012) *What money can't buy: The moral limits of markets*, New York: Farrar, Straus and Giroux.

Shearer, R., Ng, J., Berube, A. and Friedhoff, A. (2016) '*Metromonitor 2016: Tracking growth, prosperity, and inclusion in the 100 largest US metropolitan areas*', Washington, DC: The Brookings Institution.

Siu, H. and Jaimovich, N. (2015) 'Jobless recoveries', 8 April, *Third Way NEXT Initiative*. Available from: www.thirdway.org/report/jobless-recoveries [accessed 15 May 2017].

Skocpol, T. (1997) '*Civic engagement in American democracy*', 25 January, Washington, DC: National Commission on Civic Renewal.

Skocpol, T. (1999) 'Advocates without members: The recent transformation of civic life', in T. Skocpol and M. P. Fiorina (eds), *Civic engagement in American democracy*, New York: Russell Sage Foundation, pp. 461–510.

Smeeding, T. (2016) 'Gates, gaps, and intergenerational mobility: The importance of an even start', in I. Kirsch and H. Braun (eds), *The dynamics of opportunity in America*, New York: Springer, pp. 255–295.

Song, J., Price, D. J., Guvenen, F., Bloom, N. and von Wachter, T. (2015) *'Firming up inequality'*, May, NBER Working Paper no. 21199, Cambridge, MA: National Bureau of Economic Research.

Taylor, C. (1990a) 'Modes of civil society,' *Public Culture*, 3(1): 95–118.

Taylor, C. (1990b) 'Religion in a free society', in J. D. Hunter and O. Guinness (eds), *Articles of faith, articles of peace: The religious liberty clauses and the American public philosophy*, Washington, DC: Brookings Institution, pp. 1–2.

Taylor, C. (1992) 'The politics of recognition', in A. Gutmann (ed.), *Multiculturalism and 'the politics of recognition'*, Princeton, NJ: Princeton University Press, pp. 25–73.

Tipton, S. M. (1986) 'Moral languages and the good society', *Soundings: An Interdisciplinary Journal*, 69(1/2): 165–180.

Tipton, S. M. (1990) 'Republic and liberal state: The place of religion in an ambiguous polity,' *Emory Law Journal*, 39(1): 191–202.

Tipton, S. M. (2007) *Public pulpits: Methodists and mainline churches in the moral argument of public life*, Chicago, IL: Chicago University Press.

Troeltsch, E. (1960) *The social teaching of the Christian churches*, New York: Harper and Row.

US Census Bureau (2011) *The research supplemental poverty measure: 2010*, Washington, DC: US Department of Commerce.

US Census Bureau (2016) *The research supplemental poverty measure: 2015*, Washington, DC: US Department of Commerce.

Verba, S., Schlozman, K. L. and Brady, H. (1995) *Voice and equality: Civic voluntarism in American politics*, Cambridge, MA: Harvard University Press.

Vorspan, D. and Saperstein, D. (1992) *Tough choices: Jewish perspectives on social justice*, New York: Union of American Hebrew Congregations.

Walzer, M. (1991) 'The idea of civil society', *Dissent*, 38(2): 293–304.

Weintraub, J. (1997) 'The theory and politics of the public/private distinction', in J. Weintraub and K. Kumar (eds), *Public and private in thought and practice*, Chicago, IL: University of Chicago Press, pp. 1–42.

Whitmore, S. D., Bauer, L., Mumford, M. and Nunn, R. (2016) *'Money lightens the load'*, 12 December, Washington, DC: The Brookings Institution.

Williams, J. C. (2016) 'What so many people don't get about the U.S. working class', *Harvard Business Review*, November 10. Available from: https://hbr.org/2016/11/what-so-many-people-dont-get-about-the-u-s-working-class [accessed 15 May 2017].

Wilson, V. and Rodgers, W. M. III (2016) *'Black-white wage gaps expand with rising wage inequality'*, 20 September, Washington, DC: Economic Policy Institute.

Wood, R. L. (2002) *Faith in action: Religion, race, and democratic organizing in America*, Chicago, IL: University of Chicago Press.

World Economic Forum (2017) *The inclusive growth and development report 2017*, Geneva: World Economic Forum.

Wuthnow, R. (1999) 'Mobilizing civic engagement: the changing impact of religious involvement', in T. Skocpol and M. P. Fiorina, (eds), *Civic engagement in American democracy*, New York: Russell Sage Foundation, pp. 331–366.

Wuthnow, R. (2002) 'Beyond quiet influence? Possibilities for the Protestant mainline', in R. Wuthnow and J. H. Evans (eds), *The quiet hand of God: Faith-based activism and the public role of mainline Protestantism*, Berkeley, CA: University of California Press, pp. 381–404.

Wuthnow, R. (2007) *After the baby boomers: How twenty- and thirty-somethings are shaping the future of American religion*, Princeton, NJ: Princeton University Press.

INDEX